Cornerstone on Councillors' Conduct

Dedicated to the memory of
Anthony Scrivener QC
1935–2015

Cornerstone on Councillors' Conduct

Editor
Philip Kolvin QC, MA (Oxon), FRSA, Barrister

Contributors
Wayne Beglan BA (Hons), Barrister
Philip Coppel QC BA (Hons), LLB, Barrister
Estelle Dehon BA(Hons) LLB (Wits) BCL MPhil (Oxon), Barrister
Emma Dring LLB (Hons), LLM (Cantab), Barrister
James Findlay QC, MA (Cantab), Barrister
Robin Green LLB (Hons)
Ryan Kohli MA (Oxon), Barrister
Matthew Lewin, MA, Barrister
Jack Parker, BA (Hons), MSt, Barrister
Harriet Townsend, BSc (Hons), Barrister
Damien Welfare BA (Hons), MSc, FRSA, Barrister
Zoë Whittington BA (Hons), Barrister
Robert Williams, LLB (Hons), Barrister

All members of Cornerstone Barristers, London.

Bloomsbury Professional

Published by

Bloomsbury Professional Ltd, Maxwelton House, 41–43 Boltro Road, Haywards Heath, West Sussex, RH16 1BJ

© Bloomsbury Professional Ltd 2015

Bloomsbury Professional is an imprint of Bloomsbury Publishing Plc

British Library Cataloguing-in-Publication Data.

A catalogue record for this book is available from the British Library.

ISBN 978 1 78043 330 1

Typeset by Phoenix Photosetting, Chatham, Kent
Printed and bound in Great Britain by CPI Group (UK) Ltd, Croydon, CR0 4YY

Foreword

I have always believed it is a great privilege to be a councillor. It is also a significant responsibility.

Councillors can be seen as the very embodiment of local representation, one of the fundamental pillars of democracy. By living and working in the places they serve, councillors understand the needs and ambitions of local people. As elected representatives, they have the mandate to respond to those needs and make a difference for residents up and down the country.

To fulfil their role, councillors have to maintain the highest standards of conduct. They should not only remain above reproach, but also be seen to be so. The Nolan principles of public life set the standards to which representatives should adhere; residents deserve nothing less than these qualities of selflessness, integrity, objectivity, accountability, openness, honesty and leadership.

The principles are clear and easy to grasp, but what happens when they must be applied to complex, real world situations? This book helps answer the question. It provides an invaluable resource for councillors, and those who seek to understand the law that applies to councillors. It captures in one place all that anyone might need as they come to take a decision, face a dilemma or handle a complaint. By setting out the issues and providing examples and case studies, it clearly sets out what is and is not acceptable.

The whole system of local democracy ultimately depends on the knowledge and integrity of local decision makers. Councillors need to know the right thing in order to be able to do the right thing. I believe the information set out here will help the more than 20,000 councillors across England and Wales uphold the standards by which the public is protected and by which the system itself is judged.

David Sparks
Chairman of the Local Government Association
April 2015

Preface

Politicians get a bad rap in Shakespeare. Of their five mentions in the plays, three are uncomplimentary and two are downright rude: excoriating them as 'vile' and 'scurvy'. The Bard was no mean politician himself, managing to avoid offending his own Queen in plays about royalty, and tickling the belly of the audiences, from dukes to fruit-sellers, who thronged his theatres. So we can take it that, in insulting the political class, he was reflecting popular views of the time.

Not a lot has changed in the 399 years since the Bard shuffled off his mortal coil. Recent research by the independent polling company Ipsos Mori showed that only 16% of the population generally trust politicians to tell the truth. That is fewer than 1 in 6. In the North it is 11%. Among Council tenants it is an astounding 8%. Even the much blackguarded bankers poll 31%. So we have an insidious crisis in our democracy, whereby those whom we elect and fund to exercise power over our day to day lives, the education of our children and the development of our living environments, are not even trusted by us to tell the truth. More to the point, requiring only honesty is to set the bar extremely low: what price judgment, objectivity, selflessness, leadership or all the higher order virtues?

This is far from saying that only 16% of politicians are honest. It is saying that there is a huge issue of public perception, not assisted by the regular scandals which erupt volcanically onto our front pages – from cash for questions to expenses, or those who say one thing and then do another, or those who are lashed unhappily to the mast of their Party whip when voting on contentious issues.

Much of administrative law concerns appearances – what would the person on the Clapham omnibus think? What impression does the conduct in question create? While there was an enforceable Model Code and a national body to enforce it, there was a clear prospect of closing the gap between the public perception of politicians as vile and scurvy and the reality that up and down the country public spirited people give up their time and energies to work for their communities, trying to utilise the ever-diminishing resources accorded to them for the purpose in a wise and sensitive manner.

But some argue that the Code was misused to bring vexatious complaints. Others argue that the Code stopped politicians from doing their jobs of representing people, by preventing them from campaigning on issues and then carrying their mandate into Committee.

So, despite the chequered history of political conduct on these islands (and every island, and every continent) Parliament in its wisdom effectively abolished national standards, criminalised only the most serious conduct and left it to local, voluntary regulation to fill the gap. This was to take a risk. It depended on local councillors, and councils, raising their game so as voluntarily to attain and impose the standards which were previously enforced as a matter of law.

It is that gap – between the legal minimum standards enforceable by the criminal law and the high standards which we are entitled to expect from our elected politicians – which this book is principally designed to explore. What standards can we expect? What goes into local codes? What common law and statutory remedies are available against councillors and councils? How are remedies obtained?

The book is aimed not only at monitoring officers and lawyers, but at councillors themselves. We have tried to introduce as many examples of decisions as we can find, so as to populate the arid desert of legal opinion with the living greenery of real life situations. We have also tried to summarise important principles in text boxes to save the only mildly interested from having to plough through the undergrowth of legal exegesis.

We hope, therefore, that this volume, and subsequent editions, will become a signpost and friend to those councillors who want to work to the highest of standards and, at the very least, to stay out of court and the press.

This is the second book in the Cornerstone series – sandwiched between Anti-Social Behaviour and the Planning Court. The aim is to continue to serve local government with readable texts of moderate length directed specifically at their needs. We hope that the aim is being met, and welcome feedback on all of the works.

Finally, it is a joy to work with Bloomsbury Professional, the most knowledge-able, helpful, friendly, accommodating team in legal publishing. We love being published by the house which brought Harry Potter to the world. To them, and this book, we say *Wingardium Leviosa.*

Philip Kolvin QC
Cornerstone Barristers
Grays Inn,
April 2015

Contents

Table of Statutes

Table of Statutory Instruments

[References are to paragraph number]

Table of Cases

I

J

K

L

M

N

O

CHAPTER 1

Beginnings

A INTRODUCTION

1.1   The current conduct regime for local authority members dates from the Localism Act 2011, implemented from 2012. It replaced a more comprehensive regime which had been in place, with significant amendments, only since 2000. Yet the need for some form of guidance as to members' conduct has a longer history. The Redcliffe-Maud Committee on local government rules of conduct, set up in the wake of the Poulson corruption scandal,[1] proposed and drafted a code of conduct for local government in 1974. The first National Code of Local Government Conduct, based on this draft, and covering England, Wales and Scotland, was issued by three government departments in 1975. It was endorsed by the Salmon Royal Commission on Standards of Conduct in Public Life in 1976.[2] Ten years later, the Widdicombe Committee on the Conduct of Local Authority Business recommended that the code should be updated and given statutory status, and that provision should be made for new members to declare that they would be guided by it.[3] These recommendations were enacted in the Local Government and Housing Act 1989 (LGHA 1989), and a new National Code issued in 1990.

In relation to Members' interests, Part 5 of the Local Government Act 1972 (LGA 1972) required the disclosure of direct and indirect pecuniary interests, and prohibited speaking or voting on matters affected.

1.2   This chapter looks at the two regimes that have preceded the current

---

1   Report of the Prime Minister's Committee on Local Government Rules of Conduct, Cmnd 5636 (1974).
2   Royal Commission on Standards in Public Life, Cmnd 6524.
3   Cmnd 9797, paragraphs 6.7–6.23.

scheme under the Localism Act 2011: the advisory scheme in place from 1990–2000, and the largely mandatory scheme from 2000–2012. The latter may be contrasted with the present regime, which bears similarities to the position under the 1972 and 1989 Acts.

B   ADVISORY CODE, 1990–2000

National Code of Local Government Conduct

1.3   The LGHA 1989[4] for the first time gave statutory power to the Secretary of State, for 'the guidance of members of local authorities', to issue a code of recommended practice covering England, Wales and Scotland. The declaration of acceptance of office by members, whose form was prescribed in an order by the Secretary of State,[5] could include an undertaking by them to be 'guided' by the code in the performance of their functions.[6] Orders were made requiring members of local authorities other than parish and community councils to make this declaration from 3 May 1990. Members of parish and community councils followed from 1 January 1991.

1.4   The Code, which was a revised version of that produced in 1975, was issued by the Secretaries of State for the Environment, Scotland and Wales in the form of Circulars.[7] It applied to all members of local authorities, and of a number of other bodies, and included co-opted members.

1.5   In addition to the statutory code, a register of interests was required to be established under s 19 of the LGHA 1989, adding to the existing interests regime under the LGA 1972. Other provisions of the 1989 Act concerned: the political restriction of local government officers;[8] the creation of the roles of Monitoring Officer[9] and political Assistant;[10] rules requiring political balance on committees,[11] and a new scheme of members' allowances.[12]

1.6   The local Ombudsman was empowered to find, as part of an investigation, that a breach of the Code by an individual member constituted maladministration.[13] (As the Committee on Standards in Public Life (the 'Nolan' Committee, after its first Chair, Lord Nolan) later pointed out, such a finding applied to the whole of a council; even where it had made efforts to prevent the

---

4   Section 31(1).
5   For England and Wales, the LGA 1972, s 83.
6   Section 31(7) in England and Wales; Local Government (Scotland) Act 1973, s 33A in Scotland.
7   The code was an attachment to Joint Circular 8/90 from the Department of the Environment, and Circular 23/90 from the Welsh Office, issued on 10 April 1990.
8   LGHA 1989, ss 1–3.
9   LGHA 1989, s 5.
10 LGHA 1989, s 9.
11 LGHA 1989, ss 15–17.
12 LGHA 1989, s 18.
13 Nolan Committee, para 171.

bad behaviour.) The Ombudsman was required in his report to name the member or members concerned, and to give particulars of the breach, unless he was satisfied that it would be unjust to do so.[14]

1.7   The Code said that it provided, by way of guidance to members of local authorities, recommended standards of conduct in carrying out their duties, and in their relationships with the council and its officers. Key elements were as follows:

General provisions:

- members held office 'by virtue of the law, and must at all times act within the law'. They had a responsibility to make sure that what they did complied with those requirements and the guidance. They should regularly review their circumstances with this in mind;

- a member's overriding duty was to the whole community, with a special duty to constituents, including those who did not vote for the member. It was the member's duty alone to decide what view to take on any question, while acknowledging that members would be strongly influenced by the view of others, and in particular of their party;

- if a member had a 'private or personal interest' in a question which members had to decide, he or she should never take any part in the decision, save in special circumstances in the code. Where they were permitted by these circumstances to participate, they should never let the interest influence the decision;

- a member should never do anything 'as a councillor' which he or she could not justify to the public. A member's conduct, and what the public believed about his or her conduct, would affect the reputation of the member's council and any party of which they were a member;

- it was not enough to avoid actual impropriety. Members should at all times avoid any occasion for suspicion and any appearance of improper conduct.

Members' interests

1.8   Under Part 5 of the LGA 1972, members were required by law to disclose both direct and indirect pecuniary interests of themselves or a spouse, which they had in any contract, proposed contract or other matter coming before the council, a committee or sub-committee.[15] An indirect pecuniary interest arose where the member (or spouse) had a connection with a person who had a direct pecuniary interest in the matter (eg the member was employed by the proposed contractor,

---

14 LGHA 1989, s 32 (inserting s 30(3A) into the Local Government Act 1974). Repealed in England and Wales from 22 May 2012.
15 LGA 1972, ss 94(1) and 95.

or he or any nominee of his was a member of the company).[16] The member was required to disclose the interest, and was prohibited from speaking or voting on the matter. Failure to comply with this requirement was an offence, unless the member could prove that he or she did not know that the matter was under consideration at the meeting. The council's Standing Orders could require the member to withdraw from the meeting during discussion of the matter.[17] General notices of the interest, made in writing, were deemed sufficient disclosure, and were to be kept in a book by the proper officer.[18]

1.9   To these requirements, the 1989 regime added a requirement for certain direct and indirect pecuniary interests to be declared in a register.[19] These comprised: the member's employment; any sponsorship of the member (eg as to election expenses); contracts between the member (or his or her firm) and the council; land owned in the area of the authority, or where the member had a licence for use; or, corporate tenancies where the council was the landlord, and the member was a director or held shares or a partnership in the firm; shareholdings in a firm in the area, of a total nominal value of £25,000, or 1% of the total issued share capital. Breach of these obligations was a criminal offence.[20]

1.10   The Code encouraged disclosure of non-pecuniary interests (eg memberships of local bodies) although it did not did not expressly define these. Instead, it referred to 'private or personal interests', including those of family and friends, or arising through membership of, or association with, clubs, societies and other organisations. The member should not allow 'the impression to be created that you are, or may be, using your position to promote a private or personal interest rather than forwarding the general public interest'.[21]

1.11   The Code advised that any private or personal non-pecuniary interest arising at a meeting should be declared, unless it was 'insignificant'; or one which the member shared with other members of the public, as a ratepayer, a (then) community charge payer, or local inhabitant. Once declared, however, the member had to decide whether the interest was 'clear and substantial'. If it was not, the member could continue to take part in the discussion, and could vote. If the interest was clear and substantial, however, then unless the member had a dispensation, he or she should never take any further part in the proceedings, and should always withdraw from the meeting. The distinction between 'insignificant' and 'clear and substantial' was to be found in the answer to the question whether a member of the public, who knew the full facts, would reasonably think that the member <u>might</u> be influenced by the interest.[22]

1.12   Exceptional circumstances, where the member could speak or even

16 LGA 1972, s 95.
17 LGA 1972, s 94(4).
18 LGA 1972, s 96.
19 LGHA 1989, s 19; Local Authorities (Members Interests) Regulations 1992, SI 1992/618.
20 LGHA 1989, s 19(2).
21 National Code, para 9.
22 National Code, para 11.

in some cases vote, in spite of having declared a clear and substantial private personal interest, were:

- the interest arose from the member's capacity as a member of a public body, where membership of the body would not constitute an indirect pecuniary interest under the law (ie under the LGA 1972, s 94);

- the interest arose from the member having been appointed to another organisation (eg a charity, or voluntary body) by the local authority as its representative;

- the interest arose from membership of a management committee or governing body etc, of another such organisation, although the member had not been appointed to it by the council; in which case the member could speak and vote on a matter not directly affecting the finances of that organisation;

- if the member was an ordinary member or supporter of an outside organisation (but not on its management committee or governing body), the member could speak and vote on a matter in which that organisation had an interest.[23]

1.13   Certain dispensations were also available, under statute for pecuniary interests,[24] or locally in the case of non-pecuniary interests, where the work of the authority would be affected by the number of members who had interests. In relation to dispensations for non-pecuniary interests, members were expected to take advice from the Chairman or appropriate senior officer. They should then consider whether the public would regard the interest as so closely connected to the matter that the member could not be expected to put the interest out of his or her mind (eg if it affected a close relative), and finally consider any guidance from the council. The two grounds of dispensation were that the member could speak and vote, where he or she had (in the language of the Code) a 'clear and substantial private and personal non-pecuniary interest', if, but only if:

- at least half of the council or committee would otherwise be expected to withdraw because of personal interests; or,

- if their withdrawal, with that of other members for similar reasons, would upset the elected party balance on the council or committee so as to be likely to affect the decision.

1.14   If the member did speak or vote notwithstanding the interest, he or she should declare it before the decision was made, giving reasons for continuing to participate.[25]

1.15   Related expectations in the Code were that members should apply the principles of disclosure of interests to their dealings with officers, or other members (including at party or informal meetings).[26] They should avoid

---

23 National Code, para 12(a)–(d).
24 LGA 1972, s 97.
25 National Code, para 17.
26 Para 20.

membership of committees or sub-committees where they would have to make such frequent declarations that they would be of little value to it, or would be likely to weaken public confidence in it. The same applied to the leadership, or positions as the Chair of committees or sub-committees.[27]

1.16 Other paragraphs of the Code stated the following:

- mutual respect between members and officers was stated to be essential, in performing their distinct roles, but 'close personal familiarity' could damage the relationship;[28]

- confidential information should not be disclosed or used for the personal advantage of the member or anyone known to them, or to the disadvantage or discredit of the council or anyone else;[29]

- gifts and hospitality should be treated with 'extreme caution', although there were no 'hard and fast rules'.[30] The offer or receipt of gifts or invitations should always be reported to the appropriate senior officer;

- members should never seek or accept preferential dealings with the council on a personal level, and should avoid such a perception (eg by being in substantial arrears with the council, or seeking preferential treatment for friends or relatives);[31]

- council facilities should be used strictly for council duties 'and no other purpose'.[32]

1.17 Apart from the existing criminal sanctions for breach of the rules on pecuniary interests, to which the Code added the member's responsibility for registering interests, and the provision enabling the Ombudsman to treat a breach of the Code as maladministration, no express sanctions existed under the 1989 Act regime. There was uncertainty as to how members might be disciplined, and in practice this was often a matter left to the member's party whips. The only sanction open to a council itself was the exclusion of the member from committees, which itself required the co-operation of the member's party group.

1.18 The scope of the sanctions that might be available under the 1990 code was explored in the *Lashley* case,[33] where the council had anticipated the Local Government Act 2000 (LGA 2000) and introduced a standards committee in 1999. Following a complaint by a member of staff about a member's remarks to him, the Chief Executive imposed restrictions on the member's access to the council building. The restrictions were withdrawn before a first judicial review application. A decision of the standards committee to censure the member, but

---

27 Paras 21–22.
28 Para 24.
29 Para 26.
30 Paras 27–28.
31 Para 31.
32 Para 32.
33 *R v Broadland DC ex parte Lashley* [2001] 3 BGLR 264.

take no further action, was subject to a second application for judicial review; on the basis that the committee was not a lawfully constituted committee of the council, and that the decision was tainted by procedural impropriety. The Court of Appeal endorsed the approach of the High Court. Powers existed for the standards committee process. The activity of the committee was calculated to facilitate, and was conducive or incidental to, the council's functions of 'maintaining its administration and internal workings in a state of efficiency; and of furthering the welfare of its employees'. Even if the committee had mistakenly thought that it was entitled to discipline the member, there was no reason for the court to intervene. The committee's powers were restricted, but they were not non-existent. It could report an extreme case to the police or the auditors. It could recommend to the council that it should remove a member from a committee. Or it could state its findings and offer advice.

C MOVING TO A MORE COMPREHENSIVE SCHEME

1.19   The Committee on Standards in Public Life (the 'Nolan' committee) was created in October 1994, in response to the 'cash for questions' affair in Parliament. Its terms of reference were:

> 'To examine current concerns about standards of conduct of all holders of public office, including arrangements relating to financial and commercial activities, and make recommendations as to any changes in present arrangements which might be required to ensure the highest standards of propriety in public life'.

1.20   In its first report, it had produced the seven 'Nolan Principles' of public life (1995). These have remained relevant to the conduct regime, in different forms and to differing degrees, ever since; and have been incorporated into the current Act.[34]

The 'Nolan Principles'

Selflessness – Holders of public office should act solely in terms of the public interest. They should not do so in order to gain financial or other benefits for themselves, their family or their friends.

Integrity – Holders of public office should not place themselves under any financial or other obligation to outside individuals or organisations that might seek to influence them in the performance of their official duties.

Objectivity – In carrying out public business, including making public appointments, awarding contracts, or recommending individuals for rewards and benefits, holders of public office should make choices on merit.

---

34 See **Chapter 2**, para **2.10**.

Accountability – Holders of public office are accountable for their decisions and actions to the public and must submit themselves to whatever scrutiny is appropriate to their office.

Openness – Holders of public office should be as open as possible about all the decisions and actions they take. They should give reasons for their decisions and restrict information only when the wider public interest clearly demands.

Honesty – Holders of public office have a duty to declare any private interests relating to their public duties and to take steps to resolve any conflicts arising in a way that protects the public interest.

Leadership – Holders of public office should promote and support these principles by leadership and example.

The Third Nolan Committee report

1.21   The Third Report of the Nolan Committee was on aspects of the conduct of local government in England, Wales and Scotland.[35] It was highly critical of the complicated nature of the National Code (which it called 'confusing and unhelpful'), the lack of an ability for a local authority to revise or adapt its Code, and the absence of sanctions.[36] It recommended that there should be a simple statement of principles approved centrally, which local authorities could expand, combined with a 'tough but rational' regulatory system.[37] By no means all of the report's recommendations were accepted; notably that the proposed tribunals should hear appeals only, with all initial decisions taken locally by standards committees. Also, it did not propose a Standards Board. Its core recommendations, however, of a Model Code, the creation of standards committees with disciplinary powers, and of a role for tribunals, gave rise to the main features of the legislation in 2000.

White Paper 1998

1.22   The incoming Labour government set out its proposals in a White Paper ('Modern Local Government: in touch with the people'), published in 1998. Part of the White Paper constituted the government's formal response to the Third Nolan report.[38] It proposed a new 'ethical framework', in the context of a broader 'modernisation' of local government to introduce directly elected mayors, 'executive arrangements', and a new general 'power of well-being'. The local government changes sat within the context of wider constitutional change, such

35 'Standards of Conduct in Local Government in England, Scotland and Wales', Cm 3702-1, July 1997.
36 See Summary and Recommendations, especially paragraphs 14–17, and 23–25.
37 Para 57.
38 'Modern Local Government: in touch with the people', Cm 4014, paras 6.3 and following.

as devolution in Scotland and Wales, and the enactment of the Human Rights Act. The conduct of everyone in local government, the White Paper said, needed to be of the highest standard, to maintain the essential 'bond of trust' between councils and local people.[39]

1.23   The White Paper expanded the seven 'Nolan principles' of public life to fifteen, and these were expressed in the White Paper as follows:[40]

- Community leadership.
- Duty to uphold the law.
- Constituency (ie a duty to assist the council to 'act as far as possible in the interests of the whole community that it serves').
- Selflessness.
- Integrity and propriety.
- Hospitality (ie recording all gifts and hospitality, and not accepting any that might reasonably be thought to influence, or to be intended to influence, the member's judgement; or where to do so could bring discredit upon the council).
- Decisions (ie members to take their own view).
- Objectivity in decision-making.
- Accountability.
- Openness.
- Confidentiality.
- Stewardship.
- Participation.
- Declarations (ie a duty to declare any private interests relating to public duties, and to take steps to resolve any conflicts arising in a way that protected the public interest).
- Relations with officers.

1.24   These principles, and others, were to be incorporated into a Model Code, to be drawn up in discussion with the newly-formed Local Government Association, on which all local codes would be based. In relation to interests, the new regime would follow a sub-division suggested by Nolan into direct pecuniary interests (ie whether the member, or his or her spouse or partners would stand to benefit or lose financially from a decision); and all other interests.[41] The new regime was set out and enacted in Part 3 of the LGA 2000.

---

39 Para 6.1.
40 Para 6.7.
41 Cm 4014, paragraph 6.11.

D LOCAL GOVERNMENT ACT 2000: A DETAILED CONDUCT REGIME, AND THE FIRST MANDATORY CODE, 2000–2007

1.25   Part 3 of the LGA 2000 set out a regime governing conduct which relied on a central role for a Standards Board. Despite the intentions expressed for local discretion as to the code within a broad national framework, all of its text was made mandatory;[42] and the document was sufficiently detailed and comprehensive to mean that most authorities adopted it as it stood. The Code came to be criticised as overly prescriptive and complicated, and as giving rise to numerous trivial complaints. In 2007, some of its provisions, and the structure of the scheme as a whole, would be significantly recast. The scheme as a whole was amended repeatedly during its 12-year life. For that reason, this survey records only the main features.

Principles

1.26   The Secretary of State was given the power by Order to specify the principles that were (or were intended) to govern the conduct of members and co-opted members of 'relevant authorities' in England and police authorities in Wales. The National Assembly for Wales was given the equivalent power in relation to Welsh local authorities, other than police authorities. (With the passage of the Scotland Act 1998, the conduct of Scottish local members became a devolved matter for the Scottish government). The principles were set out in separate Orders in 2001,[43] and were to be reflected in the Model Code prepared under the LGA 2000, s 50. The principles applied to 'relevant authorities', which included police authorities, joint authorities, and national parks authorities, as well as all local authorities.

Model Code and duty to comply

1.27   Under the LGA 2000, s 50, the Secretary of State and the National Assembly (on the same division of labour as before) could issue a Model Code as regards the conduct expected of members and co-opted members. The Code could include mandatory and optional provisions. A later amendment to the section, occasioned by the decision of the High Court in the *Livingstone* case (see below), made clear that the principles were to apply to a member only when acting in an official capacity, unless the conduct would constitute a criminal offence.[44] An authority to which the principles applied under s 49 was required within 6 months to pass a resolution adopting a code of conduct (or a revised code).[45]

---

42 See para **1.45** below.
43 Relevant Authorities (General Principles) Order 2001, SI 2001/1401; Conduct of Members (Principles) (Wales) Order 2001, SI 2001/2276 (W.166).
44 LGA 2000, ss 49(2A)–(2D); inserted by the Local Government and Public Involvement in Health Act 2007, s 183.
45 LGA 2000, s 51(2).

The code passed by an authority had to incorporate any mandatory provisions of the Model Code. It could incorporate any optional provisions in the model, and also any other provisions (at the initiative of the local authority), provided they were consistent with the Model Code.[46] Once adopted, a Code had to be available for inspection, and a notice published in one or more local newspapers. A copy had also to be sent to the Standards Board for England (see below), or the Commissioner for Local Administration in Wales.[47] A member or co-opted member of a relevant authority was bound, within two months of the adoption of the Code, to give a written undertaking that he or she would observe it in performing his functions (as opposed to being guided by it, as before); otherwise, his membership would cease.[48]

1.28   The words 'in performing his functions' in LGA 2000, s 52(1)(a) gave rise to the most important case under the 2000 Act regime, the *Livingstone* case,[49] in which a decision by the Adjudication Panel to impose a four-week suspension was overturned. Words spoken to a journalist by the Mayor of London when leaving a reception he had hosted at City Hall, likening him to a concentration camp guard, were not spoken in an 'official capacity'; and were not even arguably spoken in the performance of his functions as Mayor for the purposes of paragraph 4 of the Code (see below).

Standards Committees

1.29   Relevant authorities (other than parish or community councils) were required to establish Standards Committees.[50] Subject to regulations, the authority could fix the number of members; provided (for a relevant authority in England or a police authority in Wales) that there was a minimum of two members, at least one of whom was an independent (ie not a member); and, that in England the elected mayor or executive Leader was not a member. Regulations required that where the committee had more than three members, at least 25% of the membership were to be independent; and that for a relevant authority in England, or a police authority in Wales, where it was operating executive arrangements, no more than one member of the Standards Committee could be a member of the executive.[51] From 1 April 2008, the Chair of the Standards Committee had to be an independent member.[52]

1.30   In Wales, the National Assembly could make Regulations as to the size of Standards Committees, including their chairing.

---

46 LGA 2000, s 51(4).
47 LGA 2000, s 51(6)(a)–(c).
48 LGA 2000, s 52(1)(a) and (b).
49 *Livingstone v Adjudication Panel for England* [2006] EWHC 2533 (Admin).
50 LGA 2000, s 53.
51 Relevant Authorities (Standards Committee) Regulations 2001, SI 2001/2812, reg 3.
52 LGA 2000, s 53(4) as amended by Local Government and Public Involvement in Health Act 2007, s 187.

1.31   Rules on political balance did not apply to a Standards Committee of a local authority in England or a police authority in Wales.

1.32   The general functions of a Standards Committee under the 2000 Act were promoting and maintaining high standards of conduct by members; and assisting members to observe the code of conduct.[53] Specific functions were to advise the authority on the adoption or revision of its Code; to monitor its operation; and to advise and train members on matters relating to the Code. The National Assembly could make provision with regard to the exercise of functions by standards committees (other than those of police committees).[54] The Standards Board and the National Assembly could issue guidance to standards committees on the exercise of their functions.[55] A relevant authority could arrange for its Standards Committee to exercise other functions (eg corporate policies on 'whistle-blowing').

1.33   Standards Committees of English district and unitary councils also acted as Standards Committees for any parish councils in their areas, as did county councils or county borough councils in Wales for community councils.

Standards Board

1.34   The Standards Board for England was created to issue advice, and to enforce the ethical framework for English local authorities and police authorities in Wales, through investigations by Ethical Standards Officers (ESOs).[56] In Wales, the functions were undertaken by the Commissioner for Local Administration in Wales (from 2005, the Public Services Ombudsman for Wales). The Board/Ombudsman did not, however, adjudicate upon complaints. These were dealt with by independent case tribunals drawn from the Independent Adjudication Panel for England (from 2010, the First-tier Tribunal); and in Wales, from the Adjudication Panel for Wales (or Panel Dyfarnu Cymru). The Standards Board was responsible, however, for the overall administration of the Panel and tribunals.

1.35   The original system was that written complaints, made by any person in England, that a member or co-opted member (including former members) had failed, or may have failed, to comply with the authority's code of conduct, were made to the Standards Board. The Board would consider whether it should be investigated, in which case it would be referred to an ESO.[57] As well as placing an immediate potential burden on the Board, this seemed an odd arrangement, requiring some initial screening of cases before a reference to an ESO. There was a considerable number of complaints, often with some appearance of political motivation, and a substantial workload developed.

---

53 LGA 2000, s 54(1)(a) and (b).
54 LGA 2000, s 54(5).
55 LGA 2000, ss 54(6) and (7).
56 LGA 2000, s 57 and Sch 4.
57 LGA 2000, s 58.

1.36   From 2008, the system was changed so that complaints were made to the Standards Committee of the authority concerned. A similar two-stage process was retained, however, in that the Standards Committee was required to refer the allegation to the Monitoring Officer or the Standards Board (if it considered it to be more serious); or decide that no action should be taken (subject to the complainant requiring it to review the latter decision). In each case, it would in practice be dependent on the Monitoring Officer or other officers to present the matter to the Standards Committee and to advise it on its options.

Ethical Standards Officers

1.37   An investigation by an ESO, on a matter referred by the Standards Board or which came to their attention from another investigation, could lead to one of four findings:

- there was no evidence of a failure to comply;

- no action need be taken;

- the matter should be referred to the Monitoring Officer of the authority; or,

- the matter should be referred to the Panel for adjudication by a tribunal.[58]

1.38   The scope of decisions referred to the Board, and thus to an ESO, was from 2008 limited to those which a Standards Committee considered to be more serious, or ones arising from another investigation at Standards Board level by an ESO. An ESO could end an investigation before its completion, and refer the matter back to the Monitoring Officer.[59] An ESO could follow such procedure for an investigation as he or she considered appropriate, subject to giving the person investigated an opportunity to comment.[60] An ESO had powers to require persons to furnish information, and rights of access to documents, backed by criminal sanctions.[61] Depending on the finding, an ESO would report less serious cases back to the Monitoring Officer, by means of a report or notification; or, in more serious cases, refer the matter to the Panel (later, the First-tier Tribunal).[62] An ESO also had power, where he or she considered it necessary in the public interest, to issue an interim report. In more serious cases, this could include recommending suspension for up to six months, after referring the matter to the Panel.

1.39   Where a matter was referred by an ESO to the Monitoring Officer, regulations made provision as to investigation by the latter, and the making by the officer of a report or recommendations to the Standards Committee, and enforcement action by the Committee. After a hearing, a Standards Committee could find that:

58 LGA 2000, s 59(4).
59 LGA 2000, s 60(2).
60 LGA 2000, s 61(1) and (2).
61 LGA 2000, s 62.
62 LGA 2000, s 64.

- there had been no failure to comply;

- there had been a failure to comply, but that no action was necessary;

- a sanction should be applied: of censure; restriction of access to the council's premises for up to three months; or, suspension or partial suspension for up to three months (or until an apology was given, or training or conciliation undertaken).[63]

1.40   A member could appeal to the Adjudication Panel. In a case where the Standards Committee considered that its powers to apply sanctions were insufficient, it could itself refer a matter to the Panel.

1.41   Chapter 3 made broadly similar provision for Wales, with a Local Commissioner for Wales (a member of the Commission for Local Administration in Wales; from 2005, the Public Services Ombudsman for Wales) exercising the same functions as the Standards Board in England, including those of Ethical Standards Officers; and with similar powers and obligations. Regulations were made by the National Assembly (see para **1.62**).

1.42   The Secretary of State took power to issue a code, as regards the conduct expected of employees of relevant authorities in England, and relevant authorities in Wales other than police authorities. Its terms fell within their terms of employment.[64]

1.43   Under LGA 2000, s 78A, from 31 January 2008, a Panel could disqualify a member from holding office for up to five years, or suspend or partially suspend the member for a 'limited period'.[65] Under the previous provision operating in England, suspension or partial suspension could be for up to a year, or disqualification for up to five years.[66]

1.44   A case tribunal which adjudicated a matter could make recommendations to a relevant authority about conduct matters. If it did, the authority was obliged to consider the matter; and, within three months, to report to the Standards Board (or Local Commissioner in Wales), detailing action taken or proposed to be taken as a result of the recommendations.[67]

First Model Code, 2001–2007

1.45   The Model Code of Conduct for local authorities in England was issued on 5 November 2001.[68] All of its provisions were made mandatory (significantly restricting the scope for any local discretion). Separate codes applied to local

---

63 See Local Authorities (Code of Conduct) (Local Determination) Regulations 2003, SI 2003/1483.
64 LGA 2000, s 82.
65 LGA 2000, s 78A.
66 LGA 2000, s 79(5).
67 LGA 2000, s 80(1) and (3).
68 Local Authorities (Model Code of Conduct) (England) Order 2001, SI 2001/3575.

authorities operating and not operating executive arrangements; although their main effects were the same. Where an authority adopted the Model Code (or the code was applied to it, if it did not do so by a deadline) the previous regime was dis-applied in relation to that authority (notably the interests rules in ss 94– 98, LGA 1972, as well as the advisory National Code of Local Government Conduct).

Code for local authorities operating executive arrangements

1.46   For those operating executive arrangements,[69] a member or co-opted member was bound by the code whenever he conducted the business of the authority, or the office to which he had been elected or appointed; or when he acted as a representative of the authority (ie his 'official capacity').[70] With two exceptions (ie conduct bringing the member's office or authority into disrepute; and improperly seeking an advantage – see below) the Code was not to apply to activities undertaken other than in an official capacity.[71]

1.47   A member representing an authority on another body should comply with his own authority's code, save to any extent that to do might conflict with a lawful obligation of that other body.[72]

General obligations in the 2001 Code

- A member should:

    – promote equality (defined as not discriminating unlawfully against any person);

    – treat others with respect; and

    – not do anything which compromised or was likely to compromise, the impartiality of those working for or on behalf of the authority.[73]

- A member must not disclose information given to him or her in confidence, or information acquired which he believed to be confidential, without the consent of a person authorised to give it; or unless he or she was required by law to do so. Nor should the member prevent others from gaining access to information to which they were entitled.[74]

- A member should not, in his 'official capacity, or any other circumstance' conduct himself in a manner which could reasonably be regarded as bringing his office or authority into disrepute.[75]

---

69 SI 2001/3575, Sch 1.
70 SI 2001/3575, Sch 1, para 1(1).
71 SI 2001/3575, Sch 1, para 1(2).
72 SI 2001/3575, Sch 1, para 1(3)(b).
73 SI 2001/3575, Sch 1, para 2.
74 SI 2001/3575, Sch 1, para 3.
75 SI 2001/3575, Sch 1, para 4.

- A member should not use his position improperly to confer on, or secure for, himself or any other person an advantage or disadvantage. When using the resources of the authority (eg office equipment or stationery), or authorising their use by others, he or she must act in accordance with any requirements made by the authority; and ensure that they were not used for party political purposes (unless doing so could reasonably be regarded as likely to facilitate or be conducive to the carrying out of the functions of the authority, or of the member's office).[76]

- The member should, in reaching decisions, have regard to any relevant advice provided to him by the authority's Monitoring Officer or Chief Financial Officer, and to give reasons for his decisions where the authority was required to do so.[77]

- Members should, if they became aware of any conduct by another member which they reasonably believed involved a failure to comply with the code of conduct, report it to the Standards Board as soon as practicable.[78]

1.48   This last provision was frequently criticised. It can be expected to have contributed to the number of cases taken to the Standards Board; and the trivial or vexatious nature of many of them.

Interests – personal interests

1.49   Part 2 of the Code dealt with members' interests. A member had to regard himself as having a personal interest in a matter if:

(i) it related to an interest which had to be declared in the register of members' interests (see below); or

(ii) if a decision on it might reasonably be regarded as affecting, to a greater extent than other council tax payers, ratepayers or local inhabitants, the well-being of himself or a relative or friend.

1.50   The same test as in (ii) above (ie whether the decision would affect the interest to a greater extent than other persons') also had to be applied to:

- any employment or business carried on by the member, by a relative (which was defined very widely) or by a friend;

- any person who employed, or had employed, the member or such other persons; or any firm in which they were a partner or director;

- any corporate body in which such persons had shares of over £5000; or

---

76 SI 2001/3575, Sch 1, para 5.
77 SI 2001/3575, Sch 1, para 6.
78 SI 2001/3575, Sch 1, para 7.

- any person (of a number of types of outside organisations listed, in relation to the register, in paragraph 15 of the Code) in which the member or his relatives or friends held a position of 'general control or management'. The list included bodies to which the member was nominated by the authority as its representative; a company, industrial and provident society; a charity, or body directed to charitable purposes; or, a body whose principal purpose was the influencing of public opinion or policy, or a trades union or professional association.[79]

1.51 Where a member had a personal interest, he or she had to disclose the existence and nature of the interest at a meeting at which the matter was considered; either at the beginning, or when the interest became apparent. A member making an executive decision (eg as an executive member, on behalf of the authority) in relation to which they had a personal interest, had to ensure that any written statement of the decision recorded the existence and nature of the interest.[80]

Interests – prejudicial interests

1.52 A personal interest was also a prejudicial interest if it was one which a member of the public, with knowledge of the relevant facts, would reasonably regard as so significant that it was likely to prejudice the member's judgement of the public interest.[81]

1.53 Notwithstanding this formulation, a member would not have a prejudicial interest in a matter if the matter related to:

- another relevant authority of which he was a member;

- another public authority in which he had a position of general control or management;

- a body on which he represented the authority;

- a matter concerning the authority's housing functions, where the member was a tenant or leaseholder of a relevant authority [not necessarily the authority of which he was a member], provided he did not have arrears of rent of for more than two months and provided that the functions of the authority did not relate particularly to his tenancy or lease;

- the authority's functions in respect of school meals, transport and travelling expenses, where the member was a parent or guardian of a child in full-time education, provided the function did not relate particularly to the school attended by the child;

79 SI 2001/3575, Sch 1, para 8(1) and (2).
80 SI 2001/3575, Sch 1, para 9(1) and 9(2) respectively.
81 SI 2001/3575, Sch 1, para 10(1).

- the functions of the authority in respect of statutory sick pay, where the member received, or was entitled to receive, sick pay from a relevant authority; or

- the functions of the authority in relation to members' allowances.[82]

1.54   A member of an Overview and Scrutiny Committee automatically had a personal and prejudicial interest in a matter before that committee, if it related to a decision made, or action taken, by another committee or sub-committee of the authority, of which he was a member – unless he was attending to answer questions or give evidence relating to that matter.[83]

1.55   The general rule in relation to prejudicial interests remained that the member should withdraw from the room whenever it became apparent that the matter was being considered (unless he had obtained a dispensation from the standards committee); or that the member should not exercise an executive function in relation to that matter, and should not seek improperly to influence the decision. The member could still participate in an Overview and Scrutiny meeting, however, unless the interest was financial; or unless the interest was of the type described above. In either case, this applied only where the committee was not exercising functions of the authority or the executive.

Register of members' interests

1.56   Within 28 days of his election (or of the Code being adopted) a member had to register his financial interests with the Monitoring Officer.[84] The Monitoring Officer was obliged to establish and maintain a register of interests of members and co-opted members, and to have it available for inspection at reasonable hours, and to advertise this fact.[85] The financial interests to be registered comprised:

(i) employment or business: the member's employment or business, the name of his or her employer, or of any firm in which the member was a partner, or of any company of which the member was a paid director;

(ii) benefactors: the names of any persons who had contributed to the member's election expenses, or expenses incurred in carrying out the member's duties;

(iii) major shareholdings: the name of any corporate body which had a place of business or land in the area of the local authority, and in which the member had a beneficial interest in shares exceeding a nominal value of £25,000, or 1% of the total issued share capital;

(iv) contracts: a description of any contract between the authority and either the member, or a firm of which the member was a partner or paid director, or in which the member had a beneficial interest in shares of the level in (iii);

82 SI 2001/3575, Sch 1, para 10(2)(a)–(g).
83 SI 2001/3575, Sch 1, para 11.
84 SI 2001/3575, Sch 1, para 14.
85 LGA 2000, s 81(1), (6) and (7).

(v) landholdings: the address or another description of land:

- in the area of the authority in which the member had a beneficial interest;

- where the landlord was the authority, and the tenant was a firm in which the member was a partner or paid director, or a body in which the member had a beneficial interest in shares of the level in (iii); or

- in the area which the member had a licence to occupy for 28 days or more.

1.57   In addition, a member had also to register, within 28 days, any membership of, or position of general control or management in any:

- body to which he was appointed as a representative of the authority;

- public authority or body exercising functions of a public nature;

- company, industrial or provident society, charity or body directed to charitable purposes;

- body whose principal purposes included the influencing of public opinion or policy; or

- trades union or professional association.

1.58   Any change to the above interests had to be notified by the member to the Monitoring Officer within 28 days of the member becoming aware of it.

1.59   Gifts and hospitality over the value of £25 had to be registered within 28 days.

1.60   The Code of Conduct for members of authorities not operating executive arrangements in Schedule 2 of the Order was the same, except for the omission of references relevant to executive arrangements, overview and scrutiny committees, and joint or area committees.[86]

1.61   Other codes of conduct were issued at the same time for parish councils, and for National Parks and the Broads Authority.[87]

1.62   The Conduct of Members (Model Code of Conduct) (Wales) Order 2001[88] applied to Welsh authorities other than police authorities, with effect from 28 July 2001. This covered broadly the same areas, although it was written in more direct language. One notable difference was that members were expressly required, in reporting misconduct, to avoid 'vexatious or malicious complaints'.[89]

---

86 SI 2001/3575, Sch 2.
87 Parish Councils (Model Code of Conduct) Order 2001, SI 2001/3576 and National Parks and Broads Authorities (Model Code of Conduct) (England) Order 2001, SI 2001/3577 respectively.
88 SI 2001/2289.
89 SI 2001/2289, para 6(1)(e).

Personal interests included visits outside the UK for which the authority had paid, or would pay.[90]

E   CRITICISMS OF THE 2000 ACT REGIME

1.63   There were a number of criticisms of the Code. The provisions concerning prejudicial interests were considered to be overly-complicated, and to have obstructed members in exercising their role as champions of their local communities; notably in relation to planning and licensing issues within their wards. There were a substantial numbers of complaints, often trivial or apparently serving a political purpose; encouraged by paragraph 7 of the Code. The *Livingstone* case exposed the uncertainty over how far the Code was applied to the behaviour of members when they were off duty.

Graham Report 2005

1.64   The 10th Report of the Committee on Standards in Public Life (the 'Graham Report', 2005) expressed the view that the ethical standards framework for local government was 'arguably the most extensive and comprehensive statutory framework for standards of conduct of any group of public office-holders in the UK'. Despite 'some flaws and problems', the Committee considered that the system was a significant improvement on the position prior to 2000. It said that, as at the time of its 1997 Report, despite 'incidences of corruption and misbehaviour, the vast majority of members and officers observe high standards of conduct'.

1.65   Nonetheless, the 'highly centralised method of handling complaints' was in its view responsible for the many complaints about the proportionality of the system, which it considered to be justified. The system ran counter to its advice in 1997. In terms of proportionality, it had generated a 'large number of apparently minor, vexatious and politically motivated complaints', which in turn caused a large backlog of national investigations, leaving members facing accusations over a long period. In terms of culture, it meant that responsibility for standards was removed from the local level, and standards committees were under-used. The devolved equivalents in Scotland and Wales had largely avoided the problems of the Standards Board.

1.66   Despite recent improvements, including the production by the Office of the Deputy Prime Minister (then the relevant government department) of long-awaited Regulations allowing referrals back to Monitoring Officers and Standards Committees, and a draft code for local government officers, the report concluded that the centralised approach held inherent flaws, and the system should be recast on a local basis. It also recommended a strengthening of the

90 SI 2001/2289, para 13(i).

independent composition of standards committees, the removal of unnecessary restrictions on members from representing their constituents, and clarification of the distinction between official and private conduct. The Standards Board should become a 'strategic regulator', setting the national framework within which Monitoring Officers and standards committees managed ethical issues primarily at local level. The Board should also provide guidance and training, and investigate (with the Adjudication Panel) the most serious complaints.

White Paper 2006

1.67   The government responded with an issues paper (Dec 2005), and then a White Paper in October 2006: 'Strong and Prosperous Communities'.[91] This reported broad support for decision-making at local level, and promised legislation to deliver a system where standards committees made initial assessments of allegations of misconduct, and most investigations and decisions were made locally. The Standards Board would move to performing a strategic role, supplying advice and guidance and ensuring consistency of standards. The Code would be made 'clearer, simpler and more proportionate', together with a new code for employees. The rules on personal and prejudicial interests would remove the 'current barriers to members speaking up for their constituents' on planning or licensing issues. Members would be able to speak and vote on such issues, unless their interests in the matter were greater than those of the majority of people in their ward.

F   THE REVISED CODE, 2007–2012

The 2007 Code

Part 1 – General provisions

1.68   The Local Authorities (Model Code of Conduct) Order 2007[92] (2007 Code) was addressed (like the 1990 Code) directly to the member. It applied whenever the member conducted the business of the authority (including the business of the office to which the member was elected or appointed); or when '[you] act, claim to act or give the impression you are acting as a representative of your authority'. References to the member's 'official capacity' were to be construed accordingly.[93] The Code made clear that it did not apply outside the member's official capacity unless the actions constituted a criminal offence, for which the member had been convicted, involving intimidation in relation to a conduct complaint (see below), the bringing of one's office or authority into disrepute, or seeking an improper advantage.[94]

---

91 Cm 6393-1. See paras 3.36–3.49.
92 SI 2007/1159.
93 SI 2007/1159, Sch 1, para 2(1).
94 SI 2007/1159, Sch 1, para 2(3)–(5).

1.69   The Code contained a number of new requirements. A member should not to do anything which might cause the authority to breach a number of equality enactments (as defined in the Equality Act 2006).[95] They should not bully any person (where previously they were expected to treat others with respect).[96] They should not intimidate or attempt to intimidate any person who was, or was likely to be, a complainant or witness concerning a conduct complaint, or a person involved in the administration of a conduct investigation or proceedings; including an allegation about that member.[97]

1.70   The rules as to confidentiality were partially relaxed (see the second bullet point in the box in para **1.47** above). Disclosure of confidential information to a third party for the purpose of obtaining professional advice was permitted, provided the third party agreed not to disclose it. A disclosure that was reasonable and in the public interest, and made in good faith and in compliance with the reasonable requirements of the authority, was also permitted under the Code.[98]

1.71   The latter amendment followed the *Dimoldenberg* case in the Adjudication Panel in May 2005. Cllr Dimoldenberg was alleged to have leaked information on three occasions to a BBC journalist, in breach of paragraph 3(a) of the 2001 Code, concerning the attempts of Westminster City Council to recover £27 million from its former Leader, following the 'homes for votes' controversy. The member claimed that he acted in the public interest to encourage the council to recover the money. The main issue concerned the role of the right to freedom of expression, under Article 10 of the European Convention on Human Rights. The Adjudication Panel found that paragraph 3(a) of the then Code did not take proper account of the Article 10 right. It also took the view that the paragraph did not allow for consideration of the circumstances surrounding a disclosure of confidential information when considering whether there had been a breach of the Code. The Panel conducted a balancing exercise, which included that the member had exercised his Article 10 right, and that he had not been self-serving in his action. It found that he had breached the Code, but that no action should be taken.

1.72   A member was obliged to have regard to any applicable code of local authority publicity made under the Local Government Act 1986, ie the prohibition on a local authority from publishing, or arranging for the publication of, any material designed to affect public support for a political party or to assist others to do so.[99]

1.73   The obligation on a member, under the previous Code, to report conduct which he or she reasonably believed to be a breach, was dropped.[100]

---

95   SI 2007/1159, Sch 1, para 3(2)(a), referring to former s 33, Equality Act 2006.
96   SI 2007/1159, Sch 1, para 3(2)(b).
97   SI 2007/1159, Sch 1, para 3(2)(c).
98   SI 2007/1159, Sch 1, para 4(a).
99   Local Government Act 1986, s 2; SI 2007/1159, para 6(c).
100 SI 2001/3575, para 7.

Part 2 – Interests

1.74 The provisions as to interests remained highly complex. Previously the test for personal interests had been whether they had to be registered, or they affected the well-being or financial position of the member, or a relative, friend or a range of other persons or bodies, to a greater extent than a council tax payer, ratepayer or inhabitant.[101] Under the 2007 Code, the list of comparators for the latter test was extended to include 'any person with whom you have a close association'; but in relation to persons or bodies in which the member held shares, the list was restricted to those in which the member had a holding with a nominal value of £25,000, rather than £5000 as before.[102] On the other hand, the extensive list of persons, activities or interests which were included where the business before the council either related to them, or was likely to affect them, was extended to the interests of any person who had given the member a gift or hospitality of at least £25 (rather than the item merely having to be registered).

1.75 Some interests required disclosure only if the member spoke on them. This applied to business relating to or affecting a body of which the member was a member or in a position of general control or management, to which they has been appointed or nominated by the authority; or a body exercising functions of a public nature, of which they were a member or held a similar position, but had not been placed there by the authority. Even the way this provision was expressed, however, referring to complicated numbering of provisions as in a legislative text, contributed to the complex nature of the Code. An interest arising from gifts or hospitality did not have to be disclosed to the meeting if it had been registered more than three years previously.

1.76 The general test for prejudicial interests was unchanged from the previous code (see para **1.52** above). The code created a broad new exception, however, where the business did not affect the financial position of the member, or of a person or body giving rise to a personal interest of the member.[103] A further wide exception was where the business did not relate to the determining or any approval, licence, permission or registration, in relation to the member or to a person or body through whom he or she had a personal interest.[104] Interests, therefore, which the public might consider would be likely to prejudice the member's judgement, but which did not affect his or her finances (or those with whom they were linked), or which were not about applications concerning them, were not prejudicial interests. This would appear to include service issues (eg social services, education) which might directly have affected the member.

1.77 The previous list of other interests which were not prejudicial interests (housing, school meals and transport, statutory sick pay, and members' allowances) was repeated; with indemnities included with the latter. The

---

101 See paras **1.49–1.50** above.
102 See para **1.50** above.
103 SI 2007/1159, Sch 1, para 10(2)(a).
104 SI 2007/1159, Sch 1, para 10(2)(b).

exclusion from the housing exception of those owing more than two months' rent was dropped. Ceremonial honours for members, and the setting of council tax, were added. The previous exceptions for membership of other relevant authorities, public authorities on which the member held a position of general control or management, or bodies to which he or she had been appointed by the authority, however, were removed.[105]

1.78   In relation to overview and scrutiny, the same position was maintained (see para **1.54** above), save that the right of a decision-maker, notwithstanding having a prejudicial interest, to attend to make presentations, answer questions or give evidence, applied only where the public were also allowed to attend for the same purpose. While understandable in promoting transparency, this was anomalous in the context of an overview and scrutiny committee which might need to ask questions of a decision-maker in a closed session.

1.79   The above restriction may have been an unintended consequence of the drafting of the main change made by the Code, which relaxed the restrictions on participation of members generally (following the lead in relation to overview and scrutiny in the previous code), where they had prejudicial interests which would otherwise prevent them from representing their constituents. A member was permitted to attend a meeting (including an overview and scrutiny meeting) where the business concerned the interest, only for the purpose of making 'representations, answering questions or giving evidence relating to the business', provided the public were allowed to attend for the same purpose. The main areas were planning and licensing, where local members (especially if they lived in their ward or division) would often have a prejudicial interest in a contentious application, and found themselves unable under the previous code to speak up for the concerns of local residents. The lifting of the restriction in those cases, to the limited extent of enabling such members to make representations before withdrawing, addressed the main element of that concern.

1.80   In relation to the register of interests, the Code recognised a category of information relating to personal interests as 'sensitive information'; meaning that its availability for inspection would create, or would be likely to create, a serious risk that the member or a person who lived with them could be subjected to violence or intimidation. In those circumstances, if the Monitoring Officer agreed, the information need not be included with the interest on the register; and its nature (as opposed to the existence of a personal interest) need not be disclosed to a meeting at which it became relevant.[106]

Welsh Code 2008

1.81   The Welsh Code, published the following year, contained significant differences from the English version.[107] The confidentiality provisions were not

105 SI 2007/1159, Sch 1, para 10(2)(c).
106 SI 2007/1159, Sch 1, paras 9(5), 14.
107 Local Authorities (Model Code of Conduct) (Wales) Order 2008, SI 2008/788 (W. 82).

amended to reflect the Article 10 exception, or the exception for disclosure to obtain third party professional advice.[108] The Code obliged members to report criminal behaviour, and retained the obligation to report misconduct (while prohibiting vexatious, malicious or frivolous complaints).[109]

1.82 Misconduct arising from improperly seeking to confer an advantage on oneself or another person applied in an official capacity or otherwise. Its scope was not limited, as in the English Code, to such behaviour where it constituted a criminal offence for which the member had been convicted.[110] The ban on misuse of the council's resources was broken down into examples.[111]

1.83 The Code banned the receipt of gifts and hospitality (other than official hospitality) or material benefits or services, which might place the member under an improper obligation; or reasonably appear to do so.[112]

1.84 In relation to interests, a Welsh member had a personal interest where the business related to or affected a firm in which he or she was a partner, or a company of which they were a remunerated director; whereas this applied to an English member only where there was a contract between the authority and such a firm or company (which the Welsh Code also covered).[113] A Welsh member likewise had a personal interest if the business related to or affected anybody to which he or she had been appointed or nominated by their authority; not merely, as in England, where they were also a member of the body, or in a position of general control or management of it.[114] On the other hand, where they did have such a position, the type of bodies which led to its counting as an interest were listed (and thus limited), whereas in the English Code they were not; and consequently the latter interest was capable of applying more widely.[115]

1.85 The Welsh Code included a general personal interest, absent from the English version, where a member of the public might reasonably perceive a conflict of interest (in determining that business) between the member's roles in the authority as a whole, and as a constituency representative.

1.86 On the test of effects on well-being or financial position, the persons who had to be taken into account were those with whom the member lived (ie not necessarily his or her family), and those with whom the member had a 'close personal association' (rather than a 'close association'). The threshold for shareholdings in companies to which the council business related, or which it

---

108 SI 2008/788, para 5.
109 SI 2008/788, para 6(b) and (c).
110 SI 2008/788, para 7(a).
111 SI 2008/788, para 7(b).
112 SI 2008/788, para 9.
113 SI 2008/788, para 10(2)(a)(ii); compare English Code SI 2007/1159, Sch 1, para 8(1)(a)(vii), which was reflected in para 10(2)(a)(v) of the Welsh Code.
114 Compare Welsh para 10(2)(a)(viii) (SI 2008/788) with English para 8(1)(a)(i) (SI 2007/1159).
115 See Welsh para 10(2)(a)(ix) (SI 2008/788) compared with English para 8(1)(a)(i) (SI 2007/1159) as above.

affected, was set at £5000, rather than £25,000 as in England.[116] Finally, unlike his English counterpart, the Welsh member had a personal interest in business affecting bodies (such as clubs, or companies) in which his close personal associates held positions of general control or management, as well as himself; where the decision might reasonably be regarded as affecting their interests to a greater extent than the majority of local taxpayers or inhabitants.[117]

1.87   Disclosure of Welsh personal interests extended to oral and written representations from members to officers.[118]

1.88   The list of exceptions from prejudicial interests was nearer to the English 2001 Code than to its contemporary replacement, with no general exclusion where the matter did not affect the member's financial position or the position of those in relation to whom he had a personal interest. There was an additional exception for school governors (save where the business related to the specific school), and another in relation to a member's role on a Local Health Board (in both cases, where the member had not been appointed by the authority).[119] There was also an exception for community members in relation to financial assistance by that council to community groups of up to £500.[120]

1.89   Five exceptions (those in paragraph 12(2)(a)), such as those for members of another public authority, or of the Local Health Board) did not apply where the decision related to any approval, consent, licence, permission or registration; partially reversing the effect in Wales of the English exception for such decisions.[121]

1.90   There was a similar right in Wales for members with prejudicial interests to make representations, but a decision-maker could only appear at an overview and scrutiny committee for that purpose if summoned to do so by the committee.[122]

1.91   There was a general obligation to register all financial and other interests within 28 days. On gifts and hospitality, the threshold was set by the authority.[123]

G   INTRODUCTION OF THE CURRENT REGIME

1.92   Following Manifesto commitments by the Conservative and Liberal Democrat parties at the General Election in 2010, the Coalition Agreement between them included a commitment to abolish 'the Standards Board regime'. In December 2010, the Government made the following announcement:

116 SI 2008/788, para 10(2)(c)(iv).
117 SI 2008/788, para 10(2)(c)(v).
118 SI 2008/788, para 11(2).
119 SI 2008/788, para 12(2)(a)(iv) and (v).
120 SI 2008/788, para 12(2)(c).
121 SI 2008/788, para 12(3).
122 SI 2008/788, para 14(2) and 14(3)(a) respectively.
123 SI 2008/788, paras 15(1) and 17 respectively.

'The Government considers that the Standards Board regime, consisting of a centrally prescribed model code of conduct, standards committees with the power to suspend a local authority member and regulated by a central quango was inconsistent with the principles of localism. In addition there is a concern that the regime is a vehicle for vexatious or politically motivated complaints.

The Government considers that it is the right and the responsibility of the electorate to determine who represents them and that the abolition of the regime will restore power to local people.'

1.93 A number of themes were reflected in this statement and others made by the Government about its policy. The approach was partly driven by a desire to reduce the number of quangos. More specifically, however, the unpopularity of the Standards Board itself (mainly amongst members) was doubtless the moving force. To this was added Ministers' desire to promote localism as they saw it. The Board was seen as a 'centrally-prescribed model', which was inconsistent with those principles. As well as having become, as Ministers in the new Government saw it, a vehicle for 'vexatious or politically motivated complaints', there was disquiet that the power to suspend or disqualify a member, wielded by a national body, removed accountability to local people. In addition, it was considered that the number and type of complaints had eroded public confidence in local members. It was argued that the risk of a complaint for bringing the council into disrepute suppressed freedom of speech; and could inhibit members from acting as whistleblowers where they perceived local decisions or actions to be wrong.

1.94 A later Impact Assessment, published in January 2011, noted that there had been over 6000 complaints between May 2008 and the end of March 2010 under the current regime, of which only 28% were recommended for investigation.[124]

1.95 The announcement in December 2010 stated that, because of the 'interdependence of the bodies, requirements and guidance' that constituted the regime, the Government proposed to abolish the regime in its entirety. The Model Code of Conduct would be revoked. The requirement for local authorities to have standards committees would be abolished, as would the Standards Board ('Standards for England'). The First-tier Tribunal (Local Government Standards in England) would lose its jurisdiction over the conduct of local authority members.

1.96 Some of the changes were made by the revocation of Orders, but the abolition of the Standards Board and Part 3 of the LGA 2000 required primary legislation. Part 1, Chapter 5 (subsequently Chapter 7) of the Localism Bill dealt with Standards. In introducing the Bill on Second Reading on 17 January 2011,

---

124 'Localism Bill: the abolition of the Standards Board regime, clarification of the law on predetermination and the requirement to register and declare interests: Impact assessment', DCLG, January 2011, p 1.

the Secretary of State, Eric Pickles, concentrated on other measures and did not mention the conduct provisions.

1.97 In the Committee stage in the House of Commons, Labour MPs moved an amendment to make it compulsory for a local authority to adopt a code of conduct. The former Local Government Minister, Nick Raynsford MP, said that, before the Standards Board, there had been complaints about 'thoroughly unsatisfactory standards of conduct'. For all the criticism of the Board – and he said that he understood the Conservative view that it had been unduly prescriptive, and that less centralisation was necessary – leaving to local discretion whether to have a code of standards in an area opened the door to 'precisely the kinds of problems and abuse that existed in the past'.[125] Without a Code, a 'minority' would 'transgress and behave inappropriately'. The public should feel confident that those elected would maintain the highest standards, and this should not be taken 'lightly' or be seen 'simply as a matter of localism and devolution: certain principles should be upheld in public life at all levels'.[126]

1.98 The Parliamentary Under-Secretary, DCLG, Andrew Stunell MP, claimed that those with experience of local government knew that the system was 'an almost constant source of irritation to almost every local authority'. He stated that between two-thirds and three-quarters of all complaints through the mechanism of the Standards Board came from parish and town councils. These complaints were 'often trivial, a waste of money and reputation, pointless and meaningless'.[127]

1.99 The Opposition also asked about the impact of cases on the Local Government Ombudsman, if his office had to deal with cases that would previously have gone through the standards system. The Minister said that the Government expected the impact to be 'slight'. Local authorities would initially resolve cases as they saw fit. If a matter went beyond that, it might or might not be a matter for criminal prosecution, action under harassment legislation, a matter for the district auditor, or a matter of maladministration for the local ombudsman.[128]

1.100 The Bill was changed in significant respects in the Lords, in the direction of the former regime, after growing pressure from a cross-party group of peers on the issue of whether local authorities should retain the discretion over whether to maintain a local code. The Government changed course at Third Reading, and moved amendments to convert the discretion into an obligation to do so (now s 27(2) of the Localism Act 2011). A code adopted by an authority should, when viewed as a whole, be consistent with the seven principles of public life, which were incorporated into the statute (Localism Act 2011, s 28(1)). There were also powers to revise or replace a local code (Localism Act 2011, s 28(5)).

---

125 Official Report, Public Bill Committee: Localism Bill, 3 February 2011, col 285.
126 Cols 285-6.
127 Col 287.
128 See cols 291-2, 299-300.

With the duty to adopt a code came a duty to have in place "arrangements under which allegations can be investigated", and "decisions on allegations can be made" (Localism Act 2011, s 28(6)) The arrangements also needed to include provision for appointment by the authority of at least one independent person whose views were to be sought and taken into account by the authority before it made a decision on an allegation; and whose views could be sought by the authority in other circumstances, or by a member facing an allegation (Localism Act 2011, s 28(7)).

1.101 The Committee on Standards in Public Life nonetheless expressed disquiet about the new Act. In a press notice, the Committee said that it had 'significant concerns about the inherent robustness of the new arrangements'. It welcomed the mandatory requirement to adopt a local code, based on the seven principles. It had 'consistently argued', however, that codes needed to be 'supported by independent scrutiny to support internal systems for maintaining standards', and by the promotion and reinforcement of such standards. Guidance, training, and the 'application of appropriate sanctions when those standards are breached are all crucial'. The committee said that the sanctions in the new arrangements were 'relatively modest', and there was a 'significantly reduced independent input' giving rise to 'inherent risks'.[129] The Secretary of State responded to the Committee's chairman that the Department would undertake a post-implementation review of the policy in three–five years (ie in 2015–2017).

1.102 The Government published guidance on making local councils more transparent, which included an Illustrative Text of a code of conduct for members (11 April 2012).[130] On 28 June 2012, the Parliamentary Under-Secretary, DCLG, Mr Robert Neill, wrote to all local authority leaders to update them on implementation and explain the role of the new independent person.[131] On 1 July 2012, all standards matters became the responsibility of local authorities. Mr Neill commented in a press release that members would now, instead of having 'hundreds of expensive and frivolous investigations hanging over their heads', be free to 'get on with their jobs'. The DCLG said in the same press release that the new rules on registering certain pecuniary interests would 'strike a common sense balance between centralised accountability, and personal privacy'.[132]

1.103 It will be clear from this summary that the revised regime places direct responsibility on local authorities to determine their own standards, how they are to be investigated and any decisions made, and how to apply the limited sanctions that are available. The role of the independent person is more limited than previously, while the Monitoring Officer is even more centrally involved. These mechanisms, and the legal issues to which they give rise, will be explored in the rest of the book. What remains unclear at this stage, however, is to what

---

129 'New standards regime for local authorities is not ready and risks public confidence', press notice, 28 June 2012.
130 'Illustrative text for local code of conduct', DCLG, 11 April 2012 (part of: 'Making local councils more transparent and accountable to local people').
131 Letter to All Local Authority Leaders, Bob Neill MP, DCLG, 28 June 2012.
132 'New Guidance to help councillors with new transparency agenda', DCLG, 2 August 2012.

extent the easing of controls will, over time, promote a greater or lesser sense of individual responsibility amongst members; and where accountability really lies within the system.

1.104　The position in Wales remains governed by Part 3 of the LGA 2000, as amended by the Localism Act 2011; and principally by Chapters 3 and 4 of Part 3.

CHAPTER 2

The standards regime

A INTRODUCTION

2.1 The previous chapter examined the history of the law relating to councillors' conduct and discussed the genesis of the new regime. This chapter will set out the legislative framework for the standards regime brought into force by Part 1, Chapter 7 of the Localism Act 2011.[1]

2.2 The purpose of the legislation was explained by His Honour Judge McKenna (sitting as a Deputy Judge of the High Court) in *R (on the application of Dennehy) v London Borough of Ealing* [2013] EWHC 4102 (Admin): '[t]he intention of the legislation is to ensure that the conduct of public life at the local government level does not fall below a minimum level which engenders public confidence in democracy as was recognised by Beatson J, as he then was, in *R (Calver) v The Adjudication Panel for Wales* [2012] EWHC 1172 (Admin) when he held that there was a clear public interest in maintaining confidence in local government whilst at the same time bearing in mind the importance of freedom of political expression or speech in the political sphere'.[2]

2.3 Whilst the intention of the legislation remains consistent with the previous regime, the means by which that intention is achieved has been altered dramatically. In accordance with the localism agenda championed by the coalition government the responsibility for establishing codes and enforcing

---

1 The Standards Board was formally abolished from 1 April 2012 in accordance with the Localism Act 2011 (Commencement No. 4) Order 2012, SI 2012/628. The duty pursuant to s 27(1) of the Localism Act 2011 came into force on 7 June 2012 but the code adopted pursuant to s 27(2) could only take effect from 1 July 2012 pursuant to the Localism Act 2011 (Commencement No. 6) Order 2012, SI 2012/1463.

2 *R (on the application of Dennehy) v London Borough of Ealing* [2013] EWHC 4102 (Admin), para 9.

their provision now rests at a local level, rather than with a centralised standards board. The rationale for such a change was explained in a DCLG press release in June 2012:

> 'These new measures, outlined in the Localism Act, will replace the bureaucratic and controversial Standards Board regime, which ministers believe had become a system of nuisance complaints and petty, sometime malicious, allegations of Councillor misconduct that sapped public confidence in local democracy.'[3]

2.4   Whilst the removal of the bureaucratic and complex regime established under the Standards Committee (England) Regulations 2008[4] ('the 2008 Regulations') is to be welcomed, it remains to be seen whether the administration of the standards regime at a local level will discourage 'nuisance complaints' and 'petty allegations'. We are somewhat sceptical as to whether the objectives of DCLG will be achieved in practice and whether the appropriate cure was the wholesale change of the previous regime. In particular the amendments have led to the loss of any real systematic independent scrutiny which had brought some distinct advantages. The lack of effective sanctions is also of concern.

B   THE DUTY

2.5   The 2011 Act places 'relevant authorities' under a statutory duty to 'promote and maintain high standards of conduct by members and co-opted members of the authority'.[5] This is the core duty imposed by the 2011 Act.

2.6   'Relevant authorities' are defined as:[6]

(a) a county council in England;

(b) a district council;

(c) a London borough council;

(d) a parish council;

(e) the Greater London Authority;

[...]

(g) the London Fire and Emergency Planning Authority;

(h) the Common Council of the City of London in its capacity as a local authority or police authority;

(i) the Council of the Isles of Scilly;

---

3 *New rules to ensure greater town hall transparency,* DCLG press release, 28 June 2012.
4 SI 2008/1085.
5 Localism Act 2011, s 27(1).
6 Localism Act 2011, s 27(6).

(j) a fire and rescue authority in England constituted by a scheme under section 2 of the Fire and Rescue Services Act 2004 or a scheme to which section 4 of that Act applies;

[...]

(l) a joint authority established by Part 4 of the Local Government Act 1985;

(m) an economic prosperity board established under section 88 of the Local Democracy, Economic Development and Construction Act 2009;

(n) a combined authority established under section 103 of that Act;

(o) the Broads Authority; or

(p) a National Park authority in England established under section 63 of the Environment Act 1995.

2.7   In discharging the core duty, relevant authorities must, in particular, adopt a code dealing with the conduct that is expected of members and co-opted members of the authority when they are acting in that capacity.[7] However, it is important to note that the adoption of the code does not necessarily exhaust the core duty.

2.8   The legislation specifically permits parish councils to comply with the duty to adopt a code of conduct simply by adopting the code of its principal authority.[8] Moreover, the parish council is entitled to assume that the code of conduct is consistent with the Nolan principles and that appropriate provision has been made in respect of the registration and disclosure of pecuniary interests and interests other than pecuniary interests.[9]

2.9   In addition to members of the relevant authorities, the codes of conduct will also apply to:

- Co-opted members, who are defined, in relation to a relevant authority, as: (a) a member of any committee or subcommittee of the authority; or (b) a member of, and represents the authority on, any joint committee or joint subcommittee of the authority; and, in the case of either (a) or (b), where the member is entitled to vote on any question that falls to be decided at any meeting of that committee or sub-committee.[10]

- Elected mayors.[11]

- The Mayor of London.[12]

- London Assembly Members.[13]

---

7 Localism Act 2011, s 27(2) In this chapter, references to 'member' should be read as including 'co-opted member' unless indicated otherwise.
8 Localism Act 2011, s 27(3)(a).
9 Localism Act 2011, s 27(3)(b).
10 Localism Act 2011, s 27(4).
11 Localism Act 2011, s 27(7)(b).
12 Ibid.
13 Ibid.

Question: Could proceedings be brought against a relevant authority for a failure to comply with the duties established by s 27(1) and (2)?

Answer: It is likely that the courts would interpret the duties imposed by s 27(1) and (2) as specific rather than 'target' duties. That is to say they would be enforceable at the suit of an individual. ('Target' duties are not directly enforceable by any individual and merely require an authority to 'do its best'.)

Section 27(2) is clearly intended to be a specific duty: it expressly requires the adoption of a code of conduct. In the absence of the adoption of a code, it is highly likely that an interested party, perhaps a councillor, could bring proceedings against a relevant authority to compel such adoption. However, it is very unlikely that any authority would consciously fail to comply with this particular duty.

While s 27(1) is framed in more general terms, it is likely that proceedings could also be brought in respect of any breach of this duty too although the circumstances in which such a claim could be brought may be limited. Firstly, there is nothing on the face of the legislation to suggest Parliament intended the duty to be a target only (contrast the duty established s 17 of the Children Act 1989 which begins 'it shall be the general duty' and is itself to be contrasted with the specific duties found in the latter provisions of the 1989 Act). Secondly, the majority of duties previously found by the courts to be target duties required the allocation of scarce resources. Thirdly, it would be surprising in the extreme if Parliament had intended only that relevant authorities 'do their best' to promote and maintain high standards of conduct by its members. However, given the clear intent of the scheme to advance the localism agenda, the Courts would likely discourage using any such claim to involve the Court in the details of how a particular case has been handled as opposed to, for example, a refusal to acknowledge the duty at all or a failure to investigate under s 28.

C LOCAL CODES

2.10   Every relevant authority must secure that its adopted code is, when viewed as a whole, consistent with the Nolan principles.[14] These are set out at s 28(1)(a) of the 2011 Act and are as follows:

- Selflessness.

- Integrity.

- Objectivity.

- Accountability.

- Openness.

---

14 Localism Act 2011, s 27(2).

- Honesty.
- Leadership.

2.11   The Nolan committee in their first report described the content of these seven principles as follows:[15]

- **Selflessness** – Holders of public office should act solely in terms of the public interest. They should not do so in order to gain financial or other benefits for themselves, their family or their friends.

- **Integrity** – Holders of public office should not place themselves under any financial or other obligation to outside individuals or organisations that might seek to influence them in the performance of their official duties.

- **Objectivity** – In carrying out public business, including making public appointments, awarding contracts, or recommending individuals for rewards and benefits, holders of public office should make choices on merit.

- **Accountability** – Holders of public office are accountable for their decisions and actions to the public and must submit themselves to whatever scrutiny is appropriate to their office.

- **Openness** – Holders of public office should be as open as possible about all the decisions and actions they take. They should give reasons for their decisions and restrict information only when the wider public interest clearly demands.

- **Honesty** – Holders of public office have a duty to declare any private interests relating to their public duties and to take steps to resolve any conflicts arising in a way that protects the public interest.

- **Leadership** – Holders of public office should promote and support these principles by leadership and example.

2.12   Although expressed in abstract terms, the Nolan principles should permeate all levels and elements of decision-making by local councillors. An example of their practical application is found within the LGA's publication 'Probity in Planning'.[16] The planning context is one in which local councillors are often responsible for decisions which are highly controversial, not least because the planning system balances the private interests in the development of land against the wider public interests. It follows that decisions on applications for planning permission are regularly the subject of legal challenge. It is unsurprising, therefore, that in the planning context compliance with the Nolan principles by councillors is often the subject of external scrutiny, including by the Local Government Ombudsman and the Courts.

15 These definitions are also reflected in the template code of conduct: http://www.local.gov.uk/ media-centre/-/journal_content/56/10180/3376577/NEWS (April 2012).
16 'Probity in Planning for Councilors and Officers' (Local Government Association and Planning Advisory Service; Published April 2013 (Updated November 2013)) http://www.pas.gov. uk/documents/332612/1099271/Probity+in+planning+guide/c2463914-db11-4321-8d38- be54c188abbe.

2.13   In order to ensure planning decisions are taken fairly, the LGA emphasises the need for councillors to comply with the Nolan principles. For example, the guidance stresses that 'serving councillors must not act as agents for people pursuing planning matters within their authority even if they are not involved in the decision making on it':[17] to do so would clearly be in breach of the principles of Integrity and Objectivity, at the very least. In relation to the decision-making itself the guidance goes on to draw a distinction between predetermination and predisposition.[18] Although the dividing line is sometimes quite thin, the former is contrary to the principle of Objectivity, whilst the latter is an inevitable feature of our democratic system. Finally, the guidance explains that, whilst it is an essential part of the planning system that local concerns are adequately ventilated and recognises that the most effective way that this can be done is through the locally elected members, nevertheless it explains that councillors must be cognisant of the possibility that inappropriate lobbying can lead to the impartiality and integrity of a member being called into question.[19]

2.14   Relevant authorities are also required to secure that their codes include provision, as they consider appropriate, for the registration and disclosure of pecuniary interests and interests other than pecuniary interests.[20] As discussed below, ss 29 to 34 of the 2011 Act set out the legislative framework for the registration and disclosure of interests. These sections do not limit what may be included in a code of conduct, save that a code cannot prejudice the operation of those sections.[21]

2.15   Relevant authorities may, at any time: (a) revise their existing codes of conduct, or (b) adopt a new code of conduct to replace their existing code of conduct.[22]

2.16   It is a requirement of the 2011 Act that relevant authorities publicise adoption, revision or replacement of a code of conduct. They must do so in such a manner as they consider is likely to bring the same to the attention of persons who live in its area.[23]

---

17 Ibid, p 6.
18 The example it gives is as follows: 'A councillor who states "Windfarms are blots on the landscape and I will oppose each and every windfarm application that comes before the committee" will be perceived very differently from a councillor who states: "Many people find windfarms ugly and noisy and I will need a lot of persuading that any more windfarms should be allowed in our area."' (p 8) The former is an example of pre-determination, the latter mere predisposition.
19 For example, in order to avoid the perception of bias the guidance advises that '[i]f councillors do express an opinion to objectors or supporters, it is good practice that they make it clear that they will only be in a position to take a final decision after having heard all the relevant arguments and taken into account all relevant material and planning considerations at committee.'
20 Localism Act 2011, s 28(2).
21 Localism Act 2011, s 28(3).
22 Localism Act 2011, s 28(5).
23 Localism Act 2011, s 28(12).

2.17   The adoption, revision or replacement of a code of conduct may not be delegated and must be discharged only by the authority.[24] The legal provisions which would otherwise permit a delegation of functions (eg s 101 of the Local Government Act 1972, or s 35 of the 2011 Act) do not apply to the adoption, revision or replacement of a code of conduct.[25]

2.18   Save that codes must: (a) when viewed as a whole be consistent with the Nolan principles, and (b) promote and maintain high standards of conduct, the 2011 Act does not prescribe their content. This is left entirely to the relevant authorities.

2.19   However, the DCLG has published an illustrative text that councils can, if they choose, use as a basis for their new local code of conduct.[26] The illustrative text is relatively brief and, in the opinion of this chapter's authors, reads more as a series of expectations rather than a formal code of conduct. Nevertheless, it includes requirements:

● to act solely in the public interest;

● never improperly to confer an advantage or disadvantage on any person;

● never act to gain financial or other material benefits;

● to make all choices, when carrying out public duties, on the basis of merit;

● to be accountable for any decisions made to the public;

● to be as open as possible about decisions and actions;

● to be prepared to give reasons for decisions;

● never to be placed under a financial or other obligation that may influence the performance of official duties;

● not to use or authorise the use of the authority's resources improperly for political purposes or party political purposes.

2.20   Examples of codes of conduct adopted by local authorities are cited in the footnote below.[27] These demonstrate the variety of approaches and content which exists among relevant authorities which may be permitted by the Act. For

---

24 Localism Act 2011, s 28(13).
25 Localism Act 2011, s 28(14).
26 https://www.gov.uk/government/publications/illustrative-text-for-local-code-of-conduct--2 (updated 20 September 2013). The Illustrative text is set out in its entirety in **Appendix D**.
27 http://www.camden.gov.uk/ccm/content/council-and-democracy/who-represents-you/camdens-councillors/conduct-of-councillors.en?page=1
https://mgov.newham.gov.uk/documents/s82616/5.1%20-%20Code%20of%20Conduct%20for%20Members.pdf
http://www.rbkc.gov.uk/councilanddemocracy/howthecouncilworks/theconstitution/constitutiontableofcontents.aspx
http://www.lambeth.gov.uk/sites/default/files/Part4CodesandProtocols.pdf
http://www.southwark.gov.uk/downloads/download/3190/southwark_council_code_of_conduct_for_members

instance, some local authorities' codes of conduct are relatively brief and reflect closely the illustrative text. On the other hand other authorities have produced more detailed codes, far exceeding the limited scope of the illustrative text. In these more detailed codes authorities have amongst other matters:

- Established a detailed Protocol for Use of Council Resources and Facilities by Councillors.

- Outlined the circumstances in which it is acceptable to accept a gift or hospitality.

- Promulgated specific codes for their Planning and Licensing Committees.

- Developed criteria for the consideration of requests for dispensation in relation to disclosable pecuniary interests.

- Established a protocol on foreign visits.

- Adopted a policy on Member and Officer relationships.

D   REGISTRATION AND DISCLOSURE OF INTERESTS

Register of interests

2.21   The monitoring officer of a relevant authority must establish and maintain a register of interests of members of the authority[28] The register of a Parish Council is the responsibility of the monitoring officer of the principal authority, which will be the relevant District Council, County Council or London Borough council.[29]

2.22   Subject to the limits on the general powers of authorities as circumscribed by Chapter 1 of the 2011 Act, it is for the relevant authority to determine the content of the register.[30] The register need not contain an entry once the member concerned: (a) no longer has an interest; or (b) is (otherwise than transitorily on re-election or re-appointment) no longer a member of the authority.[31]

2.23   The monitoring officer of a relevant authority, other than a parish council, must ensure that a copy of the register is available for inspection at a place in the authority's area at all reasonable hours and that it is published on the authority's website.[32] Monitoring officers of parish councils must, in addition, ensure the parish council's register is available for inspection at a place in the principal authority's area at all reasonable hours and is published on the principal authority's website.[33]

---

28 Localism Act 2011, s 29(1).
29 Localism Act 2011, s 29(4).
30 Localism Act 2011, s 29(2).
31 Localism Act 2011, s 29(3).
32 Localism Act 2011, s 29(5).
33 Localism Act 2011, s 29(6).

2.24   A parish council must, if it has a website, ensure the register is published on its website and the relevant monitoring officer must provide the parish council with any data it requires in order to comply with this requirement.[34]

2.25   The legislation provides for sensitive interests to be withheld from the register. An interest will be 'sensitive' for these purposes where the details of the interest could lead to the member or co-opted member (or a person connected with them) being subject to violence or intimidation. Where the monitoring officer and the member or co-opted member are both of the view that an interest is a sensitive interest, there is a prohibition on its publication, and details of the interest must not be included on any publicly available copy of the register.[35] Note that the monitoring officer has to agree in order for the interest to be treated as sensitive.

2.26   The published version of the register may state that the member has an interest the details of which are withheld.[36]

Disclosure of pecuniary interests

2.27   The 2011 Act together with the Relevant Authorities (Disclosable Pecuniary Interests) Regulations 2012[37] ('the Disclosable Pecuniary Interests Regulations') establishes those pecuniary interests which must be disclosed by members on taking office.

2.28   A member must, within 28 days of their becoming a member (or when member are re-elected or co-opted members re-appointed) notify the monitoring officer of any disclosable pecuniary interests which have not already been entered into the authority's register.[38]

2.29   The 2011 Act provides that a pecuniary interest is disclosable where it is: (i) of a type set out in the Disclosable Pecuniary Interests Regulations, and (ii) it is an interest of the member or it is an interest of the member's spouse/civil partner (or equivalent co-habitant) and the member is aware of their partner's interest.[39]

2.30   The relevant disclosable interests can be found in the Schedule to the Disclosable Pecuniary Interests Regulations. These are summarised in **Chapter 3** and a full text of these Regulations is set out in **Appendix B**.

2.31   It is notable that there is no requirement for members or co-opted members to notify the monitoring officer of any new disclosable pecuniary

---

34 Localism Act 2011, s 29(6) and (7).
35 Localism Act 2011, s 32(1)–(2).
36 Localism Act 2011, s 32(3).
37 SI 2012/1464.
38 Localism Act 2011, s 30(1) and (2).
39 Localism Act 2011, s 33.

interests when they arise, but it may be advisable to do so to ensure compliance with the requirements of s 31 of the Localism Act 2011 (for which, see below). The Department for Communities and Local Government (DCLG) has published a guide for councillors on 'Openness and transparency on personal interests',[40] which states that the principle of integrity requires councillors to give the monitoring officer responsible for the register of members' interests any information he or she requests in order to keep that register up to date.

2.32　When a member or co-opted member discloses a disclosable pecuniary interest to the monitoring officer in one of the circumstances set out above, the monitoring officer has no discretion over whether to register the interest – he or she is required to enter onto the register all interests that members and co-opted members disclose. This is so whether or not the interests are disclosable pecuniary interests. This leaves scope for an authority to require its members, through the local code or otherwise, to register interests that are additional to disclosable pecuniary interests. It may also be intended to encourage the voluntary registration by councillors of a wider range of interests than those they are required to disclose.

Consequences of members having pecuniary interests in matters considered at meetings or by single members

2.33　We have outlined below the statutory framework relevant to the impact of members having pecuniary interests in matters being considered by the authority. However, **Chapter 3** considers this issue in greater depth.[41]

2.34　Where members are: (a) present at a meeting of the authority or at any committee of the authority, (b) have a disclosable pecuniary interest in any matter to be considered, or being considered, at the meeting, and (c) aware of such an interest, then the following consequences apply:

- if the interest is not already registered, it must be disclosed to the meeting (save if it is a 'sensitive interest' (discussed at **2.25** above), in which case the member must disclose merely the fact that they have a disclosable pecuniary interest in the matter concerned);[42] and

- if the interest is not entered in the authority's register and is not the subject of a pending notification, the member must notify the monitoring officer of the interest within 28 days;[43]

---

40 September 2013. Note that this is not statutory guidance, nor is it legal opinion, so there is no obligation to follow the guide. It is nevertheless helpful in understanding what the government considers councillors are required to do.
41 See **Chapter 3**, paras **3.9–3.18**.
42 Localism Act 2011, s 31(2).
43 Localism Act 2011, s 31(3).

- most significantly, the member may not participate in the discussion of the matter at the meeting or in any vote taken on the matter at the meeting;[44] and

- a standing order of the authority may, in addition, provide for the exclusion of a member from a meeting while any discussion or vote takes place.[45]

2.35 However, the 2011 Act provides that, on written request by a member made to the proper officer of the authority, a relevant authority may grant dispensation from the third of these consequences, but only if the relevant authority considers that one or more of the following conditions are met:[46]

(a) that without the dispensation the number of persons prohibited from participating in any particular business would be so great a proportion of the body transacting the business as to impede the transaction of the business;

(b) that without the dispensation the representation of different political groups on the body transacting any particular business would be so upset as to alter the likely outcome of any vote relating to the business;

(c) that granting the dispensation is in the interests of persons living in the authority's area;

(d) that, if it is an authority to which Part 1A of the Local Government Act 2000 applies and is operating executive arrangements, then without the dispensation each member of the authority's executive would be prohibited by section 31(4) from participating in any particular business to be transacted by the authority's executive; or

(e) that it is otherwise appropriate to grant a dispensation.

2.36 Similar disclosure provisions apply in circumstances where functions are being discharged by a single member acting alone. Where they have a disclosable pecuniary interest in any matter being dealt with and they are aware of such an interest, then:

- if the interest is not entered in the authority's register and is not the subject of a pending notification, the member must notify the monitoring officer of the interest within 28 days; and

- the member may not take any further steps in relation to the matter, except for the purpose of enabling the matter to be dealt with otherwise than by that member.[47]

2.37 Most significantly, there is no dispensation provision allowing a single member to exercise the relevant function in such circumstances.

2.38 The 2011 Act establishes a number of criminal offences for contraventions of the registration and disclosure requirements. These will be discussed in **Chapter 6**.

---

44 Localism Act 2011, s 31(4).
45 Localism Act 2011, s 31(10).
46 Localism Act 2011, s 33.
47 Localism Act 2011, s 31(6)–(8).

Disclosure of non-pecuniary interests

2.39   As discussed above, the 2011 Act makes provision for the authority to include, within its code of conduct, requirements on members to register and disclose non-pecuniary interests.[48] However, the legislation expressly provides that it is for an authority to determine what is to be entered in its register.[49] A number of authorities have exercised this power and made provision for the registration and disclosure of a wide variety of non-pecuniary interests. The illustrative text from the DCLG makes provision for the disclosure of non-pecuniary interests in the following manner:

> 'You must declare any private interests, both pecuniary and non-pecuniary, including your membership of any Trade Union, that relate to your public duties and must take steps to resolve any conflicts arising in a way that protects the public interest, including registering and declaring interests...'

2.40   By way of example, the London Borough of Camden has dealt with the matter in greater detail within its code of conduct as follows:

> 'You should, in the spirit of openness disclose any other interest on a matter being, or to be, considered at a Meeting or Informal Meeting, which a member of the public with knowledge of the relevant facts, would reasonably regard to be so significant that it would materially impact upon your judgement of the public interest, and such declarations:
>
> (i)   Should include the nature and extent of your interest;
>
> (ii) Do not impact upon your ability to participate or further participate in any discussion of the matter at the meeting or participate in any vote or further vote on the matter at the meeting.'[50]

E   INVESTIGATION OF ALLEGED BREACHES AND INDEPENDENT PERSONS

2.41   The 2011 Act provides that the means by which a breach of the code is to be dealt with is in accordance with the arrangements made under s 28(6) of the Act. That section provides that relevant authorities, other than parish councils, are required to have in place (a) arrangements under which allegations can be investigated; and (b) arrangements under which decisions on allegations can be made.

'Allegations', in this context, means a written allegation that a member has failed to comply with the authority's code of conduct.[51]

---

48 Localism Act 2011, s 28(2).
49 Localism Act 2011, s 29(2).
50 http://www.camden.gov.uk/ccm/content/council-and-democracy/who-represents-you/camdens-councillors/conduct-of-councillors.en?page=1.
51 Localism Act 2011, s 28(9).

2.42   The 2011 Act does not prescribe the process by which allegations are to be investigated nor the process for making decisions on allegations, save for a requirement that arrangements put in place for making decisions on allegations must include provision for the appointment of at least one 'independent person'. The role of such a person is dealt with below.

2.43   A person cannot be appointed as an independent person if they are: (a) a member or officer of the authority (including of a parish council in the relevant area), or a relative or close friend of such a person; or (b) if at any time during the five years prior to appointment that person was a member or officer of the authority (including of a parish council in the relevant area).[52]

2.44   In a legal opinion drafted for the Association of Council Secretaries and Solicitors,[53] Clive Sheldon QC concluded that former independent members of a local authority's standards committee cannot be appointed as an independent person, at least if they have served within the previous five years. This is because the definition of 'co-opted member' (as set out above) is apt to include former independent members of a local authority's standards committee and former co-opted members are excluded from being an independent person for a period of five years.

2.45   Certain restrictions are placed on the advertisement for the post of an independent person: the post must be advertised in such a manner as is likely to bring it to the attention of the public and there must be an application process. The independent person's appointment must be approved by a majority of the members of the authority.[54] As stated above, there may be more than one independent person, which carries the merit of increasing the chance that one of them is available urgently if required.

2.46   Unlike the previous standards committees the independent member does not decide whether there has been a breach of the local code. Instead there is an obligation on a relevant authority to seek, and to take into account, the views of an independent person before it makes its decision on an allegation that it has decided to investigate.[55] Ultimately, however, the decision as to whether there has been a breach lies with the relevant authority.

2.47   In addition, the views of the independent person may be sought: (i) by the authority in relation to an allegation in circumstances where they are not obliged to do so (eg the independent person could be consulted on decisions on whether to investigate allegations or decisions on sanctions to be imposed);[56]

---

52 Localism Act 2011, s 28(8).
53 http://www.localgovernmentlawyer.co.uk/images/stories/Sanctions_and_Independent_ Persons_January_2012-2.pdf.
54 Localism Act 2011, s 28(8)(c).
55 Localism Act 2011, s 28(7)(a).
56 Localism Act 2011, s 28(7)(a).

and (ii) by a member of an authority (including a parish council member) if that person's behaviour is the subject of an allegation.[57]

Question: If a member breaches the code, does that necessarily render any decision made involving that member unlawful?

Answer: No. Section 28(4) of the Localism Act 2011 explicitly provides that a decision is not invalidated *just* because something that occurred in the process of making the decision involved a failure to comply to comply with the code. However, breaches of the code may result in decisions being quashed depending on the nature and severity of the breach. For example, if a member has a disclosable pecuniary interest of which he is aware in the subject matter being considered, but nevertheless takes part in the decision-making without securing dispensation, then it is likely that such a decision would be quashed on the basis of actual or apparent bias.

F   SANCTIONS

2.48   The 2011 Act envisages that an authority can take action against a member when it has concluded the member has breached its code of conduct. In particular s 28(11) of the Act provides:

> 'If a relevant authority finds that a member or co-opted member of the authority has failed to comply with its code of conduct (whether or not the finding is made following an investigation under arrangements put in place under subsection (6)) it may have regard to the failure in deciding –
>
> (a) Whether to take action in relation to the member or co-opted member, and
>
> (b) What action to take.'

2.49   However, although the 2011 Act establishes a number of criminal offences (which will be addressed in **Chapter 6**), it does not provide an express statutory basis for imposing sanctions on members.

2.50   The previous standards regime provided such a statutory basis, with regulation 19(c) of the 2008 Regulations[58] setting out a variety of sanctions which could then be imposed on members ranging from censure to suspension. There is no equivalent provision in the 2011 Act.

2.51   The result is a lacuna whereby it is unclear exactly what sanctions are available to local authorities when there have been breaches of their codes,

---

57 Localism Act 2011, s 28(7)(b).
58 SI 2008/1085.

but those breaches do not amount to criminal offences or, even if they do, no prosecution is brought. This uncertainty has caused a great deal of criticism, with the Committee on Standards in Public Life concluding:

> 'We have other concerns about the new arrangements which apply even in those authorities where strong leadership on standards does exist. The first is that under the previous arrangements local authorities had the power to suspend members for varying periods of time as a sanction against poor behaviour. The only sanctions now available, apart from through the use of party discipline, are censure or criminal prosecution for deliberately withholding or misrepresenting a financial interest. We do not think these are sufficient. The last few years have seen a number of examples of inappropriate behaviour which would not pass the strict tests required to warrant a criminal prosecution, but which deserves a sanction stronger than simple censure. Bullying of other members or officers is one category of offence which will be difficult to deal with adequately under the new arrangements.'[59]

2.52   In a recent independent member's report for Thanet District Council the independent member reported that there had been occasions when that authority's Councillors had 'stated that they do not intend to comply with the outcome of Standards hearings, again because there are no meaningful sanctions that can apply.'[60]

2.53   It remains to be seen whether the concerns of the Committee on Standards in Public Life and at a local level will result in the re-enactment of an equivalent to regulation 19(c) of the 2008 Regulations, perhaps in a truncated form. As far as we are aware, there is nothing of the sort on the horizon.

59 'Standards matter: A review of best practice in promoting good behavior in public life' (2013) Committee on Standards in Public Life, para 7.27. In its 2013–14 Annual Report (September 2014) the Committee concluded: '… the effectiveness of the sanctions regime for non-adherence to Local Authority codes of conduct, which apart from criminal prosecution, provides only for censure or suspension from a particular committee or committees, remains an issue of concern. We are aware that there have been recent individual cases that illustrate this, in particular the lack of a sanction to suspend councillors who have seriously breached the code of conduct. In contrast to the recent public debate on parliamentary standards calling for greater sanctions, tightening of codes of conduct, and a greater independent element, local government is now largely self regulated with no systematic approach to conduct issues and limited sanctions. There remains in our view a significant risk under these arrangements that inappropriate conduct by Local Authority members will not be dealt with effectively, eroding public confidence and trust in local government.' (At paras 44–45.)
60 Thanet District Council, Independent Members of the Standards Committee (21 November 2013) http://democracy.thanet.gov.uk/documents/s33886/Independent%20Members%20Report%20 on%20Standards.pdf.

Question: What sanctions can a local authority apply to a member who has breached its code?

Unfortunately, in lieu of any specific statutory basis for the imposing of sanctions for breaches of local codes, the answer is not clear.

It is, perhaps, easier to start with those sanctions which it would be unlawful for the authority to impose.

In his opinion for the Association of Council Secretaries and Solicitors, Clive Sheldon QC concluded that a local authority could not disqualify or suspend one of its own members for misconduct. A court is likely to find that such an action would be an interference with local democracy which could not be lawfully achieved without express statutory power (see, in particular, Munby J's judgment in *R v Broadland District Council, ex parte Lashley* (2000) 2 LGLR 933). The same conclusion is likely to apply to the sanction of excluding a member from meetings (save where there is an express power to do so, for instance by virtue of s 31(10) of the 2011 Act).

In contrast, it is likely that permissible sanctions would include: a formal letter to the member; offering advice; censure by motion; 'naming and shaming' by way of a press release and, in certain circumstances, removal of a member from committees.

G CONCLUSION

2.54   This chapter has outlined the legislative framework for the standards regime brought into force by the Localism Act 2011. At the core of the legislative framework is the duty to 'promote and maintain high standards of conduct by members and co-opted members of the authority'. However, beyond that, save for the issue of disclosable pecuniary interests, much of the detail is left to individual authorities as part of the Localism Agenda. This includes local codes of conduct and the sanction regime. Only time will tell whether local democracy is enhanced through the rigorous enforcement of local codes, or whether the upshot is a patchwork quilt of local codes without thematic consistency. Depending on one's perspective, it may be both.

CHAPTER 3

Councillors' conduct and decision-making

A INTRODUCTION

3.1   Having outlined the new standards regime in **Chapter 2**, this chapter deals with the substantive obligations which apply to councillors. What must they do? What are they not permitted to do? This chapter provides an overview of the required standards of conduct, and explains how this impacts on the way the councillor's role is discharged.

3.2   The issues of personal interests and bias/predetermination both have a direct impact on councillors' decision making functions. Both affect how and the extent to which councillors should participate. We devote sections B and C of this chapter to those issues. Section D on 'other conduct issues' looks at more generalised questions of behaviour, including interactions with others and the unique responsibilities of the elected position. These principles are of general application. Equality and diversity issues may also arise in all aspects of a councillor's work, and this is the subject of section E. Section F sets out the particular considerations which need to be borne in mind at election time.

3.2a   We also take the opportunity in this Chapter to include some Case Studies. Some are taken from appeal decisions under the former regime of the Adjudication Panel and then the First-tier Tribunal (Local Government Standards in England) ('FTT'). Decisions under the current regime are those of local standards committees. While none of these is binding on anybody, the FTT and Adjudication Panel decisions in particular give useful examples of how an independent and experienced body judged the conduct of councillors in the public interest.

47

B   PERSONAL INTERESTS

Definitions

3.3   The principle of integrity requires members to avoid acting or taking decisions in order to gain financial or other material benefits for themselves, their family or their friends. This principle underlies the requirement for members to disclose and register their personal interests. All 'relevant authorities' are obliged to ensure that their codes of conduct include appropriate provisions requiring the disclosure and registration of pecuniary interests and other interests.[1] 'Relevant authorities' are defined in s 27(6) of the Localism Act 2011 (the 2011 Act), and include county councils, district councils, parish councils, London borough councils and the Greater London Authority.

3.4   The 2011 Act and its regulations[2] stipulate the 'pecuniary interests' which must be disclosed. They are known as 'disclosable pecuniary interests' or DPIs, and are as follows:

- any employment, office, trade, profession or vocation carried on for profit or gain (so excluding unpaid work for public voluntary and charitable bodies);

- any payment received (other than from the relevant authority) in respect of any expenses incurred by the member in carrying out duties as a member, or towards his election expenses;

- outstanding contracts between the member and the relevant authority to provide goods, services or execute works;

- any beneficial interest in land in the relevant authority area;

- any licence to occupy land for more than a month in the relevant authority area;

- any tenancy where the relevant authority is the landlord and the tenant is a body in which the relevant member has an interest;

- any beneficial interest in securities of a body that has (to the knowledge of the member) a place of business or land in the area of the authority, and either the total nominal value exceeds £25,000 or one hundredth of the total issued share capital of that body; or, if the share capital of that body is of more than one class, the total nominal value of the shares of any one class in which the relevant person has a beneficial interest exceeds one hundredth of the total issued share capital of that class.

3.5   Any DPIs held by the member, the member's spouse or civil partner, or a person with whom the member is living as if they were a husband or wife or civil

---

1   Localism Act 2011, s 28(2).
2   The Relevant Authorities (Disclosable Pecuniary Interests) Regulations 2012, SI 2012/1464.

partner, must be disclosed via entry on the register of interests.[3] The requirements of disclosure and registration are set out at **Section D** of **Chapter 2**.

Question: On becoming a councillor, does Member A have to disclose his work as a landscape gardener?

Answer: Yes, so long as his work is carried on for profit or gain. In respect of employment matters, the DPI is notably wide.

Question: On becoming a councillor, does Member B have to disclose the fact he owns land outside of the relevant authority's area?

Answer: Perhaps surprisingly, no – not even land just across the border, although land in a different region of the country is probably irrelevant. A member need only disclose any beneficial interest in land which is within the area of the relevant authority.

Question: Does Member C's husband's name need to appear on the register of interests?

Answer: No. For the purposes of the register, an interest of your spouse or civil partner is your DPI. Whilst the detailed format of the register of members' interests is for your council to decide, there is no requirement to differentiate your disclosable pecuniary interests between those which relate to you personally and those that relate to your spouse or civil partner. Some councils choose to list a spouse or civil partner's interests separately (for example, in a different column); other councils do not make any differentiation.

Question: On becoming a councillor, Member D has been provided with expenses by her political party to cover the travel costs relating to her election campaign. Do these have to be disclosed?

Answer: Yes, any payment or provision of other financial benefit (other than from the relevant authority) made or provided within the previous 12 months in respect of any expenses incurred by the member in carrying out duties as a member or towards their election expenses must be disclosed. This includes any payment or financial benefit from a Trade Union.

---

3   Localism Act 2011, s 30(3).

Question: Member E owns a large number of shares in a pharmaceutical company (worth more than £25,000). The company owns a laboratory in her local area where they carry out experimentation on animals. This is very controversial and a group of animal activists in the area has carried out several attacks on the facility and on the homes of employees who work at the facility. The member is afraid that, if the group finds out about her shares, they may attack her home. Can the details of this interest be withheld from publication on the register?

Answer: Yes, so long as the monitoring officer agrees that the details of this interest could lead to the member or her family being subjected to violence or intimidation.

The answers above are subject to the proviso that local codes can themselves require the disclosure of a wider range of interests (pecuniary or otherwise) than provided for by the 2011 Act.

3.6   Interests other than pecuniary interests are not defined in the 2011 Act or its regulations, so local authorities are given a significant degree of discretion as to what other interests must be disclosed or registered. As a result, the local code should always be consulted when considering whether an interest is disclosable or registrable.

3.7   There are some manifest omissions from the list of disclosable pecuniary interests required to be disclosed under the 2011 Act. These include gifts and hospitality deriving from a member's position on the local authority; unpaid employment (including unpaid directorships); interest in land outside the authority's area; pecuniary interests of close family members; and membership of lobby or campaign groups. Authorities may wish to consider incorporating some of these as disclosable or registrable interests in their codes of conduct.

3.8   It is notable that the way in which the 2011 Act approaches personal interests is very different from the previous standards regime, which centred on 'personal' and 'prejudicial' interests, requiring a significantly broader range of interests to be declared, and which imposed administrative penalties for failures. Instead, the 2011 Act stipulates a narrower range of interests that must be registered – DPIs – but underpins them with the threat of criminal sanction,[4] ensuring that those very few councillors who deliberately abuse public office for their own financial benefit are subject to a severe penalty.

Participation in decision-making

3.9   As a basic rule, where a member or co-opted member is present at any meeting of the authority (including sub- and joint-committees) and is aware that she has a DPI in any matter being considered, then she must not participate in

4   See para **3.17** below.

discussion of the matter, nor participate in any vote on the matter, whether or not the DPI is currently on the register.[5] If the DPI is not on the register, then the member must disclose the nature and content of the DPI to the meeting, and notify the DPI to the monitoring officer within 28 days of the meeting.[6] If the undisclosed DPI is a 'sensitive interest', the member need only state to the meeting that she has a DPI, without disclosing its content.[7]

Question: You are a member of your authority's planning committee. How should you take DPIs and other interests into account when preparing for a meeting?

Answer: Prior to the meeting, you should have considered the various applications and looked at the applicants' names and addresses, their planning agents' details and the details of any objectors or supporters, and the nature of the applications, to see whether any of your DPIs are engaged. For example, if you own and run a grocery store on the High Street and an application is being made by a large supermarket chain to open a store on another street close by, you will need to declare a DPI and refrain from participating in the discussion or voting on the application. You will also need to consider whether you have a personal interest in an application (for example, if the application is being made by a close personal friend). Depending on what your code says about such interests, you may need to declare and refrain from participating. Even if your code is silent on this matter, you will need to consider how your involvement in deciding the application will be perceived by a fair-minded observer, and if your integrity may be called into question, you should consider refraining from participation. You should consult the monitoring officer if you think you may have a DPI in a matter to be considered at the meeting. See further the case study at para **3.17** below.

3.10   In order for this system to function efficiently, it helps if the agenda for a meeting gives members or co-opted members an opportunity to declare an interest early in the meeting.[8] If members or co-opted members are in any doubt as to whether they have a DPI in a matter, they should contact their council's monitoring officer for advice.

3.11   The prohibition on participation applies to any form of participation, including speaking as a member of the public.[9] However, there is no need for a member or co-opted member with a DPI in a matter being considered to leave the room, unless the council or authority's standing orders require the member to leave. Given the importance of maintaining the integrity of the decision-making process, councils and authorities should give careful consideration to whether a requirement to leave the room should be included in the standing orders. Even

---

5   Localism Act 2011, s 31(4).
6   Localism Act 2011, s 31(2).
7   Localism Act 2011, s 32(3).
8   National Association of Local Councils 'The Good Councillor's Guide – Essential Guidance for Parish and Town Councillors', p 24.
9   DCLG guide 'Openness and transparency on personal interests' (September 2013), p 7.

where the standing orders are silent, the member or co-opted member should leave the room where she considers that her presence is incompatible with her authority's code or with the seven principles of public life.[10]

Question: I am a member of the planning committee. I have registered as a disclosable interest that I am employed by a University as a technician in the medical sciences department. A planning application has been made by the University for the construction of a new School of Government. Can I participate in the debate and vote on the application?

Answer: Yes, as long as you are not involved with any part of the University that is promoting the development. If you are not so involved, you do not have a pecuniary interest in the subject matter of the discussion – the construction of a new school for a department with which you do not work. Although you clearly have a relationship with the University, which is the developer, it is not the type of relationship that gives rise to a disclosable pecuniary interest in the planning application. This has been ruled on by the High Court in *R (Freud) v Oxford City Council*.[11]

Matters would be very different if you were employed by the University in the Department of Government. Then, you would have a pecuniary interest in the application, as it may well affect your employment. You would only be able to participate in the debate and vote if you received a dispensation (see below).

3.12   Where the authority is operating executive arrangements, the requirements concerning non-participation in discussion and voting, and disclosing non-disclosed DPIs, apply to meetings of the executive and any committee of the executive.[12]

3.13   Where a member is a sole decision-taker, and is aware that she has a DPI in the matter in issue, she must not take any steps, or any further steps, in relation to the matter. She can, however, take such action as is necessary to enable the matter to be dealt with by someone else or in a different way.[13]

Dispensation allowing participation despite having a DPI

3.14   The basic rule on non-participation in meetings where a member or co-opted member has a DPI in a matter being considered is subject to an exemption. Section 33 of the 2011 Act allows the restrictions to be dispensed with following a written request by the member or co-opted member to the proper officer[14] of the

---

10 DCLG guide 'Openness and transparency on personal interests' (September 2013), p 7.
11 Localism Act 2011, s 31(5).
12 Localism Act 2011, s 31(5).
13 Localism Act 2011, s 31(8).
14 Although no definition for 'proper officer' is given in the Localism Act 2011, it is to be presumed that, pursuant to s 270(3) of the Local Government Act 1972, the proper officer of the authority is an officer appointed for the relevant purposes by the authority.

authority. The decision to award a dispensation is a matter for the authority, which may only grant such a dispensation if one or more of the following conditions are met:

- if the relevant authority considers that without the dispensation the number of people prohibited from taking part in the relevant meeting would be so great a proportion as to impede the transaction of the body's business;

- if the relevant authority considers that without the dispensation the representation of different political groups on the body transacting any particular business would be so upset as to alter the likely outcome of any vote relating to the business;

- if the relevant authority considers that granting the dispensation is in the interests of persons living in the authority's area;

- if the relevant authority is an authority to which Part 1A of the Local Government Act 2000 applies and is operating executive arrangements, and considers that without the dispensation each member of the authority's executive would be prohibited from participating in any particular business to be transacted by the authority's executive; or

- if the relevant authority considers that it is otherwise appropriate to grant a dispensation.

Any dispensation must specify a period during which it is due to take effect, which must not exceed four years.[15]

Setting council tax or setting a precept

3.15   A particular question has arisen in relation to whether councillors who are homeowners or tenants in the areas of their local authorities need a dispensation to take part in setting the council tax or a precept because they have a DPI in the matter. On the face of it, such interests seem to amount to a DPI in the subject matter of council tax and precepts, given that the level of tax payable affects homeowners and tenants in the local area. The guidance issued by DCLG specifically answers this question in the negative, on the basis that payment of, or liability to pay, council tax does not create a DPI:

> 'If you are a homeowner or tenant in the area of your council you will have registered, in accordance with the national rules, that beneficial interest in land. However, this disclosable pecuniary interest is not a disclosable pecuniary interest in the matter of setting the council tax or precept since decisions on the council tax or precept do not materially affect your interest in the land. For example, it does not materially affect the value of your home, your prospects of selling that home, or how you might use or enjoy that land.'[16]

---

15 Localism Act 2011, s 33(3).
16 DCLG guide 'Openness and transparency on personal interests' (September 2013), p 8.

3.16   It would be prudent for local authorities to consider whether their monitoring officers should issue dispensations in relation to the setting of council tax or a precept. There appears to be a clear justification for doing so, since it is unlikely that the requisite number of councillors could participate in the setting of council tax or a precept if all those liable for council tax are excluded from participating.[17]

Offences

3.17   The requirements in relation to declaration of interests have real teeth – failure to comply with a number of the duties set out above results in the commission of a criminal offence. The criminal offences are as follows:

● Without reasonable excuse, failing to comply with the duty to disclose all DPIs either 28 days after becoming a member or co-opted member; or at a meeting where a DPI is required to be disclosed; or to the monitoring officer 28 days after such a meeting.[18]

● Without reasonable excuse, to participate in a meeting in contravention of the restrictions imposed where a member or co-opted member has a DPI in a matter being considered.[19]

● Without reasonable excuse, to take steps in contravention of the Localism Act 2011, s 31(8),[20] which applies where the member is a sole decision-taker, and is aware that she has a DPI in the matter in issue.[21]

'Without reasonable excuse' is not defined in the 2011 Act, but it is a defence to a number of offences and has therefore been interpreted by the courts. At its simplest, 'without reasonable excuse' means acting culpably or in a blameworthy fashion, taking into account the standard of behaviour expected of the accused.[22] It has been held that an honest but mistaken belief may only amount to a reasonable excuse if the belief relied upon is reasonable.[23]

● If a person knowingly or recklessly provides information that is false or misleading when required to disclose an interest.[24] Acting 'recklessly' in criminal law denotes acting in a way that is careless, regardless, or heedless of the possible harmful consequences (here providing false information). It also requires that there is something in the circumstances that would have drawn the attention of an ordinary prudent individual to the possibility that his act was capable of causing the kind of harmful consequence that the section which creates the offence was intended to prevent, and that the risk of those harmful consequences occurring was not so slight that an ordinary prudent individual would feel justified in treating them as negligible.[25]

---

17 It is also notable that the previous Model Code (The Local Authorities (Model Code of Conduct) Order 2007) contained a similar dispensation, in para 10(2)(c)(vi).
18 Localism Act 2011, s 34(1)(a).
19 Localism Act 2011, s 34(1)(b).
20 See para **3.13** above.
21 Localism Act 2011, s 34(1)(c).
22 *R v L (D)* [2011] EWCA Crim 1259, at para 21.
23 *Haringey London Borough Council v Goremsandu* [2013] EWHC 3834 (Admin).
24 Localism Act 2011, s 34(2).
25 *R v Lawrence* [1982] AC 510.

Case Study

	R v Flower (Bournemouth Magistrates Court, April 2015)
Facts	Cllr Flower listed as a pecuniary interest a non-executive directorship of a housing charity, for which he received remuneration payments. He was present at a meeting about the proposed East Dorset Core Strategy and voted at the meeting. The housing charity had responded to a consultation about the Core Strategy and owned land which was being considered for development through the Core Strategy. Cllr Flower had previously attended a meeting of the charity at which the long-term future of that land had been considered. He was charged with an offence under s 34(1)(b) of the 2011 Act for participating in a discussion and vote without reasonable excuse despite having a DPI in a matter being considered.
Finding	Cllr Flower was guilty of the offence. His defence that the matters discussed at the meeting were of a broad nature and did not concern detailed issues of planning and ownership did not amount to 'reasonable excuse'. It was not right that the Core Strategy had no relevance to pecuniary matters, and it was not a defence that he did not obtain any direct benefit from the vote. The judge held that it would have been reasonable for him to have consulted the monitoring officer, and could have obtained a dispensation. He was under a duty not to participate and vote. The judge noted that Cllr Flower was of good character and the court had received a number of character references speaking highly of his abilities, his conscientiousness and his years of public service.
Decision	Conditional discharge for six months and order to pay £930 in costs.

3.18   These offences are discussed in detail in **Chapter 6**, which also covers how the offences are tried and the potential penalties on a finding of guilt.

C   BIAS AND PREDETERMINATION

Overview

3.19   'Bias' is defined as 'partiality which prevents objective consideration of an issue or situation'. It is not synonymous with 'prejudice', although it certainly includes both prejudice and preconception. 'Predetermination' is sometimes considered to be an aspect of bias, but they are conceptually distinct, as 'predetermination' means 'the act of determining or resolving in advance what is to take place'.

3.20   Avoiding bias or predetermination, or their appearance, is an essential aspect of ensuring that local decision-making upholds the seven principles of public life. It is also an important way in which local authorities can avoid challenges to their decisions.

3.21   The rule against bias has a long pedigree, stretching back to April in the year 529, when the Code of Justinian[26] proclaimed that 'no-one should be a judge in his own cause', or '*Ne quis in sua causa iudicet vel sibi ius dicat*'.[27] That maxim was adopted as a central principle of the common law of England by Chief Justice Sir Edward Coke in 1610 in *Dr Bonham's Case*,[28] since which time it has been accepted that bias both disqualifies the decision-maker and vitiates the decision. This rule prohibits two separate types of bias: 'presumed bias', which arises when the decision-maker has a direct interest in the outcome of the decision; and 'actual bias', which arises when a decision-maker has in fact been influenced by partiality or prejudice in reaching a decision.

3.22   In 1924, the courts recognised that even the appearance of bias could vitiate a decision, with Chief Justice Lord Hewart stating in *R v Sussex Justices, ex p McCarthy*: 'it is … of fundamental importance that justice should not only be done, but should manifestly and undoubtedly be seen to be done'.[29] This gave rise to the third type of bias which is prohibited: 'apparent bias', the test for which is discussed below.

3.23   Three elements have been identified[30] as underpinning these rules against bias:

- accuracy in public decision-making – an accurate decision is more likely to be achieved by a decision-maker who is impartial or disinterested in the outcome of the decision;

26 Justinian I was the Eastern Roman (Byzantine) Emperor from 527–565. He ordered a review of the Roman Empire's laws, which involved the collection of legal materials of various kinds into a single volume, then given legal force. The volume was known as the 'Corpus Iuris Civilis' or 'Body of Civil Law', and is credited as being one of the foundational documents of the Western legal tradition. The 'Codex' or 'Code' was the first of four parts of the Corpus to be completed.
27 A maxim perhaps better known in its grammatically simpler form of '*nemo iudex in causa sua*'.
28 (1610) 8 Co Rep 113b at 118. Dr Bonham had been fined and imprisoned by the Censors of the College of Physicians because he refused to stop practising as a physician despite not being a member of the College; maintaining (correctly) that he had obtained a recognised degree from the University of Cambridge and was properly qualified to practice. Coke held that the College could not be both judge and party to the case of whether Dr Bonham was required to be a member in order to practice.
29 [1924] 1 KB 256 at 259. McCarthy's conviction for dangerous driving because of a motor collision was quashed because the clerk who was assisting the Magistrates was a member of the firm of solicitors which was acting in a personal injury claim against McCarthy arising out of the accident. The clerk had retired with the Magistrates when they considered their decision, but they stated on oath that they came to their conclusion without consulting the clerk, who had in any event abstained from mentioning the personal injury case. Although it was accepted that the clerk had not in fact influenced the decision, the conviction was quashed because of the appearance of bias.
30 De Smith, Woolf and Jowell *Judicial Review* (7th edn, Sweet & Maxwell, 2013), p 414.

- absence of prejudice on the part of the decision-maker – this also feeds into accuracy, since a decision-maker who puts aside personal prejudices is more likely to make an accurate decision;

- public confidence in the decision-making process – this recognises that both bias, and its appearance, call into question the legitimacy of the decision-making process.

3.24   The rule against predetermination is a variant of the rule that, when making a decision, a public body should not fetter its discretion or 'surrender its judgment'[31] by determining the matter in advance. It was recognised as early as 1919 in *R v Port of London Authority, Ex parte Kynoch*[32] that a decision-maker must not 'shut his ears' to an application or an argument. Although the case law refers simply to 'predetermination', the test applied by the courts, which is discussed below, focuses on the appearance of predetermination.[33]

3.25   It is notable that an individual can waive his or her right to object to a decision-maker on the grounds of presumed bias, apparent bias and predetermination.

3.26   This section sets out how the courts have approached determining whether a decision is tainted by the three different types of bias, and by predetermination. It then considers how the 2011 Act addresses bias and predetermination, and finally discusses waiver.

Presumed bias

3.27   Presumed bias arises where a decision-maker has a direct financial interest (including both pecuniary and proprietary interests) in the outcome of the decision.[34] 'Direct' is understood to mean an interest which is not too remote,[35] so that financial interests of close relatives of the decision-maker, about which the decision-maker is aware, can amount to a direct financial interest. In order to give rise to presumed bias, the outcome of the decision must be such that it could realistically affect the decision-maker's interest, so a small or minimal effect will not disqualify a decision-maker.[36]

3.28   There is clearly a close relationship between the statutory regime concerning the declaration of disclosable pecuniary interests and the rule

---

31 *R v Secretary for State for the Environment, Ex p Kirkstall Valley Campaign Ltd* [1996] 3 All ER 304 at 319 per Sedley LJ.
32 [1919] 1 KB 176 at 183.
33 Auburn, Moffett, Sharland and McManus *Judicial Review, Principles and Procedure* (OUP, 2013), para 8.85.
34 *Dimes v Proprietors of the Grand Junction Canal* (1852) 3 HL Cas 759 at 793–94.
35 *R v Secretary of State for the Environment, ex p Kirkstall Valley Campaign Ltd* [1996] 3 All ER 304.
36 *Locabail (UK) Ltd v Bayfield Properties Ltd* [2000] QB 451 at paras 8 and 10.

concerning presumed bias. It is arguable that the reason for preventing participation in decision-making where a member or co-opted member has a disclosable pecuniary interest is that presumed bias disqualifies that person as a decision-maker. However, the rule concerning presumed bias is wider than the DPI regime, as it extends to financial interests of close relatives, and not just a spouse, civil partner or cohabitee.

3.29 The rule concerning presumed bias extends to a limited class of non-financial interests, where the decision concerns the promotion of a cause to which the decision-maker is strongly committed. In the *Pinochet* case,[37] the House of Lords held that Lord Hoffmann, who was a director of Amnesty International Charity Ltd (a charity wholly controlled by Amnesty International), was presumed to be biased when Amnesty International appeared as a party in a case, arguing that General Augusto Pinochet was not immune from extradition proceedings. Care must be taken in applying this category of presumed bias in the sphere of local government decision making. The courts have recognised that councillors will take public positions on issues and will commit themselves publicly to policies, as part of their democratic role, and that this should not disqualify them from participating in decision-making.[38]

Question: I am Head of Bereavement Services at a City Council. I am also the chair of the board of directors of an organisation involved in the national accreditation of stonemasons to work in cemeteries (Organisation A). Following a dispute, a longstanding national group of stonemasons that was previously part of that accreditation scheme, left and set up their own accreditation scheme (under Organisation B). The schemes are very similar. The City Council formulated a policy only permitting stonemasons accredited through Organisation A to work in cemeteries in the city. Organisation B objected and wrote to me challenging the decision. I wrote back and refused to change the decision. Were the decisions tainted by bias?

Answer: This was not considered to be presumed bias, although it was considered to amount to apparent bias: see the case of *R(National Association of Memorial Masons) v Cardiff City Council*[39], and paras **3.31–3.35** below. It is important to note that something alleged to be one type of bias can be found by the court to be a different category of bias, and can still vitiate the decision.

Actual bias

3.30 Actual bias arises where a decision-maker is shown, in fact and for whatever reason, to have been influenced in his decision-making by prejudice,

---

37 *R v Bow Street Metropolitan Stipendiary Magistrate, ex p Pinochet Ugarte (No 2)* [2000] 1 AC 119.
38 *Franklin v Ministry of Town and Country Planning* [1948] AC 87; *R (Lewis) v Redcar and Cleveland Borough Council* [2009] 1 WLR 83. This is discussed further in para **3.39** below.
39 [2011] EWHC 922 (Admin).

predilection or personal interest.[40] Such cases are rare, partly because it is difficult for those challenging decisions to prove actual bias. However, where it is proved, the law is very clear and very emphatic: a decision shown to have been tainted by actual bias cannot stand.[41]

Apparent bias

3.31   Apparent bias is the category of bias most frequently relied upon to challenge decisions. The House of Lords in *Porter v Magill*[42] established the test for apparent bias: whether 'the fair-minded and informed observer, having considered the facts, would conclude that there was a real possibility' of bias. Accordingly, the touchstone in determining whether any circumstances give rise to an appearance of bias is whether, viewed objectively by a person with knowledge of all the facts, the circumstances would lead such an observer to conclude there was a real possibility that an individual or a body was biased, in the sense of approaching the decision with a closed mind and without impartial consideration of all relevant issues.[43]

3.32   The fair-minded observer does not take the complainant's view, but an objective view.[44] She is assumed to be a 'reasonable member of the public' who is 'neither complacent nor unduly sensitive or suspicious'.[45] The fair-minded observer is thus not an insider (eg a member of a decision-making body).[46] Beyond that, the courts do not delve into the characteristics of the fair-minded and informed observer.

3.33   An allegation of apparent bias is decided on the relevant circumstances as they appear to the court after investigation, rather than being restricted to the circumstances available to a hypothetical observer when the decision was originally taken.[47] Accordingly, the informed observer is taken to know all the facts that are discovered subsequent to the decision, as a result of investigation.[48]

3.34   It is doubtful whether apparent bias on behalf of just one member is enough to undermine a decision taken by a committee. In *R (Berky) v Newport City Council*,[49] the Court of Appeal held that a more nuanced approach is required, bearing in mind the political nature of councillors and the particular circumstances in which any allegation is made. Where the decision of a committee is made by a clear majority and there is nothing to suggest that a particular councillor exercised

---

40 *R v Gough* [1993] AC 646.
41 *R v Inner West London Coroner, ex parte Dallaglio* [1994] 4 All ER 139 at 162.
42 [2001] UKHL 67, [2002] 2 AC 357 at para 103.
43 *Georgiou v Enfield LBC* [2004] EWHC 779; [2004] 2 P&CR 21 at para 31.
44 *Helow v Secretary of State for the Home Department* [2008] UKHL 62; [2008] 1 WLR 2416 at para 2.
45 *Lawal v Northern Spirit Ltd* [2003] UKHL 35, [2004] 1 All ER 187 at para 14; *R v Abdroikov* [2007] UKHL 37, [2007] 1 WLR 2679 at para 81.
46 *Belize Bank v Attorney-General of Belize* [2011] UKPC 36 at paras 37–39.
47 *R (Condron) v National Assembly for Wales* [2006] EWCA Civ 1573; [2007] 2 P&CR 4 at paras 38–40.
48 *Re Medicaments and Related Classes of Goods (No 2)* [2001] 1 WLR 700 at para 83(4).
49 [2012] EWCA Civ 378, [2012] 2 CMLR 44.

an undue degree of influence over the other members, it is unlikely that bias on the part of that councillor is sufficient of itself to render the decision unlawful.[50]

3.35   The courts have warned against attempting to define or list the factors which may or may not give rise to a real possibility of bias, as everything depends on the facts of the particular case in issue.[51] Nevertheless, it is helpful to give a few examples, drawn from the case law:

• membership by a decision-maker of internal council committees is not likely to give rise to the appearance of bias;[52] however membership of external bodies which have supported a particular proposal might do so;[53]

• substitution by a political party of a councillor physically able to attend a meeting with a different councillor (both of whom are appointed to a committee) is a political decision not challengeable before the court, and will not give rise to an appearance of bias so long as the councillor who attends is seen to have an open mind;[54]

• friendship with the individual who is the subject of the decision may be sufficient to give rise to an appearance of bias – for example, apparent bias was found where a councillor, who shared transport to and from council meetings with a fellow councillor of the same political group and who saw her socially on a relatively frequent basis, considered the fellow councillor's application for planning permission;[55]

• hostility towards someone who would be subject to or would benefit from a decision (particularly if that hostility is expressed in extreme terms) may be sufficient to give rise to an appearance of bias;[56]

• apparent bias cannot conceivably arise as a result of a decision-maker's gender, age, class, means, religion, ethnic or national origin, or sexual orientation. [57]

50 *R (Berky) v Newport City Council* [2012] 2 CMLR 44 at para 46.
51 *Locabail (UK) Ltd v Bayfield Properties Ltd* [2000] QB 451 at para 25.
52 *R (Cummins) v London Borough of Camden* [2001] EWHC 116 (Admin) at paras 260–263, where membership of a local authority's leisure and community services committee, which was in effect promoting a development on land owned by the local authority, did not preclude participation in the decision whether to grant planning permission. Support for this approach was articulated by the Court of Appeal in *R (Lewis) v Redcar and Cleveland Borough Council* [2008] EWCA Civ 746; [2009] 1 WLR 83, although the case of *Georgiou v Enfield LBC* [2004] EWHC 779; [2004] 2 P&CR 21 seems to pull in the other direction (in that case, a councillor was a member of the Conservation Advisory Committee, an advisory body that had expressed unqualified support for a proposal, and participation by the councillor in the grant of planning permission was held to give rise to an appearance of bias). The approach in *Cummins* is preferable in light of s 25 of the 2011 Act, discussed below.
53 *Bovis Homes Ltd v New Forest DC* [2002] EWHC 483 (Admin), where a councillor on a planning committee was also a member of a non-statutory committee (made up of various councils, the Forestry Commission and the Countryside Agency) which had expressed a view on the matter to be considered by the planning committee. This was held to give an appearance of bias.
54 *R (Carnegie, on behalf of Oaks Action Group) v LB Ealing* [2014] EWHC 3807 (Admin) at paras 34–42.
55 *R (Gardner) v Harrogate BC* [2008] EWHC 2942 (Admin) at paras 32–34.
56 *Locabail (UK) Ltd v Bayfield Properties Ltd* [2000] QB 451 at para 25.
57 *Locabail* at para 25.

Predetermination

3.36   Predetermination is conceptually distinct from bias in that it is an aspect of the rule that a public body must not fetter its discretion by determining a matter in advance. Nevertheless, the case law has sometimes approached bias and predetermination interchangeably,[58] and the line between the two can be difficult to draw.

3.37   The test for predetermination was established by the Court of Appeal in *R (Lewis) v Redcar and Cleveland Borough Council*:[59] whether the member or the body has made their decision with a closed mind or whether the circumstances gave rise to such a real risk of closed minds that the decision ought not in the public interest to be upheld.[60]

3.38   Unless there is positive evidence to show that a member or a body had a closed mind, prior observations or apparent favouring of a particular decision will not usually suffice to persuade a court to quash the decision.[61] 'Positive evidence' means evidence that would suggest to the fair-minded and informed observer the real possibility that the councillor in question had abandoned his or her obligations.

3.39   Predetermination is thus to be distinguished from having a predisposition towards a particular position. The courts have long recognised that councillors will take public positions on issues and will commit themselves publicly to policies, as part of their democratic role.[62] As the Court of Appeal held in *R (Lewis) v Redcar and Cleveland Borough Council*,[63] councillors are not carrying out a judicial or quasi-judicial role. Democratically accountable decision-makers who have been elected to pursue policies are entitled to be predisposed to determine matters in accordance with their political views and policies, provided they have regard to all material considerations and give fair consideration to relevant points raised with them. Councillors are also entitled to take into account the views of their constituents and to communicate with their constituents in relation to matters that fall for decision.[64]

---

58 See, for example, *Georgiou v Enfield LBC* [2004] EWHC 779; [2004] 2 P&CR 21 at para 30 and *R (Condron) v National Assembly for Wales* [2006] EWCA Civ 1573; [2007] 2 P&CR 4 at paras 11 and 43.

59 [2008] EWCA Civ 746; [2009] 1 WLR 83 at para 71.

60 [2008] EWCA Civ 746; [2009] 1 WLR 83 at paras 71 and 96.

61 *R (Island Farm Development Ltd) v Bridgend County Borough Council* [2006] EWHC 2189 (Admin) at para 31, approved of by the Court of Appeal in *R (Lewis) v Redcar and Cleveland Borough Council* [2009] 1 WLR 83 at paras 96–7.

62 *Franklin v Ministry of Town and Country Planning* [1948] AC 87.

63 [2008] EWCA Civ 746; [2009] 1 WLR 83 at para 71.

64 *R (Lewis) v Redcar and Cleveland Borough Council* [2008] EWCA Civ 746; [2009] 1 WLR 83 at para 62.

65 [2014] EWHC 2440 (Admin).

66 [1988] QB 419.

> **Question:** Can apparent bias or predetermination be alleged if there is a three line whip in place in relation to making a specific decision? For example, what if the chairman of my group tells me before a planning committee meeting that there is a whip in place for the meeting and I should vote in favour or abstain?
>
> **Answer:** This is not bias/predetermination, as long as there is a proper debate during which all members consider the important and relevant issues, so that they can weigh the whip against those issues and reach a different conclusion from the whip if they consider it is merited. For an example of a three line whip where a planning committee was considering whether to adopt a local plan, see *IM Properties Development Ltd v Lichfield District Council*.[65]
>
> Even the potential sanction of the withdrawal of the party whip is not necessarily evidence that a member no longer has discretion about how to vote: see *R v Waltham Forest London Borough Council Ex Parte Baxter*.[66]

Section 25 of the 2011 Act

3.40   Bias and predetermination are also addressed in s 25 of the 2011 Act. This applies where, as a result of an allegation of bias or predetermination, there is an issue about the validity of a decision of a 'relevant authority'[67] because an individual or body making the decision[68] allegedly had, or appeared to have, a closed mind. Section 25(2) provides that a decision-maker will not be considered to have had a closed mind, or to have given the appearance of a closed mind, just because the decision-maker has 'previously done anything that indicated what view the decision-maker took or might take in relation to a matter' which was relevant to the decision.

3.41   It is interesting to note that, although it is clearly based on the case law discussed above, the language used in s 25(2) is not drawn directly from any of those decisions. It therefore arguably creates a new statutory test where an allegation of bias or predetermination is made.

3.42   The court has suggested that s 25 of the 2011 Act will be relevant where a challenge is brought based on the appearance of bias (rather than an allegation of actual bias). In *EU Plants Ltd v Wokingham Borough Council*,[69] a statutory appeal was brought against the confirmation of a Tree Preservation Order in circumstances where a councillor had expressed 'sympathetic support' for local residents campaigning against the development of a farm. The judge said that, while s 25 will not preclude a court from looking at conduct in the round, it is relevant to whether there is an appearance of bias because of a previous expression of view.[70]

---

67 See para **3.3** above.
68 By s 25(3), this is limited to where the decision-maker is, or the body is comprised of, members or co-opted members of the relevant authority.
69 [2012] EWHC 3305 (Admin).
70 The allegation of appearance of bias in this case failed on the basis that a reasonable observer in full knowledge of these facts would not have considered that there was a real possibility of bias; see para 62.

3.43   This case shows that s 25 does not require previous statements and actions to be disregarded; rather, such statements do not, by themselves, amount to predetermination. If other 'positive evidence' of predetermination exists (for example, arising from a councillor's behaviour during a meeting or from the content of e-mails sent by the councillor), then s 25 will not prevent a finding of unlawful predetermination.

Waiver

3.44   An individual can waive his or her right to object to a decision-maker on the grounds of apparent bias[71] and predetermination.[72] Waiver is generally thought not to apply to actual bias, as it would be contrary to the public interest for such bias to be permitted as an operative force behind decision-making. In the context of decision-making by councillors, it is difficult to see how waiver in relation to presumed bias can apply, given the criminal offences imposed by the statutory regime concerning DPIs.

3.45   Waiver in relation to apparent bias and predetermination is generally only possible where those with an interest in the decision are present during the decision-making process[73] (for example, at a planning or licensing committee meeting). Waiver may also be possible if the individual or group concerned set out the waiver explicitly in writing to the decision-maker. The mere fact that an individual or group corresponds with a decision-maker will not be taken to amount to waiver, even if the issue of bias is not raised in the correspondence.[74]

3.46   For waiver to be binding, it must be clear and unequivocal, and must be made with full knowledge of all the facts relevant to the decision whether to waive or not.[75] 'Full knowledge' does not mean that information in the public domain, but not known to the individuals concerned, is imputed to them[76] – a person cannot be taken to have waived bias or predetermination if she is unaware of the relevant facts.

D   OTHER CONDUCT ISSUES

3.47   Aside from the key issues of members' interests and bias/ predetermination, a whole host of other conduct issues can and will arise in the daily life of the local authority. The model code which local authorities were required to adopt under the Local Government Act 2000 (LGA 2000) contained

---

71 *Locabail* para 26.
72 Auburn, Moffett, Sharland and McManus *Judicial Review, Principles and Procedure* (OUP, 2013) para 8.115.
73 *R v Secretary for State for the Environment, Ex p Kirkstall Valley Campaign Ltd* [1996] 3 All ER 304 at 327.
74 *R (National Association of Memorial Masons) v Cardiff City Council* [2011] EWHC 922 (Admin) at para 42.
75 *Locabail (UK) Ltd v Bayfield Properties Ltd* [2000] QB 451 at para 15.
76 *BAA Ltd v Competition Commission* [2009] CAT 35 at paras 154–156.

'general obligations' in paras 3-7.[77] These addressed issues of behaviour and use/abuse of power. Although the LGA 2000 scheme has been repealed in favour of the new local codes under the Localism Act 2011,[78] the 'general obligations' remain relevant for three reasons:

- Many local authorities will have created their local codes by revising their existing LGA 2000-compliant codes and will therefore have retained the general obligations in the same or substantially the same form.[79]

- Even where local authorities have created entirely new local codes, some elements of the LGA 2000 model code are likely to have been retained in substance if not in form. The general obligations are consistent with and can be seen as aspects of the overriding Nolan principles, which form the basis of local codes.

- The 'Illustrative Text for Local Code of Conduct', published by the Department for Communities and Local Government (DCLG) on 11 April 2012 (and updated on 20 September 2013) has reformulated some of the general obligations, eg ensuring local authority resources are not used for improper purposes and promoting high standards of conduct.

3.48   Care must be taken when applying the contents of this section of the chapter, notwithstanding the enduring relevance of the general obligations. The actual wording of the local code should always be the first port of call in the event of a potential conduct issue. The principles developed in the context of the LGA 2000 model code may be wholly or partially inapplicable, depending on the way the local code has been drafted. If in doubt, clarification should always be sought from the monitoring officer.

3.49   Where it is alleged that there has been a breach of any 'general obligation' of the local code, regard must also be had to the context in which alleged misconduct has taken place. The LGA 2000 model code was limited in scope to acts carried out in an official capacity (unless the acts constituted criminal conduct).[80] Under the Localism Act 2011, local authorities must 'in particular adopt a code dealing with the conduct that is expected of members and co-opted members of the authority when they are acting in that capacity'.[81] The illustrative text published by DCLG is limited to acts in an official capacity, and in most other cases the LGA 2000-compliant position is likely to have been retained. However, there appears to be nothing to prevent local authorities from going further and imposing obligations on the conduct of members outside their official capacity. Again, it will be important to check the local code carefully in order to ascertain whether this is the case.

77 The Local Authorities (Model Code of Conduct) Order 2007, SI 2007/1159.
78 See **Chapter 1** for a summary of the previous standards regimes.
79 As permitted by the Localism Act 2011, s 28(5).
80 Defined in para 2 of the model code. The position prior to the 2007 model code was considered in some detail in *Livingstone v Adjudication Panel for England* [2006] HRLR 45; [2006] EWHC 2533 (Admin), paras 19–30.
81 Localism Act 2011, s 27(2).

The importance of freedom of political expression

3.50   It is in the nature of local politics that elected members will hold strong views, and will sometimes express them robustly during the course of debate. This is an essential part of local democracy. It is also part of a councillor's duty to challenge the views, opinions and decisions of other·councillors and officers. Insofar as local codes can be applied to constrain the ability of councillors to express themselves as they see fit, they carry an inherent risk of stifling legitimate political discourse.

3.51   Article 10 of the European Convention on Human Rights (ECHR) protects the right to freedom of expression, including the 'freedom to hold opinions and to receive and impart information and ideas without interference'. Such freedoms may be restricted, but only to the extent which is necessary in a democratic society in response to a pressing social need. Any restriction must be proportionate to the legitimate aims being pursued by the local code (the aims being the maintenance of good administration and reasonable standards of political discourse).

Case Study	
LGS/2012/0590	*Cllr John Copeland v West Lindsey District Council Standards Committee* FTT, 5 October 2012
Facts	Cllr Copeland was a Parish Councillor. He was found by the Standards Committee to have breached the Parish Council's Code of Conduct by referring, in a number of emails, to a member of the public as a grumbler and a geriatric, which had failed to show respect to that person and had brought his office or authority into disrepute. Cllr Copeland's appeal was successful.
Finding	It was not 'necessary' within the meaning of Article 10(2) ECHR to interfere with Cllr Copeland's freedom of expression by sanctioning him for his comments. The unidentified individual had a remedy in defamation, if there was any damage to his reputation, which was doubted. Proceedings before the Standards Committee were a 'wholly disproportionate response'.
Decision	The Standards Committee's decision to censure was set aside.

3.52   Political expression – what is said or published by elected representatives – is of particular importance, and deserves enhanced protection under Article 10

ECHR.[82] It has been said that 'there is little scope … for restrictions on political speech or of debate on questions of public interest'.[83] The enhanced protection of Article 10 applies even where the speech does not concern overtly political matters such as party allegiances and views on policy. 'Political expression' is to be understood in a broad sense. It encompasses matters of public concern and public administration generally, including revealing information about public figures.[84]

3.53 In the political context, a degree of immoderate, provocative, emotive and non-rational speech is to be tolerated. Even aggressive, offensive and shocking speech may have its place as part of the cut and thrust of political life.[85] However, purely personal abuse[86] or deliberately false statements[87] do not benefit from the enhanced protection given to political expression under Article 10. That does not mean that Article 10 is irrelevant. Even abusive speech is protected by the freedom of expression. However, the protection Article 10 provides is not 'enhanced', and therefore restrictions are easier to justify as being proportionate to the aims being pursued by local codes.

3.54 Those who are responsible for enforcing local codes will need to give particularly close and careful scrutiny to allegations that a councillor has breached the local code as a result of comments made in his capacity as an elected representative. Any relevant provisions of the local code will need to be interpreted narrowly. It may be the case that, given the importance to be attached to political expression, a finding that the local code has been breached is not justified. Even where a breach is found, any sanction imposed must be the minimum which is necessary to uphold the public interest in local government being conducted to standards which maintain public confidence.

3.55 A greater degree of tolerance will be extended to the words of councillors when they are directed towards other elected members than where they are directed to officers of the local authority (or other citizens). Elected representatives voluntarily enter the political arena. They are expected and required to have thicker skins and more tolerance to criticism than ordinary citizens.[88] Officers of the local authority are not elected and do not choose to lay themselves open to criticism in the same way. The relative seniority of the officer is also likely to be a relevant factor when the local authority comes to consider any alleged breach of the local code arising out of comments made to officers. The more senior the officer, the more responsibility they can be expected to shoulder and the greater the degree of scrutiny they can expect to face in respect of their actions.

82 See eg *Castells v Spain* (1992) 14 EHRR 445, para 42.
83 *Lombardo v Malta* (2009) 48 EHRR 23, para 55.
84 *R (Calver) v Adjudication Panel for Wales* [2013] PTSR 378; [2012] EWHC 1172 (Admin), paras 61–64.
85 See the summary in *Calver*, paras 55–58 in particular.
86 *Livingstone*, para 36.
87 *Heesom v Public Service Ombudsman for Wales* [2014] EWHC 1504 (Admin), para 116.
88 *Calver*, para 58.

Case Study

[2013] EWHC 4102 (Admin)	*R(Benjamin Dennehy) v London Borough of Ealing* High Court, 20 December 2013
Facts	Cllr Dennehy posted on a blog which he maintained comments about residents of Southall in which he stated: 'It is a largely Indian community who say they deplore this behaviour but yet it is that very same community that harbours and exploits their own people in squalid third world living conditions ... The exploding population of illegal immigrants is a constant on the public purse. Illegal immigrants don't pay tax. The legitimate immigrants exploiting them in the squalid bed sheds don't pay tax on their rental income. If these are the sorts of people who exploit the desperate what other scams are they perpetrating I ask? Criminality is endemic in Southall.' He declined to issue an apology when a number of Southall residents complained because they were offended by the statements.
Finding	The Cllr failed to treat others with respect and brought the Council into disrepute because the tone and much of the content was inappropriately and unnecessarily provocative, and the comments about Southall residents were in a different part of the blog from that which raised legitimate topics of political debate. The comments were not the expression of a political view, but a personal and generic attack on a section of the public. The subjects of the speech were not politicians but ordinary members of the public, so the comments did not attract the higher level of protection applicable to political expressions. Accordingly, sanctioning the Cllr was justified and proportionate under Article 10(2) of the Convention.
Decision	The Standards Committee's decision that the Cllr breached the code and should issue an appropriate apology, was upheld.

Bullying, intimidation and failing to show respect for others

Bullying

3.56   Whilst it is important to respect the rights of councillors to make legitimate challenges and engage in robust debate, there is a line to be drawn. Behaviour which amounts to bullying or is disrespectful may attract sanction, notwithstanding the protection given to political expression under Article 10 of the ECHR.

3.57   It has been said that bullying conduct involves:

- an attempt to undermine the other person; and

- an effect on the other person (in terms of intimidation, upset or detriment to confidence, capability or health).[89]

Comments which are of an offensive nature, humiliating, or involve personal attacks are more likely to stray into the realm of bullying and intimidation. By way of illustration, consider the difference between a councillor saying to an officer 'that is an idiotic thing to say'; and telling an officer 'you are an incompetent idiot'. The former is a criticism of what the officer has said, the latter is a personal insult and is undermining.

3.58   Behaviour will not cross the line into bullying merely because the recipient feels upset or distressed by what has been said, or finds the experience unpleasant. Robust but legitimate challenges by councillors may have that effect. It is necessary to go further than simply considering the effect of the comment, and also to consider the intentions of the maker.[90]

3.59   A course of bullying conduct may be viewed as harassment, which is likely to be treated more seriously than an isolated incident; particularly where an individual councillor or officer is being repeatedly singled out for such treatment.

Intimidation

3.60   The (now abolished) Standards Board for England published guidance on the LGA 2000 model code which specifically referred to intimidation in the context of an ongoing investigation into breaches of the local code. Allegations of misconduct can sometimes be vexatious or politically motivated, but it is crucial for councillors to allow any investigation to follow its natural course. They will be able to have their say as part of the investigation process. Bullying, intimidating or attempting to put pressure on anyone involved in the investigation, whether as a complainant, witness, independent person or decision maker, is likely to attract more serious sanctions, within the limitations of the system under the 2011 Act. It has the potential to undermine confidence in the local code and in the ability of the local authority to enforce its code. In fact, councillors who are the subject of a complaint are best advised to refrain from discussing it at all with anyone involved in the case. Some communication may be necessary as part of the administration of the process, but this should be limited as far as possible and preferably conducted in writing (or confirmed in writing soon after).

Failing to treat other with respect

3.61   In the *Mullaney* case the High Court agreed that:

---

89 See eg The Code of Conduct: Guide for members May 2007, Standards Board for England, p 9 and *Heesom* para 127.
90 See eg *Heesom* at para 129.

'"the concept of respect is perfectly capable of being applied by a reasonable person. … [The] failure to treat others with respect will occur when unfair, unreasonable or demeaning behaviour is directed by one person against another". The circumstances are also relevant and can include the place where the behaviour occurred, who observed the behaviour, the character and relationship of the people involved and the behaviour of anyone who prompted the alleged act of disrespect.' [91]

3.62   Complaints about failing to treat others with respect often arise in the context of challenges or criticisms made by councillors, either of their fellow members or of officers. As already noted, councillors are entitled to question performance and must be free to make reasonable criticisms. Care should to be taken over the tone of any criticism to ensure that the language used cannot be construed as amounting to personal abuse, insult or bullying. Criticism of colleagues and officers should be based on reasonable foundations/ evidence. Councillors should generally use appropriate channels within the local authority (for example, a private meeting with a senior manager) in preference to raising such issues in public; at least in the first instance. Local authority constitutions will contain member-officer protocols, and should have procedures in place to manage such matters. These should be followed. Public criticism will often be justifiable in the interests of holding the local authority to account and ensuring performance standards, but the risk of breaching the local code will be greater since: (i) public debates of that nature can quickly degenerate and become intemperate, and (ii) any comments which are made will reach a wider audience.

Examples

3.63   Examples of conduct which has been considered to amount to a failure to show respect to others or to bullying or intimidatory behaviour include:

- Looking at senior officers in a threatening manner and declaring that a number of managers had been dispensed with and 'there are more to go', which made the officers feel threatened.[92]

- Whilst accompanying a constituent to a formal interview with housing benefit officers under the terms of the Police and Criminal Evidence Act 1984, threatening to use executive powers to overrule the officers, questioning their qualifications and reducing one to tears. Subsequently writing a letter to the officer in demeaning and intemperate terms (referring to 'bullyboy methods'

---

91 *R (Mullaney) v Adjudication Panel for England* [2009] EWHC 72 (Admin), paras 97–99, endorsing as 'plainly right' the reasoning and conclusions of the Appeals Tribunal set out at para 2(6.6), part 2 of the schedule to the judgment.
92 *Heesom.*

and suggesting that she had committed 'sins' which needed to be atoned for).[93]

- Telling a relatively new member of the housing team that the head of housing 'knows nothing about housing and her days are numbered'. This was within the context of other incidents involving the head of housing.[94]

- Trespassing on a constituent's land to film the state of his property. The film was biased against the owner and contained a variety of negative comments about him, including false allegations of breaches of planning control. The film was uploaded to YouTube and generated further disparaging comments about the owner from people who viewed it.[95]

- Engaging in a verbal attack on two officers (a director of service and a human resources representative) during a chaotic and heated meeting, in which the councillor questioned their professional capacity to recommend candidates in an appointments process and upset both.[96]

- Circulating a note to other councillors containing inaccurate and misleading comments about an officer's organisation of a day to discuss ideas for the future direction of a service. Given the member's position and prior involvement, he knew the comments were inaccurate and misleading, and that they would have an undermining effect on the officer.[97]

3.64   It is permissible for local authorities investigating allegations of misconduct to consider a number of incidents 'in the round' and to find a breach of their code on the basis of the totality of what has occurred and its overall effect.[98] The individual incidents which make up a course of conduct do not necessarily have to be isolated and a separate conclusion reached on each incident.

93 *Sanders v Kingston (No 2)* [2005] EWHC 2132 (Admin).
94 *Heesom.*
95 *Mullaney.*
96 *Heesom.*
97 *Heesom.*
98 *Sanders v Kingston (No 1)* [2005] EWHC 1145 (Admin), para 59.

Case Studies

LGS/2011/0568   *Solihull Metropolitan Borough Council Standards Committee v Cllr Patrick Nash*
FTT, 30 March 2012

Facts   This was a reference to the FTT for a determination. The FTT considered this case alongside Cllr Nash's appeal in a separate matter but arising from largely the same facts (LGS/2011/0541). Cllr Nash was chairman of the Parish Council. Mrs D, the complainant, was Clerk to the Parish Council. Their relationship deteriorated, in part because of Cllr Nash's conduct in respect of a dispute over a village hall hire agreement which resulted in findings by the FTT in case 0541 that he had not treated a Mrs J with respect and, by acting ostensibly on behalf of the Parish Council without authority, had brought his office into disrepute. Mrs D had also suffered from severe ill health. Cllr Nash, without sustainable evidence, attributed Mrs D's actions to her ill health and sought to have her examined by a doctor. The FTT found this to be 'unreasonable and oppressive'. He later disclosed this fact in a public meeting. Cllr Nash also made 'gratuitous, offensive and egregious allegations' about Mrs D in emails, the seriousness of which was aggravated because they related to her activity in a public office, and which were not protected political speech. The FTT concluded his conduct amounted to bullying and disclosure of confidential information which, when seen in the round, was 'incompatible with being a councillor'. The FTT was highly critical of other Parish Councillors who gave self-serving evidence to the FTT which showed a greater concern for their own factions than the interests of their community.

Sanction   Two years' disqualification from membership of the Parish Council and any local authority.

LGS/2012/0582 *Cllr Brian Coleman v London Borough of Barnet Standards Committee*
FTT, 27 July 2012

Facts   Cllr Coleman was a member of the Borough Council's Cabinet and held the environment portfolio. He represented the Council on the North West London Waste Authority ('NWLA'). The NWLA was considering bidders for a waste management contract. Cllr Coleman received and replied to emails from Mr C and Dr J setting out objections to a company, V, being awarded the contract. To Dr J, Cllr Coleman concluded the email exchange thus: '... I will continue to ignore this campaign from you and other anti-Zionists. In my book anti-Zionism is just a modern form of anti Semitism. I suppose 70 years ago you would have been in the Blackshirts.' The FTT found that neither Mr C nor Dr J's emails had been impolite nor raised issues they were not entitled to raise. In contrast, Cllr Coleman was found to have crossed the line from making a political point into 'personal, offensive and insulting abuse which lacked any reflective content' and failed to show respect for others.

Sanction   Written apology.

Social media: opportunities and challenges

3.65 The continued rise of social media and blogging presents a new way for councillors to engage with their constituents. These new platforms can be useful for informing constituents about local issues and the actions that their elected representatives are taking. It can raise profiles and potentially help to engage a younger demographic in local politics. However, it brings additional risks for councillors around the way in which they express themselves.

3.66 Social media and blogging are much faster than traditional methods of communication, and users are often anonymous. This can create a tendency towards knee-jerk reactions and responses and intemperate exchanges. Whilst the protections of Article 10 of the ECHR remain, councillors must be particularly careful in the way they communicate where there is any suggestion that they are using these tools in an official rather than private capacity. Comments on blogs, forums or social media are more likely to be viewed as having been made in an official capacity where the authors explicitly identify themselves as councillors, where they impart information which is known to them only by virtue of their elected position, or where they comment directly on council business rather than on wider political issues. The use of disclaimers on blogs will not necessarily mean that what is said falls outside the scope of the local code.

Question: I personally fund and distribute a monthly newsletter to my constituents, and I also run my own Twitter feed using the handle '@ CouncillorX'. I do these things in my own time and entirely separately from the council. Will the local code apply to what I write?

Answer: It is likely that the local code will apply to your Twitter feed, particularly if your tweets appear to be a means of communicating with your constituents on local or council issues. As to the newsletter, it will depend on how it is presented. If it gives the impression that it is associated with you as a councillor (eg written in first person, describes you as 'Councillor X) then the code is more likely to apply. The fact that you produce it independently will be of little weight if it is clear from the content that this is one of the ways you engage with constituents on local issues. However, what you say will usually benefit from the enhanced protection of Article 10 of the ECHR (unless you descend into personal abuse).

3.67   Care also needs to be taken where members of the public are able to make comments on what councillors have written since there may be a risk that these would become associated with the councillor if they are not removed. Use of council-run websites and social media platforms is very likely to engage the local code, since it will be immediately associated with, and treated as published by, the local authority itself. Local authorities will often have policies on the use of social media and blogs, and these should be consulted for guidance.

Case Studies

LGS/2011/0562	*Cllr Ian Smith v Knowsley Metropolitan Borough Council Standards Committee* FTT, 27 January 2012
Facts	Cllr Smith posted a series of comments on Facebook denigrating identifiable Council officers. He called them liars and accused them of manipulating a consultation and of criminality and called for their resignations. He also compared the Council to the Nazis. He then sent an email to a senior Council officer which said that a report she had published was 'criminal' and demanded she either withdraw the report or resign.
Finding	The Facebook allegations were gratuitous, unsupported by evidence and offensive. The FTT found the Nazi comparison 'particularly egregious'. They amounted to a failure to treat others with respect and bullying and brought his office or authority into disrepute. The email to the Senior Officer was, additionally, conduct which compromised, or was likely to compromise, officer impartiality.
Sanction	Suspension from attending formal Council meetings.

LGS/2012/0587	*Cllr David Allen v Surrey Heath Borough Council Standards Committee* FTT, 10 October 2012
Facts	Cllr Allen ran a Blog. A blog post he made in September 2011 made reference to another Member of the Council. That Member made a complaint.
Finding	The FTT concluded that Cllr Allen had not been acting in his official capacity when making that particular blog post. Although Cllr Allen made reference to his status as a Councillor on the Blog, it was only part of his wider profile and not an indication that he was acting in his official capacity in making the blog post.
Decision	The Standards Committee's decision to censure and require a written apology was set aside.

Compromising the impartiality of local authority employees

3.68   It has long been seen as important that those who are employed in the discharge of the local authority's statutory functions are above the political fray. Council officers are required to be loyal to the local authority as a whole and to be neutral – not least because they are required to advise councillors and implement their policies regardless of political allegiance. They must also take their decisions in the public interest, without favouring particular individuals, groups or sections of society. The LGA 2000 model code of conduct prohibited elected representatives from doing anything which compromised the impartiality of officers, and many local codes will retain specific provisions of this nature. In any event, conduct which sought to compromise the impartiality of officers would be likely to offend against the Nolan principles of objectivity, openness and leadership.

3.69   Again, there is a difficult line to be drawn between the legitimate involvement of councillors as advocates for their constituents and the illegitimate interference in administrative decision making. It is quite common, and perfectly proper, for councillors to intervene on behalf of their constituents and to take an active interest. For example, a councillor may relay complaints about problem neighbours to the housing department; or might seek an explanation as to what action the environmental health department is taking in respect of a fast food premises. In these scenarios, councillors should be particularly alert to any personal or prejudicial interests they may have. The existence of such interests creates a greater risk that councillors' interventions will be seen as attempts to influence the outcome of any decisions which have to be made.

3.70   Councillors must not use their positions to pressure officers to change their decisions or the content of reports (a particular concern in controversial areas such as planning or licensing), or to suggest to members of the public that decisions will be overturned or should be disregarded. They should not engage in conduct which crosses the dividing line between the functions of elected members and council employees. There is a further risk that, by improperly interfering with the functions of officers, councillors may additionally be judged to have used their position in an attempt to gain financial or electoral advantages (by 'currying favour' with constituents).

Question: A constituent who has been on the council's housing register for many years has asked me to intervene with the housing allocations team to match him up with an empty property. Can I do this?

Answer: Housing allocation decisions are to be taken by council officers, and the law requires that decisions are made in accordance with the published policy. You are fully entitled to ask for an explanation of your constituent's position, or ask the team to look at his case. However, you should not seek to influence the decision or put pressure on the allocations team to produce a particular outcome. Doing so might amount to an improper attempt to interfere with the impartiality of staff. It would likely be contrary to the Nolan principles of objectivity, openness and leadership.

3.71   Further examples of actions which may compromise the impartiality of officers of the authority would include asking officers to help with the preparation of party political material or in matters relating to private business; particularly where an incentive or reward is offered or provided.[99]

Bringing your office or authority into disrepute

3.72   Members can expect their actions to be the subject of scrutiny by members of the public and the media as well as by their fellow councillors and by council employees. Actions which diminish public confidence in their ability to discharge their functions will bring their office into disrepute. The concept is concerned with damage to public confidence and the reputation of both the individual and the local authority as a whole. An allegation that the council has been brought into disrepute is likely to be made in conjunction with other allegations of misconduct, and is often a consequence of other types of misconduct.

3.73   A distinction must be drawn between conduct which brings the individual into disrepute and conduct which brings the office of elected councillor, or the authority as a whole, into disrepute. Misconduct will frequently bring the reputation of the individual into disrepute. However, in the *Livingstone* case it

---

99 The Code of Conduct: Guide for members May 207, Standards Board for England, p 10.

was said that 'misuse of the office can obviously bring disrepute on the office, but personal misconduct will be unlikely to do so'.[100] In *Sanders v Kingston (No 1)* the test which was suggested was whether the conduct alleged 'was such as would cause the reputation of [the authority] to suffer in the mind of a reasonable onlooker'.[101] Corruption and sleaze may diminish public confidence in the way the local authority is run and its fitness to govern as a whole, in a way that is unlikely where a councillor has engaged in bullying or has improperly interfered in officer decision making.

3.74   Examples from the authorities include the following:

- The London Mayor saying to a Jewish journalist 'What did you do before? Were you a German war criminal? ... you are just like a concentration camp guard. You're just doing it 'cause you're paid to aren't you?': did not bring the office of Mayor into disrepute.[102]

- The publication on the internet of a film made by a councillor and containing negative and false statements about the owner of a building, acquired by trespassing onto the land: did not bring the councillor's office into disrepute.[103]

- The leader of the council used a computer provided and paid for by the local authority to download indecent images of children: did bring his office and the local authority into disrepute.[104]

- The leader of the council expressing, in correspondence with another authority and subsequently in local and national media, personal anger and engaging in an ill-tempered rant in which he uttered a mild expletive and made comments which amounted to highly offensive, personal and vulgar abuse: did bring his office and the authority as a whole into disrepute (and led to the council passing a resolution disassociating itself from his comments and to his removal as leader of the council).[105]

- A councillor secretly buying land after he had learned in a private meeting that the council was proposing to buy the land and relocate the council's offices there (a proposal he disagreed with): did bring his office and authority into disrepute.[106]

---

100 *Livingstone v Adjudication Panel for England* [2006] HRLR 45; [2006] EWHC 2533 (Admin), para 40.
101 [2005] EWHC 1145 (Admin), para 75.
102 The *Livingstone* case.
103 The *Mullaney* case.
104 *Leadbeater* (9 November 2007) Adjudication Panel for England case ref: APE 0389.
105 *Sanders (No 1)*.
106 *Gliddon* (26 November 2007) Adjudication Panel for England case ref: APE 0383.

Case Studies

Z38/68	*Re Cllr R. Brierley* Wigan Council Standards (Ad Hoc) Sub-Committee, 4 November 2014
Facts	Cllr Brierley attended a hospital, unannounced, in the early hours of the morning, and demanded confidential information about a patient, allegedly at the request of the patient's parent. He was (correctly) refused this information, but Cllr Brierley would not accept this and continued to repeat his request. He was asked to leave by the most senior manager and security officers were called in case he returned. His conduct was inappropriate, particularly as he had not obtained clear authority to make such requests, and left NHS staff feeling intimidated.
Finding	Bringing your office or authority into disrepute.
Sanction	Sanctions deferred pending further hearings into Cllr Brierley's conduct.

Z38/105	*Re Cllr Robert Bleakley* Wigan Council Standards Hearing (Ad Hoc) Sub-Committee, 5 September 2014
Facts	Cllr Bleakley was a veteran of Standards Committee hearings. In a separate hearing six months earlier, he had had already been found to have breached the Code for accessing pornography on his Council ICT equipment. In this matter, he was found to have used his Council-issued mobile phone to call premium rate sex chat lines at a cost to the Council of more than £2,000. He also sent sexist text messages to female Council officers. He described the Sub-Committee as a 'toothless Neo Nazi style labour kangaroo court'.
Finding	Contravention of the Council's Acceptable Use of ICT Policy; bringing your office or authority into disrepute.
Sanction	All Council ICT equipment withdrawn until end of term in office; oversight of, and certain restrictions on, his communications with Council officers; publication of a press release and publicity in local press.

Dishonesty and abuse of position

3.75   The Nolan principles of honesty and integrity require that councillors do not use their positions to gain improper advantages (or disadvantages) for themselves or anyone else; and do not use the resources of the local authority for improper purposes.

Use of position to gain improper advantage

3.76   The gaining of an improper advantage is generally linked to the use of the position of councillor to further private interests, rather than acting in the public interest. It is likely to be viewed as one of the most serious breaches of the local code. An example of this type of conduct was *Sloam v Standards Board for England*,[107] where a councillor had allowed his son to use a car he had been given and which still contained the disabled parking permit to which the previous owner had been entitled. The son was not disabled, and was issued with four penalty charge notices relating to his unauthorised use of the permit. The councillor wrote a letter to the authority which had issued the penalty charge notices in which he purported to suggest that the disabled permit holder had been using the car at the time. The deceitful letter was written on the headed notepaper of his own authority and signed by him as a councillor. This led to a one year period of disqualification, upheld by the High Court.[108]

Case Studies

LGS/2012/0592	*Cllr Mohinder Gill v Standards Committee of the London Borough of Hounslow* FTT, 14 June 2013
Facts	Cllr Gill sat on the Planning Committee which was asked to consider possible enforcement action. Cllr Gill adamantly opposed enforcement action. Although he had some personal and political links with the owner of the property in question, the FTT found this fell short of requiring a declaration of interest. Nevertheless, the FTT was clearly troubled by 'some factor' which had 'distorted' Cllr Gill's judgment such that he had predetermined the matter before the Committee's meeting.
Finding	Improper use of his position to secure an advantage for another person, being the property's owner.
Sanction	Six month suspension from participation in Council's planning functions, censure, written apology.

---

107 [2005] EWHC 124 (Admin).
108 Disqualification is no longer available as a sanction: see **Chapter 2, Section F**.

LGS/2011/0550	*Ethical Standards Officer v Cllr Atiq Malik* FTT, 25 January 2012
Facts	Cllr Malik perpetrated a series of frauds, by leading his victims to believe that they would be granted contracts and or council tenancies by the Council in return for payments by way of deposits and fees. The Ethical Standards Officer sought a determination from the FTT that Cllr Malik had abused his position. Only one of the frauds was found to have breached the Code because in all other cases Cllr Malik was acting in a personal capacity only. In respect of the one breach, Cllr Malik dishonestly misrepresented to Mr B that he had authority to choose three tenants for council tenancies in a new development. On the strength of that representation, Mr B introduced Mr A to Cllr Malik. Cllr Malik induced Mr A to pay him fees by way of cheques made payable to 'Brent Housing' in order to secure the tenancy. In this case, his conduct gave the clear impression he was acting with the authority of the Council. However, in another, similar council house fraud, Cllr Malik was found not to have acted in his official capacity: although his victim trusted him because of his status as a Councillor, the FTT concluded that Cllr Malik's actions did not in this case give rise to an impression he was acting on the Council's behalf. Indeed, his conduct was equally consistent with trying to subvert the Council's process which would negate any impression of authority from the Council.
Finding	Improper use of his position to secure a financial advantage for himself and a significant financial disadvantage for another.
Sanction	Maximum disqualification of five years.

Improper use of resources

3.77 The improper use of local authority resources can be divided into two discrete categories:

- Cases where resources provided to councillors are used beyond the scope of what is authorised.

- Cases where councillors use the resources of the local authority for improper political purposes.

3.78 Local authorities will generally have policies in place regarding the use of resources by members, for example IT policies which set out the terms on which the council's computers may be used by councillors and any restrictions which apply. Breach of these policies may, depending on the circumstances, amount to a breach of local codes.

3.79   The restriction on using council resources for improper political purposes is a further manifestation of the principle that the authority's business itself should be politically neutral.[109] For this reason, local authorities are prohibited from publishing materials which appear to be designed to affect support for any particular political party. There are cases, by way of exception to this general rule, where an authority may authorise the use of its resources for political purposes provided they are connected with the authority's business. An example of this would be the use of local authority computers and paper to correspond with constituents, and the use of premises and other facilities to hold surgeries for constituents. Local authorities will generally have their own policies on these matters which should be consulted.

3.80   Particular care needs to be taken around the use of websites and social media accounts which are run by the local authority. Where individual councillors have access to these, they must be aware that anything they say or post is being published by the local authority as a whole, and this is highly likely to remain the case even if councillors clearly identify themselves within the post. The risk is particularly great in the context of higher profile individuals (such as chief executives or directly elected mayors), where the distinction between the person and the role is more blurred. An example of how things can go wrong can be seen in the case of the London Mayor, who published a tweet on the mayoral twitter feed linking to the front page of a national newspaper, which had declared its support for his political party. This was found to be an improper use of the authority's resources for political purposes.[110]

3.81   In the case of particularly serious or egregious incidents of dishonesty or abuse of position, there is the possibility that the offence of misconduct in public office may also have been committed. Further information on this offence can be found in chapter 5, 'Criminal Offences'.

---

109 See also s 2 of the Local Government Act 1986, which prohibits the publication by local authorities of material which in whole or in part appears designed to affect public support for a political party.
110 Decision of Assessment Sub-Committee of the GLA Standards Committee dated 2 November 2009, GLA Reference: Oct – 01/09.

> **Case Study**
>
> | | |
> |---|---|
> | LGS/2012/0578 | *Cllr Matthew Pollard v North West Leicestershire District Council Standards Committee* FTT, 1 June 2012 |
> | Facts | Cllr Pollard chaired a meeting of Ellistown and Battleflat Parish Council at which it was decided the Council would purchase two mowers from Cllr Pollard. Cllr Pollard still had the mower(s) in his possession three years later and sought over £1,500 from the Council by way of storage charges. The Hearing Sub-Committee of the Standards Committee found this to be a misuse of his position and brought his office or authority into disrepute. Cllr Pollard appealed on the ground that Cllr W, a member of the Hearing Sub-Committee, ought to have recused himself. Cllr Pollard alleged that Cllr W had invited him to switch from the Conservative to the Labour Party and that the latter would 'pay his legal fees'. The FTT did not accept this exchange took place and found that, at the time in question, Cllr Pollard was 'tired and distraught' at the end of a long and unsuccessful polling day. There was no possibility that any conversation between the two had given rise to bias, predetermination or its appearance. Cllr Pollard had behaved reprehensibly in directly attacking Cllr W's integrity. |
> | Sanction | Six month suspension. |

Disclosing confidential information

3.82   Councillors will come into contact with a wide variety of confidential information in the course of carrying out their roles. As a result, many authorities have included within their codes of conduct a requirement that councillors should not disclose confidential information, except in certain circumstances. Some authorities have developed protocols concerning confidential information, and in some instances there may be relevant standing orders which address confidential information. Breach of confidence is also a civil wrong, which may give rise to a claim in damages.

Definition of 'confidential information'

3.83   Councillors may be familiar with the definition of 'confidential information' in the context of their right of access to information,[111] where the

---

111 See, for example, reg 21 of the Local Authorities (Executive Arrangements) (Meetings and Access to Information) (England) Regulations 2012, SI 2012/2089.

concept is narrowly defined to mean information provided to a local authority by a government department on terms which forbid disclosure of the information to the public, or information which an enactment or an order of a court prevents from being disclosed. The notion of 'confidential information' in the context of conduct includes such information, but is much broader.

3.84 Obligations of confidentiality can arise from a number of sources. The three most common are statute,[112] contract,[113] and an area of law called 'equity', which is aimed at achieving fair outcomes between people. Equitable confidentiality is described in a famous case, *Coco v A N Clark (Engineering) Ltd*,[114] which held that this type of confidentiality arises where:

- the information was imparted in circumstances that imposed an obligation of confidentiality (ie how the information was obtained);

- the information itself has a quality of confidence about it (ie the nature of the information); and

- there is unauthorised use of the information, possibly to the detriment of the person who imparted the information or who is the subject of the information.

Each of these elements is discussed below.

How the information was obtained

3.85 Information will usually have been imparted in circumstances that impose a quality of confidence if:

- the person providing it expressly states that it is being provided in confidence; or

- it has been provided to your authority in exercise of its functions (where this occurs, the authority is not permitted to use the information for an unrelated purpose).[115]

It must be remembered that, since the coming into force of the Freedom of Information Act 2000, people supplying information to public authorities have known that the authorities are subject to statutory disclosure obligations. This does not mean, however, that a councillor can disclose this information for an unrelated purpose, in the absence of a freedom of information request.

---

112 For example, the Data Protection Act 1998. There are a vast number of statutes which prohibit public authorities from disclosing certain information, ranging from the Census Act 1920 (s 8) to the Local Government Act 1974 (s 32) to the Public Services Contracts Regulations 1993, SI 1993/3228 (reg 30). For a helpful list see P Coppel *Information Rights Law and Practice* (4th edn, 2014, Hart Publishing Ltd), para 26-018.

113 For example, an employment contract or a commercial contract for the provision of services may require certain information about employees to be kept confidential.

114 *Coco v A N Clark (Engineering) Ltd* [1969] RPC 41. The information in this case was a design for a moped engine which had been provided to manufacturers, who later began producing their own moped.

115 See, for example, *Marcel v Commissioner of Police* [1992] Ch 225, where the court held that the police should not have allowed parties in a civil dispute to inspect documents seized by the police in connection with a police investigation which was subsequently dropped.

3.86   Information that is received in an exempt or private session of a committee or council may be confidential information, although it will not automatically be so[116] – everything depends on the nature of the information. It will likely have the necessary quality of confidence where:

- the information is provided on the basis that it will be kept confidential;

- there is an agreement by the members of the committee or council that it is in the public interest to keep the information confidential;

- the information is not available by any other means than through the private session.

Any confidentiality will only adhere to the information which is material to the need for confidentiality.

Nature of the information

3.87   Information will usually have a quality of confidence if it is not something that is public knowledge, and it has a 'basic attribute of inaccessibility'.[117] The fact that the information that is marked as 'classified' or 'private and confidential' is not definitive as to whether the information contained in the document is confidential.[118] The information must be such that a reasonable person would regard it as confidential. The courts have found that the following information has the requisite confidential nature:[119]

- correspondence between a person and his legal advisers;

- a person's medical records;

- statements made to the police in the course of a criminal investigation;

- tender documents;

- certain documents received in the course of commercial negotiation;[120]

- information supplied to a public authority under legal compulsion, such as a tax return;

- information supplied to a public authority which is of a highly personal and sensitive nature.[121]

---

116 See, for example, *Thomas* (17 February 2004) Adjudication Panel for England case ref: APE 0158 and *Wicking* (3 June 2009) Adjudication Panel for England case ref: APE 0420.
117 *AG v Guardian Newspapers Ltd (No 2)* [1990] 1 AC 109 at 215. This case concerned the *Spycatcher* book, written by a former member of the British security services, which contained an account of the activities of MI5.
118 *Derry City Council v Information Commissioner* (11 December 2006) First-tier Tribunal Information Rights ref: EA/2006/0014 at 34(a).
119 See P Coppel *Information Rights Law and Practice* (4th edn, 2014, Hart Publishing Ltd) para 25-015.
120 See *Derry City Council v Information Commissioner* (11 December 2006) First-tier Tribunal Information Rights ref: EA/2006/0014, where the Tribunal held that a fax from Ryanair to Derry City Council setting out financial information about Ryanair's proposed use of Derry City Airport was confidential, even though it was not part of a contract.
121 For example, *S v Information Commissioner and the General Register Office* (9 May 2007) First-tier Tribunal Information Rights ref: EA/2006/0030, which concerned notes taken by the registrar of deaths during a question and answer session of a person registering the death as they had been present at the time of death.

3.88　If information has improperly been made public, that does not mean that it always loses its confidential nature and can thereafter be recited in public with impunity.[122] This stems from the fact that the duty of confidence is imposed not only on the person to whom the information was confided, but also on any third party who acquires the information from him/her. However, the courts have indicated that a very strong public interest will be required to justify treating information that has been published as retaining its confidentiality. Where information has been widely disseminated and is well known, even if the publication was improper, the information can no longer be considered to be confidential.[123]

Detriment

3.89　The judge in *Coco v A N Clark (Engineering) Ltd* left it open whether proof of detriment is necessary to establish breach of confidence. If it is necessary, then detriment can be shown through evidence that the information was disclosed to people whom the confider would prefer not to have known of the information.[124]

Question: I am very angry about my political party's choice of a candidate for Mayor of the Council. I am aware that an officer of the Council has been driving the candidate to visit other councillors, I think to make offers of political position. I know that the officer is currently undergoing disciplinary proceedings for bringing his office into disrepute. I want to write a letter to the leadership of the party telling them all this. Can I do this?

Answer: You must not mention the disciplinary proceedings to which the officer is subject. This would amount to disclosure of confidential information. The disciplinary proceedings are an employment matter which is confidential to a council employee and which you know about because of your role as a councillor. The information has the quality of confidence about it and its disclosure would be detrimental to the employee. You should refrain from including the information about the disciplinary proceedings in your letter. See *Abbas v LB Tower Hamlets Standards Committee* (4 April 2012) First-tier Tribunal Information Rights ref: LGS/2011/0574.

---

122 *Thomas* (17 February 2004) Adjudication Panel for England case ref: APE 0158.
123 See *BBC v HarperCollins Publishers Ltd* [2010] EWHC 2424 (Ch) at paras 58–61. This case concerned an application for an injunction to prevent the publication of an autobiography revealing the identity of 'The Stig', the infamously anonymous driver in Top Gear. The application was refused because, by the time the company wished to publish the book, the identity of The Stig was generally known and anyone interested in the topic could easily discover the identity from public sources.
124 P Coppel *Information Rights Law and Practice* (4th edn, 2014, Hart Publishing Ltd) para 25–021. See also *AG v Guardian Newspapers Ltd (No 2)* [1990] 1 AC 109 at 255–56.

Definition of 'disclosure'

3.90 The Oxford English Dictionary defines 'disclosure' as 'the action or fact of disclosing or revealing new or secret information; the action of making something openly known'. A more colourful definition is given by Chief Justice Cockburn in the 1859 case of *Regina v Alfred Skeen and Archibald Freeman*:[125]

> 'But, according to Dr. Johnson[126], "disclose" may mean "to uncover; to produce from a state of latitancy to open view; to reveal; to impart what is secret". According to Richardson[127] (whose authority I much respect), "disclose" is "to uncover, or discover; to reveal; to open; to make known; to tell that which has been kept concealed."'

'Disclosure' is thus a broad term, and information can be disclosed through a very wide variety of means, including verbal communication, written communication and general publication in the news media. The number of recipients of the information is not relevant – provision of the information to even a single person amounts to 'disclosure'.

Public interest justification

3.91 Disclosure of confidential information may be justified where it is in the 'public interest' to make the disclosure. The basic principle is that the public interest in disclosing must outweigh both the public and private interests in protecting the confidentiality of the information. The paradigm instance in which this operates is to expose wrongdoing.[128] The wrongdoing does not need to amount to a criminal or a civil wrong, but must be of such a character that the public interest demands disclosure. An allegation of wrongdoing will justify exposure in the public interest if it is credible and from an apparently reliable source.[129] There is also a public interest in the public not being misled.[130] Finally,

---

125 (1859) Bell 97.
126 Dr Samuel Johnson (1709–1784), lexicographer, biographer, poet, essayist, travel writer and literary critic. Author of *A Dictionary of the English Language* (1755), completed after nine years of work and defining over 42,000 words. Dr Johnson was the first lexicographer to illustrate the meanings of words by literary quotation, most frequently citing Shakespeare, Dryden and Milton.
127 Charles Richardson (1775–1865), lexicographer and English teacher, author of the *New English Dictionary* (1834), which relied extensively on etymology and also gave copious quotations from authors to show the meanings of words.
128 P Coppel *Information Rights Law and Practice* (4th edn, 2014, Hart Publishing Ltd) paragraph 25-025. See also *Initial Services v Putterill* [1968] 1 QB 396 at 405. This case concerned an employee who resigned from a laundry company, but took with him a number of files which he then disclosed to a national newspaper. The files showed a liaison system between a group of firms in the laundry business whereby prices were kept artificially high.
129 *AG v Guardian Newspapers Ltd (No 2)* [1990] 1 AC 109 at 283.
130 See, for example, *Campbell v MGN Ltd* [2004] 2 AC 457, where the model Naomi Campbell had publicly denied taking illegal drugs or being an addict. In her subsequent claim for infringement of her privacy she accepted that these statements had been untrue, and the House of Lords accepted that a newspaper had the right to correct the false image which she had projected by publishing the information about her drug addiction and receipt of treatment.

there is a public interest in exposing damage to the environment or a health and safety risk.

3.92   The following elements are relevant in determining whether a disclosure has been made in the 'public interest':

- The disclosure must be reasonable:

  – if the person disclosing the information does not believe it to be true, then it is unlikely the disclosure is reasonable;

  – the extent of the information disclosed should not go beyond what is necessary.

- The disclosure must be made in good faith:

  – there must not be an ulterior motive, for example the achievement of political advantage;

  – disclosure for personal gain (particularly for payment) is unlikely to be made in good faith.

- The disclosure must be made in compliance with any reasonable requirements of your authority. For example, before making the disclosure, you should consult your authority's policies and protocols on matters such as whistleblowing.

3.93   Disclosure has been held to be in the public interest in the following cases:

- *London Regional Transport v Mayor of London*,[131] where disclosure of a partly redacted version of a commercially confidential interim report prepared by accountants concerning a proposed public-private partnership for the London Underground was held to be justified because there was a public interest in enabling the general public to be informed of serious criticism from a responsible source of the value for money of a such a large and potentially expensive venture;

- *Derry City Council v Information Commissioner*,[132] where disclosure of commercially confidential information about pricing was held to be in the public interest where it shed light on a debate of wide concern about the funding of an airport by a public authority. Accountability of public funding for an airport used by private operators was held to be sufficiently weighty to displace the confidentiality that attached to negotiations between the public authority and the airline operator.

---

131 [2003] EWCA Civ 1491.
132 (11 December 2006) First-tier Tribunal Information Rights ref: EA/2006/0014.

Case Study

> **Re Cllr Mark Chatburn**
> Stockton-on-Tees Borough Council Standards Panel, 7 May
> 2014

Facts   Cllr Chatburn was a member of the Planning Committee. He
published, on his blog, a legally privileged and unredacted
counsel's opinion in relation to a planning application before
the Committee. The title of the blog post was, 'How Stockton
Council is trying to manipulate its own Planning Committee'.
Cllr Chatburn was unrepentant and indicated a willingness to do
the same again.

Finding   Knowingly disclosed privileged legal advice provided to him in
confidence.

Sanction   Asked to provide written assurance he would not repeat the
breach, in default of which he would not be provided with any
exempt, confidential or legally privileged Council information
for remainder of term of office.

Data Protection Act 1998

3.94   Councillors are also under an obligation not to use or disclose personal
information in a way that is unfair or unlawful, and to keep personal information
secure. This obligation arises from the Data Protection Act 1998 (DPA 1998).
This is a much maligned piece of legislation, but a lot of the criticism directed
against it stems from misunderstanding its purpose. The impetus behind data
protection is a recognition that, in a world of increasing technical ability to store,
retrieve and share large volumes of data, there is an increased risk that information
which is private to individuals will be misused. At the heart of data protection
are several intuitively sensible principles aimed at ensuring that people's private
information is kept private, unless they consent to its use or unless its use is fair.
These principles also encapsulate what has been recognised as good business
practice: ensuring technology is secure; keeping information updated and only
keeping the information that you need.

3.95   The Information Commissioner is tasked with promoting and monitoring
data protection practices in the United Kingdom, and has produced a treasure trove
of clear, helpful and accessible guides and toolkits, tailored to particular sectors
or dealing with particular issues.[133] There is a useful guidance note for elected
and prospective members of local authorities. The Information Commissioner's
office is also able to give advice directly if contacted with specific questions.
Many local authorities will also have a Data Protection Officer who can give
guidance on data protection issues.

---

133   These are available on the Information Commissioner's website: http://ico.org.uk/.

Definitions

3.96   At the heart of data protection is the concept of 'personal data', which means information about a living individual. If you record in written or electronic form your opinions about or intentions in relation to a living individual, then this is also specifically included in the definition of that individual's personal data, in order to ensure that these opinions or intentions are used fairly and are kept securely. Obligations in relation to personal data arise when that data is being 'processed'. This means obtaining, recording, holding, transferring or disclosing the information, or carrying out any operation on the information. This definition is very wide and it is difficult to think of anything you can do with personal information that will not be processing.

3.97   The Data Protection Act also defines certain information as 'sensitive personal data', which requires particular care. This information is defined as:

- the racial or ethnic origin of the data subject;

- his political opinions;

- his religious beliefs or other beliefs of a similar nature;

- whether he is a member of a trade union;

- his physical or mental health or condition;

- his sexual life;

- the commission or alleged commission by her of any offence, proceedings for the commission or alleged commission of any offence.[134]

3.98   There are three different areas in which councillors' obligations under the Data Protection Act are likely to arise:

- When considering issues and making decisions as part of the council's business, for example in committees or working groups. This work may give you access to a considerable amount of personal information: for example, a member of a housing committee may need to access tenancy files to consider whether the local authority should proceed with an eviction; a member of a licensing committee will have access to an application for a taxi licence; a member of a planning committee with have access to an application for an extension to a house in order to house an ill parent.

- When carrying out casework in your ward/division. This will give access to personal information to timetable surgery appointments, and if a constituent complains or raises an issue, then that may entail their or other people's personal information.

- As a member of a political party canvassing for votes, electioneering and working for the party, or as an independent candidate canvassing for votes and electioneering.

134 Data Protection Act, s 2.

Question: A member of your constituency comes to you and asks for help with a noisy and intimidating neighbour. You write down the constituent's name, address and contact details; the name and address of the neighbour and details of the noisy and intimidating behaviour. You also record your opinion that this behaviour is totally unacceptable. You want to give your notes to the ward member who deals with anti-social behaviour. Can you do this?

Answer: Yes, if you have asked your constituent for permission to pass on their personal information. If the constituent objects, then you should only discuss the matter with the other member in broad terms, not giving any of your constituent's personal information. The neighbour's name and address and your opinion about their behaviour is also personal information. You can only pass on that information if it is <u>necessary</u> for the exercise of functions of a public nature exercised in the public interest.

Further question: You and the other ward member work together and find an amicable resolution to the problem. Your constituent is delighted. You want to publicise this on your blog as a good news story of local politics working, and you want to use it to progress your political party's campaign on anti-social behaviour. Can you do this?

Answer: Yes, but only if you have the consent of both the constituents involved. If they withhold consent, then you cannot use any information which may identify them.

Multi-ward authorities

3.99   In some types of local authorities councillors are elected under a multi-member system where more than one councillor represents a particular ward. As a result, there may be situations where a councillor who represents a constituent may need to pass on that individual's personal information to another councillor in the same ward. The councillor will only be allowed to disclose to the other ward councillor the personal information that is necessary either to address the constituent's concerns, or where the particular issue raises a matter which concerns other elected members in the same ward; and the constituent has been made aware that this is going to take place and why it is necessary. If a constituent objects to a use or disclosure of their information, their objections should normally be honoured. A councillor should not pass on personal information which is not connected to the constituent's case.

Fair and lawful use of information

3.100   When elected members consider using personal information for any particular purpose, they should take into account the context in which that information was collected to decide whether their use of the information will be fair and lawful. The Information Commissioner's guidance gives this helpful advice:

- Personal information held by the local authority should not be used for political or representational purposes unless both the local authority and the individuals concerned agree. It would not be possible to use a list of the users of a particular local authority service for electioneering purposes without their consent. An example would be using a local authority list of library users to canvass for re-election on the grounds that the member had previously opposed the closure of local libraries.

- When campaigning for election as the representative of a political party, candidates can use personal information, such as mailing lists, held by their parties. However, personal information they hold as elected members for casework should not be disclosed to the political party without the consent of the individual.

- Candidates for election should also be aware of the requirements of the Privacy and Electronic Communications (EC Directive) Regulations 2003[135] that regulate unsolicited electronic marketing messages sent by telephone, fax, email or text and which criminalise the use of some forms of unsolicited electoral campaigning (for example, if the person's number is registered with the Telephone Protection Service). There is a very helpful and extensive guide on this on the Information Commissioner's website.

- When campaigning for election to an office in a political party, members should only use personal information controlled by the party if its rules allow this. It would be wrong, for instance, to use personal information which the candidate might have in their capacity as the local membership secretary, unless the party itself had sanctioned this.

Security

3.101   Councillors holding personal data must keep it secure. This is particularly important when the data is of a sensitive nature. All portable devices used to store personal information – such as memory sticks, laptops and mobile phones – must be encrypted. The council must have a proper password policy (ie requiring passwords to be sufficiently complex and to be changed regularly), and computer access privileges should be job-specific. Care needs to be taken to ensure that paper files are also kept secure.

Penalties for breach and offences

3.102   Breach of the Data Protection Act can result in a monetary penalty being imposed by the Information Commissioner, and in some instances is a criminal offence. These offences include:

- Making unauthorised disclosures of personal information.[136] For example, an elected member who disclosed personal information held by the council to their party for electioneering purposes without the council's consent could commit an offence.

---

135   SI 2003/2426.
136   DPA 1998, s 55(1)(a).

- Procuring unauthorised disclosures of personal information.[137] For example, an elected member who obtained a copy of personal information apparently for council purposes, but in reality for their own personal use (or the use of his or her party) is likely to have committed an offence.

- When someone is required to notify the Information Commissioner that they hold personal information, and does not do so. There is guidance on the Information Commissioner's website about the notification requirement as it applies to councillors.[138]

E EQUALITY AND DISCRIMINATION

Breach of the equality enactments

3.103   Councillors are subject to the legal prohibitions against discrimination contained in the Equality Act 2010 (EA 2010). These proscriptions, including prohibiting harassment and victimisation, may also be included in an authority's code of conduct.

Protected characteristics under the Equality Act 2010

3.104   The EA 2010 consolidates and replaces most of the previous discrimination legislation for England, Scotland and Wales.[139] It renders unlawful various types of discrimination on the basis of nine 'protected categories', set out below.[140] The EA 2010 makes such discrimination generally unlawful in most areas of activity, including employment; housing; the provision of services, and the exercise of public functions.

Age

3.105   Age is defined by reference to a person's age group.[141] An age group can mean people of the same age or people of a range of ages. Age groups can be wide (for example, 'people under 50'; 'under 18s'). They can also be quite narrow (for example, 'people in their mid-40s'; 'people born in 1952'). Age groups may also be relative (for example, 'older than me' or 'older than us').

---

137 DPA 1998, s 55(1)(b).
138 http://ico.org.uk/for_organisations/guidance_index/~/media/documents/library/Data_ Protection/Practical_application/advice_elected_and_prospective_members_local_ authorities.ashx
139 The Race Relations Act 1976; the Sex Discrimination Act 1975; the Disability Discrimination Act 1995; the Employment Equality (Religion or Belief) Regulations 2003, SI 2003/1660; the Employment Equality (Sexual Orientation) Regulations 2003, SI 2003/1661; and the Employment Equality (Age) Regulations 2006, SI 2006/1031.
140 What follows is based on the Equality and Human Rights Commission *Code of Practice on Employment* (2011), as the principles expounded are equally applicable to councillors performing their official functions.
141 EA 2010, s 5(1).

Disability

3.106   A person has a disability if they have a physical or mental impairment which has a long-term and substantial adverse effect on their ability to carry out normal day-to-day activities.[142] Cancer, HIV infection, and multiple sclerosis are deemed disabilities under the Act from the point of diagnosis. Physical or mental impairment includes sensory impairments such as those affecting sight or hearing. An impairment which consists of a severe disfigurement is treated as having a substantial adverse effect on the ability of the person concerned to carry out normal day-to-day activities. 'Long-term' means that the impairment has lasted or is likely to last for at least 12 months or for the rest of the affected person's life. 'Substantial' means more than minor or trivial.

Gender reassignment

3.107   People who are proposing to undergo, are undergoing, or have undergone a process (or part of a process) to reassign their sex by changing physiological or other attributes of sex have the protected characteristic of gender reassignment.[143] Under the Act 'gender reassignment' is a personal process (that is, moving away from one's birth sex to the preferred gender), rather than a medical process, so a person who was born with one sex but is living as the other without the need for medical intervention is protected. Cross-dressing for purposes other than gender reassignment is, however, not protected.

Marriage and civil partnership

3.108   A person who is married or in a civil partnership has this protected characteristic.[144] Marriage will cover any formal union of a man and woman which is legally recognised in the UK as a marriage. A civil partnership refers to a registered civil partnership under the Civil Partnership Act 2004, including those registered outside the UK. People who only intend to marry or form a civil partnership, or who have divorced or had their civil partnership dissolved, are not protected on this ground.

Pregnancy and maternity

3.109   'Pregnancy' includes pregnancy-related illness. 'Maternity' refers to exercising, having exercised or seeking or having sought to exercise a right to maternity leave, whether that be compulsory, ordinary or additional maternity leave. The protected period starts when a woman becomes pregnant and continues until the end of her maternity leave, or until she returns to work, if that is earlier. Outside the protected period, unfavourable treatment of a woman in employment because of her pregnancy would be considered as sex discrimination rather than pregnancy and maternity discrimination.[145]

142 EA 2010, s 6(1).
143 EA 2010, s 7(1).
144 EA 2010, s 8(1).
145 EA 2010, s 18(7).

3.110 In the employment context, the employer's motive or intention in relation to pregnancy or maternity discrimination is not relevant, and neither are the consequences of pregnancy or maternity leave. Such discrimination cannot be justified. In some cases, employers have to treat workers who are pregnant or have recently given birth more favourably than other workers. Men cannot make a claim for sex discrimination in relation to any special treatment given to a woman in connection with pregnancy or childbirth, such as maternity leave or additional sick leave.[146]

Race

3.111 'Race' is defined as including colour, nationality and ethnic or national origins.[147] A person has the protected characteristic of race if they fall within a particular racial group. A racial group is a group of people who have or share a colour, nationality or ethnic or national origins.[148] For example, a racial group could be 'British' people. A person may fall into more than one racial group. Nationality (or citizenship) is the specific legal relationship between a person and a state through birth or naturalisation. An ethnic group is defined as a group which regards itself and is regarded by others as a distinct and separate community because of a long shared history and a cultural tradition of its own.

3.112 In addition, an ethnic group may have one or more of the following characteristics: a common language; a common literature; a common religion; a common geographical origin; or being a minority; or an oppressed group. The courts have confirmed that the following are protected ethnic groups: Sikhs, Jews, Romany Gypsies, Irish Travellers, Scottish Gypsies, and Scottish Travellers. National origins must have identifiable elements, both historic and geographic, which at least at some point in time indicate the existence or previous existence of a nation. For example, as England and Scotland were once separate nations, the English and the Scots have separate national origins.

Religion or belief

3.113 This is defined to include any religion and any religious or philosophical belief, and also the lack of any such religion or belief.[149] The term 'religion' includes the more commonly recognised religions in the UK such as the Baha'i faith, Buddhism, Christianity, Hinduism, Islam, Jainism, Judaism, Rastafarianism, Sikhism and Zoroastrianism. It is for the courts to determine what constitutes a religion. A religion need not be mainstream or well known to gain protection as a religion. However, it must have a clear structure and belief system. Denominations or sects within religions, such as Methodists within Christianity or Sunnis within Islam, may be considered a religion for the purposes of the Act.

---

146 EA 2010, s 13(6)(b).
147 EA 2010, s 9(1).
148 EA 2010, s 9(3).
149 EA 2010, s 10(1) and (2).

3.114   A belief which is not a religious belief may be a philosophical belief. Examples of philosophical beliefs include Humanism and Atheism. A belief need not include faith or worship of a God or Gods, but must affect how a person lives their life or perceives the world. To be protected, a philosophical belief must concern a weighty and substantial aspect of human life and behaviour and must be worthy of respect in a democratic society, not incompatible with human dignity and not conflict with the fundamental rights of others (so, for example, belief in racial superiority would not be protected).

3.115   While people have an absolute right to hold a particular religion or belief, manifestation of that religion or belief is a qualified right which may in certain circumstances be limited, so long as the limitation does not amount to unlawful discrimination.

Sex

3.116   This refers to a male or female of any age. In relation to a group of people it refers to either men and/or boys, or women and/or girls.[150]

Sexual orientation

3.117   This means a person's sexual orientation towards: persons of the same sex (that is, the person is a gay man or a lesbian); persons of the opposite sex (that is, the person is heterosexual); or persons of either sex (that is, the person is bisexual).[151] Sexual orientation relates to how people feel as well as their actions. Sexual orientation discrimination includes discrimination because someone is of a particular sexual orientation, and it also covers discrimination connected with manifestations of that sexual orientation. These may include someone's appearance, the places they visit or the people they associate with.

Direct and indirect discrimination[152]

3.118   The equality enactments have always drawn a distinction between direct discrimination and indirect discrimination. The distinction is important because direct discrimination can never be justified (although there are three exceptions in the EA 2010);[153] whereas there is a defence of justification available in relation to indirect discrimination. The distinction between direct and indirect discrimination can be difficult to draw. Generally, discrimination is direct where

---

150 EA 2010, s 11(a) and (b).
151 EA 2010, s 12(1).
152 What follows is based on the Equality and Human Rights Commission *Code of Practice on Employment* (2011), as the principles expounded are equally applicable to councillors performing their official functions.
153 See para **3.125** below.

a difference in treatment is based on a criterion that is either explicitly a protected characteristic or necessarily linked to a protected characteristic. It is indirect where some other criterion is applied, but a substantially higher proportion of those with the protected characteristic are affected than those who do not have that characteristic.[154]

Direct discrimination

3.119   Direct discrimination occurs when a person treats another less favourably than they treat or would treat others because of a protected characteristic.[155] To decide whether a councillor has treated someone 'less favourably', a comparison must be made with how they have treated other comparable people or would have treated them in similar circumstances. If the councillor's treatment of the person puts that person at a clear disadvantage compared with others in a comparable position, then it is more likely that the treatment will be less favourable. Less favourable treatment could also involve being deprived of a choice or excluded from an opportunity.

3.120   It is not possible to balance or eliminate less favourable treatment by offsetting it against more favourable treatment – for example, extra pay to make up for loss of job status. Direct discrimination can take place even though the councillor and the individual in issue share the same protected characteristic giving rise to the less favourable treatment. Direct discrimination also includes less favourable treatment of a person based on a stereotype relating to a protected characteristic, whether or not the stereotype is accurate. It is also direct discrimination if a councillor treats someone less favourably because the councillor mistakenly thinks that the individual has a protected characteristic.

3.121   Direct discrimination because of a protected characteristic could also occur if a person is treated less favourably because they campaigned to help someone with a particular protected characteristic or refused to act in a way that would disadvantage a person or people who have (or are believed to have) the characteristic.

---

154 *Preddy and Hall v Bull* [2013] 1 WLR 3741. In this case the Supreme Court was considering a policy instituted by the owners of a private hotel to restrict occupancy of double rooms to married couples, and to deny those in civil partnerships such rooms because they believed marriage could only be between a man and a woman. The Supreme Court held that the differentiation between marriage between heterosexuals and civil partnership between homosexuals was direct discrimination.

155 EA 2010, s 13(1).

> **Question:** A senior female officer's appraisal duties are withdrawn while her male colleagues at the same grade continue to carry out appraisals. Although she was not demoted and did not suffer any financial disadvantage, she feels demeaned in the eyes of those she managed and in the eyes of her colleagues. Is this discrimination?
>
> **Answer:** The removal of her appraisal duties may be treating her less favourably than her male colleagues. If the less favourable treatment is because of her sex, this would amount to direct discrimination.

The comparator

3.122 In comparing people for the purpose of direct discrimination, there must be no material difference between the circumstances relating to each case.[156] However, it is not necessary for the circumstances of the two people – that is, the person potentially discriminated against (P) and the comparator (C) – to be identical in every way; what matters is that the circumstances which are relevant to the treatment of P are the same or nearly the same for P as for C. In practice it is not always possible to identify an actual person whose relevant circumstances are the same or not materially different, so the comparison will need to be made with a hypothetical comparator.

3.123 Certain types of treatment do not require the identification of a comparator:

- for direct discrimination because of pregnancy and maternity, the test is whether the treatment is <u>unfavourable</u> rather than less favourable. There is no need for the woman to compare her treatment with that experienced by others in the organisation;

- when the protected characteristic is race, deliberately segregating a person or group of people from others of a different race automatically amounts to less favourable treatment.[157] There is no need to identify a comparator, because racial segregation is always discriminatory. But it must be a deliberate act or policy rather than a situation that has occurred inadvertently.

Motive

3.124 The councillor's motive or intention is irrelevant where there is direct discrimination. It is also irrelevant whether the less favourable treatment is conscious or unconscious. Councillors may have prejudices that they do not even admit to themselves or may act out of good intentions, or simply be unaware that they are treating the person differently because of a protected characteristic. This is not a defence.

---

156 EA 2010, s 23(1)
157 EA 2010, s 15(5).

Exceptions

3.125 Direct discrimination is generally unlawful. However, it may be lawful in the following circumstances:

- where the protected characteristic is age, and the less favourable treatment can be justified as a proportionate means of achieving a legitimate aim;[158]

- in relation to the protected characteristic of disability, where a disabled person is treated more favourably than a non-disabled person;[159]

- where the Act provides an express exception which permits directly discriminatory treatment that would otherwise be unlawful.

Case Studies

LGS/2012/0580	*Cllr Peter Batty v Hinckley and Bosworth Borough Council Standards Committee* FTT, 30 May 2012
Facts	Cllr Batty was the Chairman of Groby Parish Council. The local area had a history of unauthorised gypsy and traveller encampments. A plot of land was purchased in the locality and there appears to have been an anxiety that it would be cleared for the purposes of hosting an unlawful encampment. Cllr Batty played a significant role in the drafting of a leaflet distributed to his constituents which made allegations of dishonesty against the purchaser, employed emotive language which emphasised 'fear and rumour' and encouraged 'fear and suspicion of the new owners ... and of travellers and gypsies in general.' A bibliophilic FTT cited Exodus 23, Franklin D. Roosevelt and JS Mill, on its way to finding that Cllr Batty's conduct was likely to breach the Council's duties under the Race Relations Act 1976 and damage public confidence in his and the Council's likelihood of complying with equality duties and treating others with respect.
Sanction	Censure, training on race relations and a written apology.

---

158 EA 2010, s 13(2).
159 EA 2010, s 13(3).

August 2014	*Re Cllr David Silvester* Unpublished decision of South Oxfordshire District Council Monitoring Officer, BBC News Online 22 August 2014
Facts	Cllr Silvester wrote a letter to a local newspaper criticising the Prime Minister and attributing 'natural disasters ... storms and floods' in the UK to his support for, and the passage into law of, gay marriage legislation. The letter was signed, 'Councillor David Silvester'; the newspaper's letter editor added the Town Council and political party of which Cllr Silvester was a member.
Finding	Cllr Silvester was expressing his personal view and was not speaking on behalf of the Town Council, notwithstanding that he identified himself as a Councillor.
Decision	No further action, save that Members were advised not to use their official titles in personal correspondence.

Indirect discrimination

3.126 Indirect discrimination is defined as applying an apparently neutral 'provision, criterion or practice' which puts individuals sharing a protected characteristic at a particular disadvantage.[160] If it can be shown that the indirect discrimination is 'a proportionate means of achieving a legitimate aim', then the discrimination will not be unlawful.[161]

3.127 For indirect discrimination to take place, four requirements must be met:

- the councillor applies (or would apply) the provision, criterion or practice equally to everyone within the relevant group;

- the provision, criterion or practice puts, or would put, people who share a protected characteristic at a particular disadvantage when compared with people who do not have that characteristic;

- the provision, criterion or practice puts, or would put, the individual at that disadvantage; and

- the councillor cannot show that the provision, criterion or practice is a proportionate means of achieving a legitimate aim.

Provision, criterion or practice

3.128 The focus on a 'provision, criterion or practice' (termed 'PCP') indicates that indirect discrimination is not generally about specific acts of

160 EA 2010, s 19(1) and (2).
161 EA 2010, s 19(2)(d).

misconduct against an individual – there has to be some element of repetition and applicability to others as well as that individual.[162] The PCP must also be neutral on its face. If the PCP is 'indissociable' from a protected characteristic, then that will amount to direct discrimination. A helpful example is provided by *James v Eastleigh Borough Council*,[163] where the council's policy of allowing free entry to swimming pools to anyone of pensionable age was found to be direct discrimination on the grounds of sex, because the pensionable age for men was universally higher than that for women.

Question: An executive member is opposed to dreadlocks as she thinks they are unhygienic. She asks the head of a team working with her to introduce a new policy that no-one in the team can wear their hair in dreadlocks, even if the locks are tied back. Can you do this?

Answer: This is an example of a policy that has not yet been implemented but which still amounts to a provision, criterion or practice. The decision to introduce the policy could be indirectly discriminatory because of religion or belief, as it puts any Rastafarians working in the team at a particular disadvantage. The member would have to show that the provision, criterion or practice can be objectively justified in order for it to be lawful – see below.

Justification

3.129   Indirect discrimination can be justified if it can be shown to be 'a proportionate means of achieving a legitimate aim'. In order to be proportionate, the PCP must be an 'appropriate and necessary' means of achieving a legitimate aim. But 'necessary' does not mean that the PCP is the only possible way of achieving the legitimate aim; it is sufficient that the same aim could not be achieved by less discriminatory means. In order for indirect discrimination to be justified, the aim of the PCP should be legal, should not be discriminatory in itself, and must represent a real, objective consideration. The health, welfare and safety of individuals may qualify as legitimate aims provided that risks are clearly specified and supported by evidence. Reasonable business needs and economic efficiency may also be legitimate aims, but simple saving of cost has been held by the Supreme Court not to be capable of justifying a PCP.[164]

---

162   *Onu v Akwiwu* [2014] EWCA Civ 279.
163   [1990] 2 AC 751.
164   *Department for Constitutional Affairs v O'Brien* [2013] 1 WLR 522 at para 69.

> **Question:** Would the member be able to show that the dreadlock policy, set out in the previous example, was justified?
>
> **Answer:** Although the general justification for this appears to be to promote a hygienic working environment, the member would have to provide objective evidence that dreadlocks, when tied back, are unhygienic. This would likely be difficult to do. It is also questionable whether such a policy is necessary in the particular working environment (rather than, for example, a factory processing food).

Harassment and victimisation

3.130   The EA 2010 specifically prohibits harassment, which is different from other forms of discrimination because it focuses on the subject matter of the treatment rather than on the differences in treatment between people. Harassment can also be a criminal offence or give rise to a civil claim under the Protection from Harassment Act 1997 (PHA 1997). The EA 2010 also specifically prohibits victimisation, which has a narrow meaning under the Act. Local authorities may include prohibition of harassment and/or victimisation within their codes of conduct.

Harassment under the Equality Act 2010

3.131   Section 26(1) of the EA 2010 defines harassment in the following terms:

> 'A person (A) harasses another (B) if – (a) A engages in unwanted conduct related to a relevant protected characteristic, and (b) the conduct has the purpose or effect of (i) violating B's dignity, or (ii) creating an intimidating, hostile, degrading, humiliating or offensive environment for B.'[165]

This applies to each of the protected characteristics, save for pregnancy and marriage/civil partnerships. However, pregnancy and maternity harassment would amount to harassment related to sex, and harassment related to civil partnership would amount to harassment related to sexual orientation.[166] In deciding whether the conduct amounts to harassment, each of the following factors must be taken into consideration: the perception of the complainant; the

---

165 This section replaced a number of very similarly worded provisions in various pieces of equality legislation: s 3A of the Race Relations Act 1976; see s 4A of the Sex Discrimination Act 1975; s 3B of the Disability Discrimination Act 1995; reg 5 of the Employment Equality (Religion or Belief) Regulations 2003, SI 2003/1660; reg 5 of the Employment Equality (Sexual Orientation) Regulations 2003, SI 2003/1661, and reg 6 of the Employment Equality (Age) Regulations 2006, SI 2006/1031. The case law applicable to these enactments remains helpful in interpreting the Equality Act 2010.
166 Equality and Human Rights Commission *Code of Practice on Employment* (2011) para 7.5.

circumstances of the case; and whether it is reasonable for the conduct to have the effect on them.[167] Once established, there is no defence for harassment.

Unwanted conduct

3.132   A number of factors are relevant to determining whether there has been unwanted conduct. Single incidents are not considered in isolation, but rather a person's behaviour as a whole must be assessed. Some conduct will clearly be unwanted (eg offensive remarks or sexual touching), but in relation to other conduct it will be relevant that the person receiving the conduct has made clear, by words or otherwise, that the conduct is unwelcome. However, the more obviously detrimental the treatment is, the less relevant any lack of complaint about it becomes. It is well-recognised that people will sometimes go along with 'banter' that includes unwanted remarks – this will not make lawful any behaviour that breaches s 26 of the EA 2010.

Question: One of the officers in the council is an openly gay man, who regularly refers to and jokes about his sexuality. Does that mean I can engage in banter with him without any risk of breaching the equality legislation?

Answer: No. The courts have found that 'a person who parades their particular characteristic loudly and vocally might expect to receive from colleagues responses or comments which make reference to that sexuality. But that is quite distinct from the "abusive" use of references to sexual orientation or any other protected characteristic.' So, if you do engage in banter, you have to be sure that it could not be construed as abusive. Even if the officer uses quite risqué language about himself, you should not follow suit. See *Smith v Ideal Shopping Direct Ltd* UKEAT/0590/12/BA (16 May 2013).

3.133   The notion of 'conduct' is wide-ranging, and includes physical conduct, written or oral communications, email, phone calls, text messages or the use of social media, or images displayed by other means (for example, the viewing of pornographic images in the complaint's presence was held to be harassment).[168] Other examples of potential acts constituting harassment include nicknames, teasing, persistent unwarranted criticism and name-calling. Conduct can also be a single act, if sufficiently serious – there is no requirement for conduct persisting over a period of time.[169]

---

167 EA 2010, s 26(3). See also the ACAS Guide 'Harassment and Bullying in the Workplace' 03/14.
168 *Moonsar v Fiveways Express Transport Ltd* [2005] IRLR 9.
169 *Bracebridge Engineering Ltd v Darby* [1990] IRLR 3 and *Insitu Cleaning Co Ltd v Heads* [1995] IRLR 4. Note that this is one of the key differences between harassment under the Equality Act 2010 and harassment under the Protection from Harassment Act 1997: the latter requires there to be a course of conduct. See para **3.138** below.

Question: In front of her male colleagues in the enforcement team, a female officer is told by a councillor that her work is below standard and that, as a woman, she will never be competent to carry out enforcement work. The councillor goes on to suggest that she should instead move to the section of the Council dealing with children, because women are more emotional and better at dealing with that kind of work. The female officer does not respond but simply walks away.

Answer: This would likely amount to harassment related to sex. The statements made by the councillor would be self-evidently unwanted and the officer would not have to object to them before they were deemed to be unlawful harassment.

3.134   The unwanted conduct must relate to one of the protected characteristics (save for pregnancy and marriage/civil partnerships), but there is not a requirement that the person who is the target of the conduct actually possess the characteristic. For example, it may amount to harassment to direct homophobic comments at a straight man or woman.[170] Harassment is distinct from bullying because of the required link with one of the relevant protected characteristics – it is possible to intend to cause someone offence, but not to intend to do so because of a protected characteristic. In order to determine whether conduct could amount to harassment or mere bullying, it is important to look at both the intention and motives of the person whose conduct is in issue, and whether it is inherent in the conduct that it relates to a protected characteristic (for example, some words are inherently sexist, racist, homophobic or related to disability).

Purpose or effect

3.135   It is important to note that unwanted conduct can amount to harassment where someone intends to bring about an adverse environment, even if the environment does not occur, <u>or</u> where an adverse environment is brought about even though that was never anyone's intention. However, in order for an unintentional adverse environment to be brought about, it has to be reasonable that the conduct had that effect. For example, in *Heafield v Times Newspaper Ltd*[171] a senior editor had twice shouted a profanity about the Pope in asking for an update on a story concerning the Pope; the question was directed at a number of journalists who were preparing the story. He was unaware that one of the journalists was Roman Catholic. Although that journalist was upset by the editor's conduct, the tribunal held that it was not reasonable for him to be so because the editor was making a general inquiry in a heated work atmosphere, and there was no evidence of anti-Catholic settlement.

---

170   *Thomas Sanderson Blinds Ltd v English* [2011] Eq LR 688.
171   [2013] Eq LR 345.

Harassment under the Protection from Harassment Act 1997

3.136 The Protection from Harassment Act 1997 (PHA 1997) prohibits a person from pursuing a course of conduct which amounts to harassment of another and which he or she ought to know amounts to such harassment. This applies to harassment of any sort, in any context, and so is applicable to the way in which councillors conduct themselves in relation to each other, council officers or employees and members of the public. Unlike the EA 2010, there is no requirement under the PHA 1997 for the conduct to be linked to a protected characteristic.

Definition of harassment

3.137 The PHA 1997 does not define harassment. From the case law, it is clear that harassment entails, but is not limited to, alarming or causing distress to a person.[172] This can occur as a result of written or verbal conduct, and does not need to be face-to-face: it may occur through written communications, email, phone calls, text messages or the use of social media. The conduct must be 'oppressive and unacceptable' rather than merely unattractive, unreasonable or regrettable.[173] The concept of 'harassment' has been found to potentially include the following behaviour:[174]

- spreading malicious rumours, or insulting someone by word or behaviour;

- copying memos that are critical about someone to others who do not need to know;

- ridiculing or demeaning someone – picking on them or setting them up to fail;

- exclusion or victimisation;

- unfair treatment;

- overbearing supervision or other misuse of power or position;

- unwelcome sexual advances – touching, standing too close, the display of offensive materials, asking for sexual favours, making decisions on the basis of sexual advances being accepted or rejected;

- making threats or comments about job security without foundation.

Course of conduct

3.138 A 'course of conduct' must involve conduct on at least two occasions (PHA 1997, s 12). While no more than two incidents are necessary to amount to a course of conduct, the fewer the number of incidents and the wider the time lapse between them, the less likely it is that a finding of harassment can

---

172 *Coulson v Wilby* [2014] EWHC 3404 (QB).
173 *Veakins v Kier* [2009] EWCA Civ 1288 at para 11.
174 *Quarrell* (20 May 2011) Adjudication Panel for England ref: APE 0540 at paragraph 3.6.12.

reasonably be made.[175] However, it is possible that incidents occurring a year apart could constitute a course of conduct if threats are made on particular dates for a reason (for example, harassment on a religious holiday or on a birthday or anniversary).[176] A course of conduct can amount to the harassment of more than one person.[177]

3.139 A course of conduct does not amount to harassment in the following circumstances:

- The course of conduct is pursued for the purpose of preventing or detecting crime or if, in the particular circumstances the pursuit of the course of conduct is reasonable.[178] The test of a person's purpose is not wholly subjective. He or she must have thought rationally about the material suggesting the possibility of criminality and formed the view that the conduct said to constitute harassment was appropriate for the purpose of preventing or detecting it. The test of rationality imports a requirement of good faith and an absence of capriciousness.[179] Within the scheme of the PHA 1997, the test as to whether or not pursuit of a course of conduct is reasonable must be taken to be an objective one.

- The course of conduct is pursued under any statute or law or to comply with a condition or requirement imposed under a statute. Accordingly, if the law permits certain conduct, such as the service of a notice seeking possession of a property, it cannot amount to harassment.

Penalties

3.140 Harassment can be the basis for a civil claim for damages. Under the PHA 1997, s 2(1), it is also a criminal offence to pursue a course of conduct in breach of s 1 of the PHA 1997. The offence is triable in the Magistrates' Court and the maximum penalty is six months in prison or a fine not exceeding level 5 (currently £5,000).

Victimisation

3.141 EA 2010, s 27(1) defines 'victimisation' in the following terms:

---

175 *Lau v DPP* [2000] Crim LR 580. See also *Baron v Crown Prosecution Service* (13 June 2000) QBD.
176 *Lau v DPP* [2000] Crim LR 580.
177 *DPP v Dunn* [2001] 1 Cr App R 22.
178 PHA 1997, s 1(3)(a) and (c) respectively.
179 *Hayes v Willoughby* [2013] 1 WLR 935 (Supreme Court) at paras 13–17. This case concerned allegations made over a number of years by Willoughby that Hayes' management of his companies was characterised by fraud, embezzlement and tax evasion. Willoughby had sent numerous letters to the Official Receiver, the police, the Department of Trade and Industry and other public bodies. The court found that, at the outset of the campaign, there was a reasonable basis for Willoughby's suspicions, but once it became clear that the Official Receiver had examined that material and that it did not support Willoughby's case, his persistence ceased to be reasonable.

'A person (A) victimises another person (B) if A subjects B to a detriment because (a) B does a protected act, or (b) A believes that B has done, or may do, a protected act.'

It is not necessary to show that B has been treated less favourably than someone else – the emphasis is on whether a detriment has been suffered. Also, B need not have a particular protected characteristic in order to be protected against victimisation under the Act; to be unlawful, victimisation need only be linked to a 'protected act'.

Protected act

3.142   A 'protected act' is defined as bringing proceedings under the EA 2010, giving evidence or information in connection with such proceedings or making an allegation that a person has contravened the EA 2010. Making an allegation or doing something related to the Act does not have to involve an explicit reference to the legislation. A wide variety of acts could be 'protected acts':

- complaining about discrimination issues;
- encouraging others to complaint about discrimination issued;
- raising a grievance about discrimination issues;
- complaining to the monitoring officer about the conduct of a councillor because of discrimination issues;
- seeking a disclosure about pay to establish whether there is a connection between pay and a protected characteristic (under EA 2010, s 77(4));
- questioning an officer or a councillor's compliance with the public sector equality duty (of which, see below);
- generally raising awareness of equality issues in the authority.

The complaint does not have to be well-founded to be a protected act, but it is not protected if the allegation made is found to be false and made in bad faith (EA 2010, s 27(3)).

Detriment

3.143   'Detriment' in the context of victimisation is not defined by the EA 2010 and could take many forms. Generally, a detriment is anything which the individual concerned might reasonably consider changed their position for the worse or put them at a disadvantage.[180] This could include being rejected for promotion, denied an opportunity to represent the organisation at external events, excluded from opportunities to train, or overlooked in the allocation of discretionary bonuses or performance-related awards. A detriment might also include a threat made to the complainant which they take seriously and it is reasonable for them to take it seriously. There is no need to demonstrate physical

180 See Equality and Human Rights Commission *Code of Practice on Employment* (2011) at para 9.8.

or economic consequences. However, an unjustified sense of grievance alone would not be enough to establish detriment.

Question: A director in the housing department has raised a grievance arising from what she alleges is discrimination by Councillor X. One month after the grievance was raised, Councillor Y, who is very friendly with Councillor X, prevents the director from attending the Annual Cornerstone Barristers Housing Conference, which is regarded as providing the most important housing law update available to local authorities.

Answer: The raising of a grievance based on discrimination is a protected act. Blocking attendance at the conference, given its high profile, is likely to amount to a detriment and to constitute victimisation.

Causal link

3.144　There is no time limit within which victimisation must occur after a person has done a protected act. However, a complainant will need to show a link between the detriment and the protected act. In order for the necessary causal relationship between the protected act and detrimental treatment to be established, the councillor must know of the protected act. However there is no requirement that the councillor be consciously or maliciously motivated by the protected act: a sub-conscious influence is sufficient,[181] and the protected act need not be the only reason for the conduct so long as its influence is more than trivial.[182]

Positive duties – the public sector equality duty

3.145　Section 149 of the EA 2010 imposes a duty on all public authorities to have 'due regard' to three identified 'needs' in the delivery of public services and the exercise of public powers:

- the need to eliminate discrimination, harassment, victimisation and any other conduct that is prohibited by or under the EA 2010;

- the need to advance equality of opportunity between persons who share a protected characteristic (apart from marriage and civil partnership) and persons who do not share it;

181　*Nagarajan v London Regional Transport* [2000] 1 AC 501. In that case, Nagarajan had previously worked for LRT and during that time had made a number of complaints to employment tribunals alleging race discrimination and thereafter victimisation. He later applied for a position as a travel information assistant for the company, but after interview he was not appointed. One of his interviewers had given him a very low score for articulacy (which was found to be unrealistically low) and, on the basis of knowledge of the former complaints, had noted that Nagarajan was 'very anti-management'. This was held by the House of Lords to be sufficient to establish the causal link to justify a finding of victimisation.
182　*Wong v Igen Ltd (formerly Leeds Careers Guidance)* [2005] EWCA Civ 142.

- the need to foster good relations between persons who share a relevant protected characteristic and persons who do not share it.

These duties are known as the Public Sector Equality Duty (PSED). The Equality and Human Rights Commission (EHRC) has published statutory guidance on the PSED in England.[183]

3.146 The EA 2010, s 149(3) further elaborates on the need to advance equality of opportunity and makes clear that this includes the need to:

- 'remove or minimise disadvantages suffered by persons who share a relevant protected characteristic that are connected to that characteristic';

- 'take steps to meet the needs of persons who share a relevant protected characteristic that are different from the needs of persons who do not share it';

- 'encourage persons who share a relevant protected characteristic to participate in public life or in any other activity in which participation by such persons is disproportionately low'.

3.147 The EA 2010, s 149(5) further elaborates on the need to foster good relations – this involves having due regard to the need to:

- 'tackle prejudice';

- 'promote understanding'.

3.148 The PSED applies not only to the general formulation of policy but also to decisions made in individual cases where policy is applied.[184] The courts have recognised that the PSED is important and requires public authorities to consider issues of discrimination before making policy decisions or individual determinations. The Court of Appeal said in *R (Elias) v Secretary of State for Defence*:[185]

> 'It is the clear purpose of [the PSED] to require public bodies to whom that provision applies to give advance consideration to issues of ... discrimination before making any policy decision that may be affected by them. This is a salutary requirement, and this provision must be seen as an integral and important part of the mechanism for ensuring the fulfilment of the aims of anti-discrimination legislation. It is not possible to take the view that ... non-compliance with that provision [is] not a very important matter. In the context of the wider objectives of anti-discrimination legislation, [the PSED] has a significant role to play.'

---

183 EHRC *Technical Guidance on the Public Sector Equality Duty (England)* (2013).
184 *Pieretti v Enfield Borough Council* [2010] EWCA Civ 1104.
185 [2006] EWCA Civ 1293, per Arden LJ. In this case, the Secretary of State for Defence was held to have breached the forerunner of the PSED in the Race Relations Act 1976 through his decision to limit payment of compensation for 'British' civilians who were internees of the Japanese during the Second World War to those with a blood link to the UK. This was also indirect race discrimination.

3.149 It must be remembered that the PSED is not a duty to achieve a result – the promotion of equality of opportunity and good relations is not the same as the promotion of the interests of a minority.[186] The duty is to have due regard to the need to eliminate unlawful discrimination or to promote equality of opportunity and good relations between persons with protected characteristics. 'Due regard' has been defined by the courts in the following terms:

> 'What is due regard? In my view, it is the regard that is appropriate in all the circumstances. These include on the one hand the importance of the areas of life of the members of the disadvantaged racial group that are affected by the inequality of opportunity and the extent of the inequality; and on the other hand, such countervailing factors as are relevant to the function which the decision-maker is performing.'[187]

3.150 The EHRC's Guidance sets out six principles, derived from case law,[188] which comprise what a decision-maker has to do to comply with the PSED:

● In order to have due regard, those who have to take decisions that do or might affect people with different protected characteristics must be made aware of their duty to have 'due regard' to the aims of the duty.

● Due regard is fulfilled before and at the time a particular policy that will or might affect people with protected characteristics is under consideration as well as at the time a decision is taken. Due regard involves a conscious approach and state of mind.

● A body or decision-maker subject to the duty cannot satisfy the duty by justifying a decision after it has been taken. Attempts to justify a decision as being consistent with the exercise of the duty when it was not, in fact, considered before the decision are not enough to discharge the duty. The duty must be exercised in substance, with rigour and with an open mind in such a way that it influences the final decision. The duty has to be integrated within the discharge of the public functions of the body subject to the duty.

---

186 *R (Harris) v Haringey London Borough Council* [2010] EWCA Civ 703 at para 38, per Pill LJ. In this case the council was held to have breached the forerunner of the PSED in the Race Relations Act 1976 through making a planning decision to redevelop a site in an area made up predominantly of ethnic minority communities. The site incorporated an indoor market comprising a number of business and residential units. 64% of traders in the market were Latin American or Spanish speaking and the predominant occupation of homes and business units were by members of the black and ethnic minority communities. The development scheme involved the total demolition of existing buildings and erection of mixed use developments. The Council had failed to have due regard for the need to promote equality of opportunity and good relations between persons of different racial groups during the decision making process.
187 *R (Baker) v Secretary of State for Communities and Local Government* [2008] EWCA Civ 141 at para 31 per Dyson LJ. In this case the court held that a planning inspector had had due regard to the need to promote equality of opportunity between persons of different racial groups, even though he had upheld a refusal of planning permission to pitch caravans on a site in the green belt.
188 *R (Brown) v Secretary of State for Work and Pensions* [2008] EWHC 3158 (Admin).

It is not a question of 'ticking boxes'. However, the fact that a body subject to the duty has not specifically mentioned EA 2010, s 149 in carrying out the particular function is not determinative of whether the duty has been performed. It is nevertheless good practice for the policy or decision maker to make reference to s 149 and the Code in all cases where s 149 is in play. In that way the decision maker is more likely to ensure that the relevant factors are taken into account and the scope for argument as to whether the duty has been performed will be reduced.

- The duty is a non-delegable one. The duty will always remain the responsibility of the body or decision-maker subject to the duty. In practice another body may actually carry out the practical steps to fulfil a policy stated by a body subject to the duty. In those circumstances the duty to have 'due regard' to the needs identified will only be fulfilled by the body subject to the duty if: (1) it appoints a third party that is capable of fulfilling the 'due regard' duty and is willing to do so, (2) the body subject to the duty maintains a proper supervision over the third party to ensure it carries out its 'due regard' duty.

- The duty is a continuing one.

- It is good practice for those exercising public functions to keep an accurate record showing that they have actually considered the PSED and pondered relevant questions. Proper record keeping encourages transparency and will discipline those carrying out the relevant function to undertake the duty conscientiously. If records are not kept, it may make it more difficult, evidentially, for a public authority to persuade a court that it has fulfilled the duty imposed by s 149.

Question: Because of financial constraints, a local authority decides to restrict adult care services to people with critical needs. The report leading to the council's decision makes it clear that disability is an issue, but fails to refer to the PSED. The council otherwise has a good disability record. Has there been a breach of the PSED?

Answer: Yes, it is very likely a court will find that the decision was taken in breach of the PSED because there would not be any evidence that the duty and its implications had been drawn to the attention of the councillors. They should have been informed not just that disability was an issue, but also about the particular obligations which the law imposed through the PSED. The failure did not give a busy councillor any idea of the serious duties imposed on the council by the PSED. As a result, the council could not weigh matters properly in the balance. It will not be enough to refer to the Council's good record on disability and assume that the messages in the PSED had somehow got across to councillors. Based on *R (Chavda) v Harrow London Borough Council* [2007] EWHC 3064 (Admin).

F ELECTIONS

3.151   The Code of Recommended Practice on Local Authority Publicity[189] makes special provision for 'periods of heightened sensitivity', namely the period between the notice of an election and the election itself. This is commonly referred to as 'purdah'. The code states that during this period:

> 'local authorities should not publish any publicity on controversial issues or report views or proposals in such a way that identifies them with any individual members or groups of members. Publicity relating to individuals involved directly in the election should not be published by local authorities during this period unless expressly authorised by or under statute. It is permissible for local authorities to publish factual information which identifies the names, wards and parties of candidates at elections'.[190]

3.152   Following amendment of the Local Government Act 1986,[191] the Secretary of State now has a power to require local authorities (either individually by direction, or universally by order) to comply with all or part of the Code, which would include the parts relating to the purdah period.

3.153   The concept of purdah, and the provisions of the Code relating to it, are directed towards the local authority as a whole and not to individual members. However, councillors clearly need to understand the implications of the purdah period and modify their conduct in their official capacity accordingly. In particular it will be important:

- To take particular care that any comments made or publicity released around issues of policy or controversy are firmly in the context of election campaigning cannot be interpreted as representing the position of the council or members acting in their official capacities.

- To understand and respect the fact that the local authority will not publish information relating to those directly involved in the election.

- To understand and respect the fact that council premises cannot be used for party political purposes.

- Given that the business of the authority must continue as usual, to take particular care when representing the council, for example as a portfolio holder, that comments and responses to enquiries are factual and cannot give the appearance of support for any political view.

---

189   Issued by DCLG on 31 March 2011 under the Local Government Act 1986, s 4.
190   Para 34 of the Code.
191   By the Local Audit and Accountability Act 2014, s 39.

G CONCLUSION

3.154   This chapter has outlined the substantive obligations which apply to the way in which counsellors conduct themselves. Some of these obligations will of necessity appear in an authority or a council's code of conduct. Others are imposed by statute, although authorities or councils may include them within their codes. Some are derived from the seven principles of public life, which again authorities or councils may include within their codes.

3.155   It would be a gross error to assume that the abolition of the model code and the Standards Board has somehow diluted the high standards of probity required of councillors. It would be more accurate to say that councillors need to take still greater care to meet the standards required, which are not necessarily found in one single place, but are dispersed among several statutory and common law concepts and local and national codes and guidance. In the event of any doubt as to the right course to take, councillors are well-advised to consult the council's monitoring officer. That does not guarantee the right result, but greatly reduces the prospect of criticism directed at the councillors themselves.

CHAPTER 4

Complaints procedure

	What this chapter covers	
A	Introduction	4.1
B	Legal requirements	4.3
C	The complaint	4.9
D	The initial response of the authority	4.15
E	Investigation	4.18
F	Hearings	4.27
G	Outcomes and potential sanctions	4.32
H	Legal proceedings and how they may be affected	4.37
I	Conclusions	4.40

A INTRODUCTION

4.1   This Chapter describes the procedure by which members (including co-opted members) of local authorities in England[1] may be held to account for breaches of their Code of Conduct. The process is locally determined, by each of the over 350 local authorities across England,[2] and is to be distinguished from the procedure followed for complaints about service delivery. The statutory regime has been set out in **Chapter 2**, so this chapter is essentially a practical one, covering the process of complaining about a member's conduct.

4.2   The complainant may be a member of the public, an officer of the authority, or a fellow Councillor. Since the arrangements are made locally with very little in the way of express statutory requirements, they vary from authority to authority, and it is not possible to set out here a blueprint for the individual case. Nevertheless, and bearing in mind the authority's duty to promote and maintain high standards of conduct by members and co-opted members,[3] there are some principles which every authority is bound to respect,

---

1 In Wales the Public Services Ombudsman for Wales handles complaints about breaches of the relevant Code of Conduct, although he recommends that local authorities are given the opportunity to address the cause of the complaint first. Reference should therefore be made to **Chapter 7** on the procedure to follow in such cases.
2 All 'relevant authorities' other than parish councils (see s 27 of the Localism Act 2011 for definition) are required to adopt arrangements under which allegations can be investigated and decisions made (s 28(6) of the Localism Act 2011). Allegations about Parish Councils are dealt with by the relevant principal Council.
3 Localism Act 2011, s 27.

and it is worth identifying some of the features of a good procedure which some have included within the arrangements put in place under s 28(6) of the Localism Act 2011.

B LEGAL REQUIREMENTS

4.3   It is notable, first, that the statutory obligation is to have in place 'arrangements under which *allegations* can be investigated' and 'arrangements under which decisions on *allegations* can be made'.[4]

4.4   The word 'allegation' is defined in s 28(9) of the Localism Act with two essential features: (1) it is written, and (2) it concerns an alleged failure to comply with the authority's adopted code of conduct.[5]

4.5   In keeping with the policy which informed the Localism Act's provisions, there is no guidance from central government on the arrangements for investigation and decision making which are required to be made locally. As Local Authority Leaders were told at the time the statutory scheme was introduced:

> 'Our new localist approach gives councils wide freedoms to decide their own arrangements for promoting high standards of conduct for all their members, and I know that many councils have over recent months been preparing for this.
>
> To help I wrote to you in early April with an illustrative example of a simple, straightforward local code. I felt it was important that councils did not feel the need to spend money on external legal advice on drawing up a new code, and were not pressured into simply adopting the old centralist code, with all the associated problems it brought on [sic] malicious and frivolous complaints. http://www.communities.gov.uk/publications/localgovernment/localcodeconduct'[6]

4.6   There is a single statutory requirement, namely that the arrangements include the appointment of at least one 'independent person' whose views may be sought by the authority and by the member whose conduct is complained of. The Government has emphasised that the role of this person is solely advisory, as the following extract from the letter of 28 June 2012[7] emphasises:

> 'Accordingly, I would particularly draw your attention to the role of the new independent person. This is in no way similar to the role of the independent

---

4   Localism Act 2011, s 28(6) (italics added for emphasis).
5   Or the Parish Council's code in the case of an allegation about a Parish Councillor or co-opted member.
6   This is a link to the short 'illustrative example' of a 'simple, straightforward code' which was sent to relevant authorities in April 2013, and the text above is taken from the letter of 28 June 2012 from Bob Neill MP to Local Authority Leaders.
7   See letter from Bob Neill MP of 28 June 2012 to Local Authority Leaders.

chairman and independent members on the former standards committees. That former role was principally to be involved in the determination of allegations about misconduct of members. In contrast the role of the new independent person is wholly advisory, providing advice to the council on any allegation it is considering, and to a member facing an allegation who has sought the views of that person.'

4.7 Many authorities have appointed at least two independent persons either of whom might be called upon by the authority in relation to an allegation, and this is surely desirable in order that there is always a suitable person available to fulfil the statutory role. The independent person provides advice to the authority <u>and</u> to the member facing an allegation, and it is plainly desirable that they can do so without any suspicion that they might favour one side in any particular case.

4.8 It is also considered beneficial (but is not legally necessary) for the independent person to be involved at every stage of the complaints process, since it is likely to give the Monitoring Officer confidence and provide some protection for the authority in the event of a complaint as to the chosen approach to the issues. It is also likely to encourage others (the complainant and the relevant member of the authority) to respect the outcome of the process and any decisions, whether of substance or procedure, which are taken as part of it.

C THE COMPLAINT

4.9 The Council is required to make arrangements for investigating and deciding upon conduct complaints.[8]

4.10 Procedures vary from authority to authority, as does the terminology used. However, in every case the complaint should concern an alleged breach of the adopted Code of Conduct.[9] This is the core of the complaint. If there is no breach of the Council's adopted Code, while there may be good cause for a grievance, there will be no 'allegation' within the meaning of s 28(9) of the Localism Act and no basis for a complaint of this kind.

4.11 Some Councils set out in full what will not be investigated and this is considered good practice. The following is taken from the London Borough of Waltham Forest's published Complaints Procedure.

---

8 Referred to as 'allegations' within s 28(6) of the Localism Act 2011.
9 There is a legal requirement for the authority to adopt a Code of Conduct (Parish Councils may adopt their principal Council's code).

Extract from London Borough of Waltham Forest's complaints procedure

The following complaints are normally not suitable for investigation, save where the Monitoring Officer accepts there are exceptional circumstances:

1.1 Complaints that are really about Council services, its policies or performance. Such complaints will be referred to the relevant service area in accordance with the Council's Complaints Policy.

1.2 Complaints that are really about the political policies or performance of a councillor in their role. Such complaints will be referred to the councillor and/or their political group for response.

1.3 Complaints that relate to another authority or an alleged breach of another authority or body's Code of Conduct.

1.4 Vexatious or frivolous complaints or complaints which are intended to insult individuals.

1.5 Minor or 'tit-for-tat' complaints that do not justify the time and resources of an investigation.

1.6 Complaints which relate to matters or events more than three months before the date of the complaint.

1.7 Complaints by a member against another member will not normally be investigated until the Monitoring Officer considers that other processes, eg informal mediation or political group processes, have been exhausted.

1.8 Complaints by officers should be first made under the Member/Officer Protocol.

1.9 Complaints that are already subject to other internal or external processes will not be investigated until those other processes have completed to enable the complaint to be resolved by other means. Determination of such complaints will be suspended until the other process is finalised.

4.12 This extract illustrates neatly that the procedure for complaints about breaches of the code by members is only one of a range of procedures for maintaining oversight of standards, both of the conduct of individuals and in the Council's provision of services.

4.13 The main points to be aware of at the complaint stage are as follows:

● There may be a limit to the period of time within which complaint may be made (in the Waltham Forest example above it is three months). It is always helpful to those managing the process, and those who may be asked to recall events as part of an investigation, if the complainant acts reasonably promptly.

- The complaint will need to be set out in writing (the statutory definition of *allegation* requires this) and the authority is likely to have a standard form on which to complain which should be used.

- The authority's website is likely to give contact details for the person to complain to. If in doubt, the complaint should be addressed to the Monitoring Officer but always distinguished from a complaint about service delivery. Where there is also cause for complaint about service delivery, it may be necessary to make two complaints employing the procedures appropriate for each.

- The complaint and the complainant's identity are likely to be disclosed in full to the member unless a good case against such disclosure is made. This is because the investigation must meet common law standards of fairness, or natural justice. The identity of the complainant may give the subject member important information about the motivation for the complaint, and provides some context to the evidence relied upon. The Monitoring Officer is likely to be the individual who determines whether the authority should accept an anonymous complaint, and on this he may wish to consider the advice of the independent person.

- It is good practice, and may be required by some authorities,[10] for the complaint to identify the provision or provisions of the code which the member is said to have breached.

4.14 The complaint will need to be supported by evidence. Complainants should consider the exercise of legal rights to information where appropriate[11] – but not allow this to delay the complaint beyond the stated deadline.

D THE INITIAL RESPONSE OF THE AUTHORITY

4.15 The authority's published procedures are likely to state the period within which an initial response will be provided, and this is good practice. In their initial response, the authority should make it clear who is the complainant's contact for any follow up queries, and may also deal with practical points arising from the nature of the complaint itself, for example the question of disclosure of the identity of the complainant.

4.16 Naturally enough, complaints vary hugely both as to the seriousness of the allegation and as to the strength of the evidence. The authority may prefer to address the complaint in an informal way, and many complaints are successfully dealt with in this way, the Monitoring Officer facilitating perhaps an apology and/

---

10 If such a requirement is imposed it would be necessary to consider its discriminatory effect. It is considered that an authority refusing to accept a complaint which is not articulated by reference to breaches of the code but which alleges conduct which, if proved, would be a breach of the code may be acting unlawfully.
11 As to which reference should be made to Chapter 5F.

or explanation from the member concerned leading to the satisfactory resolution of the complaint.

4.17   Does the complainant or member have a remedy if they are unhappy with the authority's initial response? If, for example, the Monitoring Officer refuses to pursue a formal investigation does the complainant have a remedy? Given the statutory role of the independent person an authority may be thought unwise to refuse to investigate a complaint formally without taking that person's advice. Most, if not all, published arrangements provide for a refusal by the authority to investigate a complaint further, but will also draw attention to the right to complain to the local government ombudsman where it is believed the authority's handling of the complaint was tainted by maladministration causing injustice. This is (unless the individual authority has made some other provision within its arrangements, which is considered unlikely) the only legal remedy available to the dissatisfied complainant or member and the ombudsman's role is restricted to a complaint about the process which the authority adopted, rather than the substantive allegation which prompted the complaint.[12]

E   INVESTIGATION

4.18   It will be appreciated that many complaints, particularly those relating to comparatively minor breaches of the Code of Conduct, may be satisfactorily dealt with in an informal manner without the need for any publicity. An apology is often all that is sought and all that is required for complainant and authority to put the issue behind them.

4.19   However, those which cannot be dealt with in a consensual or an informal way, perhaps because there is a dispute over what is alleged to have been said or done, will need, in many cases to be the subject of an investigation. Many authorities leave to the Monitoring Officer a wide discretion over the handling of a complaint, a discretion which should be exercised with due regard to the Council's (and the officer's own) statutory duties.[13]

4.20   It is good practice to appoint an Investigating Officer, and the authority's procedure ought to spell out the sort of person this might be: whether an officer from within the authority, or another authority, or entirely independent of local government. It is a key role in the individual case, and it is only in rare and very straightforward cases that the Monitoring Officer is likely to be a suitable candidate (principally because of his/her proximity to the issues and personalities involved – as well as other pressures on his time). The Investigating Officer's job will be:

● to gather evidence – it may therefore involve interviewing and note taking;

---

12 See further on the ombudsman's role in England, Part 5E.
13 Notably, of course, those in s 27 of the Localism Act 2011 and ss 5 and 5A of the Local Government and Housing Act 1989.

- to reach a view on contested issues of fact and report these to the Monitoring Officer or otherwise in accordance with the Council's adopted procedure;

- to reach a view on the substance of the allegation: and in particular whether there has been a breach of the Code of Conduct by the member concerned;

- to take advice from the independent person to the extent necessary.

4.21   To meet common law standards of fairness, the Investigating Officer should give the member concerned the opportunity to comment on the allegation and the evidence before reaching any findings adverse to him or her. It is considered sensible for the Council's procedure to allow for fully informed comment by the member in every case in which a formal investigation is conducted. Where the complaint is proceeding as an anonymous complaint this may prove to be very difficult to achieve.

4.22   The Investigating Officer's report ought to be completed within a reasonable period of time. What that is will, naturally, vary – but the objective of any timeliness requirements should be to achieve a proportionately thorough investigation sufficiently promptly to satisfy all those involved.

4.23   The report should spell out any findings as to breaches of the authority's code of conduct and it is likely to be sent to the Monitoring Officer and then the member in draft for his or her comment before being finalised.[14]

4.24   It is of course quite possible that the investigation will be inconclusive as to the question whether or not there has been a breach of the authority's code of conduct. In such a case, and in any event, the Monitoring Officer may consider (and should seek the advice of the independent person on this) whether the allegation can be resolved in an informal manner even after a formal investigation. There is, it will be seen, no right to a hearing to which the complainant or the member can appeal unless this is set out within the authority's own complaints procedure.[15]

4.25   The procedure adopted by the City of York, part of which is copied below, is well considered and reflects the considerable discretion most Monitoring Officers have in relation to the conduct of complaints against members' conduct. This level of discretion is considered desirable given the need for flexibility in the light of the broad range of issues and personalities involved:

---

14 This is the practice in most of the authorities which publish detailed arrangements for the investigation of allegations.
15 An authority will generally act unlawfully if it does not follow its own published policy, *Secretary of State for the Home Department v Rahman* [2011] EWCA Civ 814 per Stanley Burnton LJ at para 42. Equally, however, from time to time the authority may review and alter its published policies (and in this case procedures for investigating complaints). Should it do so, careful attention should be given to the implications for any pending cases and avoiding unfairness in an individual case.

'36 If the monitoring officer considers local resolution is not appropriate, or the member concerned is not prepared to undertake any proposed remedial action, the monitoring officer will report the investigating officer's report to the hearing sub-committee which will conduct a hearing before deciding whether the member has failed to comply with the Code of Conduct and if so, whether to take any action in respect of the member.

37 The hearing would normally be heard within three months of the date on which the investigating officer's report is completed but not less than 10 working days after the monitoring officer sends the report to the subject member.'

4.26   Thus, the appointment of an Investigating Officer and a formal investigation by him or her, will not necessarily lead to a hearing before members of the authority. There may still be an opportunity for informal resolution on the basis of the formal report. In case this proves not to be appropriate in the Monitoring Officer's view, the authority should make arrangements for consideration of allegations by a committee or panel of members who will consider the report of the appointed Investigating Officer, hear both sides of the argument, and have available to them the advice of the Independent Person.

F   HEARINGS

4.27   Since the Standards provisions of the Localism Act are Council functions (ie may not be dealt with by the Executive) there is likely to be a Standards Committee (which may be differently named[16]), although some authorities provide for a Standards Panel (or equivalent, however named) of members to be convened on a case by case basis. It will be appreciated that the appointment of members to the panel or committee will be for the Council and not the Monitoring Officer, but he or she has a role in ensuring the committee is evenly balanced and that the authority reaches a lawful decision.

4.28   Many complaints will not require a hearing, but those which do will need to be conducted fairly, giving similar opportunities for representation to both sides of the argument. There is no legally imposed burden of proof and an authority would be unwise to impose one on either side. The hearings process should be part of an investigation by the authority into the substance of an allegation, and is fundamentally different to, for example, court proceedings between individuals. It is, therefore, possible (albeit unlikely) that the authority fails to reach a definitive finding on the evidence at the hearing and, in such a case, the authority's decision on the allegation will need to reflect that fact.

---

16 For example, in the London Borough of Waltham Forest it is called the Audit and Governance Committee.

4.29   Some authorities guarantee the right to representation, others specifically provide that the member may not be represented at a hearing, and others may expect the committee to determine the allegation on the papers and without hearing oral submissions on either side.

4.30   As with the entire process, it is the authority's own arrangements as to the procedure to be adopted which need to be considered in the light of the Constitution and the advice of the appointed Independent Person (who should be available for advice both to the authority and to the member concerned). However, since it is unlikely to have explicitly catered for all possible situations within its published procedures, the authority should be prepared to respond to requests from either side for a departure from the usual procedure if this is necessary to achieve the appropriate standard of fairness.

4.31   Decisions are usually taken at the meeting itself both as to a finding of breach and as to what the panel or committee consider is the appropriate way to set out any findings and recommendations to make in respect of the allegation.

G   OUTCOMES AND POTENTIAL SANCTIONS

4.32   If a breach of the Code is found following the final resolution of any investigation carried out under the local authority's adopted arrangements, the question arises what should be done about it.

4.33   The Act does not provide a power for those deciding upon allegations to impose sanctions and the absence of such a power has been criticised by commentators.

4.34   However, while they may lawfully decide not to follow a recommendation, it is considered that the authority would be unwise not to respond reasonably and proportionately to any recommendations of the hearing panel or other decision maker. It is considered, therefore, that the authority should give reasons to an unsatisfied complainant if departing from a recommendation.

4.35   In a case of that sort the complainant's only recourse is likely to be to the Local Government Ombudsman (the subject of Chapter 5E) and only on the basis that the authority's handling of the complaint involved maladministration causing the complainant injustice.[17]

4.36   It will only very rarely, if ever, be possible for the Councillor to prevent publication of a finding that he or she has been in breach of the Code of Conduct.

---

17 Unless and to the extent that the member's conduct contributed to a complaint of maladministration by the authority, in which case it will form part of the complaint to the ombudsman on that basis.

If he or she is aggrieved at the outcome, the only possible recourse would be by way of an application for a judicial review, since members of local authorities are not entitled to complain to the Local Government Ombudsman (save in relation to injustice suffered by them in their private capacity). As Chapter 5 makes clear, applications for judicial review may be brought on public law grounds only and are not a means by which the member can invite the court to review the merits of the authority's determination.

H LEGAL PROCEEDINGS AND HOW THEY MAY BE AFFECTED

4.37 If the alleged conduct of the Councillor is also a tort (a civil legal wrong, causing loss or harm to another, for which there is liability), the complaint and its result will be relevant evidence in any subsequent legal action. The Council may wish to consider whether the member is indemnified against liability.

4.38 If the alleged conduct of the Councillor is also a crime, the police or other appropriate prosecuting body should be informed and the relevant provisions of the Police and Criminal Evidence Act 1984 should govern any interview of the Councillor (see also Part 6 following).

4.39 The arrangements adopted by the local authority may cover this point, but not all do. In Westminster City Council, it is dealt with as follows within the written arrangements for complaint. At paragraph 4.3j the arrangements state that the Council will not investigate a complaint unless … 'If the complaint reveals a criminal offence and a complaint has been made to the police, the police investigation and any proceedings have concluded or the police have confirmed no proceedings will be issued.' On the other hand, in Oxfordshire County Council, the Council simply states that 'the Monitoring Officer has the power to call in the Police and other regulatory agencies' while the statutory arrangements published by other authorities are silent on the point.

I CONCLUSIONS

4.40 The process of holding members to account for their conduct has, as a result of the Localism Act 2011, become almost entirely a local issue. While local authorities must adopt arrangements for handling allegations about the conduct of members (which are confined to breaches of the authority's code of conduct), the content of those arrangements and the way they are applied is a matter for the local authority to determine, provided they observe common law standards of fairness and impartiality and an Independent Person is available to advise.

4.41 This means that the procedure a complainant should follow, and the support available to him and the subject member, will vary widely from authority to authority.

4.42   Many complaints are addressed in an informal way to the satisfaction of all parties, and for others the adverse publicity involved is an effective deterrent. However, if the member is found to have breached the code of conduct, so that the allegation is well founded, there is no power to impose a sanction on the member concerned, and this is widely seen to be a deficiency of the current statutory scheme.

CHAPTER 5

Challenging council decisions

A INTRODUCTION

5.1 The effectiveness of duties and standards in relation to councillors' conduct relies on the ability to scrutinise and police compliance with them. Three mechanisms for doing so will be examined in this chapter: judicial review, which may involve the courts in scrutinising decisions of local authorities in relation to councillors' conduct; ombudsmen, who offer a complaints handling service in relation to maladministration; and, Freedom of Information, which may provide an external investigative tool for individuals in relation to possible misconduct by councillors.

B JUDICIAL REVIEW: INTRODUCTION

5.2 Judicial review is the mechanism by which the courts exercise control over the legality of actions of public authorities. These include local authorities, such that judicial review is a primary tool by which to challenge the exercise of power by local authority councillors. The scope of the control provided by judicial review is potentially very wide: it can apply to any area of local authority decision-making, including decisions of councils and their committees and sub-committees, as well as power exercised under delegated authority by officers. Common examples include judicial review of decisions to close facilities such as libraries or schools, to grant planning permission, and to revoke licences. The process relies on a claimant (or 'applicant': the phrases 'claim for judicial review' and 'application for judicial review' are used more or less interchangeably) bringing a challenge before the court; the courts themselves do not instigate the procedure.

5.3 The defendant to a judicial review claim in the local government context is the local authority itself. Although the decision under challenge may have been taken by a committee, sub-committee, a single councillor or an officer, the function will have been delegated from those of the local authority. Responsibility for the decision, which is the target of the judicial review, ultimately lies with the local authority. Judicial review is concerned with the actions or decisions of the council, not of individual councillors (save where they are a decision-maker on behalf of the council). However, circumstances may arise where a council's decision making could become liable to successful challenge by way of judicial review based upon the acts of individual councillors; and so judicial review can also be relevant to conduct issues. Some examples of when such an issue may arise are: (a) all the members (or a sufficient number of them to affect the decision) act in the same or similar ways, amounting to misconduct (eg they participate in a decision in which they have a DPI); (b) a highly persuasive member, who has a DPI in a matter, attends a committee and affects the result by his advocacy, even though he has no vote; or (c) a single decision-maker for an Executive decision (or a backbench member acting under powers in s 236, Local Government and Public Involvement in Health 2007) makes a decision in respect of which s/he is biased.

5.4   Another type of judicial review may arise where a person wishes to challenge a decision of a Standards Committee, on one of the grounds below (eg that it has exceeded its powers, or not followed correct procedure). In other cases, judicial review may not be the direct cause of action in relation to misconduct, but may coincide with a misconduct matter; or the alleged misconduct may be evidence of a wider failure by the council that is tested by judicial review. An example of the latter might be a judicial review of a planning decision on grounds of bias, where one or more members have failed to disclose DPIs connecting them to the developer, leading to a conduct investigation.

5.5   The subsequent sections deal first with the grounds on which a judicial review can be brought, focusing on the likely application to local authorities, before turning to the procedure for applying for judicial review and finally the remedies available on a successful challenge.

C JUDICIAL REVIEW: GROUNDS

5.6   The grounds on which a claim for judicial review may be brought are overlapping and expressed in a variety of different ways. The classic categorisation is threefold: illegality, irrationality, and procedural unfairness. In practice the grounds are broken down further. The following is a list of the principal ones, any of which could be relevant in the context of a particular decision concerning a councillor's conduct:

- *Ultra vires* ('beyond its powers').

- Improper purpose.

- Taking into account irrelevant considerations/not taking into account relevant considerations.

- Irrationality/perversity.

- Procedural unfairness: the right to be heard and the rule against bias.

It is important to be clear, however, that judicial review could potentially apply to the manner in which a council has handled a conduct matter; not to the alleged misconduct itself.

Ultra vires

5.7   Local authorities are creatures of statute, being set up by statute and with their powers limited to those which statute confers. The courts will enforce these limits by way of judicial review, pronouncing where the limits lie and whether they have been exceeded, and potentially requiring the authority to act within the limits. The scope of the doctrine extends to all functions of local authorities. Challenges on this ground often involve difficult questions of statutory interpretation to ascertain whether the statutory power encompasses the particular activity in question, which may have taken place in a context far removed from that existing at the time of the drafting of the power.

5.8   By way of example, *Credit Suisse v Waltham Forest BC*[1] concerned the Council's formation of a company to discharge its duties of providing housing for the homeless under the Housing Act 1985. The Council purported to guarantee the obligations of the company under a loan agreement which the company entered into with a bank. On the bank trying to enforce the guarantee, the courts held that the Council had no power to give the guarantee. It went beyond any statutory powers the Council had to provide housing, such that the guarantee could not be enforced.

Improper purpose

5.9   Powers conferred on a local authority may be exercised for the public purpose for which the powers were conferred and not otherwise. If a local authority contravenes this principle the court will intervene on a claim for judicial review. The principle of limiting a power to the use for which it was intended is, like the *ultra vires* principle, founded on giving effect to the will of the legislator.

5.10   Identifying the public purpose for which a specific power has been conferred is often a difficult exercise in statutory interpretation. Certain general limitations are clear however. Powers conferred on a local authority may not be lawfully exercised to promote the electoral advantage of a political party, as illustrated by the cause célèbre of *Porter v Magill*.[2] Westminster City Council had power to sell council properties pursuant to s 32 of the Housing Act 1985. A policy was formulated to further the majority party's electoral chances by

1   [1997] QB 362 (CA).
2   [2001] UKHL 67.

exercise of this power, such that the subsequent exercise of the power was held to be unlawful on grounds of improper purpose.

5.11   The position is complicated by reason of the fact that councillors may have multiple motivations for exercising a power, including the fact that it is the policy of the councillor's party and the councillor wishes to earn the gratitude of the electorate by exercise of the power. The House of Lords in the Porter case was clear that such considerations are legitimate and indeed the law needs to recognise as much to avoid parting company with the realities of party politics. At the same time, the councillor's support for the policy must be for valid local government reasons and the councillor must not abdicate his responsibility and duty of exercising personal judgement when performing the statutory function.

Taking into account irrelevant considerations/not taking into account relevant considerations

5.12   Statutory powers must be exercised with the decision-maker having taken into account all relevant considerations and excluded all irrelevant considerations. Relevant and irrelevant considerations are sometimes listed in the statute itself. Often, however, the court will need to determine what does and does not constitute a relevant consideration. This will be determined having regard to the purpose of the statutory power.

5.13   By way of example, in deciding whether to grant planning permission local authorities are required by s 70 of the Town and Country Planning Act 1990 to take into account 'material considerations'. In *Tesco Stores Ltd v Secretary of State for the Environment* it was held: 'An offered planning obligation which has nothing to do with the proposed development, apart from the fact that it is offered by the developer, will plainly not be a material consideration and could be regarded as only an attempt to buy planning permission'.[3]

Irrationality/perversity

5.14   A public authority may not make a decision which is so unreasonable that no reasonable authority, properly directing itself, could reach such a decision. This is known as 'Wednesbury unreasonableness' from *Associated Provincial Picture Houses Ltd v Wednesbury Corp.*[4]

5.15   The principle involves the court exercising its own judgement about the rationality of the decision of a local authority. In this way it goes beyond the narrower function of the *ultra vires* ground, whereby a court is simply confining a local authority to its powers as spelled out in legislation. The *Wednesbury* role is heavily circumscribed however: the court will not explore the merits of

3   [1995] 2 All ER 636 at 647.
4   [1948] 1 KB 223.

the decision, and it will not substitute itself for the decision-maker, either by stating what the decision should be or re-making the decision itself. In this way the separation of the judicial role of the court and the administrative role of the local authority is maintained. It also means that judicial review is fundamentally different to an appeal on the merits. The Wednesbury principle is justified on the basis that Parliament when conferring a statutory power could not have intended it to be exercised in a wholly irrational or perverse way.

5.16   Irrationality is a high hurdle and the ground is difficult to make out, not only because of the courts' refusal to step into the shoes of the decision maker but because of the potential advantage that a decision-maker will have over a Judge in terms of assessing the relevant factual material.

Procedural unfairness: the right to be heard and the rule against bias

5.17   The procedural fairness of administrative decision-making is regulated both by statutory procedures and the common law requirements of natural justice. A claimant will be able to make out this ground of challenge where the procedure adopted by the local authority fell short of these standards. In respect of statutory procedures, assessing compliance is relatively straightforward. Assessing compliance with natural justice (which extends to administrative decision-making as a duty to act fairly, despite the non-judicial context) is less so because the duty is highly flexible and varies considerably in differing contexts.

5.18   There are two principal aspects of the duty to act fairly. First, there is the right to be heard. Whether this right applies and the extent to which it applies will be fact sensitive, having regard in particular to whether a sanction is being applied, rights interfered with, or livelihoods affected (for example a local authority sub-committee deciding upon the revocation of a taxi licence).

5.19   The second aspect of the duty to act fairly is the rule against bias, which is of great significance in the context of councillors' conduct. It is explored in more detail in **Chapter 3** of this book but in summary the principle is a common law one which is further divided into categories of presumed, actual, and apparent bias. If bias is made out, the decision is unlawful and may be quashed. The availability of apparent bias means it is not necessary to establish actual bias.

5.20   The rule against bias is qualified by the concept of waiver. A person who was fully aware of the nature of the disqualification and his right to object, and who had the opportunity to object but did not, will be considered to have acquiesced in the participation of the disqualified decision-maker.[5]

---

5   *Smith v Kvaerner Cementation Foundations Ltd* [2006] 3 All ER 593. For an example in the local authority context (failure of an interested party to object to participation of a councillor on a planning committee), see *EU Plants Ltd v Wokingham BC* [2012] EWHC 3305.

5.21   Further protection from allegations of bias or predetermination against councillors is provided by s 25 of the Localism Act 2011. This provides, so far as relevant:

> '(1) Subsection (2) applies if-
>
> > (a)   As a result of an allegation of bias or predetermination, or otherwise, there is an issue about the validity of a decision of a relevant authority, and
> >
> > (b)   It is relevant to that issue whether the decision-maker, or any of the decision-makers had or appeared to have had a closed mind (to any extent) when making the decision.
>
> (2) A decision-maker is not to be taken to have had, or to appeared to have had, a closed mind when making the decision just because –
>
> > (a)   The decision-maker had previously done anything that directly or indirectly indicated what view the decision-maker took, or would or might take, in relation to the matter, and
> >
> > (b)   The matter was relevant to the decision.
>
> [...]'

5.22   The section is intended to make clear that despite a councillor having campaigned on an issue or made public statements about their approach to an item of council business, the councillor will be able to participate in discussion on that issue in the council and to vote on it if it arises in an item of council business requiring a decision.

D   JUDICIAL REVIEW: PROCEDURE AND REMEDIES

5.23   The Civil Procedure Rules ('CPR') contain in Part 54 the main procedural rules applying to judicial review. In order to bring a claim the claimant must have some connection to the subject matter of the dispute. In shorthand, they must have standing. The current approach of the courts to the issue of standing is comparatively relaxed. So, for example, it is possible for representative bodies to take claims on behalf of their members. Commercial competitors will normally have sufficient standing where one of them is advantaged or disadvantaged by a reviewable decision.[6] Bodies representing the public interest in a particular area may also be found to have sufficient standing.[7] In order to bring a claim relying on the provisions of the Human Rights Act 1998 the claimant must be a 'victim'.[8] There are specific rules dealing with environmental claims falling

---

6   *R v A-G ex p ICI plc* [1987] 1 CMLR 72.

7   *R v HM Inspector of Pollution ex p Greenpeace (No 2)* [1994] 4 All ER 329.

8   As to which see *Klass v Federal Republic of Germany* (1979-80) 2 EHRR 214; *Loizidou v Turkey (Preliminary Objections)* (1995) 20 EHRR 99; *R v Broadcasting Standards Commission ex p BBC*, The Times 12.4.00.

within the Aarhus Convention[9] and procurement related claims made under the Public Contracts Regulations 2015.[10] It will not normally be an abuse of process to select from a pool of aggrieved individuals an individual who is eligible for public funding.

5.24 It is not necessary for the claimant to have a particular interest in the grounds of challenge advanced in a case so long as he has a sufficient interest in whether the actual decision stands or falls. Whilst an authority cannot bring a claim to strike down one of its own decisions (because it cannot be both claimant and defendant), it may authorise an individual such as a member to bring a claim.[11]

5.25 It is important that any claim for judicial review is brought promptly.[12] Claims which are not brought promptly may fail for that reason alone: CPR 54.5.[13] Whether a claim is brought promptly will ultimately depend on all the circumstances.

5.26 Claims must also be brought not later than three months after the grounds to make the claim first arose. In cases involving the planning acts as defined by s 336 of the Town and Country Planning Act 1990 that requirement is tightened, requiring any claim to be made not later than six weeks after the grounds to make the claim first arose: CPR 54.5(5). The 'first arose' formulation means that it may be both appropriate and necessary to challenge a decision or resolution relating to strategy or selection criteria before they are applied to a particular case.[14] However, in cases involving planning permissions it is well settled that an aggrieved claimant is entitled to wait until the formal grant of planning permission, but may, if they prefer, challenge the earlier resolution to grant.[15]

5.27 The time limits set out above may not be extended by agreement between the parties: CPR 54.5(2). In cases where it was not possible or practicable to bring the claim promptly or within the time limits in the rules then an application can be made to extend time within form N461 (below). It is important to bear in mind that some statutory challenges have time limits which are effectively absolute (for example s 288 of the Town and Country Planning Act 1990). It is therefore important to be clear from an early stage under which specific provision any challenge is being made.

---

9 Art 9(2) of the Convention.
10 Reg 91 of the 2015 Regulations, SI 2015/102.
11 *R (Gardner) v Harrogate BC* [2008] EWHC 2941 (Admin); [2009] JPL 873.
12 Save that the requirement may be disapplied in cases involving procurement or points of EU law: *R (Buglife) v Medway Council* [2011] EWHC 746 (Admin); [2011] 3 CMLR 39.
13 See for example *R (007 Stratford Taxis Ltd) v Stratford on Avon DC* [2011] EWCA Civ 160; [2012] RTR 53.
14 *R (Parker Rhodes Hickmotts Solicitors) v Legal Services Commission* [2011] EWHC 1323 (Admin); [2011] ACD 88; *R (Nash) v Barnet LBC* [2013] EWCA Civ 1004; [2013] PTSR 1457.
15 *R v Hammersmith and Fulham LBC ex p Burkett* [2002] UKHL 23; [2002] 1 WLR 1593; *R (Catt) v Brighton and Hove CC* [2013] EWHC 1977 (Admin); [2013] PTSR D29.

5.28   Before issuing a claim there are three other matters for consideration. Firstly a claimant should satisfy themselves that there is no other avenue through which they might achieve the same relief, because judicial review is recognised as a remedy of last resort and claims can be refused permission on the basis that an alternative remedy is available. This might, therefore, apply if a conduct investigation has not been completed. The most common examples of satisfactory alternative remedies include statutory provisions or rules adopted by a local authority which provide for an internal review or reconsideration of a decision. Secondly, a claimant should comply with the pre-action protocol relating to judicial review claims (unless the claim is one of emergency to which the protocol does not apply). However, it is clear that a claimant should not breach the time limits above in order to secure compliance with the protocol, because merely seeking to comply with the protocol is very unlikely to amount to a good excuse for failing to commence proceedings promptly and in any event within the necessary period.[16] Thirdly, it is important for the claimant to identify any interested parties who are directly affected by the claim so that they can be served with pre-action correspondence and any issued claim: CPR 54.1(2)(f).

5.29   The CPR provides for specific court forms to be used in judicial review claims. Such a claim will normally have two main stages being the permission stage and the full hearing stage. Claims which are not considered by the court to be arguable (or otherwise such as to justify a full hearing on the basis of their importance) will be rejected at the permission stage. Claims which are considered to be arguable will proceed to a full hearing. Defendants to a judicial review claim may choose not to participate until the issue of permission has been decided, and still participate in the full hearing; but such an approach is rare. In deciding whether to participate at the permission stage it is important to bear in mind that the question of delay cannot normally be re-opened by a defendant at the full hearing stage once permission has been granted (although questions of whether granting relief would cause detriment to good administration remain open).[17]

5.30   A claim should be commenced by form N461 setting out in full the facts and grounds in support of the claim. The claimant owes the court a duty of full and frank disclosure and accordingly all material facts including those adverse to the claimant's case should be included in the statement of facts and grounds and any supporting evidence. The duty of full and frank disclosure is a continuing one. Failure to comply with the duty can be a ground in itself for interim relief to be set aside[18] or, in an extreme case, for the court to refuse to exercise its discretion to grant any relief.

5.31   Applications for urgent relief including a stay on further decision making or other action by the authority can be made using form N463 and the court will

---

16 *Finn-Kelcey v Milton Keynes BC* [2008] EWCA Civ 1067; [2009] Env LR 17.
17 *R v Criminal Injuries Compensation Board ex p A* [1999] 2 AC 330; *R (Lichfield Securities Ltd) v Lichfield DC* [2001] EWCA Civ 304; [2011] PLCR 32.
18 See, for example, *R (Lawer) v Restormel BC* [2007] EWHC 2299 (Admin); [2008] HLR 20.

generally consider such applications on paper in the first instance, and within the time requested on the N463 form. Therefore, if a defendant or interested party wishes to respond to such an application they will need to do so in writing (circulated to all parties) within the time requested for a decision on the N463 form. However, there is also now a specific form a defendant may use for seeking reconsideration of the grant of interim relief (Form AC002). A claimant making such an urgent application is subject to a heightened duty of full and frank disclosure and must identify, for example, any material in which the defendant further explains or justifies its decision making or any other circumstances which militate against the grant of urgent relief. An important element of that duty is a duty to make sufficient enquiries to establish accurately the factual position upon which the claimant relies.

5.32   Applications for urgent relief can include a claim for a mandatory injunction requiring an authority to take some action. For such an application to be successful it is normally necessary to satisfy the court that the claimant has a strong prima facie case.[19]

5.33   In appropriate cases it is possible for judicial review claims to be swiftly determined. A party may seek, or the parties may agree, for example: (i) that permission should be granted for the claim because it is arguable, (ii) that the normal directions should be substantially abridged, (iii) that the hearing of the claim should be expedited due either to its consequences of it being upheld or quashed; (iv) to a 'rolled up' hearing. In cases where the parties agree to any of those courses the court will normally adopt the proposal. A 'rolled up' hearing is one in which the court will consider the question of permission and, if satisfied permission should be granted, proceed immediately to hear the claim in full. All such applications can be made within form N463 with an additional rider if necessary.

5.34   A defendant to a judicial review claim may file summary grounds of response ('SGR') on form N462, not more than 21 days after being served with the claim form, seeking to persuade the court that a claim is unarguable. The SGR should, accordingly, be limited to making points which the defendant considers to be 'knock out' points. The finer merits may safely be left to be debated later if permission is granted. The rules do not make provision for the claimant to file any reply to the SGR, but that course is now often taken.

5.35   If permission is refused the claimant may apply for permission to be reconsidered at a short oral hearing. If permission is again refused then the claim is at an end, save that an appeal may be made to the Court of Appeal to seek to overturn the refusal of permission. Permission may be granted generally or limited to particular grounds, and may be granted subject to conditions. If permission is granted then the defendant will have a further 35 days to file its detailed grounds and any written evidence: CPR 54.14. The case will then be listed for full hearing. In preparing the SGR and any detailed grounds and

19 *De Falco v Crawley* [1980] QB 460.

evidence, the defendant owes the court a duty of candour requiring it to explain fully the decision arrived at and the basis for it.

The defendant's evidence

5.36   Evidence filed on behalf of the defendant should normally be limited to setting the background, contextualising and giving reasons for the impugned action. If appropriate evidence may also set out circumstances relevant to whether the court should decline to grant relief as a matter of discretion or on the basis of substantial detriment to good administration. Evidence may legitimately specify what matters were taken into account in cases where there is an allegation that relevant matters were left out of account.[20]

5.37   Where reasons have already been provided (especially reasons provided pursuant to a statutory duty) the evidence should be limited to elucidation and clarification of the reasons given.[21] However, in a case where it is clear that the reasons recorded on the face of a decision are not the true reasons, the record may be corrected by evidence.[22] In cases where all statute requires is a summary of the reasons, it follows that the summary may be substantially amplified in evidence.[23]

Relief

5.38   While any remedies for misconduct will be directed to the individual member, those in judicial review operate at the level of the council. A claimant who demonstrates that a decision was reached based upon or affected by a material error of law can generally expect the court to quash the relevant decision.[24] Declarations may be sought as to the validity, for example, of policies underlying the decision made in an individual application of the policy.

5.39   If an error of law is demonstrated, but the defendant demonstrates the error did not influence the process because, for example, the merits of the decision were otherwise overwhelming or a flaw in procedure was overcome by later corrective action, the court will normally refuse relief so long as the procedure, looked at as a whole, was fair.[25]

5.40   In rare cases it may be possible for a claimant to say that in fact there was only one conclusion that the defendant could have reached on a proper

---

20 *Hijazi v Kensington & Chelsea RLBC* [2003] EWCA Civ 692; [2003] HLR 72.
21 *R v Westminster CC ex p Ermakov* [1996] 2 All ER 302; *R (Lanner PC) v Cornwall Council* [2013] EWCA Civ 1290.
22 *Westminster CC v Secretary of State for Communities and Local Government* [2014] EWHC 708 (Admin).
23 *R (Siraj) v Kirklees MBC* [2010] EWCA Civ 1286; [2011] JPL 571.
24 *R (Edwards) v Environment Agency (No 2)* [2008] UKHL 22; [2008] 1 All ER 1587.
25 *Calvin v Carr* [1980] AC 574; *Bolton MDC v Secretary of State* (1996) 71 P& CR 309; *Holmes-Moorhouse v Richmond upon Thames LBC* [2009] UKHL 7; [2009] 1 WLR 413.

consideration of the matter. In such a case the claimant can seek a declaration to that effect and/or an order requiring the defendant to make that decision and act on the basis of that conclusion, known as a mandatory order.[26]

5.41   It is also possible to seek damages within a judicial review claim in an appropriate case. In such circumstances the court will normally deal with the normal judicial review issues arising and then make any necessary consequential directions for a damages hearing.[27] In order to award damages the court must be satisfied that an award would have been made if the claim had been made in a conventional private law claim.[28] Thus, damages may potentially be claimed in cases involving negligence,[29] breach of statutory duty,[30] misfeasance in public office[31], reparation under EU law,[32] and just satisfaction under the Human Rights Act 1998.[33]

5.42   All relief in judicial review lies in the discretion of the court, and accordingly there are a number of situations where relief may be refused. A court may consider the claim is academic, that it is premature, or that due to the conduct of the claimant relief should be refused. Another well recognised basis for refusing relief is where in a case involving undue delay granting relief would be likely to: (1) cause substantial hardship to, or substantially prejudice the rights of, any person, or (2) cause substantial prejudice to good administration.[34]

Costs

5.43   Costs in judicial review follow similar principles to those in general litigation.[35] The winner will normally recover costs from the unsuccessful party. It is rare for interested parties (or additional defendants to statutory challenges) to recover a second set of costs in cases where the defendant is successful unless they can demonstrate an interest requiring separate representation.[36] A defending party successfully appearing at a permission hearing will not normally recover the costs of that hearing, but can claim the costs of preparing its acknowledgment of service.[37]

---

26 Senior Courts Act 1981, s 31(5A).
27 *R (Kurdistan Workers Party) v Secretary of State for the Home Department* [2002] EWHC 644 (Admin).
28 Senior Courts Act 1981, s 31; *R (Quark Fishing Ltd) v Secretary of State for Foreign and Commonwealth Affairs* [2005] UKHL 57; [2006] 1 AC 529.
29 *Stovin v Wise* [1996] AC 923.
30 *M v Home Office* [1994] 1 AC 377.
31 In relation to the high requirements for a successful misfeasance claim see *Three Rivers DC v Bank of England* [2003] 2 AC 1.
32 *Francovich v Italian Republic* [1991] ECR I-5357.
33 *R (Bernard) v Enfield LBC* [2002] EWHC 2282 (Admin); [2003] UKHRR 148.
34 Senior Courts Act 1981, s 31(6).
35 *M v LB Croydon* [2012] EWCA Civ 595; [2012] 1 WLR 2607 as explained in *Speciality Produce Ltd v Secretary of State for the Environment, Food and Rural Affairs* [2014] EWCA Civ 225; [2014] CP Rep 29.
36 *Bolton MDC v Secretary of State for the Environment* [1995] 1 WLR 1176.
37 *R (Mount Cook Land Ltd) v Westminster CC* [2004] CP Rep. 12.

5.44   The Aarhus Convention has important implications for costs. The general rule is that public access to litigation involving environmental issues should not be prohibitively expensive. The rules are now codified within the CPR at rules 45.41–45.44. The claim form must set out that the claim is an Aarhus claim (if the claimant wishes to rely on the Aarhus costs rules) and the basis for that contention: CPR 45.41, 54.6. If the defendant fails to challenge the application of the convention then the claim will continue as an Aarhus claim: CPR 45.44. The effect of the rules is that a party to such a claim may not be ordered to pay costs exceeding the amount prescribed in Practice Direction 45: CPR 45.43. Those amounts for claimants are currently set at £5,000 where the claimant is claiming only as an individual and not as, or on behalf of, a business or other legal person; and £10,000 in all other cases. The amount set for a defendant is £35,000.

5.45   However, the rules do not attempt to define what may fall within an Aarhus claim and so the extent of Article 9 of the convention will continue to be discussed in the courts. There have been a number of recent cases exploring the width of what may fall within Article 9.[38]

E   OMBUDSMAN

5.46   'Ombudsman' is a Swedish word meaning 'representative of the people'. References to 'the Ombudsman' are so frequently used in so many different areas of public and commercial life, that it might be tempting to think that there is but one. There are in fact several different Ombudsman schemes, some statutory and others based solely on contract.

5.47   They share the essential characteristic of being a complaints handling service. For present purposes there are three ombudsmen of direct relevance to complaints about local authorities in England and Wales and they are all creatures of statute. They are:

- The Local Government Ombudsman ('the LGO') who, together with the Parliamentary Commissioner for Administration (as an 'ex officio' member), comprise the Commission for Local Administration created by s 23 of the Local Government Act 1974.[39] They are responsible for the investigation of complaints about local authorities (and certain other bodies) within England (see s 25 of the 1974 Act).

- The Parliamentary Commissioner for Administration to be referred to as the Parliamentary Ombudsman ('the PO') created by the Parliamentary

---

38 *R (Edwards) v Environment Agency (No 2)* Case C-260/11 [2013] 1 WLR. 2914; *European Commission v United Kingdom of Great Britain and Northern Ireland* (Case C-530/11) [2014] 3 WLR 853; *Coventry v Lawrence* [2014] UKSC 46; [2014] 3 WLR 555.

39 Strictly, the Act establishes 'a body of commissioners' numbering at least two. However, the Commission has moved to a system headed by a single Ombudsman, so facilitating more effective governance and consistency. Note, too, amendments in the Local Government and Public Involvement in Health Act 2007, Health Act 2009, Education Act 2011, and Localism Act 2011.

Commissioner Act 1967 and responsible for complaints about central Government, its various departments and Parliamentary Committees (see Schedule 2 to the 1967 Act).[40]

- The Public Services Ombudsman for Wales ('the PSOW') created by the Public Services Ombudsman (Wales) Act 2005 and responsible for complaints about public bodies and their services in Wales, as well as complaints about the conduct of Councillors in Wales (under Part III of the Local Government Act 2000). This is dealt with in **Chapter 7**.

5.48–5.50 If an MP refers a complaint to the PO and it covers areas which fall within the jurisdiction of the LGO as well, a joint investigation and report should be prepared. By way of an example, when a complaint was made by a young victim of crime about the response of the Youth Offending Team and the complaints handling process of the local authority (the Trafford Metropolitan Borough Council) it led to a joint report laid before Parliament and published on both the LGO's and the PO's websites.

5.51 The Ombudsman is, in essence, a service for handling complaints where it is claimed that a member of the public has suffered injustice as a result of a local authority's alleged maladministration, service failure or failure to provide a service (see, for the LGO, s 26(1) of the Local Government Act 1974). Another important role for the LGO is the provision of advice and guidance on good administrative practice (s 23(12A) of the Local Government Act 1974).

5.52 The LGO shares many similarities with other statutory Ombudsman schemes, and may conduct joint investigations with either the Parliamentary and Health Service Ombudsman,[41] or the Housing Ombudsman.[42]

5.53 There are three obvious ways in which a Councillor may come into contact with the LGO. First, the Councillor may have acted or failed to act in a way that is relevant to an allegation of maladministration concerning service delivery. Allegations of bias, for example, have led to such findings. Secondly, a complaint about a Councillor may be handled by the authority in a way which leads to a complaint of maladministration to the LGO. Thirdly, Councillors may wish to make use of the service themselves (only in their private capacity as user of a local authority service), or may refer a complaint by a member of the public about one or other of the authority's services to the LGO.

5.54 The LGO website is a valuable source of information about the Ombudsman's role, and all LGO decisions are now published there. Also included is the Annual Report and Accounts which the LGO is required to lay before Parliament, and this document includes a digest of the work of the LGO

---

40 The role of the PO is carried out by the same organisation as that of the Health Service Ombudsman created in 1993, and is therefore often referred to as the Parliamentary and Health Service Ombudsman.
41 Regulatory Reform (Collaboration etc between Ombudsmen) Order 2007, SI 2007/1889.
42 Local Government Act 1974, s 33ZA.

over the year including analysis of trends in the subject matter of complaints and a list of reports prepared over the year. For the 2013–14 year, the LGO received 20,306 complaints, of which 11,725 were referred to the assessment team, the vast majority of which were dealt with without the need for detailed investigation and report. Since 99% of cases are dealt with within 12 months it is instructive to look at the number of reports published in the same period, a mere 58 during 2013–14 of which five reports were published jointly with the PHSO.

5.55   Complaints about Councillor's conduct do not frequently form the main subject of investigation. This falls within the 'Corporate or other' category for reporting in the Annual Report and Accounts for 2013–14, and there are no reports for the year under the subheading 'councillor conduct and standards'. There need be no surprise about this – on the one hand, as this book has explained, local authorities are required to have in place arrangements for investigating complaints about conduct themselves; and on the other hand, as explained above, the High Court (unlike the LGO) is – in the context of an application for judicial review – able to quash decisions which are dependent upon unlawful conduct by Councillors. However, where the conduct of a Councillor has contributed to maladministration, the LGO will have a role.[43]

5.56   The Advice and Guidance currently available on the website is extensive. Fact Sheets give a brief overview of how the LGO may be able to help with complaints arising in a number of different contexts. The Fact Sheet on Parish Councils, for example, advises that the LGO will not investigate a complaint about a Councillor, since that must be dealt with via the Standards Committee,[44] and continues 'The Ombudsman may then be able to look at how the Standards Committee considered your complaint about a parish councillor. But she will not investigate the issues that prompted your complaint'.

5.57   There are also a series of **Reports** which identify and advise on a local authority's response to matters of particular concern, or matters which may come up particularly often. For example, the Focus Report 'School Admissions Procedures: Are Parents Being Heard?' published in September 2014, its preparation perhaps a reflection of the fact that Education and Children's Services has consistently provided the largest number of complaints to the LGO (16% in 2013–14).

5.58   The following are of particular interest in the handling of complaints within a local authority and are found under 'Publications':

- The 2011 Joint Publication with the charity Centre for Public Scrutiny entitled 'Aiming for the Best: Using lessons from complaint to improve public services'.

- Guidance on Running a Complaints System, updated in 2014.

---

43 As is mentioned in **Chapter 1**, para **1.99**, the effect of the abolition of the Standards Board on the workload of the Ombudsman was expected by the Government to be 'slight', and this appears to be borne out by experience to date.

44 Part 4 discusses the process for bringing a complaint under locally determined arrangements for considering allegations about Councillors which are referred to here.

5.59 Following a Law Commission Report, the LGO has been implementing a Transformation Plan in recent years, under which its governance and service delivery have been improved in ways capable of being achieved without legislation. However, further amendments of its governance are to be expected in the future. Reference may usefully be made to:

- LGO (2012) A Transformation Plan for the Local Government Ombudsman 2011–2015.

- CLG (2012) The Work of the LGO (2012–2013) HC 431.

- External Evaluation of the Local Government Ombudsman in England by Richard Thomas CBE, Jim Martin and Richard Kirkham dated April 2013.

- CLG Governance Review of the Local Government Ombudsman Service. A report for the Secretary of State for Communities and Local Government November 2013.

Complaining to the Ombudsman

5.60 The best and most up to date source of guidance on how to complain is the LGO website itself and an appropriate form is provided there. This section identifies the legal barriers to a complaint.

5.61 First, the body complained of must be one subject to the Local Government Act 1974. This includes (see s 25) any local authority, defined as a County Council, a District Council, a London Borough, the Broads Authority, the Common Council of the City of London, and the Council of the Isles of Scilly. It includes a joint authority established under Part IV of the Local Government Act 1985, the Greater London Authority, and a National Park Authority. However, Parish and Town Councils are excluded from the LGO's jurisdiction, although it may be possible to complain about a service they provide if it is provided on behalf of a body which is subject to the Act (see the LGO's Factsheet on Parish Councils, found under Publications on the LGO website).

5.62 It should be noted that both members and officers are included within the definition of local authority, as are any committee and (if relevant) the executive (s 25(4) and (4ZA)).

5.63 Secondly the LGO may not conduct an investigation unless one of three conditions are met:

- a complaint meeting the requirements of s 26A and s 26B has been made; or

- such a complaint has been made to the authority concerned and is referred or treated as referred under s 26C; or

- the matter comes to the attention of the LGO during the course of another investigation and the provisions of s 26D are satisfied.

5.64   Investigations are most often begun by the first of these, by complaint direct to the LGO. Complainants are members of the public or persons authorised in writing by such a person to act on his behalf (s 26A) and (although the LGO retains a residual discretion to dis-apply this requirement) the complaint should be made in writing within 12 months of the date the person affected first had notice of the matter (s 26B).

5.65   So, as the LGO website advises 'Councillors can help their constituents to make a complaint against a council, but they cannot make a complaint against their own council themselves, except about any services they receive in common with other service users (for example, if they are council tenants).' Councillors can also refer complaints made to them on to the LGO (s 26A), the second condition referred to above.

5.66–5.73   Even when it is clear that one of the statutory conditions for an investigation is met, the LGO retains a broad discretion whether or not to investigate a complaint and whether to end an investigation that has begun (s 30(1C) and (1D)).

The subject matter of investigations

5.74   The LGO may only investigate allegations of maladministration; failures in a service it was the authority's function to provide; and failures to provide such a service at all (see s 26(1) of the LGA 1974).

5.75   The term 'maladministration' warrants further comment. It is not defined by statute and is given a broad interpretation (*R v Local Commissioner for Administration for the North and East Area of England Ex p Bradford City Council* [1979] QB 287). In adopting a passage from the then current edition of Wade on Administrative Law Lord Denning MR said this (at 311H):

> 'It will cover "bias, neglect, inattention, delay, incompetence, ineptitude, perversity, turpitude, arbitrariness and so on". It "would be a long and interesting list", clearly open-ended, covering the *manner* in which a decision is reached or discretion is exercised; but excluding the *merits* of the decision itself or of the discretion itself. It follows that "discretionary decision, properly exercised which the complainant dislikes but cannot fault the manner in which it was taken, is excluded": see Hansard, 734 HC Deb, col. 51.
>
> In other words, if there is no maladministration, the Ombudsman may not question any decision taken by the authorities. He must not go into the merits of it or intimate any view as to whether it was right or wrong. This is explicitly declared in s 34(3) of the Act of 1974. He can inquire whether there was maladministration or not. If he finds none, he must go no further. If he finds it, he can go on and inquire whether any person has suffered injustice thereby.'

5.76   A list of matters included in the term maladministration, couched in more modern terms perhaps but considered consistent with Lord Denning's dictum in 1979, is found on the LGO website and copied below:

- delay;

- incorrect action or failure to take any action;

- failure to follow procedures or the law;

- failure to provide information;

- inadequate record-keeping;

- failure to investigate;

- failure to reply;

- misleading or inaccurate statements;

- inadequate liaison;

- inadequate consultation;

- broken promises.

5.77   There are specific exclusions from the remit of the LGO which are set out within s 26 and Schedule 5 to the LGA 1974. They include, most notably, cases in which the person affected has a right of appeal or a right to a remedy in court unless the LGO is satisfied that it would not be reasonable to expect the person affected to avail themselves of the right or remedy (s 26(6)).

5.78   With this in mind, the LGO's finding of maladministration was challenged in *R (Liverpool City Council) v Local Commissioner for Administration*.[45] Interestingly, this was a case in which the complaint of maladministration arose in circumstances which would also be a conduct issue: the Council had permitted an extension to a city football stadium and, as the Ombudsman found, six were season ticket holders of the relevant club (and had not declared their interest) while others had voted in favour out of 'a misplaced loyalty for their political party'. The Council argued that the complaint could and should be raised on a judicial review, in relation to which Henry LJ said this (paragraph 23):

> 'What may not have been recognised back in 1974 was the emergence of judicial review to the point where most if not almost all matters which could form the basis for a complaint of maladministration are matters for which the elastic qualities of judicial review might provide a remedy. In that situation, the proviso in sub-section (6) becomes of greater importance: "Provided that a Local Commissioner may conduct an investigation notwithstanding the existence of such a right or remedy if satisfied that in the particular circumstances it is not reasonable to expect the person aggrieved to resort or to have resorted to it."'

45 [2001] 1 All ER 462.

5.79   The Judge went on to endorse the LGO's application of the proviso in that case on account of: (a) the fact finding powers of the LGO which would be denied the complainants in the context of a challenge by way of judicial review, and (b) the modest means of the complainants.

5.80   Also excluded from the LGO's remit is any action which affects all or most of the inhabitants of the area covered by the authority; matters relating to the commencement of civil or criminal proceedings; and matters relating to the appointment of personnel (s 26(7) and Sch 5 of the LGA 1974).

The investigation and report

5.81   The LGO has extensive powers to enable him to conduct a thorough investigation of the facts. Councillors associated with the matter of complaint should expect to be interviewed, and to provide to the Ombudsman any papers considered relevant to the investigation. On the other hand, an Ombudsman must not interfere with any further action considered appropriate by the authority.

5.82   The Ombudsman's investigation includes the following mandatory provisions:[46]

- that the investigation is conducted in private;

- that the authority, and all those who are alleged in the complaint (or otherwise appear to the Ombudsman) to have taken or authorised the action under investigation, are given an opportunity to comment.

5.83   Meanwhile his powers are considerable. They include the power to obtain information from those considered appropriate by the Ombudsman and to pay those who furnish him with information their expenses and compensation. His powers in relation to disclosure and attendance of witnesses are equivalent to the High Court, and even capable of overriding the all statutory and other sources of Crown immunity where correspondence between the authority and any Government Department is concerned.

5.84   Obstruction of the Ombudsman's investigation is capable of being treated in like manner to contempt of court in the High Court, and the 1974 Act (England) provides for transfer of such offences to the High Court for inquiry.

5.85   At the conclusion of an investigation, in the general case, the LGO must prepare a report of the results of the investigation to the complainant, the referrer (if referred) and the authority concerned (s 30(1) of the LGA 1974). The Act provides for an exception where the Ombudsman is satisfied with action

46 See ss 28 and 29 of the LGA 1974 generally on the investigation process.

the authority concerned have taken or propose to take, and considers it is not appropriate to prepare a report. In such a case he must prepare a statement of reasons for this decision and send a copy to all those concerned (s 30(1B) of the LGA 1974).

5.86 During the investigation, the circumstances may change to the point where the investigation is halted. For example:

- the investigation does not affect any power or duty the authority may have to continue to deal with the matters which are the subject of the investigation and this could lead to a satisfactory resolution of issues;

- the authority may offer redress which satisfies the LGO and may render further investigation unnecessary.

5.87 The decision whether to discontinue an investigation is for the LGO alone to make.

5.88 Naturally, the investigation process must be fair and seen to be fair. The principles of natural justice apply to the investigation and to the report, which is sent in draft to the authority and to the complainant before being published.

5.89 In the case of *R (on the application of Kay) v Health Service Commissioner*[47] the Court of Appeal applied the approach of Collins J in *Turpin v Commissioner for Local Administration*[48] to a complainant's demand to see all the material sent by the investigated body to the Commissioner. Collins J had said this:

> 'The law as to the requirements of fairness in conducting an investigation is, as it seems to me, clear. The general rule is that a person or body which has to make a decision based on an issue raised by one person against another should normally disclose the material on which it is going to rely or which comes into its possession which may influence its decision to each of the parties so that each party can know what material is available, what matters are likely to be held against them and whether it is necessary for that party to itself put forward material or to make representations to deal with such matters. If that is not done, it is clear that there is a risk – I put it no higher – that injustice will be occasioned to such party.'

5.90 As Sullivan LJ went on to say in *Kay*:

> 'In Turpin Collins J was considering a refusal by the Ombudsman to disclose interview notes on which the Ombudsman proposed to rely when deciding that an investigation was not required to the complainant.

---

47 [2009] EWCA Civ 732.
48 [2001] EWHC Admin 503.

In those circumstances it is unsurprising that Collins J concluded that the failure to disclose those interview notes to the complainant on which the Ombudsman was proposing to rely was not fair. Collins J said in paragraph 69:

> "One cannot deal with every possible situation and it must be a matter left always to the discretion of the Ombudsman, but it is a discretion which ought, prima facie, in my judgment, to be exercised in favour of disclosure unless there are good reasons not to disclose. I see no justification for giving the Ombudsman a general right to refuse to disclose whatever the circumstances. It is not suggested here, no could it be suggested, that there was any good reason not to give the interview notes to the Turpins, no doubt on an undertaking that they would only be used for the purposes of the complaint which they were making to the Ombudsman."

> The circumstances in the present case are very different. We are not concerned with material on which the Ombudsman does propose to rely; rather we are concerned with whether there is any obligation to disclose to the complainant material on which the Ombudsman does not propose to rely. In other words the Ombudsman, having sorted out the wheat from the chaff, is obliged to disclose the wheat under the Turpin principle to the complainant. But Turpin was not concerned with what happened to the chaff. Should the chaff, in the Ombudsman's view, or any part of it be disclosed to the complainant? While the statutory procedures accord a very broad measure of discretion to the Ombudsman, the authorities establish that that discretion must be exercised in a fair manner. In my judgment the procedure envisaged by the Act should ensure fairness because the draft report is sent to the complainant.'

5.91   The LGO is required to prepare a report whenever he completes an investigation of a matter (s 30(1) of the LGA 1974) and will send a draft copy of the report to the complainant and the investigated body before publishing it.

5.92   In reporting on the outcome of a complaint, the LGO will both reach findings as to the substance of the complaint <u>and</u> (where considered appropriate) make recommendations as to redress or change within the Authority concerned. There is no right of appeal against the Ombudsman's findings and an aggrieved complainant can only make use of the Ombudsman's own complaints service or, on public law grounds, seek judicial review.

5.93–5.96   In the following boxes three cases in which the conduct of Councillors has led to findings of maladministration are given by way of example.

A case of delay

March 2013 report into a complaint concerning Derbyshire Dales District Council. This was a case in which a particularly difficult former Councillor had held up the process of issuing a noise abatement notice against him, so extending the period during which complainants suffered noise nuisance at night by two years (this was in addition to an earlier complaint which had led to an express reassurance by the Council to the LGO that the matter would be resolved by 2011). By the time of the report the noise abatement notice had been served but the LGO recommended a payment be made of £1,820 representing £10 per night of nuisance beyond the period by which the Council had assured the LGO the matter would be resolved.

A case of the appearance of bias

A 2008 report into two complaints concerning Forest Heath District Council. This was a case in which planning permission had been granted for development against the advice of professional officers. The applicant's father was a member of the planning committee and did not take part in the decision. However his substitute showed bias. The LGO recommended that the complainants were paid £1,000, that the Council apologised to them, and that it put in place appropriate training for Councillors.

A case of prejudicial interest in a planning decision

2006 report into a complaint concerning Harrogate Borough Council. The Chairman of the Planning Committee had exercised his casting vote in favour of a scheme (to construct a house on the site of a caravan) promoted by another Councillor whom he gave a lift to and from Council meetings and occasionally socialised with. As the LGO reported 'the only Councillors who should have considered and voted on the application were those whose relationship with (the applicant) would not lead a member of the public to think that their decision, because of that relationship, would be biased'. The LGO recommended that the Council consider what action it should take to cancel the planning permission 'which was improperly obtained', and provide training. In due course the Leader of the Council applied to the High Court for a Quashing order, granted by Sullivan J in *R (Gardner) v Harrogate BC* [2008] EWHC 2942 (Admin).

The response of the Authority concerned to the report

5.97   Where the LGO reports that there has been maladministration or service failure it must be laid before the authority concerned, which must notify within three months (or such longer period as may be agreed in writing) what action the authority have taken or propose to take in the light of the report (LGA 1974, s 31).

5.98   Section 31 sets out in detail what action is required in a variety of scenarios following an adverse report. These include provision for making a further report where the authority's response does not satisfy the Ombudsman (s 31(2A)), and a further sanction (preparing and publishing a statement under s 31(2E)–(2G) where the authority's response to the further report is inadequate.[49]

5.99   There is no right of appeal against the Ombudsman's report and findings of maladministration, injustice and loss are binding unless successfully challenged by judicial review. As was said in 1988 by Lord Donaldson MR[50] in a passage explicitly approved by the Court of Appeal in 2009[51] 'Whilst I am very far from encouraging councils to seek judicial review of an Ombudsman's report, which, bearing in mind the nature of his office and duties and the qualifications of those who hold that office, is inherently unlikely to succeed, in the absence of a successful application for judicial review and the giving of relief by the court, local authorities should not dispute an Ombudsman's report and should carry out their statutory duties in relation to it'. This is itself a challenging task and the High Court will not readily intervene.[52]

5.100   On the other hand, the authority's response to the recommendations of the Ombudsman is not so constrained:

> 'The authority is not obliged to accept and act on the recommendations as to remedy made by the LGO. The authority's decision how to respond is governed by usual, general public law requirements of good faith, rationality, fairness and so on. The rationality of a proposed response has to be assessed taking account of the binding findings of maladministration, injustice and loss which have been made.'[53]

5.101   Local authorities decline to accept and act on recommendations regarding remedy made by the LGO in only a tiny proportion of cases.[54] Whilst this serves to emphasise the seriousness with which a local authority should approach a LGO recommendation as to remedy for maladministration, it does

---

49 The facts of *Nestwood Homes v South Holland* [2014] EWHC 863 (Admin) illustrate the way these provisions can operate in practice.

50 In *R v Local Commissioner for Administration for England Ex p Eastleigh BC* [1988] QB 855.

51 See *R (Bradley) v Secretary of State for Work and Pensions* [2008] EWCA Civ 36 [2009] QB 114 at 139 distinguishing the LGO from the Parliamentary Ombudsman whose finding of maladministration by a minister who is subject to the disciplines of Parlimaent is not binding on the minister.

52 See Morison J in *R (Doy) v Local Commissioner for Administration* [2002] Env LR 11, and Sullivan J (as he then was) in *R (Gardner) v Harrogate Borough Council and Atkinson* [2008] EWHC 2942 at para 12.

53 *Nestwood Homes* at para 57. See also *R (Gallagher) v Basildon DC* [2010] EWHC 2824 (Admin) at para 27.

54 See *Gallagher* at para 15.

not in itself indicate that an authority is required to treat itself as bound to accept and act upon such a recommendation.

F   FREEDOM OF INFORMATION

5.102   This section deals with requests for recorded information about councillors' conduct, such as for information that records whether:

'Cllr X is under investigation.'

'Cllr Y met developer Z socially outside council duties.'

'Cllr R has a disclosable pecuniary interest, through owning shares in the council's contractor for waste services, which she has not declared.'

Information requests

5.103   The Freedom of Information Act 2000 ('FOIA 2000') confers an entitlement on any person making a request for information to a public authority (in this context, a local authority) to be informed in writing whether it holds information of the description requested; and, if so, to have that information communicated to him or her (FOIA 2000, s 1(1)). The public authority is obliged to satisfy the entitlement, and what it must do in terms of communicating the information is set out in s 11 of the FOIA. Where the information is 'environmental information' (which could in certain instances include information on conduct matters) the public authority has a duty to make the information held available on request (reg 5(1) of the Environmental Information Regulations 2004;[55] 'the EIR')[56] Although not express, there is considered by inference to be an analogous duty to 'confirm or deny' under the EIR, as under the FOIA, since there is a limited exception to it in reg 12(6)).

5.104   The duties are to be complied with promptly, and in any event not later than the twentieth working day following the date of receipt of the request (s 10(1) of the FOIA); although there can be an extension of time under FOIA to 'until such time as is reasonable in the circumstances' to consider the public interest test (s 10(3) of the FOIA). Under the EIR, the information is to be made available 'as soon as possible' and not later than the twentieth working day after the date of receipt of the request (reg 5(2) of the EIR); an extension may only be given to 40 working days, if the authority reasonably believes that the 'complexity and volume' of the request makes it impracticable to comply sooner; both elements (ie complexity and volume) being required to be met (reg 7(1) of the EIR).

---

55 SI 2004/3391.

56 For the definition of 'environmental information', see EIR, reg 2(1)(a)–(f). The definition, especially of 'measures' in reg 2(1)(c) is broadly applied. An example might be information about a decision on a planning application about which a member is alleged to have had a pre-determined view.

5.105   These duties under the FOIA are disapplied in certain circumstances. There is no duty to comply with a request, for example, where the cost of locating or retrieving it would exceed a limit set in regulations (s 12(1) of the FOIA). The limit is currently £450, assessed at £25 per hour per person, in a local authority; or 18 hours' work. There is also no duty to comply with a request for information which is vexatious (s 14(1) of the FOIA). There are no similar exclusions under the EIR, but it may be possible – on cost or vexatiousness grounds – to claim an exception under reg 12(4)(b) of the EIR, that the request is 'manifestly unreasonable", subject to the public interest test.

5.106   In both the Act and the Regulations there is a suite of exemptions/ exceptions to protect recognised supervening interests. 'Exemptions' under the FOIA, and 'exceptions' under the EIR, overlap in some cases but differ quite markedly in others. Under the FOIA, about one third of the exemptions are 'absolute' (ie they apply in all cases, where the facts support it); the remainder being commonly known as 'qualified' exemptions, although the term does not appear in the Act. A qualified exemption is one in which it is not enough for the information to be captured by the terms of the exemption/exception. The public authority must also show that the public interest in upholding the exemption/ exception outweighs the public interest in disclosure. An example of an absolute exemption is the duty not to disclose information that has been entrusted to the public authority by a third party on confidential terms, where its disclosure would be a breach of that duty of confidence, actionable by the other person (s 41(1) of the FOIA). Its partial equivalent under the EIR is restricted to commercial or industrial information that is confidential, where the confidentiality is provided by law to protect a legitimate economic interest (although the confidentiality need not arise from a duty to the third party).[57] No EIR exceptions (other than those concerned with personal data under reg 13) are absolute, and they apply only where, or to the extent that, the public interest test is satisfied.

Subject access right

5.107   As a separate right, any individual is entitled under s 7 of the Data Protection Act 1998 ('DPA 1998') to be informed what personal data of that individual (ie information about that person that distinguishes him or her from others)[58] is being 'processed' (ie used, kept, disclosed etc) by or on behalf of the 'data controller'. The data controller is the legal person who controls the processing; in this context, the local authority. Personal data include expressions of opinion about, or intention towards, the individual concerned (the 'data subject').

---

57 It is possible in certain cases of confidential information that other EIR exceptions may apply (eg if disclosure would harm the confidentiality of proceedings, where the confidentiality is provided by law; subject to the public interest test – reg 12(5)(d)).

58 See guidance 'Determining what is Personal Data' by the Information Commissioner; partially endorsed by the Court of Appeal in *Edem v Information Commissioner and FSA* [2014] EWCA Civ 92); and definition of personal data in DPA 1998, s 1(1).

5.108   The 'subject access right' is exercisable subject to the provision by the requester of evidence of identity and, in the case of most data controllers, payment of a statutory fee (generally set at £10). The duty is to comply promptly, and in any event within 40 days (s 7(8) and (10) of the DPA 1998). A number of exemptions apply (see below). It should be noted that non-compliance with the s 7 claim constitutes a breach of s 4(4) of the DPA 1998 (duty of data controller to comply with data protection principles) – ie a statutory trust – actionable in the county court or the High Court. It can also sound in damages if there is resultant distress.

Requests relating to conduct

5.109   Individuals or journalists, or possibly councillors other than the individual member involved, may attempt to use the FOIA or EIR to find out more about a suspected course of misconduct, or about the investigation of a past conduct matter. A councillor facing allegations or an investigation may also seek to use the subject access right in the DPA to seek to discover more about the matter or the investigation.

5.110   The starting point in either case should be that the requester is entitled to the information but that, in a number of these cases, there will also be a number of exemptions or exceptions which may apply. The proper approach by the authority would be to recognise the rights of requesters, while also giving due weight to the need to protect the proper privacy rights of individuals, and the integrity and effectiveness of the investigation. The latter will require identification of an applicable exemption (if any) and, depending on whether it is absolute or not, the public interest balance. Withholding some information may be necessary to enable further facts relevant to a matter under investigation to be identified. Full disclosure of what is held at the time of a request could, dependent on the content and timing, prejudice the right to a fair hearing of a councillor who has been accused of misconduct. 'Fishing expeditions', made under the FOIA in the hope of finding a conduct issue would doubtless be undesirable. There are no blanket exemptions, however, and a local authority will always need to examine the scope of statutory exemptions, and the public interest considerations, closely to establish whether, in the specific circumstances, any might apply to a given piece or type of information. On the other hand, processes within an authority for investigating allegations, and taking action in relation to any breach, need to be sufficiently transparent and accountable that they can properly command public confidence. It will be important, therefore, to have clearly in mind the purpose and limits of, and justification for, any exemptions that are claimed.

FOI exemptions

Personal data exemption

5.111   The most critical information about a conduct matter is likely to constitute the personal data of the councillor concerned. (It may well also be the personal data of others involved, including the complainant). The most likely exemption to consider, whether in relation to a live investigation or one that has been concluded, will be ss 40(2) and (3)(a)(i) of the FOIA. This confers an absolute exemption from disclosure on the personal data of any third party (ie a person who is not the requester), where such disclosure to the public, otherwise than under the FOI Act, would contravene any of the data protection principles. In practice, this focusses on whether the first data protection principle would be contravened. The principle requires any processing of personal data (including its disclosure) to be conducted 'fairly' and 'lawfully', and for at least one of the data processing conditions in Schedule 2 and, if the data are 'sensitive' personal data, also one of the conditions in Schedule 3, to be met.

Case Study (Part 1) – background

You are the Monitoring Officer of Notown BC. Cllr Smith is the Cabinet member for Resources. The council has recently let its office supplies contract to NewOffices Ltd. This has been controversial. The bid from NewOffices was not the lowest, although its service was considered in certain respects to be preferable to that of the lowest tenderer. Cllr Smith is said to have unfairly favoured the successful tenderer, and a complaint has been made that he was biased in its favour and wrongly influenced the Cabinet to agree its bid.

Officers who were present believe that he did not unduly influence the discussion, and that the successful tender was satisfactory.

The complaint is at an early stage of investigation, but it appears that Cllr Smith has had previous business dealings with some of the directors of the company, including possibly working for one of them, which he did not disclose to you. These dealings were 7–8 years ago, and were unrelated to his council work, or to this company.

The requester asks:

'(a) Are you investigating Cllr Smith for misconduct in relation to the letting of the office supplies contract to NewOffices Ltd?

(b) if so, what facts are held that give rise to any allegations of misconduct?

(c) if so, under which provisions of your conduct code is any investigation of Cllr Smith taking place?'

The investigation is still at an early stage, but your preliminary view is that it will be necessary to take a report to your standards committee, although you do not at present expect it to recommend that any action be taken.

Case Study (Part 2) – confirming or denying

The first thing to note is that the FOIA does not confer a right to interrogate a public authority – in other words, to force a public authority to answer questions about matters. The Act is concerned with disclosing information that answers a specific description. However, a public authority must help a requester. Therefore, even though the request may read like an interrogation of the public authority, it must read it as best it can as a request for information. If it is unclear, the correct response is to speak or write to the requester to get clarification.

The majority of the file on the investigation will constitute the personal data of Cllr Smith; and possibly also of other persons. The exemption in s 40 of the FOIA, is therefore relevant.

If, on the basis of the considerations below, you conclude that confirming to the public that Cllr Smith is under investigation would be a breach of the first data protection principle (eg on the ground that it was unfair to Cllr Smith, for reputational reasons, to disclose this fact before you have established that he has a case to answer), the duty to confirm or deny would not arise, under s 40(5) of the FOIA.

On the other hand, if you conclude that it would not be unfair to confirm that the information is held, perhaps because the fact of the investigation is already public knowledge, or because he has robustly denied the allegations publicly or to fellow councillors, you would confirm that information on this matter was held, and move to consider what, if anything, should be disclosed.

Fairness

5.112   The Information Commissioner (ICO) recommends that the issue of fairness should be considered first. The considerations relevant to fairness are set out in Part II of Schedule 1 to the DPA 1998. They are also examined at some length in the guidance of the Information Commission on s 40, which should be examined in its current form when a case arises. Part II of Schedule 1 lays down prescriptive requirements as to whether personal data have been obtained fairly, and how data subjects should be enabled to be aware, or kept informed, of who is processing their personal data and for what purpose (often met by 'Privacy Policies'; previously known as 'Fair Processing Notices'). The ICO's guidance in this context can be summarised under four headings:

● whether the information is 'sensitive personal data' (eg as to an individual's physical or mental health; or, the commission or alleged commission by him of an offence – see s 2 of the DPA 1998);

● the possible consequences of disclosure;

● the reasonable expectations of the data subject;

- any legitimate interests in the public having access to the information, balanced with the rights and freedoms of the data subject.[59]

Lawfulness

5.113 The requirement of lawfulness is that the processing should not be unlawful (eg under statute or common law), so that a disclosure which breached an implied or express obligation of confidence would be unlawful (unless, for example, there were an overwhelming argument in the public interest to disclose the information – eg because it disclosed the commission of an offence).

Data processing conditions

5.114 In terms of data processing conditions, Schedule 2 contains only two that are likely to be relevant in this context. Condition 1 is that the data subject has consented to the disclosure, which must be freely given in relation to the specific disclosure. More likely to apply is condition 6, that the processing is necessary for the purposes of the legitimate interests pursued by the third party to whom the disclosure is to be made (in this context, the requester), except where disclosure would be unwarranted in the particular case by reason of prejudice to the rights and freedoms or legitimate interests of the data subject. There is thus a three-part test:

- whether there is a legitimate (public) interest in the disclosure;

- whether the disclosure is 'necessary' to meet that legitimate interest;

- the disclosure should not cause unwarranted harm to the interests of the individual.

5.115 The first part will normally be met, on standard FOI grounds of openness and accountability, as well as any particular factors relevant to the case. The second, the test of necessity, is now to be interpreted as meaning whether there is a 'pressing social need' for any interference with privacy rights, and that the interference must be proportionate. (To some extent, in the writer's view, this test now effectively overlaps with the first and third parts, and contributes little to them. The second part may, however, depend on the identity of the requester or the purpose of the request. For example, if the requester is an investigative reporter who needs the information for legitimate journalistic purposes, that will strengthen the legitimate interest in the disclosure.)[60] The third part, usually the most important, will cover similar (but perhaps not identical) ground to that assessed in relation to fairness. The relevant factors will be:

- whether the information relates to the individual's public or private life;

---

59 See: 'Personal Information (s 40 and Reg 13)', Information Commissioner, Version 1.3 (August 2013), pp 13–29.
60 See the guidance on s 40, paras 101–112 on the three-part test.

- the potential harm or distress that may be caused by disclosure;

- whether the individual has objected to disclosure;

- the reasonable expectations of the individual as to disclosure or otherwise.

5.116   In relation to any sensitive personal data, a condition in Schedule 3 of the DPA will also need to be satisfied before the information can be disclosed. There is no general condition (as a counterpart to the 6th condition in Schedule 2), and so any disclosure of sensitive information has to be considered with care. The ICO advises that only two are relevant: where the data subject has given 'explicit consent' (condition 1); or, where the information has already been made public by the data subject (condition 5).[61] Outside these situations, on this basis, sensitive personal data of a third party should not be disclosed in response to an FOI request.

Case Study (Part 3) – disclosure or otherwise

In terms of fairness, the information does not appear to include any sensitive personal data.

The possible consequences of disclosure at this stage, while the investigation is current, could be expected to be severe for Cllr Smith in terms of reputation. His reasonable expectations are of privacy during the investigation, albeit the full facts are likely to need to go to the committee. There is a legitimate public interest in local residents knowing the facts, but this is balanced (and probably outweighed) by the member's right to privacy while the investigation is current. On balance, the fairness test for disclosure is not met.

In terms of a data processing condition, it is assumed that Cllr Smith will not consent to disclosure of his personal data. The three-part test under condition 6 produces similar reasoning to the consideration of fairness: there is a legitimate public interest in disclosure, although it may be necessary to disclose only part of the information held at this stage if that need is to be met. The intrusion on the privacy interests of Cllr Smith would, however, be unwarranted; especially before any hearing has taken place and before he has had an opportunity to respond to the allegations.

The timing of the request is, therefore, in this case critical to your response.

You refuse to disclose any of the information concerning Cllr Smith, under ss 40(2)(a) and 40(3)(a)(i), FOIA.

FOIA, s 40 – further exemption

5.117   A further ground of exemption under s 40 arises where, if the data subject were hypothetically to request the information himself or herself under their right to subject access, the authority would have a ground of exemption on

61 See guidance, paras 88–92.

which to deny them access under the DPA (FOIA, s 40(4)). Thus, as a general example, if a data subject asks under his subject access right to see the personal data held on about him by a data controller, but disclosure to him of some of the information held would be likely to prejudice the prevention or detection of crime (eg by tipping him off that he is under investigation by the police, alerting him to remove evidence), the data controller may apply an exemption under s 29(1) of the DPA, and avoid disclosure.

5.118   Where this exemption would apply under the DPA to a request from the data subject, it constitutes an exemption to an FOI request from another person; subject to the public interest test. The logic is that, if the data subject could not have the information, there is likely to be a good argument that an outside requester should not be able to require it to be placed in the public domain either. This will not always be the case, however; on occasion it may be important in the public interest that a matter is disclosed, even if previously regarded as confidential. For that reason, the exemption in s 40(4) is subject to the public interest test.

5.119   In the context of conduct investigations, it is possible that the following DPA 1998 exemptions from subject access may be relevant:

- ss 29(1) (as above) or 29(2): prejudice to crime prevention, or apprehension or prosecution of offenders;

- s 31(2)(a)(iii): prejudice from disclosure to proper discharge of functions designed to protect public against dishonesty, malpractice, or other seriously improper conduct;

- s 31(4)(a)(ii): prejudice from disclosure to proper discharge of functions of the local Ombudsman;

- Schedule 7, paragraph 7: prejudice to negotiations with data subject (where the information is a record of the intentions of the data controller);

- Schedule 7, paragraph 10: where the information is covered by legal professional privilege.

Case Study (Part 4) – additional s 40 exemption

You consider what would happen if Cllr Smith were to make a subject access request while the investigation is underway. You would be likely to refuse, since it would prejudice your investigation designed to protect the public from seriously improper conduct (DPA 1998, s 31(2)(a)(iii)). There may also be legal advice which you would expect to withhold under Schedule 7, paragraph 10 of the DPA. You therefore have one or more further potential grounds of exemption under s 40(4) of the FOIA. On the public interest test, you would be likely to conclude that the public interest in disclosure was outweighed by the public interest in not compromising the investigation.

5.120   It may be that the tests for disclosure in s 40 of the FOIA, and particularly those relating to the first data protection principle, may be difficult to meet in specific instances in relation to conduct allegations, matters being investigated, or (at least in some cases) past investigations.

Other FOI exemptions

5.121 Other FOI exemptions which may be relevant, in particular cases, to other information than personal data in relation to a conduct matter, may include the following:

- Section 22: information is held with a view to its publication at some future date, and it is reasonable in all the circumstances to withhold it until that date. (*Example*: where you will publish the investigation report after the conclusion of the process. In the case study above, however, the request is wider and the exemption would be unlikely to cover the whole of it, It would perhaps relate only part (b) of the request, for 'what facts are held that give rise to any allegations of misconduct', and would apply only to those facts that would be published in the report.)

- Section 30(2)(a)(iii) and (b), and s 31(2)(b): information was obtained or recorded by the authority from confidential sources, for the purposes of its functions relating to investigation under statutory powers of improper conduct. (*Example*: the authority's misconduct investigation includes some information supplied from its trading standards surveillance records.)

- Section 31(1)(g) and s 31(2)(b): information does not fall under s 30 (eg is not from a confidential source) but disclosure would be likely to prejudice the exercise by the authority of its functions for the purposes of ascertaining whether any person is responsible for improper conduct (*Example*: the authority concludes that disclosure in this case would be likely to harm its function of investigating allegations of improper conduct; perhaps by discouraging future whistleblowers, or persons willing to co-operate with an investigation.)

- Section 36(2)(b) or (c): in the reasonable opinion of the 'qualified person' (eg the Monitoring Officer), disclosure would be likely to inhibit the free and frank provision of advice, or would be likely otherwise to prejudice the effective conduct of public affairs. (*Example*: you (if you are the qualified person), or the officer in that role, reach the view on the facts that disclosure at this point will harm either the investigation concerned, or a future similar such process, by weakening the protection for a 'safe space' in which it can be conducted; so that views expressed are likely to be less open.)

- Section 41(1)(a): information was obtained by the public authority from any other person (including another public authority) and its disclosure to the public (otherwise than under the FOI Act) would constitute a breach of confidence actionable by that or another person (absolute exemption). (*Example*: the investigation has received information from a junior officer to whom an undertaking of confidentiality has been given.)

- Section 42(1): information is covered by legal professional privilege.

5.122   In each case, other than that in s 41, whether the exemption applies is subject to the public interest test (ie whether the public interest in maintaining the exemption outweighs the public interest in disclosure).

5.123   Depending on the facts, some (but not all) of the above exceptions may also give rise to an exemption from the duty to confirm or deny that the information is held; provided, where it applies, that the public interest test is met in relation to that aspect as well.

EIR exceptions

5.124   The EIR exception for third party personal data (Reg 13) is effectively the same as s 40 of the FOIA. Other exceptions that may be relevant may be:

- Reg 12(4)(d): material is still in course of completion, unfinished documents, or incomplete data (where the key public interest consideration will be harm to the authority's 'safe space' for consideration of issues). (*Example*: this exception may apply to a draft report to a standards committee, or one awaiting its approval, on a similar basis to s 36 of the FOIA, above.)

- Reg 12(4)(e): internal communications (very broad application in principle, but limited in practice by main public interest consideration above). (*Example*: this may apply to a report (if it is environmental information, and to any extent that the information is not personal data), or to other internal documents containing environmental information that have been shared with others in the authority; but the likely harm to the 'safe space' would need to be identified, and the public interest argument for non-disclosure carefully weighed.)

- Reg 12(5)(b): harm to ability of public authority to conduct an inquiry of a disciplinary nature (if found to be applicable to a conduct matter under the new regime). This exception also covers information subject to legal professional privilege (*Example*: this could be considered in support of the above exception.)

- Reg 12(5)(d): confidentiality of proceedings, where the confidentiality is provided by law (if found to apply to conduct proceedings under the new regime). (*Example*: this exception could have significance for conduct proceedings, where held in camera.)

- Reg 12(5)(f): harm from disclosure to the interests of a volunteer of the information, where the authority could not oblige him to provide it, it has no other entitlement to disclose it, and the supplier of the information has not consented to its disclosure. (*Example*: this may apply in cases where an investigating officer has been given information which the informant wishes to keep confidential, where there would be likely to be harm to the latter's interests if it were disclosed.)

  This might also apply in a case where a whistleblower was employed by an outside supplier of grounds maintenance services to the authority, and an allegation had been made of improper involvement of a councillor in the contract; or that a DPI was held in the company by the councillor that had not been disclosed. Although the whistleblower could not be sacked for making the disclosure, the authority might conclude that there would nonetheless be likely to be long-term harm to his employment prospects, which it could not protect; and thus conclude that the exemption applied.

5.125 Each of the above exceptions in Reg 12 of the EIR is subject to the public interest test.[62]

5.126 It does not appear that these exceptions would apply to the duty under the EIR to confirm or deny; since there is only one exception that is enabled to do so expressly.[63] It would appear, therefore, likely that an authority would be obliged to confirm or deny, in response to a request considered under the EIR, that information was held on a conduct matter, where (or to the extent that) the information concerned was environmental information as defined in the Regulations; although instances where this was the case are thought to be rare.

Subject access exemptions

5.127 Where the request comes from the person who is the subject of the information – typically from the person who is the subject of the investigation – the exemptions from subject access identified above in para **5.119** could also be relevant. The same would be the case if the request came from another person affected by a conduct allegation, whose personal data were amongst the recorded information on the matter.

General

5.128 The above considers the position from the point of view of the requester, whether it is personal information relating to him/herself or non-personal information. A public authority must be astute to the other side of the coin in relation to third-party personal information – in other words, personal information where the data subject is not (or not only) the requester. Where a public authority discloses the information in response to a request without being obliged to do so, that will constitute a breach of s 4(4) of the DPA, potentially sounding in damages. In short, there is a fine line to tread and the public authority must get it right.

5.129 A further important consideration for local authorities is the role of Part VA of the Local Government Act 1972, in giving the public rights of access to

---

62 Where more than one exception under the EIR is engaged, the authority may aggregate the public interest arguments against disclosure: *Office of Communications v Information Commissioner*, Case C-71/10, 28 July 2011.

63 Reg 12(6), referring to the exception in Reg 12(5)(a) for information whose disclosure would adversely affect international relations, defence, national security or public safety.

meetings and information, and also in enabling them to deliberate privately on certain conduct matters where these fall within the exemptions in Schedule 12A of that Act. The FOIA will recognise the operation of a regime such as Part VA, and may exempt such information under s 44 (prohibition on disclosure), at least where it is 'confidential' information within the narrow terms of that Schedule; or, more likely, the exemption in s 36 (prejudice to conduct of public affairs) will apply to the information as a whole that is 'exempt' under the 1972 Act.

5.130   Regulation 5(6) of the EIR provides, however, that any enactment or rule of law that would prevent the disclosure of information in accordance with those regulations shall not apply. This has been taken to reflect the status of the Regulations as giving effect to an EU provision. The provision has been stated in guidance to exclude Part VA from having effect as a barrier in itself to the disclosure of environmental information. If an EIR exception applies to the facts, however, the application of the exempt information regime in a given case may be taken to be a strong public interest factor against disclosure. An example would be the exception for internal communications (Reg 12(4)(e)), which could apply to the report or internal documents relating to the investigation; or, arguably, the exception for the confidentiality of proceedings of the authority provided by law (Reg 12(5)(d)); although the issue would be whether exempt proceedings were 'confidential' in these terms.

5.131   There is no suggestion that Reg 5(6) would limit the operation of the exception in Reg 13 of the EIR, in relation to disclosure of third party personal data; presumably because that provision, in reflecting the DPA, is itself giving effect to an EU provision.

G   CONCLUSION

5.132   This Chapter has outlined the main processes, and considerations relating to them, through which councils may face challenges in relation to decisions on conduct: by judicial review of a decision tainted by unlawful conduct; by a complaint of maladministration to the Ombudsman on a conduct matter; or, and more likely as a preliminary step in a conduct matter, by requesting information held relating to a member's conduct. Prudent councils, and councillors, will be aware of the potential for all of them in their day to day decision-making, and when considering not only whether their conduct is above reproach, but is demonstrably so.

CHAPTER 6

Offences

> 'To every subject in this land, no matter how powerful, I would use Thomas
> Fuller's words over 300 years ago:
> "Be you ever so high, the law is above you."'

Lord Denning MR[1]

	What this chapter covers	
A	Introduction	6.1
B	Offences under s 34 of the Localism Act 2011	6.3
C	Misconduct in public office	6.23
D	Offences under the Bribery Act 2010	6.30
E	Restrictions on voting on council tax matters	6.39
F	Disqualification by reason of criminal conviction	6.40
G	Conclusion	6.41

A INTRODUCTION

6.1   The law expects that councillors who exercise power and influence in their councils do so for the public good, not maliciously or for their own benefit. Where they act improperly, or fail to act when they should, the law provides both criminal sanction and civil redress. This chapter is primarily concerned with the statutory and common law offences that may be committed by councillors when performing their public functions.

6.2   Elected members are required to observe various ethical principles of public life (see **Chapters 2** and **7**), including: selflessness, integrity, objectivity, accountability, openness, honesty and leadership. The Localism Act 2011 (the Act) and the Bribery Act 2010 (the 2010 Act) criminalise behaviour that is directly contrary to those principles and which is likely to undermine trust in local government. They do not provide a complete code, however, focusing instead on financial non-disclosure and corruption. Other serious abuses are covered by the common law offence of misconduct in a public office. Where a councillor's misconduct has caused loss to an individual he may be liable in damages for the tort of misfeasance in public office. These offences – although

---

1   *Gouriet v Union of Post Office Workers* [1977] QB 729, 761–762.

important in underpinning the standards regimes – are intended to be reserved for the worst types of conduct. In all other cases, the conduct of councillors is a matter for non-criminal investigation and determination.

B OFFENCES UNDER S 34 OF THE LOCALISM ACT 2011

6.3   Under s 34 of the Act, councillors in England who fail to meet their obligations in relation to disclosable pecuniary interests (DPIs)[2] may be guilty of a criminal offence. These obligations are discussed in more detail in **Chapter 3** but may be summarised as follows:

- if a councillor, or their partner, has a DPI then they are required to register that DPI with the monitoring officer;[3]

- if a councillor is present at a meeting and has an unregistered DPI (including any DPIs of his/her partner) then the councillor must declare the DPI and not participate in any discussion or vote on the matter without a dispensation to do so;[4]

- if a councillor is to act alone in a matter and is aware that they have a DPI in that matter they must not take any steps or further steps in the matter and must register the DPI.[5]

6.4   The introduction of criminal sanctions for non-compliance strengthens the above obligations for councillors to disclose their personal financial interests and not to participate in council business when they have such an interest.[6] The aim is, of course, to ensure that councillors are acting in the public interest rather than using their position for their own financial benefit, and – perhaps just as importantly – to ensure that the public have confidence that this will be the case. Councillors must not only do the right thing but must also be seen to be doing the right thing. The duties to disclose interests are about being open and transparent and the criminalisation of non-compliance with those duties serves to emphasise the seriousness with which transparency in public office is to be taken. The message is clear: transparency is essential and councillors who abuse their position for personal gain will not get away with it lightly.

6.5   Albeit the addition of criminal liability suggests a tougher approach than the previous standards regime, as discussed further at para **6.12**, these criminal

---

2 Localism Act 2011, s 30(3) and Relevant Authorities (Disclosable Pecuniary Interests) Regulations 2012, SI 2012/1664. In summary, the specified DPIs are: paid employment; member sponsorship; an ongoing contract with the authority; a beneficial interest in or licence to occupy land in the authority's area; a tenancy granted by the authority to a corporate body in which a beneficial interest is held; and beneficial interests in securities of a business in the authority's area that exceed a certain value.

3 Localism Act 2011, s 30.

4 Localism Act 2011, s 31(1), (2) and (4).

5 Localism Act 2011, s 31(6), (7) and (8).

6 Localism Act 2011, ss 30(1), 31(2), 31(3), 31(4), 31(7) and 31(8). See also **Chapter 3**.

offences are in fact reserved for a relatively narrow range of circumstances as they only relate to what councillors must do about DPIs, ie those interests specified in the Relevant Authorities (Disclosable Pecuniary Interests) Regulations (2012 Regulations).[7] The offences do not relate to any responsibilities there might be in relation to broader interests. They are limited to what appear to have been deemed the more serious and influential financial matters and, as such, it may well be right to say that it is unlikely there will be vast numbers of prosecutions under these provisions. That said, these are still relatively new offences and it is not yet fully known the extent to which they might be invoked.

6.6   Councillors reading this book may consider that these offences do not apply to them because they are honest and acting in the public interest, whereas the offences are intended to catch those who are not. Whilst stamping out dishonest motives might be the primary intention of s 34, however, there are certainly some conceivable scenarios in which a councillor might, at least on the face of things, meet the elements of the s 34 offences without having acted in a deliberate or corrupt manner (see para **6.16**) and it cannot be assumed that in those circumstances there will be no attempt to prosecute (whether ultimately a prosecution will succeed or not). Councillors do therefore need to be aware of the requirements, be vigilant in compliance and ensure that they do not open up any possibility for prosecution as a result of carelessness.

Section 34(1): failure to disclose a DPI and/or participation in council business despite having a DPI

6.7   S 34(1) of the Act provides:

'(1) A person commits an offence if, without reasonable excuse, the person—

(a)   fails to comply with an obligation imposed on the person by section 30(1) or 31(2), (3) or (7),

(b)   participates in any discussion or vote in contravention of section 31(4), or

(c)   takes any steps in contravention of section 31(8).'

6.8   Under this section, it is a criminal offence if a councillor does any of the following without reasonable excuse:

* fails to comply with any of the duties to disclose DPIs as set out in ss 30(1), 31(2), 31(3) and 31(7);[8]

* participates in a meeting (by discussion or vote) when he/she has a DPI in a matter being, or to be, considered at the meeting contrary to s 31(4);[9]

---

7   SI 2012/1664, see Sch 1. See also **Chapter 3**.
8   Localism Act 2011, s 34(1)(a). See also **Chapter 3** for a description of the requirements.
9   Localism Act 2011, s 34(1)(b).

• takes steps in a matter in which he/she is acting alone when he/she is aware of having a DPI in the matter, in contravention of s 31(8).[10]

6.9 An offence will only be committed under s 34(1) if any of the contraventions listed above are 'without reasonable excuse'. From the construction of the provision it appears that the absence of a reasonable excuse is probably one of the definitional elements of the offence which the prosecution must prove.[11] In light of this and based on other statutes which use the same or similar wording – for example, s 7(6) of the Road Traffic Act 1988 – it is likely that for the s 34(1) offence, the defendant will have an evidential burden to raise the issue of reasonable excuse but once raised the prosecution must disprove it to the criminal standard.[12]

6.10 What constitutes a reasonable excuse is not prescribed in the Act and, in the absence of any judicial guidance on the s 34(1) offence, there will be scope for debate about whether a defence of reasonable excuse can be made out. The inclusion of this element does suggest that for a successful prosecution there may need to be a degree of culpability or blame attributable to the councillor. Certainly, in cases concerning the offence of misconduct in public office the courts[13] have found that the words 'without reasonable excuse or justification' denote some culpability[14] and it may be reasonable to conclude that the same would apply to the similar wording in the s 34(1) offence (which of course also relates to the conduct of persons in public office). Having said that, it should be noted that the other elements of the offence of misconduct in public office do expressly denote culpability (as for that offence the defendant must have 'wilfully' neglected to perform his duty or 'wilfully' misconducted himself). That is in contrast to the offence under s 34(1) of the Act which simply provides that the defendant is guilty if he commits the prohibited conduct without reasonable excuse thus not obviously requiring a mental element (eg dishonesty, intention, recklessness) which might be taken to suggest that culpability is not necessarily required.

6.11 That there ought to be a degree of blameworthiness for the s 34(1) offence to be made out would accord with the Government's clear intentions in introducing the offences – that is, to deter and punish any councillors who might *intentionally* abuse their position in public office for personal financial gain. In a press release issued by the Department of Communities and Local Government (DCLG) in June 2012 the offences were described as 'Tough new measures that

---

10 Localism Act 2011, s 34(1)(c).
11 That has been the approach to the inclusion of similar wording for other statutory offences, for example the offence of assisting an offence under s 4(1) of the Criminal Law Act 1967, which was considered in *R v Brindley* 55 CR App R 258 in which it was said that all four elements of the offence (including that the act was done 'without lawful authority or reasonable excuse') have to be proved.
12 See, in the context of the offence under s 7(6) of the Road Traffic Act 1988, *McKeon v DPP* [2008] RTR 14, DC; *Rowland v Thorpe* [1970] 3 All ER 195; and *DC and R v Harling* [1970] RTR 441, CA.
13 See **Section C** below.
14 *R v L (D)* [2011] EWCA Crim 1259; [2011] Cr App R 14 and *A-G's Ref (No 3 of 2003)* [2005] QB 73.

crack down on genuine corruption and increase transparency in public life'.[15] Another slightly earlier DCLG press release quoted Bob Neill MP as saying:

> 'Instead of having hundreds of expensive and frivolous investigations hanging over their heads local councillors will be free to get on with the job of getting the best for their local area. But far from letting councillors off the hook without any checks we are ensuring that they conform to the highest standards and anyone who abuses their position for personal gain can expect to face the full force of the law.'[16]

6.12   Whilst the offences may have been primarily aimed at those who deliberately abuse their position – and the inclusion of the 'without reasonable excuse' element in s 34(1) may tend to support that – there is still uncertainty over precisely what would constitute a reasonable excuse for this offence. The phrase 'without reasonable excuse' in some other statutory offences has been construed quite narrowly. For example, the Court of Appeal has considered the offence of failing without reasonable excuse to provide an evidential specimen contrary to s 9(3) of the Road Traffic Act 1972 (now s 7(6) of the Road Traffic Act 1988) and said that to be capable of being a 'reasonable excuse' the factor relied on must arise out of a physical or mental inability to provide a specimen (of urine or blood) or would entail a substantial risk to health to give it.[17] The courts have thus, quite significantly, limited what is even *capable* of being a reasonable excuse for this offence.

6.13   Similarly, the courts have restricted what constitutes a 'reasonable excuse' for the offence of having an offensive weapon in a public place contrary to s 1 of the Prevention of Crime Act 1953. The Court of Appeal has specifically said that the cases of this offence where the defence of reasonable excuse will be available are restricted[18] although it has also said that the words 'reasonable excuse' should not be fettered to the extent of saying that only self-defence could constitute reasonable excuse.[19] Various cases have considered what might be a reasonable excuse for this offence (eg carrying a weapon as part of a fancy dress outfit[20]) and what could not be (eg carrying a weapon as a general precaution[21]), such that in the context of this offence there is judicial guidance about what would be sufficient.

---

15 DCLG press release 'New rules to ensure greater town hall transparency' (28 June 2012) available at https://www.gov.uk/government/news/new-rules-to-ensure-greater-town-hall-transparency.

16 DCLG press release 'New reforms will stop town hall corruption and culture of malicious complaints' (11 April 2012) available at https://www.gov.uk/government/news/new-reforms-will-stop-town-hall-corruption-and-culture-of-malicious-complaints--2.

17 *R v Lennard* [1973] 1 WLR 483, CA. See also *R v John (Graham)* [1974] 1 WLR 624 in which it was held that religious beliefs, however sincerely held, could not, in law, amount to an excuse for failing to supply a specimen.

18 *Densu* [1998] 1 Cr App R 400.

19 *DPP v Patterson* [2004] EWHC 2744 (Admin).

20 *Houghton v Chief Constable of Greater Manchester* (1987) 84 Cr App R 319.

21 *Evans v Hughes* [1972] 3 All ER 42.

6.14   It is not yet known the extent to which the courts will restrict the offence in s 34(1) of the Act and it may not be possible to rely on the case law dealing with other offences to demonstrate what the words should mean in the Act offence. What these other cases can tell us, however, is that the courts have sought to limit what at first seems to be a very wide range of matters that might constitute a reasonable excuse. The basis for such limitation has generally been an attempt to discern what parliament must have intended and is thus driven by the underlying policy reasons for the creation of the statutory offence. In the two examples of other statutory offences (failing to provide a specimen and having an offensive weapons), it is clear that the need to protect the public from drink drivers and dangerous persons is the reason for limiting the scope of the reasonable excuse defence.[22] As noted above, the government's intentions in introducing the offences in s 34 of the Localism Act appears to have been primarily to ensure that councillors do not abuse their position for their own gain. This might suggest that a more liberal approach to the 'reasonable excuse' element of the offence would be appropriate where there is no evidence of intention or other culpability. However, since at the time of writing there is not yet any case law on these offences and in light of the stricter approach taken in some of the other statutory offences, it is prudent to assume that matters which people might generally think of as reasonable excuses for behaviour (eg honest mistake) may not be sufficient. That is to say, it may not necessarily only be deliberate behaviour that will be caught by the s 34 offences. Councillors who have acted honestly but nevertheless failed to register or declare a DPI in accordance with ss 30 and 31 may have no 'reasonable excuse' and thus may face prosecution.

6.15   If, for example, a councillor forgot to register a DPI within 28 days of becoming a member, contrary to s 30(1), he/she may technically have committed an offence under s 34(1)(a). Whether or not the councillor in that scenario would be guilty of the offence would depend upon whether it was considered, in all of the circumstances of the case, that forgetting to register the DPI amounted to a 'reasonable excuse'. There may have been good reasons for forgetting (eg being ill or suffering a bereavement) but whether those reasons (which in day to day life may be good ones) would be sufficient to constitute reasonable excuse is far from certain.[23] Alternatively, whilst not deliberate, it might have been due to carelessness or oversight which is obviously less likely to be considered to constitute a reasonable excuse. The point is that it may be arguable either way. Although in this particular example – unless some harm came from the non-disclosure – it may be fairly unlikely that there would be

---

22 See for example the discussion in *R v John (Graham)* at 629.

23 In the context of the offence of having an offensive weapon in a public place (s 1 of the Prevention of Crime Act 1953), the issue of forgetfulness has been considered and it has been held that whilst simple forgetfulness would not be sufficient to amount to a reasonable excuse, the combination of forgetfulness and other circumstances may be relevant to the issue of whether there is a reasonable excuse: see for example *Glidewell* [1999] EWCA Crim 1221; also *Hilton v Canterbury Crown Court* [2009] EWHC 2876. It has also been said that factors causing forgetfulness such as illness or the taking of medication would be relevant: *Tsap* [2008] EWCA Crim 2679. These issues are discussed in Archbold 2015 at 24–184 and Blackstone's Criminal Practice 2015 at B12.161.

a prosecution, there remains a risk if councillors do not comply with the disclosure requirements in ss 30 and 31 of the Act, whether or not they are acting deliberately or dishonestly. Such 'excuses', would of course at least be mitigating factors and may reduce the sentence imposed even though the reason was insufficient as a defence.

6.16   Given the criminalisation of these conduct issues, it is perhaps not surprising that the Act has limited the criminal offences to disclosure failures in relation to the relatively narrow range of interests that are DPIs. Authorities may of course go further than the legislation in their own codes of conduct and may require councillors to disclose, and not participate in council business concerning, a far broader range of interests (financial or otherwise) than just DPIs. Whether to do so, however, is now left to individual authorities to decide for themselves – which of course accords wholly with the policy of localism. In practice many authorities have decided to include a far broader range of interests than those prescribed by the Act and councillors must therefore ensure that they know what their own code requires of them. In any event it ought not to be forgotten that councillors have a duty to act in accordance with the seven principles of public life and must disclose any interests that they consider necessary in order to do that, even if those do not fall within the Act or their code of conduct. Whilst breach of any additional disclosure requirements or the seven principles will not be a criminal offence, there may still be some form of sanction imposed (see **Chapter 2, Section F**).

Section 34(2): providing false or misleading information when registering and declaring DPIs

6.17   Section 34(2) provides:

'(2) A person commits an offence if under section 30(1) or 31(2), (3) or (7) the person provides information that is false or misleading and the person—

(a)   knows that the information is false or misleading, or

(b)   is reckless as to whether the information is true and not misleading.'

6.18   In addition to the s 34(1) offence of failing to disclose a DPI, by s 34(2), if a councillor does register or declare a DPI but, in doing so, knowingly or recklessly provides information that is false or misleading then he/she will be guilty of an offence. This offence is perhaps more straightforward than s 34(1) in that it simply provides a means to punish councillors who act deliberately and dishonestly or – at best – recklessly with regards to the information they disclose. The concept of recklessness as the mental element in an offence carries with it a degree of culpability such as to make the behaviour unacceptable for councillors and thus punishable by criminal sanction. There is no defence of reasonable excuse available for the s 34(2) offence.

Prosecutions

6.19   A prosecution for an offence under s 34 can only be instituted by or on behalf of the Director of Public Prosecutions.[24] The authority cannot therefore bring its own prosecution and must instead report any breaches (or potential breaches) to the police or CPS so that a decision on whether to charge can be made. Some authorities have in place a published protocol between the authority's monitoring officer and the local police constabulary for the reporting of potential offences and sharing of information, setting out the responsibilities and agreed approach of both parties. For example, some protocols stipulate that the monitoring officer will not inform the councillor or other persons when a possible breach is first identified by them or the police in case doing so should jeopardise any investigations or potential prosecution.

6.20   The time limit for bringing a prosecution under s 34 is 12 months from the date on which the prosecuting authority was satisfied that it had the evidence to warrant prosecution. No proceedings may, however, be brought more than three years after the commission of the offence or, where the contravention is a continuing one, after the last date on which the offence was committed.[25]

Penalties

6.21   The offences in s 34 are summary only offences which will be dealt with by the magistrates' court. The criminal penalties available to the court on a conviction are:

● A fine not exceeding level 5 on the standard scale, currently £5000 (s 34(3)).

● Disqualification from being or becoming a councillor for up to 5 years (s 34(4)).

In addition to the criminal penalties there is also of course the mere fact of a criminal record and the reputational damage that prosecution is likely to cause whether or not a conviction is ultimately secured.

6.22   The existence of the offences in s 34 of the Act is intended to provide nationwide consistency when it comes to councillors who deliberately abuse their position for personal financial gain, ensuring that a tough line is taken against them to the extent that they may be prosecuted and fined for their behaviour. Beyond that, however, central government has taken a back seat and left it to individual authorities to determine what is or is not necessary to be disclosed and what sanctions, if any, are to apply where councillors do not comply. As highlighted by the example at para **6.15** above, the inclusion of the 'reasonable excuse' defence in s 34(1) means that there is some degree of uncertainty about whether councillors who have mistakenly, as opposed to deliberately, failed to comply with the statutory obligations will be guilty of an offence. Given those

24 Localism Act 2011, s 34(5).
25 Localism Act 2011, s 31(7).

uncertainties and the potentially severe consequences, councillors need to be vigilant about ensuring their compliance. If there is any doubt it is certainly advisable to register the interest.

Question: Some months after Councillor X was elected her husband, Y, bought a small restaurant in the town centre with the intention of expanding it into a bigger restaurant so as to increase his profit. Y makes a planning application to the local authority. The application is to be discussed at a meeting of the planning committee on which Councillor X sits. Councillor X discloses her interest to the meeting and does not participate in any discussion or vote. In fact, she decides to leave the room whilst the matter is discussed. She thereafter forgets about it and does not notify the monitoring officer of her disclosure to the meeting. Has Councillor X done enough to avoid potential prosecution?

Answer: Possibly not. Although Councillor X has properly complied with her duties under s 31(2) and (4) (ie she disclosed her interest to the meeting and did not participate in any discussion or vote on the matter at the meeting), she did not however notify the monitoring officer within 28 days of her disclosure to the meeting thereby acting in contravention of s 31(3). She may therefore be guilty of an offence under s 34(1)(a). Whether or not the offence could be made out would depend upon whether Councillor X could establish that she had a reasonable excuse (see above).

C MISCONDUCT IN PUBLIC OFFICE

6.23   Where a councillor, acting as a councillor, wilfully neglects to perform his duty or wilfully misconducts himself in a way which amounts to an abuse of the public trust, he commits the offence of misconduct in a public office.[26] It is a serious offence with a maximum sentence of life imprisonment. The offence can be tried only on indictment (in other words, only in the Crown Court). In essence, the offence involves a serious abuse of the powers and responsibilities of office.

6.24   The elements of the offence[27] are:

- a public officer acting as such;

- wilfully neglects to perform his duty and/or wilfully misconducts himself;

- to such a degree as to amount to an abuse of the public's trust in the office holder;

- without reasonable excuse or justification.

---

26 *Attorney General's Reference (No 3 of 2003)* [2005] QB 73.
27 See *Attorney General's Reference (No 3 of 2003)* [2005] QB 73, para 61; *R v ABC* [2015] EWCA Crim 539, paras 17–19.

6.25   There is no doubt that councillors are public officers for these purposes.[28] Wilful misconduct means 'deliberately doing something which is wrong knowing it to be wrong or with reckless[29] indifference as to whether it is wrong or not'.[30] For an offence to be committed there must be an awareness of the duty to act or a subjective recklessness as to the existence of the duty. The recklessness test will apply to: (a) the question whether in particular circumstances a duty arises at all, (b) the conduct of the defendant if it does, (c) the legality of the defendant's act or omission, and (d) the consequences of the act or omission.[31]

6.26   When the offence of misconduct in public office is alleged to have been committed in circumstances which involve the acquisition of property by theft or fraud, and in particular when the holder of a public office is alleged to have made improper claims for public funds in circumstances which are said to be criminal, an essential ingredient of the offence is proof that the defendant was dishonest.[32] A defendant is dishonest if according to the ordinary standards of reasonable and honest people what he did was dishonest and the defendant must have realised that.[33]

6.27   The offence relates only to serious misconduct. In *Attorney General's Reference (No 3 of 2003)*,[34] the Court of Appeal held:

> '56 ... there must be a serious departure from proper standards before the criminal offence is committed; and a departure not merely negligent but amounting to an affront to the standing of the public office held. The threshold is a high one requiring conduct so far below acceptable standards as to amount to an abuse of the public's trust in the office holder. A mistake, even a serious one, will not suffice. The motive with which a public officer acts may be relevant to the decision whether the public's trust is abused by the conduct. ...

> 57 ... the element of culpability "must be of such a degree that the misconduct impugned is calculated to injure the public interest so as to call for condemnation and punishment". The constitutional context has changed but the rationale for the offence remains that stated by Lord Mansfield CJ in *R v Bembridge* 3 Doug KB 327: those who hold public office carry out their duties for the benefit of the public as a whole and, if they abuse their office, there is a breach of the public's trust. ...

> 58 It will normally be necessary to consider the likely consequences of the breach in deciding whether the conduct falls so far below the standard of conduct to be expected of the officer as to constitute the offence. The

---

28 *R v William James Speechley* [2005] Cr App R (S) 15.
29 A person acts recklessly with respect to a circumstance when he is aware of a risk that it exists or would exist. A person acts recklessly with respect to a result when he is aware of a risk that it would occur, and it was, in the circumstances known to him, unreasonable to take that risk: *R v G* [2004] 1 AC 1034.
30 *Attorney General's Reference (No 3 of 2003)*, para 28.
31 *Attorney General's Reference (No 3 of 2003)*, para 30.
32 *R v W* [2010] QB 787, para 14.
33 *R v Ghosh* [1982] QB 1053.
34 [2005] QB 73.

conduct cannot be considered in a vacuum: the consequences likely to follow from it, viewed subjectively as in *R v G* [2004] 1 AC 1034, will often influence the decision as to whether the conduct amounted to an abuse of the public's trust in the officer. A default where the consequences are likely to be trivial may not possess the criminal quality required; a similar default where the damage to the public or members of the public is likely to be great may do so. ...'

6.28　In *R v ABC*,[35] the Court of Appeal held that the conduct must be worthy of condemnation and punishment, and must have the effect of harming the public interest.[36] For the holder of a public office to be convicted of misconduct in a public office, he must know of the facts and circumstances which would lead the right-thinking member of the public to conclude that the misconduct was such as to amount to an abuse of the public's trust in the office holder, although it need not be shown that the office holder had himself reached that conclusion.[37] Fortunately, there have been few prosecutions brought against local authority members for misconduct in public office. The only recent case of note is *R v William Speechley* [2005] 2 Cr App R (S) 15, in which the defendant, a county council leader, was convicted of seeking to influence the route of a road improvement scheme so as to enhance the value of land he owned. As a county councillor the defendant should have declared his interest in the land, but in discussions with officers and at meetings of the county, district and parish councils which he attended the defendant failed to do so. In rejecting his appeal against an 18-month sentence of imprisonment, the Court of Appeal said:

'55 If the new by-pass followed the off-line route many people, including the Appellant, believed that it would substantially increase the value of the Appellant's land. That is clear from the finding of the jury, having regard to the way in which they were directed by the judge. With that knowledge the Appellant, as Leader of the County Council, chose to conceal his interest and to press for the off-line route using the full weight of his office and his personality to further the case. This was not a case of oversight. His conduct, as the jury found, involved dishonesty. Indeed, it was dishonesty that was the driving force. Advice was ignored. Any official who attempted to withstand the Appellant had also to consider his own position. As the judge said, the public must have confidence in our public institutions. When someone in a high position is convicted of this sort of misconduct a severe sentence is entirely appropriate. But for the mitigating factors to which Mr Harbage referred, the sentence could well have been longer.'

6.29　The offence of misconduct in public office is allied to the civil tort of misfeasance in public office.[38] Where a claimant has suffered loss or damage by

---

35 [2015] EWCA Crim 539.
36 Para 34.
37 Paras 48–49.
38 As to which, see *Three Rivers DC v Governor and Company of the Bank of England (No 3)* [2003] 2 AC 1; *Watkins v Secretary of State for the Home Department* [2006] 2 AC 395.

reason of the misconduct of a member acting as such, and the member acted with intent to injure the claimant or with knowledge that he had no power to do the act complained of and that the act would probably injure the claimant, the claimant can seek damages from the member or, depending on the circumstances, the authority.[39]

D OFFENCES UNDER THE BRIBERY ACT 2010

6.30   The Bribery Act 2010 prohibits the offering, giving, soliciting and acceptance of money or other advantages in order to induce or reward the improper performance of public and other functions. The explanatory notes to the Act summarise it in this way:

> '4. The Act replaces the offences at common law and under the Public Bodies Corrupt Practices Act 1889, the Prevention of Corruption Act 1906 and the Prevention of Corruption Act 1916 (known collectively as the Prevention of Corruption Acts 1889 to 1916 and which will be repealed …) with two general offences. The first covers the offering, promising or giving of an advantage (broadly, offences of bribing another person). The second deals with the requesting, agreeing to receive or accepting of an advantage (broadly, offences of being bribed). The formulation of these two offences abandons the agent/principal relationship on which the previous law was based in favour of a model based on an intention to induce improper conduct. …'

6.31   The 2010 Act applies to offences committed on or after 1 July 2011. The common law and statutory provisions referred to in the explanatory notes above will continue to apply to offences committed before that date.

6.32   Section 1 of the 2010 Act creates the offence of bribing another person. It does so by reference to two sets of circumstances (called Case 1 and Case 2) in which the offer, promise or giving of money or other advantage is unlawful. It states:

> '(1) A person ("P") is guilty of an offence if either of the following cases applies.
>
> (2) Case 1 is where—
>
>> (a) P offers, promises or gives a financial or other advantage[40] to another person, and

---

39 A local authority may be liable for misfeasance in public office where a group of councillors in committee act with malice: see *Jones v Swansea City Council* [1990] 1 WLR 1453; *Barnard v Restormel Borough Council* [1998] 3 PLR 27. The same is likely to be the case where one or more members on an authority's executive act with malice.

40 The Act does not define 'financial or other advantage'. As to this, the explanatory notes to the Act state: 'The meaning of "financial or other advantage" is left to be determined as a matter of common sense by the tribunal of fact.'

    (b)   P intends the advantage—

        (i)   to induce a person to perform improperly a relevant function or activity, or

        (ii) to reward a person for the improper performance of such a function or activity.

  (3) Case 2 is where—

    (a)   P offers, promises or gives a financial or other advantage to another person, and

    (b)   P knows or believes that the acceptance of the advantage would itself constitute the improper performance of a relevant function or activity.

  (4) In case 1 it does not matter whether the person to whom the advantage is offered, promised or given is the same person as the person who is to perform, or has performed, the function or activity concerned.

  (5) In cases 1 and 2 it does not matter whether the advantage is offered, promised or given by P directly or through a third party.'

6.33   A 'relevant function' is defined in s 3 of the 2010 Act in these terms:

'(1) For the purposes of this Act a function or activity is a relevant function or activity if—

    (a)   it falls within subsection (2), and

    (b)   meets one or more of conditions A to C.

  (2) The following functions and activities fall within this subsection—

    (a)   any function of a public nature,

    (b)   any activity connected with a business,

    (c)   any activity performed in the course of a person's employment,

    (d)   any activity performed by or on behalf of a body of persons (whether corporate or unincorporate).

  (3) Condition A is that a person performing the function or activity is expected to perform it in good faith.

  (4) Condition B is that a person performing the function or activity is expected to perform it impartially.

  (5) Condition C is that a person performing the function or activity is in a position of trust by virtue of performing it.

  ...'

6.34   Section 4(1)(a) of the 2010 Act states that a relevant function or activity is performed improperly if it is performed in breach of a relevant expectation.

A relevant function or activity is to be treated as being performed improperly if there is a failure to perform the function or activity and that failure is itself a breach of a relevant expectation (s 4(1)(b)). Section 4(2) goes on to say that a 'relevant expectation':

> '(a) in relation to a function or activity which meets condition A or B, means the expectation mentioned in the condition concerned, and
>
> (b) in relation to a function or activity which meets condition C, means any expectation as to the manner in which, or the reasons for which, the function or activity will be performed that arises from the position of trust mentioned in that condition.'

6.35   For the purposes of the Act the test of what is expected is a test of what a reasonable person in the United Kingdom would expect in relation to the performance of the type of function or activity concerned (s 5(1)).

Example of offence under s 1 – Case 1

A property developer offers money to a member of a planning committee to vote in favour of his development scheme. Here the developer is offering a financial advantage to another person to perform improperly a relevant function or activity – the determination of planning applications, being a function of a public nature and an activity performed by and on behalf of a body of persons. The relevant function would be performed improperly because to vote in favour of a development scheme in return for money would breach the expectation that members of the planning committee would cast their vote in good faith and impartially. It would make no difference to the developer's criminal liability if the offer was made through an intermediary, nor if the money was to be given to the member's spouse.

Example of offence under s 1 – Case 2

A member of a council offers to support an increase in the chief executive's remuneration in return for the chief executive's agreement to favour a tender submitted to the council by a company in which the member has an interest. Here the member is offering a financial or other advantage to another person to perform improperly a relevant function or activity – the selection of tenders, being a function of a public nature, a business activity and an activity performed in the course of a person's employment. The relevant function would be performed improperly because to favour a tender in anticipation of a reward would breach the expectation that a council officer would take procurement decisions in good faith and impartially. The chief executive may also be said to be in a position of trust in which he would also be expected to act in good faith and impartially.

6.36   Section 2 of the Act creates offences relating to the soliciting or receipt of bribes. In a similar fashion to s 1, it does so by reference to four sets of circumstances (Cases 3–6) in which the person who benefits or might benefit from a bribe commits an offence. It states:

'(1) A person ("R") is guilty of an offence if any of the following cases applies.

(2) Case 3 is where R requests, agrees to receive or accepts a financial or other advantage intending that, in consequence, a relevant function or activity should be performed improperly (whether by R or another person).

(3) Case 4 is where—

(a) R requests, agrees to receive or accepts a financial or other advantage, and

(b) the request, agreement or acceptance itself constitutes the improper performance by R of a relevant function or activity.

(4) Case 5 is where R requests, agrees to receive or accepts a financial or other advantage as a reward for the improper performance (whether by R or another person) of a relevant function or activity.

(5) Case 6 is where, in anticipation of or in consequence of R requesting, agreeing to receive or accepting a financial or other advantage, a relevant function or activity is performed improperly—

(a) by R, or

(b) by another person at R's request or with R's assent or acquiescence.

(6) In cases 3 to 6 it does not matter—

(a) whether R requests, agrees to receive or accepts (or is to request, agree to receive or accept) the advantage directly or through a third party,

(b) whether the advantage is (or is to be) for the benefit of R or another person.

(7) In cases 4 to 6 it does not matter whether R knows or believes that the performance of the function or activity is improper.

(8) In case 6, where a person other than R is performing the function or activity, it also does not matter whether that person knows or believes that the performance of the function or activity is improper.'

Example of offence under s 2 – Case 3

A member who sits on a council's licensing committee offers to vote in favour of a football club's application for an alcohol licence in return for the gift of a season ticket. Here the member requests a financial or other advantage intending that, in consequence, a relevant function or activity – the determination of licensing applications, being a public function and an activity performed by or on behalf of a body of persons – should be performed improperly. The relevant function or activity would be performed improperly because to vote in favour of a licensing application in return for a gift would breach the expectation that members of the licensing committee would determine licensing applications in good faith and impartially.

Example of offence under s 2 – Case 4

A member demands that an environmental health officer ends an investigation into clear breaches by a restaurant of food hygiene legislation. Under duress, the officer does so. The member acted with the intention of approaching the restaurant proprietor afterwards to ask for discounted dining rates. Here, in anticipation of the member requesting a financial or other advantage, a relevant function or activity – the investigation of food hygiene offences, being a function of a public nature, an activity performed in the course of a person's employment and an activity performed by or on behalf of a body of persons – is performed improperly by the officer at the member's request. The relevant function or activity would be performed improperly because for the officer to discontinue an investigation without good reason under pressure from a member would breach the expectation that officers investigating food hygiene offences would act in good faith.

Prosecution

6.37 No proceedings for an offence under the 2010 Act may be instituted in England and Wales except by or with the consent of the Director of Public Prosecutions or the Director of the Serious Fraud Office.[41]

Penalties

6.38 A person guilty of an offence under ss 1 or 2 of the 2010 Act is liable: (a) on summary conviction, to imprisonment for a term not exceeding six months, or to a fine not exceeding the statutory maximum (currently £5,000), or to both; (b) on conviction on indictment, to imprisonment for a term not exceeding ten years, or to a fine, or to both.[42]

E   RESTRICTIONS ON VOTING ON COUNCIL TAX MATTERS

6.39 Section 106 of the Local Government Finance Act 1992 provides that a member of a local authority who has not paid an amount due in respect of council tax for at least two months after it became due and who attends a meeting at which the level of council tax is considered must: (a) disclose that s 106 applies to him, and (b) refrain from voting on any question with respect to that matter. A failure to comply with either of these requirements is an offence,[43] unless the member proves that he did not know that: (a) the section applied to him at the time of the meeting, or (b) the matter in question was the subject of consideration at the meeting. The offence is punishable in the magistrates' court by a fine not exceeding level 3 on the standard scale (currently £1000).

---

41 Bribery Act 2010, s 10(1).
42 Bribery Act 2010, s 11(1).
43 *DPP v Burton, The Times,* June 8, 1995.

F DISQUALIFICATION BY REASON OF CRIMINAL CONVICTION

6.40   Section 80(1)(d) of the Local Government Act 1972 disqualifies a person from being elected or being a member of a local authority if he has within five years before the day of election or since his election been convicted in the United Kingdom, the Channel Islands or the Isle of Man of any offence and has had passed on him a sentence of imprisonment (whether suspended or not) for a period of not less than three months without the option of a fine.

G CONCLUSION

6.41   As outlined in this chapter, there are a number of criminal offences (both statutory and common law) with which a councillor may be charged as a result of his conduct in office. There is also the potential for civil redress if the conduct has caused someone loss. There is a degree of overlap between the statutory offences and the common law offence of misconduct in public office, although it is likely that the latter would be relied on only where the former were deemed to be inapplicable or inadequate.

6.42   In most cases, a criminal offence will be charged only where there has been serious misconduct, in particular where a councillor has behaved dishonestly and abused his position. If, however, the new standards regime in England is seen to be insufficiently robust, there may be public or political pressure to expand the use of the criminal law.

CHAPTER 7

Wales

	What this chapter covers	
A	Introduction	7.1
B	The standards regime in Wales	7.5
C	Councillors' conduct and decision-making	7.26
D	Making and handling complaints about conduct issues	7.28
E	Challenging council decisions	7.38
F	Offences	7.39

A INTRODUCTION

7.1   The purpose of this chapter is to consider the law relating to councillors' conduct in Wales. It mirrors the approach taken in previous chapters, but where the law in Wales is the same as that in England the reader will be directed to the relevant commentary in the earlier chapters.

7.2   The Welsh Ministers have rejected the principal changes to the local government ethical framework implemented in England under the Localism Act 2011. In their view the scheme established by Part 3 of the Local Government Act 2000 does not require significant reform and is sufficiently robust to deal with minor, vexatious and politically motivated complaints.[1] There are, however, aspects of the conduct regime that the Welsh Government intends to modify. In its White Paper *Reforming Local Government: Power to Local People* (February 2015) the Government gave the following summary of changes that lie ahead:

> 'The Local Government (Democracy) (Wales) Act 2013 makes provision for the establishment of joint Standards Committees, the electronic publication of registers of interests and powers to enable the transfer of misconduct reports and Member dispensation requests between Standards Committees to overcome potential conflicts of interest. These provisions will be brought into effect later this year. Also, this year, we will bring forward legislation to modify the model code of conduct for Local Authority Members to facilitate the operation of local resolution policies and to clarify the position of Members with constituency interests. We will also exempt Local Authorities from publishing misconduct reports during ongoing proceedings.'[2]

---

1   The views of the Welsh Ministers were referred to by Hickinbottom J in *Heesom v The Public Services Ombudsman for Wales* [2014] EWHC 1504 (Admin), [2014] 4 All ER 269, at para 30.
2   *Reforming Local Government: Power to Local People* (February 2015), p 30.

7.3 In conjunction with these relatively modest changes, local government structures in Wales are to be recast. Following the Welsh Government's July 2014 White Paper *Reforming Local Government* and the *Invitation to Principal Local Authorities in Wales to submit proposals for voluntary merger* published in September 2014, the Local Government (Wales) Bill was introduced into the Assembly in January 2015, providing for certain preparatory arrangements to enable a programme of local government mergers and reform and to facilitate the voluntary early merger of two or more principal local authorities by April 2018. In the process that will eventually see 12 or so merged authorities in Wales, a substantial number of councillors may find themselves surplus to requirement.[3]

7.4 In these circumstances councillors, and the standards regime as a whole, might be expected to come under a degree of pressure.

B   THE STANDARDS REGIME IN WALES

7.5 **Chapter 1** traces the history of the current standards regimes in England and Wales. Until 2012 the means by which standards were set and enforced in each country were in all essential respects the same. The coalition government's localism agenda, given flesh in the Localism Act 2011, has seen a parting of the ways. While England has embarked on a new and arguably less stringent system, Wales has stuck with the standards regime put in place by the Local Government Act 2000.

7.6 The main elements of the statutory regime in Wales as at the date of this work are as follows.[4]

The principles and code of conduct

7.7 Under the 2000 Act the National Assembly for Wales has power[5] to specify the principles which are to govern the conduct of members and co-opted members of 'relevant authorities' (county councils, county borough councils, community councils, fire and rescue authorities and National Park Authorities).[6] In exercise of that power the Assembly made the Conduct of Members (Principles) Order 2001, which specifies ten principles:

● Selflessness: Members must act solely in the public interest. They must never use their position as members to improperly confer advantage on themselves or to improperly confer advantage or disadvantage on others.

---

3   *Reforming Local Government: Power to Local People* (February 2015), p 34.
4   For a judicial summary see the judgment of Hickinbottom J in *Heesom v The Public Services Ombudsman for Wales* [2014] EWHC 1504 (Admin), [2014] 4 All ER 269, paras 11–24.
5   A power exercisable by the Welsh Ministers since 2006.
6   LGA 2000, s 49(2), (6).

- Honesty: Members must declare any private interests relevant to their public duties and take steps to resolve any conflict in a way that protects the public interest.

- Integrity and Propriety: Members must not put themselves in a position where their integrity is called into question by any financial or other obligation to individuals or organisations that might seek to influence them in the performance of their duties. Members must on all occasions avoid the appearance of such behaviour.

- Duty to Uphold the Law: Members must act to uphold the law and act on all occasions in accordance with the trust that the public has placed in them.

- Stewardship: In discharging their duties and responsibilities members must ensure that their authority's resources are used both lawfully and prudently.

- Objectivity in Decision-making: In carrying out their responsibilities including making appointments, awarding contracts, or recommending individuals for rewards and benefits, members must make decisions on merit. Whilst members must have regard to the professional advice of officers and may properly take account of the views of others, including their political groups, it is their responsibility to decide what view to take and, if appropriate, how to vote on any issue.

- Equality and Respect: Members must carry out their duties and responsibilities with due regard to the need to promote equality of opportunity for all people, regardless of their gender, race, disability, sexual orientation, age or religion, and show respect and consideration for others.

- Openness: Members must be as open as possible about all their actions and those of their authority. They must seek to ensure that disclosure of information is restricted only in accordance with the law.

- Accountability: Members are accountable to the electorate and the public generally for their actions and for the way they carry out their responsibilities as a member. They must be prepared to submit themselves to such scrutiny as is appropriate to their responsibilities.

- Leadership: Members must promote and support these principles by leadership and example so as to promote public confidence in their role and in the authority. They must respect the impartiality and integrity of the authority's statutory officers and its other employees.

7.8   Drawing on those principles, the Assembly (now, the Welsh Ministers) may issue a model code as regards the conduct which is expected of members and co-opted members of relevant authorities.[7] A model code of conduct must be consistent with the principles specified by the Assembly and may include mandatory and optional provisions.[8] The current model code of conduct was

---

7   LGA 2000, s 50(2).
8   LGA 2000, s 50(4)(a).

issued in 2008[9] and it applies to each relevant authority in Wales. All its provisions are mandatory.[10]

7.9   Where a model code of conduct applying to a relevant authority is issued by the Assembly, that authority must within six months pass a resolution adopting a code of conduct incorporating any mandatory provisions in the model code and such other optional provisions or other provisions consistent with the model code as it chooses.[11]

7.10   Every member of a local authority must undertake that in performing his functions he will observe the authority's code of conduct for the time being.[12] The current model code of conduct requires that each member must observe its provisions when involved in the business of the authority or acting or purporting to act as a member or representative of the authority.[13] Certain provisions of the model code of conduct must be observed by members at all times and in any capacity.[14]

The standards committee

7.11   Every relevant authority, save for a community council, must establish a standards committee.[15] The general functions of a standards committee are to promote and maintain high standards of conduct by the members and co-opted members of the authority, and to assist members and co-opted members to observe the authority's code of conduct.[16] Its specific functions are to advise the authority on the adoption or revision of a code of conduct; monitor the operation of the code of conduct; and advise, train or arrange to train members and co-opted members of the authority on matters relating to the code of conduct.[17]

7.12   The standards committee of a county or county borough council also performs the same functions in relation to the community councils and their members within the county or county borough council's area.[18]

---

9   See the Local Authorities (Model Code of Conduct) (Wales) Order 2008, SI 2008/788, which is reproduced at the end of this work.
10 Local Authorities (Model Code of Conduct) (Wales) Order 2008, art 3(2).
11 LGA 2000, s 51.
12 LGA 2000, s 52; LGA 1972, s 83; Local Elections (Declaration of Acceptance of Office) (Wales) Order 2004, SI 2004/1508.
13 Local Authorities (Model Code of Conduct) (Wales) Order 2008, art 2(1).
14 Local Authorities (Model Code of Conduct) (Wales) Order 2008, art 2(1)(d).
15 LGA 2000, s 53. The composition and workings of a standards committee are governed by the Standards Committees (Wales) Regulations 2001, SI 2001/2283.
16 LGA 2000, s 54(1).
17 LGA 2000, s 54(2).
18 LGA 2000, s 56.

The Public Services Ombudsman for Wales

7.13   The Public Services Ombudsman for Wales is the primary investigator of complaints made against councillors. He may: (a) investigate cases in which a written allegation is made to him by any person that a member or co-opted member (or former member or co-opted member) of a relevant authority has failed, or may have failed, to comply with the authority's code of conduct; and (b) also investigate other cases in which he considers that a member or co-opted member (or former member or co-opted member) of a relevant authority has failed, or may have failed, to comply with the authority's code of conduct and which have come to his attention as a result of an investigation under (a).[19]

7.14   The Ombudsman is not obliged to investigate a complaint and may decide that a written allegation should not be investigated.[20] If he conducts an investigation, he may arrive at one of the following findings:

(a) that there is no evidence of any failure to comply with the code of conduct of the relevant authority concerned;

(b) that no action needs to be taken in respect of the matters which are the subject of the investigation;

(c) that the matters which are the subject of the investigation should be referred to the monitoring officer of the relevant authority concerned; or

(d) that the matters which are the subject of the investigation should be referred to the president of the Adjudication Panel for Wales for adjudication by a tribunal falling within s 76(1).[21]

7.15   The Ombudsman may, and in certain circumstances must, produce reports, including interim reports, on his investigations.[22] In serious cases, where he considers that it is in the public interest that the subject of an interim report should be suspended immediately, the Ombudsman may make a recommendation to that effect and must then refer the matter to the Adjudication Panel for Wales.[23]

Referral of a complaint to the authority concerned

7.16   Where a complaint is referred by the Ombudsman to the monitoring officer of the authority concerned,[24] the monitoring officer must, depending on the circumstances, conduct an investigation and then report to the authority's standards committee, or consider any report sent to him by the Ombudsman and

19 LGA 2000, s 69(1).
20 LGA 2000, s 69(2).
21 LGA 2000, s 69(3), (4).
22 LGA 2000, ss 71, 72.
23 LGA 2000, s 72(1)–(4).
24 Which may be done before or following the completion of an investigation: LGA 2000, ss 70(3), (4), 71(2).

make recommendations to the authority's standards committee.[25] Unless the standards committee determines that there is no evidence of a breach of the code of conduct, it must give the subject of the investigation an opportunity to make representations.[26] Following consideration of any representations the standards committee must determine:

(a) that there is no evidence of any failure to comply with the code of conduct of the relevant authority and that therefore no action needs to be taken in respect of the matters which are the subject of the investigation;

(b) that a member or co-opted member (or former member or co-opted member) of a relevant authority has failed to comply with the relevant authority's code of conduct but that no action needs to be taken in respect of that failure;

(c) that a member or co-opted member (or former member or co-opted member) of the relevant authority has failed to comply with the authority's code of conduct and should be censured; or

(d) that a member or co-opted member of a relevant authority has failed to comply with the authority's code of conduct and should be suspended or partially suspended from being a member or co-opted member of that authority for a period not exceeding six months.[27]

There is a right of appeal to the Adjudication Panel for Wales.[28]

7.17 The standards committee must produce a report on the outcome of the investigation, which must be publicised.[29]

Referral of a complaint to the Adjudication Panel for Wales

7.18 Where a complaint is referred by the Ombudsman to the Adjudication Panel for Wales[30] a tribunal is formed to adjudicate on the matter.[31] The tribunal has power to summon witnesses and arrange for expert evidence to be given.[32] The adjudication is determined at a hearing, usually in public,[33] unless the

---

25 Local Government Investigations (Functions of Monitoring Officers and Standards Committees) (Wales) Regulations 2001 SI 2001/2281, reg 3.
26 Local Government Investigations (Functions of Monitoring Officers and Standards Committees) (Wales) Regulations 2001, reg 7.
27 Local Government Investigations (Functions of Monitoring Officers and Standards Committees) (Wales) Regulations 2001, reg 9(1).
28 Local Government Investigations (Functions of Monitoring Officers and Standards Committees) (Wales) Regulations 2001, regs 10–12.
29 Local Government Investigations (Functions of Monitoring Officers and Standards Committees) (Wales) Regulations 2001, reg 13.
30 Which may be done following the production of a report or interim report: LGA 2000, ss 71(3), 72(4).
31 LGA 2000, s 76.
32 The Adjudications by Case Tribunals and Interim Case Tribunals (Wales) Regulations 2001, SI 2001/2288, regs 8, 10.
33 The Adjudications by Case Tribunals and Interim Case Tribunals (Wales) Regulations 2001, reg 16(1).

person the subject of the investigation agrees to dispense with a hearing or has indicated that he will not take part in the hearing or dispute the contents of the Ombudsman's report.[34]

7.19   In adjudicating on any of the matters which are the subject of an interim report recommending immediate suspension, an interim case tribunal must reach one of the following decisions:

(a) that the person recommended for suspension should not be suspended or partially suspended from being a member or co-opted member of the relevant authority concerned;

(b) that that person should be suspended or partially suspended from being a member or co-opted member of the relevant authority concerned for a period which does not exceed six months or (if shorter) the remainder of the person's term of office.[35]

There is a right of appeal to the High Court against a decision to suspend, but only with the leave of the court.[36]

Disclosure and registration of members' interests

7.20   The monitoring officer of each relevant authority must establish and maintain a register of interests of the members and co-opted members of the authority.[37] Copies of the register must be made available at an office of the authority for inspection by members of the public at all reasonable hours.[38] Members must register their financial and other interests specified in the code of conduct in the register by providing written notification to the monitoring officer.[39] With the agreement of the monitoring officer, members need not register 'sensitive information', defined as 'information whose availability for inspection by the public creates, or is likely to create, a serious risk that [the member] or a person who lives with [him] may be subjected to violence or intimidation'.[40]

7.21   Within 28 days of receiving any gift, hospitality, material benefit or advantage above a value specified in a resolution by the authority, a member must provide written notification to the monitoring officer of the existence and nature of the gift, etc.[41]

7.22   Part 3 of the model code of conduct defines personal and prejudicial interests. Where a member has a personal interest in any business before the

---

34 The Adjudications by Case Tribunals and Interim Case Tribunals (Wales) Regulations 2001, regs 3(3), 15(1).
35 LGA 2000, s 78(1).
36 LGA 2000, s 78(10), (11).
37 LGA 2000, s 81(1).
38 LGA 2000, s 81(6).
39 The model code of conduct, para 15.
40 The model code of conduct, para 16.
41 The model code of conduct, para 17.

authority in which he is involved, he must disclose that fact.[42] Subject to certain exceptions, a member who has a personal interest will also have a prejudicial interest if the interest is one which a member of the public with knowledge of the relevant facts would reasonably regard as so significant that it is likely to prejudice the member's judgement of the public interest.[43]

7.23　A member will also have a prejudicial interest in any business before an overview and scrutiny committee where that business relates to a decision made or action taken by the authority's executive or board, or a committee, and at the time the decision was made or action was taken the member was a member of that body and was present when the decision was made or action was taken.[44]

7.24　The Ombudsman has issued two guidance documents: *The Code of Conduct for members of local authorities in Wales: Guidance from the Public Services Ombudsman for Wales for members of county and county borough councils, fire and rescue authorities, and national park authorities* and *The Code of Conduct for members of local authorities in Wales: Guidance from the Public Services Ombudsman for Wales for members of community councils*, which are helpful in understanding the provisions of the model code of conduct and what is meant by personal and prejudicial interests.

7.25　A member who has a prejudicial interest in any business of the authority must, unless he has obtained a dispensation from the standards committee, withdraw from any meeting where the business is being considered and must not seek to take part in or influence, by way of representations or otherwise, the decision about that business.[45] If the meeting is a public meeting, a member with a prejudicial interest may attend, but only for the purpose of making representations, answering questions or giving evidence relating to the business, and must withdraw immediately afterwards.[46] A member with a prejudicial interest may also participate in a meeting of the overview and scrutiny committee if he is required to attend the meeting by the committee exercising its statutory powers.[47] A member with a prejudicial interest cannot circumvent the prohibition or restrictions on attending meetings by claiming to attend in his private capacity.[48]

C　COUNCILLORS' CONDUCT AND DECISION-MAKING

7.26　In **Chapter 3** there is a discussion of the principles of law governing the way councillors discharge their responsibilities. Although the standards regimes are now different in Wales and England, the principles that have emerged over the

---

42　The model code of conduct, para 11.
43　The model code of conduct, para 12.
44　The model code of conduct, para 13.
45　The model code of conduct, para 14(1). As to dispensations, see subparas (3)(b), (4).
46　The model code of conduct, para 14(1)(a)(i), (2).
47　The model code of conduct, para 14(3)(a).
48　*R (Richardson) v North Yorkshire County Council* [2003] EWCA Civ 1860, [2004] 1 WLR 1920.

years are equally relevant (in some respects more relevant now than in England) to the way Welsh councillors go about their business. The Data Protection Act 1998, the Equality Act 2010 and the Protection from Harassment Act 1997 also extend to both Wales and England.

7.27   Save for:

- the commentary in section B on personal interests (instead, see above);

- the mention, in the context of elections, of *The Code of Recommended Practice on Local Authority Publicity* (for present purposes it should be *The Code of Recommended Practice on Local Authority Publicity in Wales*[49], but the relevant provisions are much the same); and

- the reference to the Secretary of State's power under the Local Government Act 1986 to require compliance with the *Code of Recommended Practice on Local Authority Publicity*,

the discussion in **Chapter 3** is equally applicable to Wales and will not be repeated here.

D   MAKING AND HANDLING COMPLAINTS ABOUT CONDUCT ISSUES

7.28   This section describes parts of the process by which members (including co-opted members) of local authorities in Wales may well be held to account for breaches of their Code of Conduct. As set out in **section B** above the Public Service Ombudsman for Wales is the primary investigator of complaints made against councillors. As the statutory regime has also been summarised above, this section is essentially a practical one, covering elements of the process of complaining about a member's conduct.

7.29   **Section B** identifies the two Codes of Guidance issued by the Ombudsman which provide useful guidance as to his approach. In addition, the Ombudsman publishes various leaflets relating to the complaints procedure which are freely available on his website.

7.30   The Ombudsman encourages all public bodies to take a common approach to the resolution of complaints, with a model concerns and complaints policy involving a two stage process, the first informal and the second formal. It is only after following this process that a complainant, if still unsatisfied, should approach the Ombusdman.

7.31   The complainant may be a member of the public, an officer of the authority, or a fellow councillor; but the Ombudsman has made it clear he requires the complainant to have direct knowledge of the behaviour they are complaining

---

49 Issued in August 2014.

about, and will not investigate a complaint simply based on what the complainant has been told by a third party.

7.32   The complaint must be made in writing and the Ombudsman provides a form for that purpose which requires the details of the complainant, the subject of the complaint, the precise and specific evidence that is relied upon to claim that a breach of the code of conduct has occurred, when the incident took place, and the identification and contact details of any witnesses who can confirm the allegations in the complaint. The form encourages as much detail as possible to be given in relation to the evidence supporting the complaint. It also contains a declaration which makes clear that the information will be shared with the subject of the complaint and may become public knowledge. The declaration requires the complainant to confirm that they are prepared to give oral evidence in public in support of their complaint.

7.32   The Ombudsman's practice is to acknowledge complaints once received and then assess the complaint to determine if an investigation is required. The Ombudsman may seek further information from the complainant before making that determination. The determination follows the Ombudsman's assessment of the seriousness of the complaint applying a two stage test. He looks first to see whether there is evidence that a breach of the Code actually took place; and then whether the breach, if proved, would be likely to lead to a sanction being imposed on the member. In making his decision the Ombudsman takes into account the outcomes of previous cases considered by standards committees and Adjudication Panels across Wales. In appropriate cases therefore, both those complaining and those the subject of complaint may wish to refer to particular such decisions in support of their respective cases. The Ombudsman publishes a code of conduct casebook twice a year which is freely available on his website. The casebook is divided into four substantive sections covering the four possible outcomes of an investigation set out at para **7.14** above, in summary: (1) complaints where it was found that there was no evidence of breach; (2) those complaints where no action was held necessary; (3) complaints referred to the standards committee; and (4) those referred to the panel or decided by the panel on appeal.

7.33   In cases where the Ombudsman decides not to investigate he will inform the complainant as to the reasons for that decision. The Ombudsman points out, in particular, that the Code is not meant to prevent robust political debate. The introduction of the third issue of his casebook is to similar effect and points out that he takes a dim view of vexatious complaints.[50] If the Ombudsman concludes that there has been a breach of the code but that the breach is unlikely to lead to a sanction being imposed he will write to the monitoring officer of the local authority stating that he does not intend to investigate the complaint and asking the monitoring officer whether the local authority wishes to carry out an investigation. At that point the monitoring officer may decide that no

---

50 His observation was made against the background of half of the cases dealt with in that issue disclosing no evidence of breach (more than double the number of such cases in the previous issue of the casebook).

investigation is called for, at which stage, subject to any legal challenge that will be an end of the complaint. If the monitoring officer decides to investigate then a local investigation will take place. The approach to a local investigation is set out in para **7.16** above.

7.34 The Ombudsman has to balance the need to investigate matters thoroughly and fairly with the need to avoid undue delay in concluding cases. He expects in a normal case to complete his consideration of a complaint within nine months of it being made. When the investigation is complete, if the Ombudsman decides either that the complaint should be referred to the monitoring officer of the relevant authority concerned, or that the complaint should be referred to the Adjudication Panel for Wales for adjudication, then he must produce a report on the outcome of his investigation.[51] In the first case he must send copies of his report to the monitoring officer and the standards committee of the relevant local authority. In the second case he must send a copy of the report to the monitoring officer and to the president of the Adjudication Panel. The procedure followed by the Adjudication Panel is set out at para **7.18** above. The Ombudsman may also decide, in certain circumstances, that it is appropriate to issues interim reports as described in **section B** above.

7.35 The maximum penalty that a standards committee can apply following a local investigation is suspension for six months. The Adjudication Panel can impose a penalty of up to five years' disqualification from office. All the decisions made by the panel are available to view online. In addition, the panel publishes as document APW16 a register of tribunal decisions which is regularly updated. The register provides information about the nature of the allegation in each case and a summary of the tribunal decision. It therefore provides a useful resource for those involved in a complaints process.

7.36 In relation to matters referred to the Adjudication Panel there is a standard form for the complainant to reply to the reference – form APW01 which is supported by guidance on contesting a reference contained in booklet APW02. The Adjudication Panel has an established procedure for dealing with appeals from a decision of a standards committee which is set out in its procedural guidance booklet APW03. The Adjudication Panel has issued guidance for its case tribunals to apply when considering on a referral what if any sanction ought to be imposed. The guidance applies both to interim case tribunals and final decisions. The guidance is contained in booklet APW04. The guidance does not provide a firm tariff but gives broad guidance as to when disqualification, suspension, partial suspension, or no action might be taken on a referral. It also contains a non-exhaustive list of mitigating and aggravating factors. The guidance sets out the aims of both the interim case tribunal and the case tribunal and those purposes will also be relevant to how the guidance on sanction should be applied, and therefore should be closely considered by those involved in the complaints process.

51 Local Government Act 2000, s 71.

7.37   Similar forms and guidance are available in relation to appeals to the Adjudication Panel from a decision of a standards committee. The panel has an established procedure for dealing with such appeals which is set out in its procedural guidance booklet APW07. There is a standard notice of appeal – form APW06 which is supported by the guidance on appealing contained in booklet APW07. The Adjudication Panel has issued guidance for its case tribunals to apply when considering on appeal what if any sanction ought to be imposed. The guidance is contained in booklet APW08. The guidance does not provide a firm tariff but gives broad guidance as to when suspension, partial suspension, or no action might be taken on an appeal. It also contains a non-exhaustive list of mitigating and aggravating factors.

7.38   In terms of the outcomes from complaints in 2013–14 the Ombudsman handled just under 2,000 cases dealing with service provision and issued 245 investigation reports. The majority of complaints (891) were about County Councils and County Borough Councils, with 23 about Community Councils and 15 about National Park Authorities. Unlike complaints about service provision, Code of Conduct complaints have fallen in the past year and stood at 228 in 2013–14, split approximately 50:50 between County Councils/County Borough Councils and Community Councils. Of the 229 code cases closed in 2013–14, the great majority did not warrant an investigation (171 were closed following the initial consideration) and only sixled to the issue of a report, five to the authority's standards committee, and one to the Adjudication Panel for Wales.

E   CHALLENGING COUNCIL DECISIONS

7.39   The discussion in **Chapter 5** on the main grounds for challenging council decisions by way of judicial review proceedings, the procedure involved, and the possible outcomes of such litigation, is equally applicable to Wales and will not be repeated here. In most cases a challenge to a decision of a Welsh local authority would be expected to be brought in Wales and would be heard in Cardiff (CPR PD 54D, paras 2.2, 5.2).

7.40   The Public Service Ombudsman for Wales is also responsible for complaints about public bodies and their service in Wales. This power, which is directed at the corporate body of the local authority, is in addition to his jurisdiction to investigate conduct complaints against individual councillors dealt with above. The governing legislation is Part 2 of the Public Service Ombudsman (Wales) Act 2005. The procedures are broadly similar to those applying to England and dealt with in **Chapter 5**. For a recent and authoritative comparison of the two statutory schemes as they apply to the conduct of Councillors, reference may be made to *Heesom v Public Service Ombudsman for Wales*,[52] a statutory appeal to the High Court from the Adjudication Panel for Wales which had upheld a complaint

---

52 [2014] EWHC 1504 (Admin).

about the conduct of a County Councillor. In general, the Ombudsman's website includes useful guidance on making a complaint and a complaint form.

7.41   The Ombudsman has jurisdiction in respect of 'listed authorities', which include the Welsh Government itself, county councils, county borough councils, community councils, and various other public authorities.[53] The matters which may be investigated include not only alleged maladministration but also alleged failures in, or failures to provide, a relevant service, which in the case of a local authority include any service which it was the authority's function to provide.[54]

7.42   If, having investigated, the Ombudsman prepares a report under s 16 of the Act, the authority concerned must publicise it in accordance with s 17 (unless it receives a direction to contrary effect under that section). Within the 'permitted period' (generally a month) the authority must notify the Ombudsman of the action it has taken or proposes to take in response to the report.

7.43   The Ombudsman may then prepare a special report under s 22 setting out his own recommendations for action. Wilful disregard of the Ombudsman's s 16 report entitles the Ombudsman to refer the authority to the High Court under s 20 of the Act.

7.44   Although there has not been a single reported case of judicial review of the Ombudsman's report or the response of an authority to it, a similar approach to that applying in England may be expected in the event of such a challenge, namely that findings are final, unless successfully challenged by judicial review, and that they therefore must set the context within which the adequacy of the authority's response to any recommendations would be judged

F   OFFENCES

7.45   Save for **section B** (offences under s 34 of the Localism Act 2011), the discussion in **Chapter 6** of offences particularly relevant to councillors is equally applicable to Wales and will not be repeated here.

---

53 See ss 28, 41, Sch 3. Exclusions are set out in ss 9 and 11, and Sch 2.
54 Section 7.

Statutes

LOCALISM ACT 2011, PART 1, CHAPTER 7, SS 27–37

27 Duty to promote and maintain high standards of conduct

(1) A relevant authority must promote and maintain high standards of conduct by members and co-opted members of the authority.

(2) In discharging its duty under subsection (1), a relevant authority must, in particular, adopt a code dealing with the conduct that is expected of members and co-opted members of the authority when they are acting in that capacity.

(3) A relevant authority that is a parish council—

(a) may comply with subsection (2) by adopting the code adopted under that subsection by its principal authority, where relevant on the basis that references in that code to its principal authority's register are to its register, and

(b) may for that purpose assume that its principal authority has complied with section 28(1) and (2).

(4) In this Chapter 'co-opted member', in relation to a relevant authority, means a person who is not a member of the authority but who—

(a) is a member of any committee or sub-committee of the authority, or

(b) is a member of, and represents the authority on, any joint committee or joint sub-committee of the authority,

and who is entitled to vote on any question that falls to be decided at any meeting of that committee or sub-committee.

(5) A reference in this Chapter to a joint committee or joint sub-committee of a relevant authority is a reference to a joint committee on which the authority is represented or a sub-committee of such a committee.

(6) In this Chapter 'relevant authority' means—

(a) a county council in England,

(b) a district council,

(c) a London borough council,

(d) a parish council,

(e) the Greater London Authority,

[...]

(g) the London Fire and Emergency Planning Authority,

(h) the Common Council of the City of London in its capacity as a local authority or police authority,

(i) the Council of the Isles of Scilly,

(j) a fire and rescue authority in England constituted by a scheme under section 2 of the Fire and Rescue Services Act 2004 or a scheme to which section 4 of that Act applies,

[...]

(l) a joint authority established by Part 4 of the Local Government Act 1985,

(m) an economic prosperity board established under section 88 of the Local Democracy, Economic Development and Construction Act 2009,

(n) a combined authority established under section 103 of that Act,

(o) the Broads Authority, or

(p) a National Park authority in England established under section 63 of the Environment Act 1995.

(7) Any reference in this Chapter to a member of a relevant authority—

(a) in the case of a relevant authority to which Part 1A of the Local Government Act 2000 applies, includes a reference to an elected mayor;

(b) in the case of the Greater London Authority, is a reference to the Mayor of London or a London Assembly member.

(8) Functions that are conferred by this Chapter on a relevant authority to which Part 1A of the Local Government Act 2000 applies are not to be the responsibility of an executive of the authority under executive arrangements.

(9) Functions that are conferred by this Chapter on the Greater London Authority are to be exercisable by the Mayor of London and the London Assembly acting jointly on behalf of the Authority.

(10) In this Chapter except section 35—

(a) a reference to a committee or sub-committee of a relevant authority is, where the relevant authority is the Greater London Authority, a reference to—

(i)   a committee or sub-committee of the London Assembly, or

(ii) the standards committee, or a sub-committee of that committee, established under that section,

(b) a reference to a joint committee on which a relevant authority is represented is, where the relevant authority is the Greater London Authority, a reference to a joint committee on which the Authority, the London Assembly or the Mayor of London is represented,

(c) a reference to becoming a member of a relevant authority is, where the relevant authority is the Greater London Authority, a reference to becoming the Mayor of London or a member of the London Assembly, and

(d) a reference to a meeting of a relevant authority is, where the relevant authority is the Greater London Authority, a reference to a meeting of the London Assembly;

and in subsection (4)(b) the reference to representing the relevant authority is, where the relevant authority is the Greater London Authority, a reference to representing the Authority, the London Assembly or the Mayor of London.

28 Codes of conduct

(1) A relevant authority must secure that a code adopted by it under section 27(2) (a 'code of conduct') is, when viewed as a whole, consistent with the following principles—

(a) selflessness;

(b) integrity;

(c) objectivity;

(d) accountability;

(e) openness;

(f) honesty;

(g) leadership.

(2) A relevant authority must secure that its code of conduct includes the provision the authority considers appropriate in respect of the registration in its register, and disclosure, of—

(a) pecuniary interests, and

(b) interests other than pecuniary interests.

(3) Sections 29 to 34 do not limit what may be included in a relevant authority's code of conduct, but nothing in a relevant authority's code of conduct prejudices the operation of those sections.

(4) A failure to comply with a relevant authority's code of conduct is not to be dealt with otherwise than in accordance with arrangements made under subsection (6); in particular, a decision is not invalidated just because something that occurred in the process of making the decision involved a failure to comply with the code.

(5) A relevant authority may—

(a) revise its existing code of conduct, or

(b) adopt a code of conduct to replace its existing code of conduct.

(6) A relevant authority other than a parish council must have in place—

(a) arrangements under which allegations can be investigated, and

(b) arrangements under which decisions on allegations can be made.

(7) Arrangements put in place under subsection (6)(b) by a relevant authority must include provision for the appointment by the authority of at least one independent person—

(a) whose views are to be sought, and taken into account, by the authority before it makes its decision on an allegation that it has decided to investigate, and

(b) whose views may be sought—

    (i) by the authority in relation to an allegation in circumstances not within paragraph (a),

    (ii) by a member, or co-opted member, of the authority if that person's behaviour is the subject of an allegation, and

    (iii) by a member, or co-opted member, of a parish council if that person's behaviour is the subject of an allegation and the authority is the parish council's principal authority.

(8) For the purposes of subsection (7)—

(a) a person is not independent if the person is—

    (i) a member, co-opted member or officer of the authority,

    (ii) a member, co-opted member or officer of a parish council of which the authority is the principal authority, or

    (iii) a relative, or close friend, of a person within sub-paragraph (i) or (ii);

(b) a person may not be appointed under the provision required by subsection (7) if at any time during the 5 years ending with the appointment the person was—

    (i) a member, co-opted member or officer of the authority, or

    (ii) a member, co-opted member or officer of a parish council of which the authority is the principal authority;

(c) a person may not be appointed under the provision required by subsection (7) unless—

    (i) the vacancy for an independent person has been advertised in such manner as the authority considers is likely to bring it to the attention of the public,

    (ii) the person has submitted an application to fill the vacancy to the authority, and

    (iii) the person's appointment has been approved by a majority of the members of the authority;

(d) a person appointed under the provision required by subsection (7) does not cease to be independent as a result of being paid any amounts by way of allowances or expenses in connection with performing the duties of the appointment.

(9) In subsections (6) and (7) 'allegation', in relation to a relevant authority, means a written allegation—

(a) that a member or co-opted member of the authority has failed to comply with the authority's code of conduct, or

(b) that a member or co-opted member of a parish council for which the authority is the principal authority has failed to comply with the parish council's code of conduct.

(10) For the purposes of subsection (8) a person ('R') is a relative of another person if R is—

(a) the other person's spouse or civil partner,

(b) living with the other person as husband and wife or as if they were civil partners,

(c) a grandparent of the other person,

(d) a lineal descendant of a grandparent of the other person,

(e) a parent, sibling or child of a person within paragraph (a) or (b),

(f) the spouse or civil partner of a person within paragraph (c), (d) or (e), or

(g) living with a person within paragraph (c), (d) or (e) as husband and wife or as if they were civil partners.

(11) If a relevant authority finds that a member or co-opted member of the authority has failed to comply with its code of conduct (whether or not the finding is made following an investigation under arrangements put in place under subsection (6)) it may have regard to the failure in deciding—

(a) whether to take action in relation to the member or co-opted member, and

(b) what action to take.

(12) A relevant authority must publicise its adoption, revision or replacement of a code of conduct in such manner as it considers is likely to bring the adoption, revision or replacement of the code of conduct to the attention of persons who live in its area.

(13) A relevant authority's function of adopting, revising or replacing a code of conduct may be discharged only by the authority.

(14) Accordingly—

(a) in the case of an authority to whom section 101 of the Local Government Act 1972 (arrangements for discharge of functions) applies, the function is not a function to which that section applies;

(b) in the case of the Greater London Authority, the function is not a function to which section 35 (delegation of functions by the Greater London Authority) applies.

29 Register of interests

(1) The monitoring officer of a relevant authority must establish and maintain a register of interests of members and co-opted members of the authority.

(2) Subject to the provisions of this Chapter, it is for a relevant authority to determine what is to be entered in the authority's register.

(3) Nothing in this Chapter requires an entry to be retained in a relevant authority's register once the person concerned—

(a) no longer has the interest, or

(b) is (otherwise than transitorily on re-election or re-appointment) neither a member nor a co-opted member of the authority.

(4) In the case of a relevant authority that is a parish council, references in this Chapter to the authority's monitoring officer are to the monitoring officer of the parish council's principal authority.

(5) The monitoring officer of a relevant authority other than a parish council must secure—

(a) that a copy of the authority's register is available for inspection at a place in the authority's area at all reasonable hours, and

(b) that the register is published on the authority's website.

(6) The monitoring officer of a relevant authority that is a parish council must—

(a) secure that a copy of the parish council's register is available for inspection at a place in the principal authority's area at all reasonable hours,

(b) secure that the register is published on the principal authority's website, and

(c) provide the parish council with any data it needs to comply with subsection (7).

(7) A parish council must, if it has a website, secure that its register is published on its website.

(8) Subsections (5) to (7) are subject to section 32(2).

(9) In this Chapter 'principal authority', in relation to a parish council, means—

(a) in the case of a parish council for an area in a district that has a district council, that district council,

(b) in the case of a parish council for an area in a London borough, the council of that London borough, and

(c) in the case of a parish council for any other area, the county council for the county that includes that area.

(10) In this Chapter 'register', in relation to a relevant authority, means its register under subsection (1).

30 Disclosure of pecuniary interests on taking office

(1) A member or co-opted member of a relevant authority must, before the end of 28 days beginning with the day on which the person becomes a member or coopted member of the authority, notify the authority's monitoring officer of any disclosable pecuniary interests which the person has at the time when the notification is given.

(2) Where a person becomes a member or co-opted member of a relevant authority as a result of re-election or re-appointment, subsection (1) applies only as regards disclosable pecuniary interests not entered in the authority's register when the notification is given.

(3) For the purposes of this Chapter, a pecuniary interest is a 'disclosable pecuniary interest' in relation to a person ('M') if it is of a description specified in regulations made by the Secretary of State and either—

(a) it is an interest of M's, or

(b) it is an interest of—

    (i)   M's spouse or civil partner,

    (ii)   a person with whom M is living as husband and wife, or

    (iii) a person with whom M is living as if they were civil partners,

and M is aware that that other person has the interest.

(4) Where a member or co-opted member of a relevant authority gives a notification for the purposes of subsection (1), the authority's monitoring officer is to cause the interests notified to be entered in the authority's register (whether or not they are disclosable pecuniary interests).

31 Pecuniary interests in matters considered at meetings or by a single member

(1) Subsections (2) to (4) apply if a member or co-opted member of a relevant authority—

(a) is present at a meeting of the authority or of any committee, subcommittee, joint committee or joint sub-committee of the authority,

(b) has a disclosable pecuniary interest in any matter to be considered, or being considered, at the meeting, and

(c) is aware that the condition in paragraph (b) is met.

(2) If the interest is not entered in the authority's register, the member or co-opted member must disclose the interest to the meeting, but this is subject to section 32(3).

(3) If the interest is not entered in the authority's register and is not the subject of a pending notification, the member or co-opted member must notify the authority's monitoring officer of the interest before the end of 28 days beginning with the date of the disclosure.

(4) The member or co-opted member may not—

(a) participate, or participate further, in any discussion of the matter at the meeting, or

(b) participate in any vote, or further vote, taken on the matter at the meeting,

but this is subject to section 33.

(5) In the case of a relevant authority to which Part 1A of the Local Government Act 2000 applies and which is operating executive arrangements, the reference in subsection (1)(a) to a committee of the authority includes a reference to the authority's executive and a reference to a committee of the executive.

(6) Subsections (7) and (8) apply if—

(a) a function of a relevant authority may be discharged by a member of the authority acting alone,

(b) the member has a disclosable pecuniary interest in any matter to be dealt with, or being dealt with, by the member in the course of discharging that function, and

(c) the member is aware that the condition in paragraph (b) is met.

(7) If the interest is not entered in the authority's register and is not the subject of a pending notification, the member must notify the authority's monitoring officer of the interest before the end of 28 days beginning with the date when the member becomes aware that the condition in subsection (6)(b) is met in relation to the matter.

(8) The member must not take any steps, or any further steps, in relation to the matter (except for the purpose of enabling the matter to be dealt with otherwise than by the member).

(9) Where a member or co-opted member of a relevant authority gives a notification for the purposes of subsection (3) or (7), the authority's monitoring officer is to cause the interest notified to be entered in the authority's register (whether or not it is a disclosable pecuniary interest).

(10) Standing orders of a relevant authority may provide for the exclusion of a member or co-opted member of the authority from a meeting while any discussion or vote takes place in which, as a result of the operation of subsection (4), the member or co-opted member may not participate.

(11) For the purpose of this section, an interest is 'subject to a pending notification' if—

(a) under this section or section 30, the interest has been notified to a relevant authority's monitoring officer, but

(b) has not been entered in the authority's register in consequence of that notification.

32 Sensitive interests

(1) Subsections (2) and (3) apply where—

(a) a member or co-opted member of a relevant authority has an interest (whether or not a disclosable pecuniary interest), and

(b) the nature of the interest is such that the member or co-opted member, and the authority's monitoring officer, consider that disclosure of the details of the interest could lead to the member or co-opted member, or a person connected with the member or co-opted member, being subject to violence or intimidation.

(2) If the interest is entered in the authority's register, copies of the register that are made available for inspection, and any published version of the register, must not include details of the interest (but may state that the member or co-opted member has an interest the details of which are withheld under this subsection).

(3) If section 31(2) applies in relation to the interest, that provision is to be read as requiring the member or co-opted member to disclose not the interest but merely the fact that the member or co-opted member has a disclosable pecuniary interest in the matter concerned.

33 Dispensations from section 31(4)

(1) A relevant authority may, on a written request made to the proper officer of the authority by a member or co-opted member of the authority, grant a dispensation relieving the member or co-opted member from either or both of the restrictions in section 31(4) in cases described in the dispensation.

(2) A relevant authority may grant a dispensation under this section only if, after having had regard to all relevant circumstances, the authority—

(a) considers that without the dispensation the number of persons prohibited by section 31(4) from participating in any particular business would be so great a proportion of the body transacting the business as to impede the transaction of the business,

(b) considers that without the dispensation the representation of different political groups on the body transacting any particular business would be so upset as to alter the likely outcome of any vote relating to the business,

(c) considers that granting the dispensation is in the interests of persons living in the authority's area,

(d) if it is an authority to which Part 1A of the Local Government Act 2000 applies and is operating executive arrangements, considers that without the dispensation each member of the authority's executive would be prohibited by section 31(4) from participating in any particular business to be transacted by the authority's executive, or

(e) considers that it is otherwise appropriate to grant a dispensation.

(3) A dispensation under this section must specify the period for which it has effect, and the period specified may not exceed four years.

(4) Section 31(4) does not apply in relation to anything done for the purpose of deciding whether to grant a dispensation under this section.

34 Offences

(1) A person commits an offence if, without reasonable excuse, the person—

(a) fails to comply with an obligation imposed on the person by section 30(1) or 31(2), (3) or (7),

(b) participates in any discussion or vote in contravention of section 31(4), or

(c) takes any steps in contravention of section 31(8).

(2) A person commits an offence if under section 30(1) or 31(2), (3) or (7) the person provides information that is false or misleading and the person—

(a) knows that the information is false or misleading, or

(b) is reckless as to whether the information is true and not misleading.

(3) A person who is guilty of an offence under this section is liable on summary conviction to a fine not exceeding level 5 on the standard scale.

(4) A court dealing with a person for an offence under this section may (in addition to any other power exercisable in the person's case) by order disqualify the person, for a period not exceeding five years, for being or becoming (by election or otherwise) a member or co-opted member of the relevant authority in question or any other relevant authority.

(5) A prosecution for an offence under this section is not to be instituted except by or on behalf of the Director of Public Prosecutions.

(6) Proceedings for an offence under this section may be brought within a period of 12 months beginning with the date on which evidence sufficient in the opinion of the prosecutor to warrant the proceedings came to the prosecutor's knowledge.

(7) But no such proceedings may be brought more than three years—

(a) after the commission of the offence, or

(b) in the case of a continuous contravention, after the last date on which the offence was committed.

(8) A certificate signed by the prosecutor and stating the date on which such evidence came to the prosecutor's knowledge is conclusive evidence of that fact; and a certificate to that effect and purporting to be so signed is to be treated as being so signed unless the contrary is proved.

(9) The Local Government Act 1972 is amended as follows.

(10) In section 86(1)(b) (authority to declare vacancy where member becomes disqualified otherwise than in certain cases) after '2000' insert 'or section 34 of the Localism Act 2011'.

(11) In section 87(1)(ee) (date of casual vacancies)—

(a) after '2000' insert 'or section 34 of the Localism Act 2011 or', and

(b) after 'decision' insert 'or order'.

(12) The Greater London Authority Act 1999 is amended as follows.

(13) In each of sections 7(b) and 14(b) (Authority to declare vacancy where Assembly member or Mayor becomes disqualified otherwise than in certain cases) after sub-paragraph (i) insert—

'(ia) under section 34 of the Localism Act 2011,'.

(14) In section 9(1)(f) (date of casual vacancies)—

(a) before 'or by virtue of' insert 'or section 34 of the Localism Act 2011', and

(b) after 'that Act' insert 'of 1998 or that section'.

35 Delegation of functions by Greater London Authority

(1) The Mayor of London and the London Assembly, acting jointly, may arrange for any of the functions conferred on them by or under this Chapter to be exercised on their behalf by—

(a) a member of staff of the Greater London Authority, or

(b) a committee appointed in accordance with provision made by virtue of this section.

(2) Standing orders of the Greater London Authority may make provision regulating the exercise of functions by any member of staff of the Authority pursuant to arrangements under subsection (1).

(3) Standing orders of the Greater London Authority may make provision for the appointment of a committee ('the standards committee') to exercise functions conferred on the Mayor of London and the London Assembly by or under this Chapter in accordance with arrangements under subsection (1).

(4) Standing orders of the Greater London Authority may make provision about the membership and procedure of the standards committee.

(5) The provision that may be made under subsection (4) includes—

(a) provision for the standards committee to arrange for the discharge of its functions by a sub-committee of that committee;

(b) provision about the membership and procedure of such a subcommittee.

(6) Subject to subsection (7), the standards committee and any sub-committee of that committee—

(a) is not to be treated as a committee or (as the case may be) subcommittee of the London Assembly for the purposes of the Greater London Authority Act 1999, but

(b) is a committee or (as the case may be) sub-committee of the Greater London Authority for the purposes of Part 3 of the Local Government Act 1974 (investigations by Commission for Local Administration in England).

(7) Sections 6(3)(a) (failure to attend meetings) and 73(6) (functions of monitoring officer) of the Greater London Authority Act 1999 apply to the standards committee or any sub-committee of that committee as they apply to a committee of the London Assembly or any sub-committee of such a committee.

(8) Part 5A of the Local Government Act 1972 (access to meetings and documents) applies to the standards committee or any sub-committee of that committee as if—

(a) it were a committee or (as the case may be) a sub-committee of a principal council within the meaning of that Part, and

(b) the Greater London Authority were a principal council in relation to that committee or sub-committee.

(9) Arrangements under this section for the exercise of any function by—

(a) a member of staff of the Greater London Authority, or

(b) the standards committee,

do not prevent the Mayor of London and the London Assembly from exercising those functions.

(10) References in this section to the functions of the Mayor of London and the London Assembly conferred by or under this Chapter do not include their functions under this section.

(11) In this section 'member of staff of the Greater London Authority' has the same meaning as in the Greater London Authority Act 1999 (see section 424(1) of that Act).

36 Amendment of section 27 following abolition of police authorities

In section 27(6) (which defines 'relevant authority' for the purposes of this Chapter) omit—

(a) paragraph (f) (the Metropolitan Police Authority), and

(b) paragraph (k) (police authorities).

37 Transitional provision

(1) An order under section 240(2) may, in particular, provide for any provision made by or under Part 3 of the Local Government Act 2000 to have effect with modifications in consequence of any partial commencement of any of the amendments to, or repeals of, provisions of that Part made by Schedule 4.

(2) An order under section 240(2) may, in particular, make provision for an allegation or a case that is being investigated under Part 3 of the Local Government Act 2000 by the Standards Board for England or an ethical standards officer—

(a) to be referred to an authority of a kind specified in or determined in accordance with the order;

(b) to be dealt with in accordance with provision made by the order.

(3) The provision that may be made by virtue of subsection (2)(b) includes—

(a) provision corresponding to any provision made by or under Part 3 of the Local Government Act 2000;

(b) provision applying any provision made by or under that Part with or without modifications.

Regulations

RELEVANT AUTHORITIES (DISCLOSABLE PECUNIARY INTERESTS) REGULATIONS 2012, SI 2012/1464

1. Citation, commencement and interpretation

(1) These Regulations may be cited as the Relevant Authorities (Disclosable Pecuniary Interests) Regulations 2012 and shall come into force on 1st July 2012.

(2) In these regulations—

'the Act' means the Localism Act 2011;

'body in which the relevant person has a beneficial interest' means a firm in which the relevant person is a partner or a body corporate of which the relevant person is a director, or in the securities of which the relevant person has a beneficial interest;

'director' includes a member of the committee of management of a registered society within the meaning given by section 1(1) of the Co-operative and Community Benefit Societies Act 2014, other than a society registered as a credit union;

'land' excludes an easement, servitude, interest or right in or over land which does not carry with it a right for the relevant person (alone or jointly with another) to occupy the land or to receive income;

'M' means a member of a relevant authority;

'member' includes a co-opted member;

'relevant authority' means the authority of which M is a member;

'relevant period' means the period of 12 months ending with the day on which M gives a notification for the purposes of section 30(1) or section 31(7), as the case may be, of the Act;

'relevant person' means M or any other person referred to in section 30(3)(b) of the Act;

'securities' means shares, debentures, debenture stock, loan stock, bonds, units of a collective investment scheme within the meaning of the Financial Services and Markets Act 2000 and other securities of any description, other than money deposited with a building society.

2. Specified pecuniary interests

The pecuniary interests which are specified for the purposes of Chapter 7 of Part 1 of the Act are the interests specified in the second column of the Schedule to these Regulations.

Schedule 1

Subject	Prescribed description
Employment, office, trade, profession or vocation	Any employment, office, trade, profession or vocation carried on for profit or gain
Sponsorship	Any payment or provision of any other financial benefit (other than from the relevant authority) made or provided within the relevant period in respect of any expenses incurred by M in carrying out duties as a member, or towards the election expenses of M
	This includes any payment or financial benefit from a trade union within the meaning of the Trade Union and Labour Relations (Consolidation) Act 1992
Contracts	Any contract which is made between the relevant person (or a body in which the relevant person has a beneficial interest) and the relevant authority— (a) under which goods or services are to be provided or works are to be executed; and (b) which has not been fully discharged
Land	Any beneficial interest in land which is within the area of the relevant authority
Licences	Any licence (alone or jointly with others) to occupy land in the area of the relevant authority for a month or longer
Corporate tenancies	Any tenancy where (to M's knowledge)— (a) the landlord is the relevant authority; and (b) the tenant is a body in which the relevant person has a beneficial interest

Securities	Any beneficial interest in securities of a body where—
	
	(a) that body (to M's knowledge) has a place of business or land in the area of the relevant authority; and
	
	(b) either—
	
	   (i) the total nominal value of the securities exceeds £25,000 or one hundredth of the total issued share capital of that body; or
	
	   (ii) if the share capital of that body is of more than one class, the total nominal value of the shares of any one class in which the relevant person has a beneficial interest exceeds one hundredth of the total issued share capital of that class

European Convention on Human Rights

Article 10 of the ECHR provides (so far as is relevant):

'(1) Everyone has the right to freedom of expression. This right shall include freedom to hold opinions and to receive and impart information and ideas without interference by public authority and regardless of frontiers ....

(2) The exercise of these freedoms, since it carries with it duties and responsibilities, may be subject to such formalities, conditions, restrictions or penalties as are prescribed by law and are necessary in a democratic society, in the interests of ... the protection of the reputation or rights of others, ...'

Guidance

Contents	
Department of Communities and Local Government: Illustrative text for code dealing with the conduct expected of members and co-opted members of the authority when acting in that capacity	203
Openness and transparency on personal interests: A guide for councillors	205
Probity in planning for councillors and officers	213
Positive engagement: a guide for planning councillors	227

DEPARTMENT OF COMMUNITIES AND LOCAL GOVERNMENT: ILLUSTRATIVE TEXT FOR CODE DEALING WITH THE CONDUCT EXPECTED OF MEMBERS AND CO-OPTED MEMBERS OF THE AUTHORITY WHEN ACTING IN THAT CAPACITY

You are a member or co-opted member of the [name] council and hence you shall have regard to the following principles – selflessness, integrity, objectivity, accountability, openness, honesty and leadership.

Accordingly, when acting in your capacity as a member or co-opted member:

You must act solely in the public interest and should never improperly confer an advantage or disadvantage on any person or act to gain financial or other material benefits for yourself, your family, a friend or close associate.

You must not place yourself under a financial or other obligation to outside individuals or organisations that might seek to influence you in the performance of your official duties.

When carrying out your public duties you must make all choices, such as making public appointments, awarding contracts or recommending individuals for rewards or benefits, on merit.

You are accountable for your decisions to the public and you must co-operate fully with whatever scrutiny is appropriate to your office.

You must be as open as possible about your decisions and actions and the decisions and actions of your authority and should be prepared to give reasons for those decisions and actions.

You must declare any private interests, both pecuniary and non-pecuniary, including your membership of any Trade Union, that relate to your public duties and must take steps to resolve any conflicts arising in a way that protects the public interest, including registering and declaring interests in a manner conforming with the procedures set out in the box below.

You must, when using or authorising the use by others of the resources of your authority, ensure that such resources are not used improperly for political purposes (including party political purposes) and you must have regard to any applicable Local Authority Code of Publicity made under the Local Government Act 1986.

You must promote and support high standards of conduct when serving in your public post, in particular as characterised by the above requirements, by leadership and example.

Registering and declaring pecuniary and non-pecuniary interests

You must, within 28 days of taking office as a member or co-opted member, notify your authority's monitoring officer of any disclosable pecuniary interest as defined by regulations made by the Secretary of State, where the pecuniary interest is yours, your spouse's or civil partner's, or is the pecuniary interest of somebody with whom you are living with as a husband or wife, or as if you were civil partners.

In addition, you must, within 28 days of taking office as a member or co-opted member, notify your authority's monitoring officer of any disclosable pecuniary or non-pecuniary interest which your authority has decided should be included in the register or which you consider should be included if you are to fulfil your duty to act in conformity with the Seven Principles of Public Life. These non-pecuniary interests will necessarily include your membership of any Trade Union.

If an interest has not been entered onto the authority's register, then the member must disclose the interest to any meeting of the authority at which they are present, where they have a disclosable interest in any matter being considered and where the matter is not a 'sensitive interest'.[1]

Following any disclosure of an interest not on the authority's register or the subject of pending notification, you must notify the monitoring officer of the interest within 28 days beginning with the date of disclosure.

Unless dispensation has been granted, you may not participate in any discussion of, vote on, or discharge any function related to any matter in which you have a pecuniary interest as defined by regulations made by the Secretary of State. Additionally, you must observe the restrictions your authority places on your involvement in matters where you have a pecuniary or non-pecuniary interest as defined by your authority.

---

1   A 'sensitive interest' is described in the Localism Act 2011 as a member or co-opted member of an authority having an interest, and the nature of the interest being such that the member or co-opted member, and the authority's monitoring officer, consider that disclosure of the details of the interest could lead to the member or co-opted member, or a person connected with the member or co-opted member, being subject to violence or intimidation.

OPENNESS AND TRANSPARENCY ON PERSONAL INTERESTS: A GUIDE FOR COUNCILLORS

September 2013

Department for Communities and Local Government

© *Crown copyright, 2013*

Copyright in the typographical arrangement rests with the Crown.

You may re-use this information (not including logos) free of charge in any format or medium, under the terms of the Open Government Licence. To view this licence, www.nationalarchives.gov.uk/doc/open-government-licence/ or write to the Information Policy Team, The National Archives, Kew, London TW9 4DU, or email: psi@nationalarchives.gsi.gov.uk.

This document/publication is also available on our website at www.gov.uk/dclg.

If you have any enquiries regarding this document/publication, email contactus@ communities.gov.uk or write to us at:

Department for Communities and Local Government
Eland House
Bressenden Place
London
SW1E 5DU

Telephone: 030 3444 0000

For all our latest news and updates follow us on Twitter: https://twitter.com/ CommunitiesUK

September 2013

ISBN: 978-1-4098--3604-9

The Guide

This guide on personal interests gives basic practical information about how to be open and transparent about your personal interests. It is designed to help councillors, including parish councillors, now that new standards arrangements have been introduced by the Localism Act 2011.[2]

Why are there new rules?

Parliament has abolished the Standards Board regime and all the rules under it. It has done this because that centrally-imposed, bureaucratic regime had become a vehicle for petty, malicious and politically-motivated complaints against councillors. Rather than creating a culture of trust and openness between councillors and those they represent, it was damaging, without justification, the public's confidence in local democratic governance.

---

2 The Guide should not be taken as providing any definitive interpretation of the statutory requirements; those wishing to address such issues should seek their own legal advice.

The new standards arrangements that Parliament has put in place mean that it is largely for councils themselves to decide their own local rules. It is essential that there is confidence that councillors everywhere are putting the public interest first and are not benefiting their own financial affairs from being a councillor. Accordingly, within the new standards arrangements there are national rules about councillors' interests.[3]

Such rules, in one form or another, have existed for decades. The new rules are similar to the rules that were in place prior to the Standards Board regime. Those rules, originating in the Local Government Act 1972 and the Local Government and Housing Act 1989, involved local authority members registering their pecuniary interests in a publicly available register, and disclosing their interests and withdrawing from meetings in certain circumstances. Failure to comply with those rules was in certain circumstances a criminal offence, as is failure to comply in certain circumstances with the new rules.

Does this affect me?

Yes, if you are an elected, co-opted, or appointed member of:

- a district, unitary, metropolitan, county or London borough council;
- a parish or town council;
- a fire and rescue authority;
- a transport or other joint authority;
- a combined authority or an economic prosperity board;
- the London Fire and Emergency Planning Authority;
- the Broads Authority;
- a National Park authority;
- the Greater London Authority;
- the Common Council of the City of London;
- the Council of the Isles of Scilly.

How will there be openness and transparency about my personal interests?

The national rules require your council or authority to adopt a code of conduct for its members and to have a register of members' interests.

The national rules require your council's code of conduct to comply with the Seven Principles of Public Life, and to set out how, in conformity with the rules, you will have to disclose and register your pecuniary and your other interests.

---

3   The national rules are in Chapter 7 of the Localism Act 2011 and in the secondary legislation made under the Act, particularly in The Relevant Authorities (Disclosable Pecuniary Interests) Regulations 2012 (S.I. 2012/1464).

Within these rules it is for your council to decide what its code of conduct says. An illustrative text for such a code is available on the Department's web site.[4]

Your council's or authority's monitoring officer (or in the case of a parish council the monitoring officer of the district or borough council) must establish and maintain your council's register of members' interests. Within the requirements of the national rules it is for your council or authority to determine what is to be entered in its register of members' interests.

What personal interests should be entered in my council's or authority's register of members' interests?

Disclosable pecuniary interests, and any other of your personal interests which your council or authority, in particular through its code of conduct, has determined should be registered.

Any other of your personal interests which you have asked the monitoring officer, who is responsible for your council's or authority's register of members' interests, to enter in the register.

As explained in the following section, your registration of personal interests should be guided by your duty to act in conformity with the seven principles of public life. You should ensure that you register all personal interests that conformity with the seven principles requires. These interests will necessarily include your membership of any Trade Union.

What must I do about registering my personal interests?

Under your council's code of conduct you must act in conformity with the Seven Principles of Public Life. One of these is the principle of integrity – that 'Holders of public office must avoid placing themselves under any obligation to people or organisations that might try inappropriately to influence them in their work. They should not act or take decisions in order to gain financial or other material benefits for themselves, their family, or their friends. **They must declare and resolve any interests and relationships.**'[5]

Your registration of personal interests should be guided by this duty and you should give the monitoring officer who is responsible for your council's or authority's register of members' interests any information he or she requests in order to keep that register up to date and any other information which you consider should be entered in the register.

All sitting councillors need to register their declarable interests – both declarable pecuniary interests, and other interests that must be declared and registered as required by your authority's code, or your duty to act in conformity with the Seven Principles of Public Life, such as your membership of any Trade Union. Any suggestion that you should tell the monitoring officer about your pecuniary interests only in the immediate aftermath of your being elected is wholly incompatible with this duty, with which you must comply.

4   https://www.gov.uk/government/publications/illustrative-text-for-local-code-of-conduct--2
5   http://www.public-standards.gov.uk/about-us/what-we-do/the-seven-principles/

If you have a disclosable pecuniary interest which is not recorded in the register and which relates to any business that is or will be considered at a meeting where you are present, you must disclose[6] this to the meeting and tell the monitoring officer about it, if you have not already done so, so that it can be added to the register. You must tell the monitoring officer within 28 days of disclosing the interest. For this purpose a meeting includes any meeting of your council or authority, of its executive or any committee of the executive, and of any committee, sub-committee, joint committee or joint sub-committee of your authority.

If you have a disclosable pecuniary interest which is not shown in the register and relates to any business on which you are acting alone, you must, within 28 days of becoming aware of this, tell the monitoring officer about it, if you have not already done so, so that it can be added to the register. You must also stop dealing with the matter as soon as you become aware of having a disclosable pecuniary interest relating to the business.

When you are first elected, co-opted, or appointed a member to your council or authority, you must, within 28 days of becoming a member, tell the monitoring officer who is responsible for your council's or authority's register of members' interests about your disclosable pecuniary interests. If you are re-elected, re-co-opted, or reappointed a member, you need to tell the monitoring officer about only those disclosable pecuniary interests that are not already recorded in the register.

What are pecuniary interests?

A person's pecuniary interests are their business interests (for example their employment, trade, profession, contracts, or any company with which they are associated) and wider financial interests they might have (for example trust funds, investments, and assets including land and property).

Do I have any disclosable pecuniary interests?

You have a disclosable pecuniary interest if you, or your spouse or civil partner, have a pecuniary interest listed in the national rules (see annex). Interests or your spouse or civil partner, following the approach of the rules under the 1972 and 1989 Acts, are included to ensure that the public can have confidence that councillors are putting the public interest first and not benefiting the financial affairs of themselves or their spouse or civil partner from which the councillor would stand to gain. For this purpose your spouse or civil partner includes any person with whom you are living as husband or wife, or as if they were your civil partner.

Does my spouse's or civil partner's name need to appear on the register of interests?

No. For the purposes of the register, an interest of your spouse or civil partner, which is listed in the national rules, is your disclosable pecuniary interest. Whilst

---

6   If the interest is a sensitive interest you should disclose merely the fact that you have such a disclosable pecuniary interest, rather than the interest. A sensitive interest is one which the member and the monitoring officer, who is responsible for the register of members' interests, consider that disclosure of its details could lead to the member, or a person connected to the member, being subject to violence or intimidation.

the detailed format of the register of members' interests is for your council to decide, there is no requirement to differentiate your disclosable pecuniary interests between those which relate to you personally and those that relate to your spouse or civil partner.

Does my signature need to be published online? Won't this put me at risk of identity theft?

There is no legal requirement for the personal signatures of councillors to be published online.

Who can see the register of members' interests?

Except for parish councils, a council's or authority's register of members' interests must be available for inspection in the local area, and must be published on the council's or authority's website.

For parish councils, the monitoring officer who is responsible for the council's register of members' interests must arrange for the parish council's register of members' interests to be available for inspection in the district of borough, and must be published on the district or borough council's website.

Where the parish council has its own website, its register of members' interests must also be published on that website.

This is in line with the Government's policies of transparency and accountability, ensuring that the public have ready access to publicly available information.

Is there any scope for withholding information on the published register?

Copies of the register of members' interests which are available for inspection or published must not include details of a member's sensitive interest, other than stating that the member has an interest the details of which are withheld. A sensitive interest is one which the member and the monitoring officer, who is responsible for the register of members' interests, consider that disclosure of its details could lead to the member, or a person connected to the member, being subject to violence or intimidation.

When is information about my interests removed from my council's register of members' interests?

If you cease to have an interest, that interest can be removed from the register. If you cease to be a member of the authority, all of your interests can be removed from the register.

What does having a disclosable pecuniary interest stop me doing?

If you are present at a meeting of your council or authority, of its executive or any committee of the executive, or of any committee, sub-committee, joint committee, or joint sub-committee of your authority, and you have a disclosable pecuniary interest relating to any business that is or will be considered at the meeting, you must not:

- participate in any discussion of the business at the meeting, or if you become aware of your disclosable pecuniary interest during the meeting participate further in any discussion of the business; or

- participate in any vote or further vote taken on the matter at the meeting.

These prohibitions apply to any form of participation, including speaking as a member of the public.

In certain circumstances you can request a dispensation from these prohibitions.

Where these prohibitions apply, do I also have to leave the room?

Where your council's or authority's standing orders require this, you must leave the room. Even where there are no such standing orders, you must leave the room if you consider your continued presence is incompatible with your council's code of conduct or the Seven Principles of Public Life.

Do I need a dispensation to take part in the business of setting council tax or a precept?

Any payment of, or liability to pay, council tax does not create a disclosable pecuniary interest as defined in the national rules; hence being a council tax payer does not mean that you need a dispensation to take part in the business of setting the council tax or precept or local arrangements for council tax support.

If you are a homeowner or tenant in the area of your council you will have registered, in accordance with the national rules, that beneficial interest in land. However, this disclosable pecuniary interest is not a disclosable pecuniary interest in the matter of setting the council tax or precept since decisions on the council tax or precept do not materially affect your interest in the land. For example, it does not materially affect the value of your home, your prospects of selling that home, or how you might use or enjoy that land.

Accordingly, you will not need a dispensation to take part in the business of setting the council tax or precept or local arrangements for council tax support, which is in any event a decision affecting the generality of the public in the area of your council, rather than you as an individual.

When and how can I apply for a dispensation?

The rules allow your council or authority in certain circumstances to grant a dispensation to permit a member to take part in the business of the authority even if the member has a disclosable pecuniary interest relating to that business. These circumstances are where the council or authority considers that:

- without the dispensation so great a proportion of the council or authority would be prohibited from participating in that business as to impede the council's or authority's transaction of that business;

- without the dispensation the representation of different political groups dealing with that business would be so upset as to alter the likely outcome of any vote;

210

- the granting of the dispensation is in the interests of people living in the council's or authority's area;

- without the dispensation each member of the council's executive would be prohibited from participating in the business; or

- it is otherwise appropriate to grant a dispensation.

If you would like your council or authority to grant you a dispensation, you must make a written request to the officer responsible for handling such requests in the case of your council or authority.

What happens if I don't follow the rules on disclosable pecuniary interests?

It is a criminal offence if, without a reasonable excuse, you fail to tell the monitoring officer about your disclosable pecuniary interests, either for inclusion on the register if you are a newly elected, co-opted or appointed member, or to update the register if you are re- elected or re-appointed, or when you become aware of a disclosable pecuniary interest which is not recorded in the register but which relates to any matter:

- that will be or is being considered at a meeting where you are present; or

- on which you are acting alone.

It is also a criminal offence to knowingly or recklessly provide false or misleading information, or to participate in the business of your authority where that business involves a disclosable pecuniary interest. It is also a criminal offence to continue working on a matter which can be discharged by a single member and in which you have a disclosable pecuniary interest.

If you are found guilty of such a criminal offence, you can be fined up to £5,000 and disqualified from holding office as a councillor for up to five years.

Where can I look at the national rules on pecuniary interests?

The national rules about pecuniary interests are set out in Chapter 7 of the Localism Act 2011, which is available on the internet here:

http://www.legislation.gov.uk/ukpga/2011/20/part/1/chapter/7/enacted

and in the secondary legislation made under the Act, in particular The Relevant Authorities (Disclosable Pecuniary Interests) Regulations 2012 which can be found here:

http://www.legislation.gov.uk/uksi/2012/1464/contents/made

Annex A

Description of disclosable pecuniary interests

If you have any of the following pecuniary interests, they are your **disclosable pecuniary interests** under the new national rules. Any reference to spouse or civil partner includes any person with whom you are living as husband or wife, or as if they were your civil partner.

- Any employment, office, trade, profession or vocation carried on for profit or gain, which you, or your spouse or civil partner, undertakes.

- Any payment or provision of any other financial benefit (other than from your council or authority) made or provided within the relevant period in respect of any expenses incurred by you in carrying out duties as a member, or towards your election expenses. This includes any payment or financial benefit from a trade union within the meaning of the Trade Union and Labour Relations (Consolidation) Act 1992. The relevant period is the 12 months ending on the day when you tell the monitoring officer about your disclosable pecuniary interests following your election or re-election, or when you became aware you had a disclosable pecuniary interest relating to a matter on which you were acting alone.

- Any contract which is made between you, or your spouse or your civil partner (or a body in which you, or your spouse or your civil partner, has a beneficial interest) and your council or authority:

  – under which goods or services are to be provided or works are to be executed; and

  – which has not been fully discharged.

- Any beneficial interest in land which you, or your spouse or your civil partner, have and which is within the area of your council or authority.

- Any licence (alone or jointly with others) which you, or your spouse or your civil partner, holds to occupy land in the area of your council or authority for a month or longer.

- Any tenancy where (to your knowledge):

  – the landlord is your council or authority; and

  – the tenant is a body in which you, or your spouse or your civil partner, has a beneficial interest.

- Any beneficial interest which you, or your spouse or your civil partner has in securities of a body where:

  – that body (to your knowledge) has a place of business or land in the area of your council or authority; and

  – either –

    (i) the total nominal value of the securities exceeds £25,000 or one hundredth of the total issued share capital of that body; or

    (ii) if the share capital of that body is of more than one class, the total nominal value of the shares of any one class in which you, or your spouse or your civil partner, has a beneficial interest exceeds one hundredth of the total issued share capital of that class.

PROBITY IN PLANNING FOR COUNCILLORS AND OFFICERS

This publication was prepared by Trevor Roberts Associates for the Planning Advisory Service. It also includes contributions from officers from various councils.

Published April 2013

Updated November 2013: text updated on page 14 to remove reference to discussing applications at a 'call-over' meeting

Foreword

This 2013 update to the 2009 version of the Local Government Association's Probity in Planning guide reflects changes introduced by the Localism Act 2011. It clarifies how councillors can get involved in planning discussions on plan making and on applications, on behalf of their communities in a fair, impartial and transparent way.

This guide has been written for officers and councillors involved in planning. Councillors should also be familiar with their own codes of conduct and guidance.

This guide is not intended to nor does it constitute legal advice. Councillors and officers will need to obtain their own legal advice on any matters of a legal nature concerning matters of probity.

Introduction

Planning has a positive and proactive role to play at the heart of local government. It helps councils to stimulate growth whilst looking after important environmental areas. It can help to translate goals into action. It balances social, economic and environmental needs to achieve sustainable development.

The planning system works best when officers and councillors involved in planning understand their roles and responsibilities, and the context and constraints in which they operate.

Planning decisions involve balancing many competing interests. In doing this, decision makers need an ethos of decision-making in the wider public interest on what can be controversial proposals.

It is recommended that councillors should receive regular training on code of conduct issues, interests and predetermination, as well as on planning matters.

Background

In 1997, the Third Report of the Committee on Standards in Public Life (known as the Nolan Report) resulted in pressures on councillors to avoid contact with developers in the interests of ensuring probity. In today's place-shaping context, early councillor engagement is encouraged to ensure that proposals for sustainable development can be harnessed to produce the settlements that communities need.

This guidance is intended to reinforce councillors' community engagement roles whilst maintaining good standards of probity that minimizes the risk of legal challenges.

Planning decisions are based on balancing competing interests and making an informed judgement against a local and national policy framework.

Decisions can be controversial. The risk of controversy and conflict are heightened by the openness of a system which invites public opinion before taking decisions and the legal nature of the development plan and decision notices. Nevertheless, it is important that the decision-making process is open and transparent.

One of the key aims of the planning system is to balance private interests in the development of land against the wider public interest. In performing this role, planning necessarily affects land and property interests, particularly the financial value of landholdings and the quality of their settings. Opposing views are often strongly held by those involved.

Whilst councillors must take account of these views, they should not favour any person, company, group or locality, nor put themselves in a position where they may appear to be doing so. It is important, therefore, that planning authorities make planning decisions affecting these interests openly, impartially, with sound judgement and for justifiable reasons.

The process should leave no grounds for suggesting that those participating in the decision were biased or that the decision itself was unlawful, irrational or procedurally improper.

This guidance is not intended to be prescriptive. Local circumstances may provide reasons for local variations of policy and practice. Every council should regularly review the way in which it conducts its planning business.

This guidance refers mainly to the actions of a local authority planning committee as the principal decision-making forum on planning matters. It is recognised, however, that authorities have a range of forms of decision-making: officer delegations; area committees; planning boards, and full council.

This guidance applies equally to these alternative forms of decision-making. Indeed, it becomes very important if the full council is determining planning applications referred to it, or adopting local plans and other policy documents, that councillors taking those decisions understand the importance of this guidance. The guidance also applies to councillor involvement in planning enforcement cases or the making of compulsory purchase orders.

The general role and conduct of councillors and officers

Councillors and officers have different but complementary roles. Both serve the public but councillors are responsible to the electorate, whilst officers are responsible to the council as a whole. Officers advise councillors and the council and carry out the council's work. They are employed by the council, not by individual councillors. A successful relationship between councillors and officers will be based upon mutual trust, understanding and respect of each other's positions.

Both councillors and officers are guided by codes of conduct. The 2011 Act sets out a duty for each local authority to promote and maintain high standards of conduct by councillors and to adopt a local code of conduct. All councils had to adopt a local code by August 2012.

The adopted code should be consistent with the principles of selflessness, integrity, objectivity, accountability, openness, honesty and leadership.

It should embrace the standards central to the preservation of an ethical approach to council business, including the need to register and disclose interests, as well as appropriate relationships with other councillors, staff, and the public. Many local authorities have adopted their own, separate codes relating specifically to planning although these should be cross referenced with the substantive code of conduct for the council.

Staff who are chartered town planners are subject to the Royal Town Planning Institute (RTPI) Code of Professional Conduct, breaches of which may be subject to disciplinary action by the Institute. Many authorities will have adopted a code of conduct for employees and incorporated those or equivalent rules of conduct into the contracts of employment of employees.

In addition to these codes, a council's standing orders set down rules which govern the conduct of council business.

Councillors and officers should be cautious about accepting gifts and hospitality and should exercise their discretion. Any councillor or officer receiving any such offers over and above an agreed nominal value should let the council's monitoring officer know, in writing, and seek advice as to whether they should be accepted or declined. Guidance on these issues for both councillors and officers should be included in the local code of conduct Employees must always act impartially and in a politically neutral manner. The Local Government and Housing Act 1989 enables restrictions to be set on the outside activities of senior officers, such as membership of political parties and serving on another council. Councils should carefully consider which of their officers are subject to such restrictions and review this regularly.

Officers and serving councillors must not act as agents for people pursuing planning matters within their authority even if they are not involved in the decision making on it.

Whilst the determination of a planning application is not a 'quasi-judicial' process (unlike, say, certain licensing functions carried out by the local authority), it is a formal administrative process involving the application of national and local policies, reference to legislation and case law as well as rules of procedure, rights of appeal and an expectation that people will act reasonably and fairly. All involved should remember the possibility that an aggrieved party may seek a Judicial Review and/or complain to the Ombudsman on grounds of maladministration or a breach of the authority's code.

Finally, as planning can sometimes appear to be complex and as there are currently many changes in planning taking place, the LGA endorses the good practice of many councils which ensures that their councillors receive training on planning when first appointed to the planning committee or local plan steering group, and regularly thereafter. The Planning Advisory Service (PAS) can provide training to councillors (contact pas@local.gov.uk).

Registration and disclosure of interests

Chapter 7 of the 2011 Act places requirements on councillors regarding the registration and disclosure of their pecuniary interests and the consequences for a councillor taking part in consideration of an issue in the light of those interests. The definitions of disclosable pecuniary interests are set out in The Relevant Authorities (Disclosable Pecuniary Interests) Regulations 2012. A failure to register a disclosable pecuniary interest within 28 days of election or co-option or the provision of false or misleading information on registration, or participation in discussion or voting in a meeting on a matter in which a councillor or co-opted member has a disclosable pecuniary interest, are criminal offences.

For full guidance on interests, see Openness and transparency on personal interests: guidance for councillors, Department for Communities and Local Government, March 2013. (This guidance note does not seek to replicate the detailed information contained within the DCLG note). Advice should always be sought from the council's monitoring officer. Ultimately, responsibility for fulfilling the requirements rests with each councillor.

The provisions of the Act seek to separate interests arising from the personal and private interests of the councillor from those arising from the councillor's wider public life. Councillors should think about how a reasonable member of the public, with full knowledge of all the relevant facts, would view the matter when considering whether the councillor's involvement would be appropriate.

Each council's code of conduct should establish what interests need to be disclosed. All disclosable interests should be registered and a register maintained by the council's monitoring officer and made available to the public. Councillors should also disclose that interest orally at the committee meeting when it relates to an item under discussion.

A councillor must provide the monitoring officer with written details of relevant interests within 28 days of their election or appointment to office. Any changes to those interests must similarly be notified within 28 days of the councillor becoming aware of such changes.

A disclosable pecuniary interest relating to an item under discussion requires the withdrawal of the councillor from the committee. In certain circumstances, a dispensation can be sought from the appropriate body or officer to take part in that particular item of business.

If a councillor has a (non-pecuniary) personal interest, he or she should disclose that interest, but then may speak and vote on that particular item. This includes being a member of an outside body; mere membership of another body does not constitute an interest requiring such a prohibition.

It is always best to identify a potential interest early on. If a councillor thinks that they may have an interest in a particular matter to be discussed at planning committee he or she should raise this with their monitoring officer as soon as possible.

See Appendix for a flowchart of how councillors' interests should be handled.

Predisposition, predetermination, or bias

Members of a planning committee, Local Plan steering group (or full Council when the local plan is being considered) need to avoid any appearance of bias or of having predetermined their views before taking a decision on a planning application or on planning policies.

The courts have sought to distinguish between situations which involve predetermination or bias on the one hand and predisposition on the other. The former is indicative of a 'closed mind' approach and likely to leave the committee's decision susceptible to challenge by Judicial Review.

Clearly expressing an intention to vote in a particular way before a meeting (predetermination) is different from where a councillor makes it clear they are willing to listen to all the considerations presented at the committee before deciding on how to vote (predisposition). The latter is alright, the former is not and may result in a Court quashing such planning decisions.

Section 25 of the Act also provides that a councillor should not be regarded as having a closed mind simply because they previously did or said something that, directly or indirectly, indicated what view they might take in relation to any particular matter.

This reflects the common law position that a councillor may be predisposed on a matter before it comes to Committee, provided they remain open to listening to all the arguments and changing their mind in light of all the information presented at the meeting. Nevertheless, a councillor in this position will always be judged against an objective test of whether the reasonable onlooker, with knowledge of the relevant facts, would consider that the councillor was biased.

For example, a councillor who states 'Windfarms are blots on the landscape and I will oppose each and every windfarm application that comes before the committee' will be perceived very differently from a councillor who states: 'Many people find windfarms ugly and noisy and I will need a lot of persuading that any more windfarms should be allowed in our area.'

If a councillor has predetermined their position, they should withdraw from being a member of the decision-making body for that matter.

This would apply to any member of the planning committee who wanted to speak for or against a proposal, as a campaigner (for example on a proposal within their ward).

If the Council rules allow substitutes to the meeting, this could be an appropriate option.

Authorities will usually have a cabinet/executive member responsible for development and planning. This councillor is able to be a member of the planning committee. Leading members of a local authority, who have participated in the development of planning policies and proposals, need not and should not, on that ground and in the interests of the good conduct of business, normally exclude themselves from decision making committees.

Development proposals submitted by councillors and officers, and council development

Proposals submitted by serving and former councillors, officers and their close associates and relatives can easily give rise to suspicions of impropriety. Proposals could be planning applications or local plan proposals.

Such proposals must be handled in a way that gives no grounds for accusations of favouritism. Any local planning protocol or code of good practice should address the following points in relation to proposals submitted by councillors and planning officers:

- if they submit their own proposal to their authority they should play no part in its consideration;

- a system should be devised to identify and manage such proposals;

- the council's monitoring officer should be informed of such proposals;

- such proposals should be reported to the planning committee and not dealt with by officers under delegated powers.

A councillor would undoubtedly have a disclosable pecuniary interest in their own application and should not participate in its consideration. They do have the same rights as any applicant in seeking to explain their proposal to an officer, but the councillor, as applicant, should also not seek to improperly influence the decision.

Proposals for a council's own development should be treated with the same transparency and impartiality as those of private developers.

Lobbying of and by councillors

Lobbying is a normal part of the planning process. Those who may be affected by a planning decision, whether through an application, a site allocation in a development plan or an emerging policy, will often seek to influence it through an approach to their ward member or to a member of the planning committee.

As the Nolan Committee's 1997 report stated: 'It is essential for the proper operation of the planning system that local concerns are adequately ventilated. The most effective and suitable way that this can be done is through the local elected representatives, the councillors themselves'.

Lobbying, however, can lead to the impartiality and integrity of a councillor being called into question, unless care and common sense is exercised by all the parties involved.

As noted earlier in this guidance note, the common law permits predisposition but nevertheless it remains good practice that, when being lobbied, councillors (members of the planning committee in particular) should try to take care about expressing an opinion that may be taken as indicating that they have already made up their mind on the issue before they have been exposed to all the evidence and arguments.

In such situations, they could restrict themselves to giving advice about the process and what can and can't be taken into account.

Councillors can raise issues which have been raised by their constituents, with officers. If councillors do express an opinion to objectors or supporters, it is good practice that they make it clear that they will only be in a position to take a final decision after having heard all the relevant arguments and taken into account all relevant material and planning considerations at committee.

If any councillor, whether or not a committee member, speaks on behalf of a lobby group at the decision-making committee, they would be well advised to withdraw once any public or ward member speaking opportunities had been completed in order to counter any suggestion that members of the committee may have been influenced by their continuing presence. This should be set out in the authority's code of conduct for planning matters.

It is very difficult to find a form of words which conveys every nuance of these situations and which gets the balance right between the duty to be an active local representative and the requirement when taking decisions on planning matters to take account of all arguments in an open-minded way. It cannot be stressed too strongly, however, that the striking of this balance is, ultimately, the responsibility of the individual councillor.

A local code on planning should also address the following more specific issues about lobbying:

- Planning decisions cannot be made on a party political basis in response to lobbying; the use of political whips to seek to influence the outcome of a planning application is likely to be regarded as maladministration.

- Planning committee or local plan steering group members should in general avoid organising support for or against a planning application, and avoid lobbying other councillors.

- Councillors should not put pressure on officers for a particular recommendation or decision, and should not do anything which compromises, or is likely to compromise, the officers' impartiality or professional integrity.

- Call-in procedures, whereby councillors can require a proposal that would normally be determined under the delegated authority to be called in for determination by the planning committee, should require the reasons for call-in to be recorded in writing and to refer solely to matters of material planning concern.

As previously outlined, councillors must always be mindful of their responsibilities and duties under their local codes of conduct. These responsibilities and duties apply equally to matters of lobbying as they do to the other issues of probity explored elsewhere in this guidance.

Pre-application discussions

Pre-application discussions between a potential applicant and a council can benefit both parties and are encouraged. However, it would be easy for such discussions to become, or be seen by objectors to become, part of a lobbying process on the part of the applicant.

Some councils have been concerned about probity issues raised by involving councillors in pre-application discussions, worried that councillors would be accused of predetermination when the subsequent application came in for consideration. Now, through the Localism Act and previously the Audit Commission, the LGA and PAS recognise that councillors have an important role to play in pre-application discussions, bringing their local knowledge and expertise, along with an understanding of community views. Involving councillors can help identify issues early on, helps councillors lead on community issues and helps to make sure that issues don't come to light for the first time at committee. PAS recommends a 'no shocks' approach.

The Localism Act, particularly s 25, by endorsing this approach, has given councillors much more freedom to engage in pre-application discussions. Nevertheless, in order to avoid perceptions that councillors might have fettered their discretion, such discussions should take place within clear, published guidelines.

Although the term 'pre-application' has been used, the same considerations should apply to any discussions which occur before a decision is taken. In addition to any specific local circumstances, guidelines should include the following:

- Clarity at the outset that the discussions will not bind a council to making a particular decision and that any views expressed are personal and provisional. By the very nature of such meetings not all relevant information may be at hand, nor will formal consultations with interested parties have taken place.

- An acknowledgement that consistent advice should be given by officers based upon the development plan and material planning considerations.

- Officers should be present with councillors in pre-application meetings. Councillors should avoid giving separate advice on the development plan or material considerations as they may not be aware of all the issues at an early stage. Neither should they become drawn into any negotiations, which should be done by officers (keeping interested councillors up to date) to ensure that the authority's position is co-ordinated.

- Confirmation that a written note should be made of all meetings. An officer should make the arrangements for such meetings, attend and write notes. A note should also be taken of any phone conversations, and relevant emails recorded for the file. Notes should record issues raised and advice given. The note(s) should be placed on the file as a public record. If there is a legitimate reason for confidentiality regarding a proposal, a note of the non-confidential issues raised or advice given can still normally be placed on the file to reassure others not party to the discussion.

- A commitment that care will be taken to ensure that advice is impartial, otherwise the subsequent report or recommendation to committee could appear to be advocacy.

- The scale of proposals to which these guidelines would apply. Councillors talk regularly to constituents to gauge their views on matters of local concern. The Nolan Committee argued that keeping a register of these conversations would be impractical and unnecessary. Authorities should think about when, however, discussions should be registered and notes written.

Authorities have other mechanisms to involve councillors in pre-application discussions including:

- committee information reports by officers of discussions to enable councillors to raise issues, identify items of interest and seek further information;

- developer presentations to committees which have the advantage of transparency if held in public as a committee would normally be (with notes taken);

- ward councillor briefing by officers on pre-application discussions.

Similar arrangements can also be used when authorities are looking at new policy documents and particularly when making new site allocations in emerging development plans and wish to engage with different parties, including councillors, at an early stage in the process.

The Statement of Community Involvement will set out the council's approach to involving communities and other consultees in pre-application discussions. Some authorities have public planning forums to explore major pre-application proposals with the developer outlining their ideas and invited speakers to represent differing interests and consultees. As well as being transparent, these forums allow councillors and consultees to seek information and identify important issues for the proposal to address, although still bearing in mind the need to avoid pre-determination.

Officer reports to committee

As a result of decisions made by the courts and ombudsman, officer reports on planning applications must have regard to the following:

- Reports should be accurate and should include the substance of any objections and other responses received to the consultation.

- Relevant information should include a clear assessment against the relevant development plan policies, relevant parts of the National Planning Policy Framework (NPPF), any local finance considerations, and any other material planning considerations.

- Reports should have a written recommendation for a decision to be made.

- Reports should contain technical appraisals which clearly justify the recommendation.

- If the report's recommendation is contrary to the provisions of the development plan, the material considerations which justify the departure must be clearly stated. This is not only good practice, but also failure to do so may constitute maladministration or give rise to a Judicial Review challenge on the grounds that the decision was not taken in accordance with the provisions of the development plan and the council's statutory duty under s 38A of the Planning and Compensation Act 2004 and s 70 of the Town and Country Planning Act 1990.

Any oral updates or changes to the report should be recorded.

Public speaking at planning committees

Whether to allow public speaking at a planning committee or not is up to each local authority. Most authorities do allow it. As a result, public confidence is generally enhanced and direct lobbying may be reduced. The disadvantage is that it can make the meetings longer and sometimes harder to manage.

Where public speaking is allowed, clear protocols should be established about who is allowed to speak, including provisions for applicants, supporters, ward councillors, parish councils and third party objectors.

In the interests of equity, the time allowed for presentations for and against the development should be the same, and those speaking should be asked to direct their presentation to reinforcing or amplifying representations already made to the council in writing.

New documents should not be circulated to the committee; councillors may not be able to give proper consideration to the new information and officers may not be able to check for accuracy or provide considered advice on any material considerations arising. This should be made clear to those who intend to speak.

Messages should never be passed to individual committee members, either from other councillors or from the public. This could be seen as seeking to influence that member improperly and will create a perception of bias that will be difficult to overcome.

Decisions which differ from a recommendation

The law requires that decisions should be taken in accordance with the development plan, unless material considerations (which specifically include the NPPF) indicate otherwise (s 38A of the Planning and Compensation Act 2004 and s 70 of the Town and Country Planning Act 1990).

This applies to all planning decisions. Any reasons for refusal must be justified against the development plan and other material considerations.

The courts have expressed the view that the committee's reasons should be clear and convincing. The personal circumstances of an applicant or any other material or non-material planning considerations which might cause local controversy will rarely satisfy the relevant tests.

Planning committees can, and often do, make a decision which is different from the officer recommendation. Sometimes this will relate to conditions or terms of a s 106 obligation. Sometimes it will change the outcome, from an approval to a refusal or vice versa. This will usually reflect a difference in the assessment of how a policy has been complied with, or different weight ascribed to material considerations.

Planning committees are advised to take the following steps before making a decision which differs from the officer recommendation:

- if a councillor is concerned about an officer reccommendation they should discuss their areas of difference and the reasons for that with officers in advance of the committee meeting;

- recording the detailed reasons as part of the mover's motion;

- adjourning for a few minutes for those reasons to be discussed and then agreed by the committee;

- where there is concern about the validity of reasons, considering deferring to another meeting to have the putative reasons tested and discussed.

If the planning committee makes a decision contrary to the officers' recommendation (whether for approval or refusal or changes to conditions or s 106 obligations), a detailed minute of the committee's reasons should be made and a copy placed on the application file. Councillors should be prepared to explain in full their planning reasons for not agreeing with the officer's recommendation. Pressure should never be put on officers to 'go away and sort out the planning reasons'.

The officer should also be given an opportunity to explain the implications of the contrary decision, including an assessment of a likely appeal outcome, and chances of a successful award of costs against the council, should one be made.

All applications that are clearly contrary to the development plan must be advertised as such, and are known as 'departure' applications. If it is intended to approve such an application, the material considerations leading to this conclusion must be clearly identified, and how these considerations justify overriding the development plan must be clearly demonstrated.

The application may then have to be referred to the relevant secretary of state, depending upon the type and scale of the development proposed (s 77 of the Town and Country Planning Act 1990). If the officers' report recommends approval of such a departure, the justification for this should be included, in full, in that report.

Committee site visits

National standards and local codes also apply to site visits. Councils should have a clear and consistent approach on when and why to hold a site visit and how to conduct it. This should avoid accusations that visits are arbitrary, unfair or a covert lobbying device. The following points may be helpful:

- visits should only be used where the benefit is clear and substantial; officers will have visited the site and assessed the scheme against policies and material considerations already;

- the purpose, format and conduct should be clear at the outset and adhered to throughout the visit;

- where a site visit can be 'triggered' by a request from the ward councillor, the 'substantial benefit' test should still apply;

- keep a record of the reasons why a site visit is called.

A site visit is only likely to be necessary if:

- the impact of the proposed development is difficult to visualise from the plans and any supporting material, including photographs taken by officers;

- the comments of the applicant and objectors cannot be expressed adequately in writing; or

- the proposal is particularly contentious.

Site visits are for observing the site and gaining a better understanding of the issues. Visits made by committee members, with officer assistance, are normally the most fair and equitable approach. They should not be used as a lobbying opportunity by objectors or supporters.

This should be made clear to any members of the public who are there.

Once a councillor becomes aware of a proposal they may be tempted to visit the site alone. In such a situation, a councillor is only entitled to view the site from public vantage points and they have no individual rights to enter private property. Whilst a councillor might be invited to enter the site by the owner, it is not good practice to do so on their own, as this can lead to the perception that the councillor is no longer impartial.

Annual review of decisions

It is good practice for councillors to visit a sample of implemented planning permissions to assess the quality of the decisions and the development. This should improve the quality and consistency of decision-making, strengthen public confidence in the planning system, and can help with reviews of planning policy.

Reviews should include visits to a range of developments such as major and minor schemes; upheld appeals; listed building works and enforcement cases. Briefing notes should be prepared on each case. The planning committee should formally consider the review and decide whether it gives rise to the need to reconsider any policies or practices.

Scrutiny or standards committees may be able to assist in this process but the essential purpose of these reviews is to assist planning committee members to refine their understanding of the impact of their decisions. Planning committee members should be fully engaged in such reviews.

Complaints and record keeping

All councils should have a complaints procedure which may apply to all council activities. A council should also consider how planning-related complaints will be handled, in relation to the code of conduct adopted by the authority.

So that complaints may be fully investigated and as general good practice, record keeping should be complete and accurate. Every planning application file should contain an accurate account of events throughout its life. It should be possible for someone not involved in that application to understand what the decision was, and why and how it had been reached. This applies to decisions taken by committee and under delegated powers, and to applications, enforcement and development plan matters.

List of references

Probity in planning: the role of councillors and officers – revised guidance note on good planning practice for councillors and officers dealing with planning matters Local Government Association, May 2009

http://www.local.gov.uk/web/guest/publications/-/journal_content/56/10171/3378249/PUBLICATION-TEMPLATE

The Localism Act 2011

http://www.legislation.gov.uk/ukpga/2011/20/ contents/enacted

National Planning Policy Framework Department for Communities and Local Government, March 2012

https://www.gov.uk/government/uploads/system/uploads/attachment_data/file/6077/2116950.pdf

Committee on Standards in Public Life (1997) Third Report: Standards of Conduct in Local Government in England, Scotland and Wales, Volume 1 Report Cm 3702-1:

http://www.public-standards.gov.uk/our-work/inquiries/previous-reports/third-report-standards-of-conduct-of-local-government-in-england-scotland-and-wales/

Royal Town Planning Institute Code of Professional Conduct:

http://www.rtpi.org.uk/membership/ professional-standards/

The Relevant Authorities (Disclosable Pecuniary Interests) Regulations 2012

http://www.legislation.gov.uk/uksi/2012/1464/ contents/made

Openness and transparency on personal interests: guidance for councillors, Department for Communities and Local Government, March 2013

https://www.gov.uk/government/publications/openness-and-transparency-on-personal-interests-guidance-for-councillors

The Planning System – matching expectations to capacity

Audit Commission, February 2006

http://archive.audit-commission.gov.uk/auditcommission/sitecollectiondocuments/ AuditCommissionReports/NationalStudies/ Planning_FINAL.pdf

'Standards Matter' Kelly Committee Jan 2013

http://www.official-documents.gov.uk/ document/cm85/8519/8519.pdf

Flowchart of councillors' interests

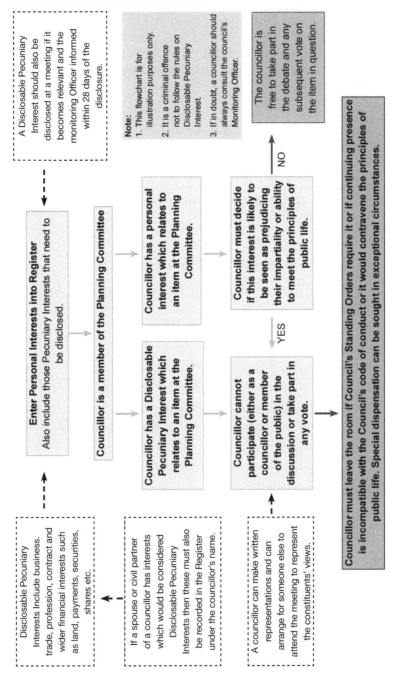

Local Government Association

Local Government House
Smith Square
London SW1P 3HZ

Telephone 020 7664 3000

Fax 020 7664 3030

Email info@local.gov.uk www.local.gov.uk

© Local Government Association, April 2013

For a copy in Braille, larger print or audio, please contact us on 020 7664 3000.

We consider requests on an individual basis.

POSITIVE ENGAGEMENT: A GUIDE FOR PLANNING COUNCILLORS

Updated version

> 'The engagement of local councillors as leaders and representatives of the community is vital in the delivery of positive outcomes from the planning process.'

A message from Iain Wright MP Parliamentary Under Secretary of State, DCLG and Paul Bettison, Environment Board Chairman, LGA.

> 'There have been some considerable changes over the last few years in how the planning process is delivered within England with a move away from an often adversarial, reactive and conflict based system towards a more pro-active, inclusive and creative approach.

> As a local councillor involved in planning matters, whether as a ward councillor representing your area's constituents as a councillor responsible for drawing up the spatial plan for your area, or as a councillor responsible for deciding upon application you have a crucial role to play in both making the planning system work and ensuring the best possible outcomes for your community for both now and in the future. The engagement of local councillors as leaders and representatives of the community is vital in the delivery of positive outcomes from the planning process.

> However, concerns are sometimes expressed about the compatibility of councillors meeting developers and interest groups and then taking decisions on an impartial basis.

> This leaflet is an updated version of the positive engagement for elected members launched in 2005. It is intended to summarise the principles that should be observed to enable you to both participate in and lead the system.'

In broad terms, the success of the planning system will depend on:

- establishing and taking forward a clear spatial vision for the area based on the sustainable community strategy;

- effective dialogue between applicants, local authority, local people and other interests to help define and realise the vision;

- ensuring that the spatial plan for an area embodies the aspirations of the community;

- effective communication and ownership of policy between executive and planning committee;

- the planning service being focused on outcomes;

- early and effective community engagement in discussions on plans and development proposals, in accordance with the authority's Statement of Community Involvement;

- upholding the ACSeS Model Members Planning Code.

As a community leader and local representative you will want to be involved in relevant public meetings, pre-application discussions and policy production. However, this may create some risks for councillors, particularly those who are members of the planning committee, and for the integrity of the decision making process. You should familiarise yourself with guidance found in the LGA guide Probity in Planning (update) – the role of councillors and officers, guidance from the Standards Board for England which provides an overview of the Model Code of Conduct which applies to all members and co-opted members of local authorities and the ACSeS Model Members Planning Code (see the weblinks at the end of this leaflet).

Councillors can involve themselves in discussions with developers, their constituents and others about planning matters. However, difficulties can be avoided if you follow these useful general hints:

Do:

- always involve officers and structure discussions with developers;

- inform officers about any approaches made to you and seek advice;

- familiarise yourself with your authority's Code of Conduct and follow it when you are representing your authority;

- keep your register of interests up to date;

- follow your local authority's planning code;

- be aware of what predisposition, predetermination and bias mean in your role – ask your monitoring or planning officer and refer to the Standards Board Occasional Paper on Predetermination, Predisposition and Bias if unsure;

- be prepared to hold discussions with an applicant and your officers before a planning application is made, not just after it has been submitted to your authority;

- preface any discussion with disclaimers; keep a note of meetings and calls; and make clear at the outset that discussions are not binding;

- be aware of what personal and prejudicial interests are – refer to your monitoring officer and the Standards Board's website if you are unsure;

- recognise the distinction between giving advice and engaging in negotiation and when this is appropriate in your role;

- stick to policies included in adopted plans, but also pay heed to any other considerations relevant to planning;

- use meetings to show leadership and vision;

- encourage positive outcomes;

- ask for training from your authority in probity matters;

- recognise that you can lobby and campaign but that this may remove you from the decision making process;

- feed in both your own and your local community's concerns and issues;

- be aware that you can engage in discussions but you must have and be seen to have an open mind at the point of decision making.

Do not:

- use your position improperly for personal gain or to advantage your friends or close associates;

- meet developers alone or put yourself in a position where you appear to favour a person, company or group – even a 'friendly' private discussion with a developer could cause others to mistrust your impartiality;

- attend meetings or be involved in decision-making where you have a prejudicial interest under the Model Code of Conduct – except when speaking when the general public are also allowed to do so;

- accept gifts or hospitality;

- prejudge or be seen to prejudge an issue if you want to be a decision maker on a proposal;

- seek to influence officers or put pressure on them to support a particular course of action in relation to a planning application;

- compromise the impartiality of people who work for your authority;

- invent local guides on probity in planning which are incompatible with current guidance – look for commonly held and common sense parallels in other authorities or the principles set out in national guidance.

This simple guide has been produced by a number of organisations who have shared interest in maximising the effectiveness of councillor involvement in planning.

They include: the Local Government Association, Association of Council Secretaries and Solicitors, the Standards Board for England, Planning Advisory Service and The Department of Communities and Local Government and Planning Officers Society.

Weblinks

The Association of Council Secretaries and Solicitors

Model Members Planning Code www.acses.org.uk/documents/category/4

Department of Communities and Local Government

www.communities.gov.uk

Local Government Association

Probity in planning (update): the role of councillors and officers

www.lga.gov.uk/planning

A LGA update to the highly successful original guidance (published in 1997) on preparing a local code of good practice for those dealing with planning matters will be available shortly

National Planning Forum

Pre-application advice for town and country planning:

National Planning Forum good practice note 2 one of a series of 'inspiring planning' good practice notes www.natplanforum.org.uk/good%20practice.html

Planning Advisory Service

Member development modules

www.pas.gov.uk/membertraining

Planning Officers Society

Members and Planning

www.planningofficers.org.uk/article.cp/articleid/176

The Standards Board for England

Guidance on the Model Code of Conduct, including personal and prejudicial interests

www.standardsboard.gov.uk/TheCodeofConduct/Guidance/

Fact sheets and Frequently Asked Questions

www.standardsboard.gov.uk/TheCodeofConduct/
Factsheetsandfrequentlyaskedquestions/

Paper on predisposition, predetermination or bias, and the Code

www.standardsboard.gov.uk/Publications/OccasionalPaper/

Key cases

Contents

PERSONAL AND PREJUDICIAL INTERESTS ON THE PART OF COUNCILLORS

R v Kirklees MBC Ex p Beaumont [2001] 3 LGLR 12

Facts

Pupils at a school challenged a decision by the Council to close the school on the basis of a surplus of places in the area. It was alleged that two councillors involved in the decision had a private or personal interest because they were governors of another school which was to replace the school due to be closed by means of an expansion programme, and that such interest should have been disclosed.

Issue

Whether the Councillors should have disclosed their interest in the matter and withdrawn from the meeting at which the decision was taken.

Decision

The court held that each of the councillors concerned had a clear and substantial interest in the outcome of the voting process and that accordingly they should have declared their interest and withdrawn from the voting process.

R (on the application of Richardson) v North Yorkshire CC [2003] EWCA Civ 1860

Facts

Councillor Richardson objected to an application for planning permission to extend a quarry in circumstances where his property was one of a handful likely to be most affected by the proposed development.

On the basis that he had a prejudicial interest in the subject matter of the meeting, he was excluded from the Council's planning and regulatory functions committee meeting at which it was resolved that planning permission would be granted subject to conditions.

Cllr Richardson challenged the grant of planning permission.

Issues

(1) Which members with a prejudicial interest in a particular matter were required by the Code to withdraw from a meeting to consider the matter: whether all members or only members of the committee holding the relevant meeting.

(2) Whether a member, who was required to withdraw from the meeting in his role as a councillor, was entitled to attend it in his 'personal capacity'.

(3) Whether Cllr Richardson was properly to be regarded as having a 'prejudicial interest' in the matter of this planning application.

Decision

The Code required Cllr Richardson to withdraw on the basis of his membership of the authority alone and even though he was not a member of the planning committee deciding the application.

Furthermore, where a councillor was prevented by the code from attending the meeting in his official capacity, it was not open to him to declare that he would attend the meeting solely in his private capacity to defend his own personal interests.

As to whether the councillor was in breach of the code the judge stated that:

> 'A member of the public with knowledge of the relevant facts would reasonably have regarded Mr Richardson's personal interest as so significant that it was likely to prejudice his judgment of the public interest. I reject [the] submission that a knowledgeable member of the public would reasonably have regarded him as simply putting forward the views of the people he represented, or making a contribution to the debate based on his perception of the public interest, rather than being influenced by the potential impact of the development on his own home. However conscientious a councillor might be in his representative role and his concern to protect the public interest, the personal interest was a highly material additional consideration.'

Scrivens v Ethical Standards Officer [2005] EWHC 529 (Admin)

Facts

Councillor Scrivens was found to have breached the code by failing to declare personal and prejudicial interests in relation to various Council meetings, including a failure to declare a prejudicial interest in an Amenities Committee meeting to determine an application for funding made by a theatre company to whom Cllr Scrivens' theatrical clothes hire business had hired out costumes at cost and given them box office space in his shop free of charge.

Issue

Whether, in determining whether a councillor has failed to comply with the requirements of the Code as regards personal and prejudicial interests, the proper test to be applied by a case tribunal of the Adjudication Panel is subjective or objective:

(a) whether the councillor, on the information available to him on the occasion in question, could rationally have taken the view he did as to whether he had a personal or (if so) prejudicial interest in the matter under consideration; or

(b) whether, viewed objectively, the councillor had a personal or a prejudicial interest in the matter.

Decision

The court held that the issue of whether there had been a breach was to be assessed objectively by reference to a 2-stage test:

(1) whether the member in question had a personal or prejudicial interest; and, if so

(2) whether there had been a breach of the code.

The court rejected Cllr Scrivens' argument that test was subjective. In other words, it was irrelevant whether a councillor reasonably but mistakenly believed that he did not have a personal or prejudicial interest.

The judge stated that:

> 'In my judgment, a subjective test would confer considerable latitude on the conduct of members. It would seriously detract from the express object of the Act and the purpose of the code, namely the promotion and maintenance of high standards of conduct by members. The effect of the Appellant's contention, which is that a member of a local authority may participate with impunity in its consideration of a matter in which a fair-minded person would think that he has a disqualifying prejudicial interest, if the member wrongly but reasonably believes that he does not have such an interest, would be to damage public confidence in the affairs of local authorities.'

R (on the application of Port Regis School Ltd) v North Dorset DC [2006] EWHC 742 (Admin)

Facts

The Council granted planning permission for agricultural land to be used as a showground and to erect a pavilion, as part of which it was proposed provide a dedicated room in the pavilion for the use of a local Masonic Lodge.

233

Two members of the meeting at which the decision was taken were freemasons, had declared their interest and had signed declarations to abide by the Code (which allowed them to speak and vote at the meeting). They were not members of the particular Masonic Lodge in question and therefore did not declare a prejudicial interest (which would have precluded them from speaking and voting).

The Claimant challenged the decision, arguing that they should have declared a prejudicial interest, rather than just a personal interest on the basis of their membership such that the decision was unlawful by reason of apparent bias.

Issue

Whether there was apparent bias in the decision as a result of the fact that freemasonry was a 'secretive' and 'fraternal' society and that a freemason was required (irrespective of membership of a particular lodge) to pledge to form a 'column of mutual defence' with brother masons and to 'succour his [fellow mason's] weakness and relieve his necessities, so far as may fairly be done.'

Decision

The judge stated that:

> '[...] it would be unrealistic to believe that the firmly held suspicion, that being a member requires partiality to be shown to freemasons and to freemasonry, has been dispelled. Without information which illuminates what is meant by "a column of mutual support", the perception that freemasonry will give rise to apparent bias in decision making will prevail.
>
> I am conscious that the extent of the suspicion is such as to make it likely that a large section of fair minded people would agree with the claimant's expressed position and subscribe to a belief that there is always a real possibility that a freemason will assist another freemason or freemasonry, whatever may be called for by the merits of a decision which has to be taken in connection with local government, but I have concluded that a fair minded observer, informed of the facts in connection with freemasonry which have been placed before this court and having regard to the circumstances of this case, would not conclude that there was a real possibility of apparent bias affecting the decision [...]'

In particular the judge took into account the fact that in addition to the obligation of mutual assistance, a freemason must assume a number of other obligations which included being '... exemplary in the discharge of ... civil duties ... by paying due obedience to the laws'. A freemason was not required, when all the oaths were read to together in context, to be partial to any other freemason or to the interests of freemasonry in a local government context.

Further, oaths of mutual assistance were not incompatible with the judicial oath (*Locabail (UK) Ltd v Bayfield Properties Ltd* (Leave to Appeal) [2000] QB 451).

EU Plants Limited v Wokingham Borough Council [2012] EWHC 3305 (Admin)

Facts

The Claimant challenged the Council's decision to confirm a Tree Preservation Order, which protected all trees on land within a 5 metre strip adjacent to a specified permissive path on a farm which produced soft fruit plants for commercial fruit farms. The Claimant wanted to expand its activities at the farm.

The Chairman of the planning committee that made the decision lived in close proximity to the farm and, prior to the making of the Order, had made various statements to the Claimant's Managing Director, which included a veiled threat to use a Tree Preservation Order to stop development, and an expression of sympathetic support for local residents campaigning against development of the farm.

The Claimant challenged the decision on the basis that the Councillor had a personal interest in the matter and that he had demonstrated bias or apparent bias. It was said that the Councillor was, operating from behind the scenes, the driving force behind the Order.

Issue

(1) Whether the decision to confirm the Order was unlawful by reason of the Councillor's personal interest in the matter.

(2) Whether the decision was tainted by bias.

Decision

The challenge was dismissed. The Councillor only learnt of the Order when he received notice of it. He was entitled to take into account the views of his constituents and members of the residents' group, provided he took into account and had regard to all material considerations and gave fair consideration to the application. He didn't actually vote for the Order at the meeting.

An appeal to the Court of Appeal failed on other grounds ([2013] EWCA Civ 1542).

R (Freud) v Oxford City Council [2013] EWHC 4613 (Admin)

Facts

Mr Freud challenged the grant of planning permission in favour of the University of Oxford for the redevelopment of one its buildings. The proposal was controversial locally by reason of its uncompromisingly modern design. One of the Claimant's grounds was that the chairman of the planning committee and others ought not to have participated in the debate because of their connection with the university. In particular, one councillor was employed by the university.

Issue

Whether, by reason of his employment by the university which had applied for planning permission, a member of the planning committee had a disclosable pecuniary interest in the planning application and should not have taken part in the debate at the meeting to discuss it.

Decision

The challenge failed. The councillor was not in any part of the university which was promoting the application. He had no contract to deal with it. He had nothing in that respect which could amount to a disclosable pecuniary interest in that matter.

While there might have been a basis on which it might be said that everybody who is employed by an employer has some pecuniary interest, however indirect, in how that employer does under ss 94-98 of the Local Government Act 1972, the law had changed and, by reference to the relevant provisions (ss 25, 30–31 of the Localism Act 2011), there was no longer any basis for such an argument.

PREDETERMINATION

R v Waltham Borough Council, ex parte Baxter [1988] QB 419

Facts

Prior to a council meeting at which the forthcoming rate was to be set, members of the majority group discussed and decided, at a private meeting, on a proposed increase in the rate, which was significant. The group's standing orders provided that members were prohibited from voting against decisions of the group, with the sanction of withdrawal of the party whip.

Several members who had opposed the level of increase and voted against the proposal in the private meeting nevertheless voted for the resolution at the council meeting and accordingly the decision to increase the rate taken.

The applicants challenged the decision on the basis that those members had voted contrary to their personal views and that, had they abstained or voted against the resolution, the decision would not have been passed.

Issue

Whether the decision was unlawful by reason of the fact that some councillors had voted for the resolution, notwithstanding that it was contrary to their personal view, thereby fettering their discretion and in breach of their duty to consider the issues involved and to reach their own decision.

Decision

The claim was dismissed.

If the councillors had voted as they did, not because they considered that the resolution should be passed, but because, in the light of the majority group's private vote, their discretion had been fettered and they had no option but to vote as they did, the decision would be unlawful.

However, the evidence did not show that this was the case. Each councillor, despite having opposed the increase at the earlier policy meeting, had voted as they had after making up their own minds on the issue.

The Court said, 'bearing in mind that it must always be open to a member of the council to change his mind at any time before the actual vote in council, the fact that he expressed a different view at an earlier time does not, of itself, give rise to any inference that his discretion was fettered or that he voted contrary to his genuinely held views'.

Further, that a councillor faced the sanction of the withdrawal of the party whip should he vote contrary to group policy was not evidence that his discretion had been fettered. What would be objectionable would be a provision that a member had forthwith to resign his membership of the council if, in the absence of a conscience situation, he intended to vote contrary to group policy.

Party loyalty or party policy were relevant considerations provided they did not dominate so as to exclude other considerations or deprive the councillor of a real choice.

R (Island Farm Development Ltd) v Bridgend County Borough Council [2006] EWHC 2189 (Admin)

Facts

The Council owned land designated as a specialist site for high technology usage designed to attract employers. The Claimant had planning permission to develop adjoining land and entered into preliminary negotiations to purchase the Council's land to facilitate its development plans. No binding agreement was reached.

Elections then resulted in a change in control of the Council and the new administration froze all sale negotiations pending a review. Following a review meeting, the local authority decided not to sell the land in order to preserve future employment opportunities.

The members of the cabinet which decided not to proceed with the sale had been active and vociferous opponents of the development. Their manifesto had stated:

> '... Island Farm was planned in part to accommodate a valuable extension to a business park [...] We would not allow these community assets to be reduced by uncertain and speculative ventures of the kind recently proposed [...]'

One Councillor had, prior to his election, been an active member and secretary of the Island Farm Action Group (IFAG), which had opposed the proposed development.

The Claimant challenged the decision not to sell the land on the basis that it was predetermined and tainted by apparent bias.

Issue

Whether the decision was predetermined and tainted by bias.

Decision

The challenge was dismissed.

The Councillor who had been a member of the Action Group had produced a speaking note at the meeting setting out the pros and cons of the options. This did not support the claim that he had closed his mind to any arguments that a sale was the appropriate option.

> 'The reality is that Councillors must be trusted to abide by the rules which the law lays down, namely that, whatever their views, they must approach their decision-making with an open mind in the sense that they must have regard to all material considerations and be prepared to change their views if persuaded that they should.'

The evidence before the judge demonstrated that each member was prepared to and did consider the relevant arguments and each was prepared to change his or her mind if the material persuaded him or her to do so.

R (Lewis) v Redcar and Cleveland BC [2008] EWCA Civ 746

Facts

A local resident challenged the decision by the Council to grant planning permission for a mixed use development, alleging that the committee had approached the matter with a closed mind.

The planning decision was made when the Council was under the control of a coalition cabinet which had expressed support for the development. The proposal was politically controversial and the decision was made during the purdah period prior to an election, contrary to the council's own guidance and in the face of opposition from the opposition party (which subsequently won the election). One of the coalition councillors who spoke and voted at the planning meeting was a member of the cabinet which had previously signed the heads of agreement and had also more recently had made forceful public statements in support of the project. Despite the formidable arguments on both sides, not a single member of the coalition abstained or voted against the motion. Just two days before the election and also before the Secretary of State had reached a decision about whether to call the application in (which would take the application out of the hands of the Council), the Council entered into a binding development agreement with the developer.

Issue

Whether any of the matters set out above showed that the Council had approached the decision with a closed mind (ie that it was pre-determined).

Decision

The Court of Appeal (reversing the decision of the High Court) held that, in the particular circumstances of the case, none of the factors highlighted above were sufficient to establish that the decision had been made with a closed mind.

In the context of local planning authority decision making, an allegation that a decision was biased or predetermined must be approached by asking whether 'from the point of view of the fair-minded and informed observer, there was a real possibility that the planning committee or some of its members were biased in the sense of approaching the decision with a closed mind and without impartial consideration of all relevant planning issues', a test which derives in part from the test for bias set out in *Porter v Magill* [2001] UKHL 67.

The Court held that the Porter v Magill test needed to take into account the particular role of local planning authorities, the fact that councillors 'are elected to provide and pursue policies' and that 'members of a Planning Committee would be entitled, and indeed expected, to have and to have expressed views on planning issues'.

Rix LJ stated that 'there is no escaping the fact that a decision-maker in the planning context is not acting in a judicial or quasi-judicial role but in a situation of democratic accountability. He or she will be subject to the full range of judicial review, but in terms of the concepts of independence and impartiality, which are at the root of the constitutional doctrine of bias, whether under the European Convention for the Protection of Human Rights and Fundamental Freedoms or at common law, there can be no pretence that such democratically accountable decision-makers are intended to be independent and impartial just as if they were judges or quasi-judges. They will have political allegiances, and their politics will involve policies, and these will be known'.

Unless there is positive evidence to show that there was indeed a closed mind on the part of councillors, prior observations or apparent favouring of a particular decision would not usually suffice to justify quashing a decision.

It should be noted that s 25 of the Localism Act 2011 now makes provision in relation to things previously done that directly or indirectly indicate what view the decision-maker took, or would or might take, in relation to a decision.

R (Berky) v Newport City Council [2012] EWCA Civ 378

Facts

The Claimant challenged a decision to grant planning permission to a developer for mixed development of a site on a number of grounds, most of which related to the way in which the Council had dealt with the requirements of the EIA Regulations. It was also alleged that the decision was tainted by real or apparent bias.

One of the committee members had been referred to in literature circulated by the developer as supporting the proposal, although the councillor denied any direct involvement in promoting the development.

In particular, a 48-page petition to 'welcome and support the proposals for' the development was submitted to the Council shortly before the decision. The petition appeared to have been put together by the councillor concerned. A leaflet had also been circulated by councillors explaining 'Why your councillors are backing this project'. At the committee meeting, the councillor spoke in favour of the development and challenged the suggestion that there should be a debate about it, saying that Councillors supported the scheme and that they should simply vote on it.

Issue

Whether the decision making process was tainted by real or apparent bias on the part of one of the members of the planning committee.

Decision

The Court of Appeal upheld the High Court's decision that the matters set out above were not, in light of the guidance contained in *Lewis v Redcar*, sufficient to demonstrate apparent bias.

That the Councillor was 'inclined to support the development, and that this was known in the area, was not itself objectionable since such a state of affairs "is not uncommon in the world of local politics". Nor was it significant that his name appeared on a ward newsletter supportive of the proposal.'

As to his comments at the committee meeting, 'although regrettable I do not consider it enables a submission of bias, apparent bias or pre-determination on the part of the decision maker – the whole planning committee – to be made good. Rather it should be seen as an example of an ill considered remark by a single member of a democratically accountable political decision maker made in the heat of the moment.'

R (Bishop's Stortford Civic Federation) v East Hertfordshire District Council [2014] EWHC 348 (Admin)

Facts

The Council had agreed to sell land to developers for redevelopment, subject to the grant of planning permission.

At a subsequent meeting to consider the planning application, one councillor, who was a member of the executive and who had been involved with the land sale negotiations, attended the meeting, although he was not a member of the planning committee, and addressed the committee members. He summarised the agreement reached in principle with the developers and said that to renege on the agreement would be 'morally bankrupt' because it would undermine the decision made by the full council.

The planning committee voted by six votes to five to grant outline permission.

Following complaints about the councillor's intervention at the meeting, an independent investigator appointed by the Council's monitoring officer found that he should not have addressed the meeting and that in so doing he had brought his office into disrepute contrary to the Code.

The Claimant challenged the grant of permission.

Issues

(1) Whether it was open to a member who was not a member of the relevant committee to attend its meetings and make representations to it.

(2) Whether, as a result of the councillor's interventions, the planning committee had been misled into believing that the principle of mixed development on the site had already been established by a favourable vote in favour of selling the land.

Decision

The claim for judicial review was dismissed.

In the absence of an express prohibition in the council's constitution or some other document, it was in principle open to any councillor to attend the planning committee and address its members, so long as: (1) the committee had given it permission; and (2) he had no prejudicial interest in the outcome of the subject matter.

The motive of the non-committee member addressing the committee was irrelevant. The court would be slow to intervene in policy judgments reached by experienced and democratically elected planning committees. Excessive forensic analysis of the debate before the committee, the views expressed and the language used was unnecessary, inappropriate and could fetter the democratic process. What had to be considered was the general tenor of the discussion and debate to ascertain whether the decision making process had improperly been influenced.

The planning officer's report had directed the planning committee to the relevant planning issues and the majority had followed its recommendation in favour of granting permission. There was no basis for suggesting that experienced members would none the less have acted contrary to their training which emphasised the importance of approaching decisions with an open mind, having regard to the relevant considerations.

IM Properties Development Limited v Lichfield District Council [2014] EWHC 2440 (Admin)

Facts

This was a challenge to a decision by the Council to endorse modifications to the draft Lichfield Local Plan Strategy which involved releasing two sites from the Green Belt. The sites were subject to interests on the part of housing developers and the Claimant had an interest in a third site, outside the Green Belt, in respect of which the Council had previously refused an application for planning permission for 750 homes. The Claimant did not want the other sites to be released from the Green Belt.

The Claimant challenged the decision to release the sites from the Green Belt on a number of bases, which included an allegation that the actions of the leader of the Council amounted to predetermination.

Prior to the meeting, the chairman of the Council's planning committee sent an e-mail to the Conservative group members on the committee which read, which said '[…] the group decided in government parlance to have a three line whip in

241

place at the council meeting on Tuesday. In plain terms group members either vote in favour of the report I will be giving regarding the local plan or abstain. Also if you are approached by anyone promoting alternative sites, please make no comment. If group members are reported making negative comments it would without any doubt derail our local plan. Sorry if you find this a little heavy handed but there is an awful lot at stake.'

Issue

The claim was dismissed on a separate ground (that the Court did not have jurisdiction to hear the claim). However, the Court also considered whether the e-mail from the Chairman of the Council's planning committee amounted to predetermination of the decision.

Decision

The e-mail was covered by s 25 of the Localism Act 2011, which provides that a decision-maker is not to be taken to have had, or to have appeared to have had, a closed mind when making the decision just because the decision-maker had previously done anything that directly or indirectly indicated what view the decision-maker took, or would or might take, in relation to a matter.

The Court dismissed the submission that s 25 of the 2011 Act only applied when a councillor makes a public statement. The statutory wording was broadly phrased and referred to a councillor having done 'anything' in relation to the matter which was the subject of the decision.

In any event, the judge stated that 'I do not find that the tenor of the email was so strident as to remove the discretion on the part of the recipient as to how he or she would vote. Neither the language used nor the absence of any sanction support that contention. The debate shows a far reaching discussion between members and displays no evidence of closed minds in relation to the decisions that had to be taken. A fair minded and reasonable observer in possession of all of the facts would not be able to conclude on the basis of the evidence that there was any real possibility of predetermination as a result of the email […]'

COUNCILLOR MISCONDUCT

Murphy v Ethical Standards Officer of the Standards Board for England [2004] EWHC 2377 (Admin)

Facts

Councillor Murphy was vehemently opposed to proposals for a large scale development. He had publicly declared his opposition and was alleged to have put together alternative proposals for the development of the site. Following a complaint to the Local Government Ombudsman that Cllr Murphy had wrongly participated in the proceedings of the Council's Planning Committee when it refused planning permission, the Ombudsman produced a report which found that Cllr Murphy had a non pecuniary interest in the proposals because he entered the planning meeting with his mind already made up that he would refuse the application.

The Ombudsman's report was due to be discussed at a subsequent meeting of the Council. Cllr Murphy was informed by the Council that he was considered to have a personal and prejudicial interest in the matter and would therefore be required to declare the interest and withdraw from the meeting. Despite this advice, Cllr Murphy did not withdraw from the meeting and, indeed, spoke about the report although he abstained from voting.

Following a referral to the Standards Board for England, Cllr Murphy was found to have breached the Code of Conduct and he was suspended from the Council for one year.

Issues

(1) Whether this was a matter which affected Cllr Murphy's 'well-being'.

(2) Whether the Tribunal was right to find that Cllr Murphy had a personal and prejudicial interest as prescribed by the Code.

(3) Whether the finding infringed Cllr Murphy's human rights (Articles 6, 8 and 10 ECHR).

(4) Whether the sanction of a year's suspension was disproportionate.

Decision

The court dismissed Cllr Murphy's challenge. In particular, the court held that:

(1) The Tribunal was correct to find that 'well-being' was a broad concept that could be said to affect a person's quality of life, either positively or negatively. In this case, the matter affected Cllr Murphy's well-being because:

> 'His reputation is tarnished. It would be entirely natural for the council-lor to want to salvage his reputation by getting his Council to express dissatisfaction with the report. The councillor would be likely to have had a strong sense of satisfaction about the restoration of his reputation locally if the Council had expressed dissatisfaction with it. In that sense, it is likely that the councillor's sense of well-being would have been en-hanced. That, at least, is what an informed outsider would think, which is the standpoint which […] the Code contemplates ("might reasonably be regarded as").'

(2) The Tribunal correctly considered the five elements that it was required to consider by reference to the Code of Conduct, namely whether the Council's decision on the report could (1) be reasonably regarded as (2) affecting his well-being (3) more than it affected other local people and whether a member of the public (4) with knowledge of the relevant facts (5) reasonably regard his interest in the report as so significant that it was likely to prejudice his judgment of the public interest?

(3) As to Cllr Murphy's human rights:

  (a) Article 6: There was nothing contrary to Article 6 in the way in which the proceedings before the Tribunal were conducted. Although Cllr Murphy did not give evidence on oath, he had not asked to give evidence. Although Cllr Murphy had asked the Tribunal in advance whether he might bring witnesses in support of his case, the President of the Tribunal responded that the witnesses were not witnesses of fact to the events in question and Cllr Murphy would have to make an application to the Tribunal if he wanted them to give evidence. No application was made thereafter. Finally, the fact that the Tribunal was composed of solicitor with a London Borough, a retired local government officer and a retired civil servant did not make them more likely to share the Ethical Standards Officer's interpretation of the Code.

  (b) Article 8: Contrary to Cllr Murphy's submission, the Tribunal had not sought to explore his private feelings about the Ombudsman's report. His private feelings were not relevant. What was relevant was whether a decision on the Ombudsman's report might reasonably be regarded as affecting his well-being. Article 8 was not engaged.

  (c) Article 10: Cllr Murphy argued that if the Code prevented him from speaking at the meeting about the Ombudsman's report, his right to freedom of expression was impinged. This was not the case:

   'The exercise of one's right to freedom of expression is expressly subject to such conditions as are necessary in a democratic society and for the protection of the rights of others. There is an obvious need to protect the reputation of local authorities as one of the democratic elements of society. In that connection, there is a need to maintain public trust and confidence in the decision-making process of local authorities. The provisions of the Code which are engaged in the present case are plainly intended to ensure that that trust and confidence is not misplaced. They must, of course, go no further than is necessary for the achievement of that purpose, but it cannot seriously be gainsaid that the decision-making process of local authorities, and public confidence in it, would be substantially undermined if councillors who have an interest in the outcome of the process could remain at a meeting at which the topic in which they have an interest is to be discussed and could influence the Council's decision on the topic by speaking at the meeting on it.

   I can see how a possible infringement of Art. 10 might arise if what amounts to an interest of such a kind as to prevent a councillor from speaking on the topic is defined too widely. But I do not think that the definition of a councillor's personal or prejudicial interest is drawn too widely in the Code. In any event, it is important to remember that Cllr. Murphy was only prevented from talking about the Ombudsman's report at a meeting of the Council. There was nothing to prevent him from talking about it on any other occasion, or from circulating his views on the Ombudsman's report to his constituents and to the other Members of the Council.'

(4) As to the sanction, the Court 'hesitantly' found that the period of suspension was too long. There were unusual features in the case which the Tribunal had paid insufficient attention to, namely that Cllr Murphy's interest in the Ombudsman's report was known to everyone and that he had received conflicting and confusing advice. These facts, coupled with the mitigating features which the Case Tribunal expressly recognised (his long public service and the evidence that no-one had called his integrity into question) meant that the period of suspension should be four months.

Sanders v Kingston (No. 1) [2005] EWHC 1145 (Admin)

Facts

In 2001, Carrickfergus Borough Council, a local authority in Northern Ireland, wrote to all UK local authorities for support in its call for an inquiry into the suicide at army barracks of a soldier, Paul Cochrane, whose family resided in Carrickfergus, as well as into the deaths of other army personnel.

In response to the request, the leader (as he then was) of Peterborough City Council, Mr Sanders, wrote in hand on the letter – 'Members of the Armed Forces DO get killed be it accident or design – THAT is what they are paid for' – and returned it to the Carrickfergus Chief Executive. In response to a private and confidential letter, Mr Sanders again wrote in hand 'PCC was elected to look after the local affairs of Peterborough, NOT indulge in matters relating to the armed forces. Many things happen in Ireland that defy common sense BUT that is a matter for the IRISH people not PCC'.

In a subsequent telephone interview with a newspaper journalist, Mr Sanders made comments (disputed by Mr Sanders) which were described as 'both foul mouthed, potentially racist and personally abusive. It appears that, at least to some extent, [Mr Sanders] remained under the misapprehension that the "unexplained deaths" the concern of Carrickfergus arose from the Troubles and not from the way in which young recruits were being treated in training camps'.

In an interview with the BBC, Mr Sanders said 'I believe in my heart of hearts that Paul Cochrane's family owe me an abject apology for the amount of time that I have spent on this particular cause because it is absolutely nothing to do with me [...]You've killed hundreds of my friends. You've killed people in Peterborough. You've caused distress to hundreds of families in England. Now that one of your own has committed suicide – I presume in your own country – yet it suddenly becomes an Englishman's fault. ... When do I get my apology from the Cochrane family and when will the English people get an apology from the people of Northern Ireland for killing so many of our soldiers over the past 25 years? I think you should all hang your heads deeply in shame for involving the English people in your own quarrel.'

Mr Sanders was found by a Case Tribunal to have breached the council's Code of Conduct because: (1) his comments in correspondence and in interviews were disrespectful and deeply offensive to any reasonable person, particularly to the Cochrane family, the family of the young soldier who committed suicide; and (2) that he brought his office and authority into disrepute.

Issues

Mr Murphy sought to challenge the decision on a number of bases. The principal contention was that the Tribunal failed to have regard to the fact that the right to freedom of expression under Article 10 was engaged.

Decision

The court held that wherever a member is found to have breached the code by reason of statements made and is sanctioned as a result, Article 10 ECHR was necessarily engaged. The Case Tribunal had erred in failing to consider Article 10 at all.

The correct approach for a panel or standards committee in such circumstances is to ask:

(1) whether the panel was entitled to find as a matter of fact that there had been a breach of the Code; and

(2) if so, whether the finding in itself or the imposition of a sanction was prima facie a breach of Article 10(1);[1] and

(3) if so, whether the restriction involved one which was justified by reason of the requirements of Article 10(2).[2]

As to stage 3, the Court acknowledged, in accordance with ECHR authority (see, for example, *Castells v Spain* (1992) 14 EHRR 445) that an extremely high level of protection must be given to political expression because of its fundamental importance for the maintenance of a democratic society.

However, in this case none of the statements made by Mr Sanders were a political expression of views at all. His responses in correspondence and in interviews were 'the ill-tempered response of a person who thought that he should not be being troubled by the request of Carrickfergus and who has chosen to express his annoyance in personal and abusive terms directed, in the main to Carrickfergus council and to the Cochrane family, as a by-product to the Irish people and, to an even more insignificant degree, reflecting at all on the question of the Troubles'.

As such, the restriction placed on Mr Sanders by the panel was justified by reference to Article 10(2) and there had been no breach of Article 10.

Mr Sanders' appeal against the sanction imposed (18 month disqualification) was allowed on the basis that the panel had failed to have regard to the relevant guidance. The disqualification was disproportionate by reference to Article 10(2) and the court instead imposed a partial suspension.

1   See above.
2   See above.

Livingstone v Adjudication Panel for England [2006] EWHC 2533 (Admin)

Facts

The Mayor of London, Ken Livingstone, following a reception at City Hall in London was confronted outside the venue by a newspaper journalist. During the conversation, Mr Livingstone asked the journalist 'What did you do before? Were you a German war criminal?', and stated '... you are just like a concentration camp guard. You're just doing it 'cause you're paid to aren't you?'

The Panel found that the Mayor had conducted himself in a manner which could reasonably be regarded as bringing his office or authority into disrespect.

Issue

The Panel had found that at the time Mr Livingstone made the comments, he was not acting in an official capacity. The issue was therefore whether the Code could apply to only to acts not done in an official capacity, but as a private individual.

Decision

The reference in s 52 of the Local Government Act 2000 to the fact that a member 'in performing his functions' would declare to observe the Code of Conduct, meant that the Code could not affect what a member did in his private life.

However, the words of limitation 'in performing his functions' did not cover the same conduct as 'in his official capacity' but might extend further: 'They must cover activities which are apparently within the performance of a member's functions. Thus misuse of the position for personal advantage will appear to whoever is affected by it to have been in the performance of functions.'

The Code therefore covered conduct where the member was 'acting in his official capacity' and conduct where the member was misusing his position as a member.

> 'It is important to bear in mind that the electorate will exercise its judgment in considering whether what might be regarded as reprehensible conduct in a member's private life should bring his membership to an end in due course. Equally, it is important that the flamboyant, the eccentric, the positively committed – one who is labelled in the somewhat old fashioned terminology, a character – should not be subjected to a Code of Conduct which covers his behaviour when not performing his functions as a member of a relevant authority.'

The words spoken by the Mayor were not spoken in an official capacity, nor was he misusing his position as a member.

The restraint of the Mayor's conduct in the circumstances was not a proportionate interference with the Mayor's Article 10 ECHR rights to freedom of expression, given that he was off duty.

That said, the Mayor was not entitled to the enhanced protection afforded to political expression as he was not expressing a political opinion but rather 'indulging in offensive abuse'.

The words spoken were not such as to bring the office into disrepute, although they did bring him into disrepute personally.

R (Mullaney) v Adjudication Panel for England [2009] EWHC 72 (Admin)

Facts

Councillor Mullaney trespassed onto land to film a historic building which led to a scuffle with the owner of the land. He (and another councillor) then made the film available on the internet so as to force Council officers to take action in respect of alleged breaches of planning control.

He was found to have breached the Code by failing to treat others with respect. The standards committee decided that the Councillors should apologise or be suspended for one month. The Appeals Tribunal changed the sanction so as to no longer offer the option of an apology being given to avoid suspension, whilst noting that it considered that an apology was still appropriate. However, the Tribunal did not invite Cllr Mullaney to make submissions to it on the point that (or in the light of a view that) it might increase the sanction (by removing the option of apologising to avoid suspension) or by reference to its preliminary view that it would (or might) do so.

Issues

(1) whether the Councillor was acting in an official capacity;

(2) whether he had failed to treat others with respect; and

(3) whether the failure of the Appeal Tribunal acted unfairly in the circumstances in failing to give Cllr Mullaney an opportunity to make representations in respect of the sanction.

Decision

Cllr Mullaney was acting in his official capacity at the time because: (1) the taking and publication of the video was a continuum of steps taken in respect of the building by the councillor on behalf of a constituent in which he identified himself as a councillor and made 'Councillor Enquiries'; (2) the councillor was a member of the planning committee and he had a legitimate and keen interest in the building as a councillor (who is interested in planning matters); and (3) he identified himself as a councillor on the video and in its publication.

Even though the councillor was in his view acting on public interest grounds, he had failed to strike a balance between the various relevant aspects of the public interest in all the circumstances of the case and had failed to treat others with respect thereby breaching the code.

However, the Tribunal's failure to alert Cllr Mullaney that it was considering the removal of the opportunity to avoid a suspension without giving him an opportunity to make submissions on the point was procedurally unfair and thus an error of law. The matter was remitted to a differently constituted Appeal Tribunal.

R (Calver) v Adjudication Panel for Wales [2012] EWHC 1172 (Admin)

Facts

Councillor Calver posted various sarcastic and mocking comments about the running of the council and other councillors on his blog expressing the view that the council was acting beyond its proper role, was producing minutes which failed to represent what it was doing, was wasting money and was involved in secret dealings. The claimant also criticised one council member for gaining her place without a contested election, and he stated that the conduct of another council member had entailed the 'disgraceful manipulation of children'.

The Panel upheld a decision by the Council's standards committee that Cllr Calver had breached the Code of Conduct by publishing derogatory comments about two fellow community councillors, and by bringing his office and/or the Council into disrepute.

Issues

In accordance with *Sanders v Kingston* (above), the issues were:

(1) Whether the standards committee and the panel were entitled as a matter of fact to conclude that the claimant's conduct in respect of the comments was in breach of the Code of Conduct.

(2) If so, whether the finding in itself or the imposition of a sanction was prima facie a breach of Article 10.

(3) If so, whether the restriction involved was one which was justified by reason of the requirements of Article 10(2).

Decision

The High Court allowed Cllr Calver's claim.

While the committee and tribunal were entitled to conclude that Cllr Calver's comments breached the code of conduct, the Court found that the restriction imposed on the councillor by reason of the finding that he was in breach of the code would, pursuant to stage 3 of the 3-stage approach, be a disproportionate interference with the right to freedom of expression in Article 10.

In allowing the claim, the court noted that:

(1) There was a fundamental common law right to freedom of expression which meant that there was a narrower approach to the interpretation of legislation and instruments which restricted freedom of speech.

(2) Where Article 10 was under consideration, while the court must have due regard to the judgment of the statutory regulator, the approach involves scrutiny of greater intensity than in a judicial review not involving a Convention right, and the decision whether Article 10 is infringed is ultimately one for the court.

(3) There were no 'bright lines' in this area of the law: 'Neither freedom of speech nor the principle reflected in the exceptions under consideration (eg reputation or privacy) can be given effect in an unqualified way without restricting the other [...] The matters that have to be balanced, in the present case, on one side of the balance a councillor's right to freedom of expression and the public interest in such freedom, and on the other side of the balance the public interest in proper standards of conduct by members of local authorities, are not easily commensurable.'

(4) The Article 10 balancing process was a highly fact-sensitive one. While other decisions provided valuable guidance as to the general approach, 'it is important to keep in mind their particular facts'.

(5) Freedom of expression 'includes the right to say things which "right thinking people" consider dangerous or irresponsible or which shock or disturb.'

Furthermore, 'the recognition of the importance of expression in the political sphere and that the limits of acceptable criticism are wider in the case of politicians acting in their public capacity than they are in the case of private individuals [...]. This recognition involves both a higher level of protection ("enhanced protection") for statements in the political sphere and the expectation that if the subjects of such statements are politicians acting in their public capacity, they lay themselves open to close scrutiny of their words and deeds and are expected to possess a thicker skin and greater tolerance than ordinary members of the public.'

The conduct in this case was nowhere near as egregious as was the case in *Sanders v Kingston* or *(R) Mullaney v Adjudication Panel for England*. Further, most of the statements were not purely personal abuse of the kind seen in *Livingstone v Adjudication Panel for England* and were directed at members of the Council.

The panel had also taken an overly narrow approach to what amounted to 'political expression': [The comments] 'were in no sense "high" manifestations of political expression. But, they (or many of them) were comments about the inadequate performance of councillors in their public duties.' The comments therefore attracted the high level of protection afforded to political expression.

It would be disproportionate to impose a sanction.

R (Dennehy) v London Borough of Ealing [2013] EWHC 4102 (Admin)

Facts

Councillor Dennehy made the following comments on his blog:

'[Southall] is home to the worst concentration of illegal immigrants in the UK. It has gambling, drinking, drug, prostitution and crime issues unlike many other parts of London. It is a largely Indian community who say they deplore this behaviour but yet it is that very same community that harbours and exploits their own people in squalid third world living conditions.

The exploding population of illegal immigrants is a constant on the public purse. Illegal immigrants don't pay tax. The legitimate immigrants exploiting them in the squalid bed sheds don't pay tax on their rental income.

If these sorts of people exploit the desperate what other scams are they perpetrating I ask?

Criminality is endemic in Southall'

The Council's standards committee found that the comments had breached the Council's Code because he had not treated others with respect and had brought the Council and the office of Councillor into disrepute. The Committee resolved that the councillor should issue an apology and that the decision would be published in the local newspaper and on the Council's website.

The findings of the committee were that, although the subject matter of the blog was a legitimate topic for debate, 'the tone, style and choice of wording in the post was written in such a way that it did cause offence to some residents and councillor Dennehy could reasonably have expected that to be the case had he reflected on the particular way in which he chose to raise the issues'.

Issue

The councillor challenged this finding on the basis that the committee failed to have regard to his rights under Article 10 of the ECHR.

Decision

In accordance with the 3 stage approach in *Sanders v Kingston*, the Court held that the committee was plainly entitled to find, as it did, that as a matter of fact, what the claimant had said about Southall residents had failed to treat others with respect and had brought the council and the office of councillor into disrepute.

On the face of it the finding and the sanctions did constitute a breach of Article 10. However, they were justified under Article 10(2) since, as the report explained, the comments about Southall residents were contained in a separate section of the blog from those which raised legitimate topics of political debate.

'They were not the expression of a political view, but an unjustified personal and generic attack on a section of the public. The subjects of the speech were not politicians but ordinary members of the public and, as such, the comments did not attract the higher level of protection applicable to political expressions and the comments would plainly have undermined confidence in local government, the preservation of which is a recognised aim of the code.'

Further, the extent of the interference was 'on any view very limited indeed'.

In terms of sanctions following the finding, the claimant was 'merely requested, not required, to apologise and as I understand it, he has not done so and in addition the committee's findings were neutrally reported in the local press and on the council's website'.

Heesom v Public Service Ombudsman for Wales [2014] EWHC1504 (Admin)

Facts

Councillor Heesom was found to have breached the Code on a number of occasions, which included describing the Adult Social Care Directorate as 'a shambles' and 'shambolic'; and, whilst looking at two Council officers in a threatening manner, saying that a number of managers at the Council had been dispensed with and 'there are more to go'. He was also found to have improperly sought to interfere with the housing allocation decision-making process. There were other findings of bullying and failures to show respect and consideration for others.

The tribunal published their decision after hearing 48 witnesses over 58 days of hearings and consideration of 7000 pages of evidence. Their Findings of Fact, which was just one of three parts of the judgment was a document of over 400 pages.

The Councillor appealed to the High Court.

Issues

(1) What is the appropriate standard of proof in an adjudication by a case tribunal of the Adjudication Panel for Wales.

(2) What is the scope of and legitimate restrictions to a politician's right of freedom of expression under Article 10 of the European Convention for on Human Rights ('the ECHR') and at common law, particularly in relation to civil servants' rights and interests which might be adversely affected by the purported exercise of those rights.

(3) Did the case tribunal err in its findings as to breaches of the Code and were any breaches such as to justify the sanction imposed

Decision

(1) The appropriate standard of proof was the civil standard, rather than the criminal standard.

(2) As to whether politicians were entitled to the enhanced protection afforded to political expression in the criticism of civil servants, the Court found that:

    (i)   Civil servants are, of course, open to criticism, including public criticism; but they are involved in assisting with and implementing policies, not (like politicians) making them. As well as in their own private interests in terms of honour, dignity and reputation [...] it is in the public interest that they are not subject to unwarranted comments that disenable them from performing their public duties and undermine public confidence in the administration. Therefore, in the public interest, it is a legitimate aim of the State to protect public servants from unwarranted comments that have, or may have, that adverse effect on good administration.

(ii) Nevertheless, the acceptable limits of criticism are wider for non-elected public servants acting in an official capacity than for private individuals, because, as a result of their being in public service, it is appropriate that their actions and behaviour are subject to more thorough scrutiny. However, the limits are not as wide as for elected politicians, who come to the arena voluntarily and have the ability to respond in kind which civil servants do not […].

(iii) Where critical comment is made of a civil servant, such that the public interest in protecting him as well as his private interests are in play, the requirement to protect that civil servant must be weighed against the interest of open discussion of matters of public concern and, if the relevant comment was made by a politician in political expression, the enhanced protection given to his right of freedom of expression

(3) As to the individual findings, the Court, allowing the appeal in part, found that three of the findings of breach should be quashed, but the remainder upheld.

In particular, the court upheld a finding that comments directed towards to civil servants to the effect that their jobs were at risk comprised comments of political expression and were therefore entitled to enhanced protection but that the finding of a breach was nonetheless a necessary interference with his Article 10 rights:

'Appropriate challenges to the manner in which non-elected senior public servants do their job, even in very robust terms, are protected by article 10. However, here, the Appellant intentionally sought to undermine [the officers] by publicly threatening them that their jobs would go, without reference to other councillors or the procedures that are in place to deal with such employment issues […] These comments were a deliberate challenge and threat to the mutual trust and confidence between councillors and officers, which suffered as a result. Consequently, they did not just adversely impact on the rights and interests of [the officers] as individuals, but upon the public interest in good administration.'

The court overturned the panel's finding that comments made in the context of the appointment of a new Director of Planning were not political expression.

The court also overturned a finding of bullying, on the basis that there was no finding that the councillor had intended to intimidate or undermine the relevant officer.

As to the sanction, the court noted that it would have been preferable for the panel to have referred to the need to justify any sanction imposed under Article

10(2). That said, the panel in this case did impliedly consider the proportionality of the sanction such that there was no breach of Article 10.

Further, while the subsequent re-election of a councillor may be a relevant factor for the panel to take into account in determining the appropriate sanction, whether it is material (and, if so, the weight to be given to it as a factor) is a matter – just one of many – for the panel to consider, particularly if it is unclear whether the electorate was aware of the full details of the misconduct.

SANCTION

Sloam v Standards Board for England [2005] EWHC 124 (Admin)

Facts

Councillor Sloam was given a car by a friend. The former owner was entitled to display a disabled parking permit in that car. Cllr Sloam kept the permit in the car, attempted to renew it and used it to attempt to avoid parking fines. He pleaded guilty to a criminal charge of attempting, by deception, dishonestly to evade a liability.

He was found to have breached the Code by bringing the office into disrepute and was disqualified for one year.

Issue

Whether the sanction imposed was excessive and the just decision would have been suspension.

Decision

The Court dismissed Cllr Sloam's appeal.

Cllr Sloam had argued that this was a first offence. He had pleaded guilty in front of the Magistrate's court. The level of his remorse was extreme and deeply genuine. The effect that it had had upon him and his family he could not begin to talk about. It was the wish of many other people, who had paid testimony to his dedication through many years as a councillor and his excellent work that he has done over many years, that he should continue as a councillor. The decision of disqualification, when measured against his record, was extreme and given that he was 68 years old, disqualification at his age might well be, and was likely to be, effectively the end of his public life.

The judge noted that the court should be slow to intervene in matters that have been decided by a specially trained Tribunal which had had the benefit of hearing the evidence over an extended period of time. The Tribunal did not only have to take into account the effect of any decision that they might make upon the individual in front of it, but also that it have in mind the wider picture, which included the importance of discouraging similar action by others.

The Tribunal took into account that under normal circumstances for a serious breach of the Code, which this was, a period of two years' disqualification would appropriately have been imposed but that in light of Cllr Sloam's record of public service and the testimonials presented on his behalf, it was appropriate to impose the minimum period of disqualification of one year.

The Tribunal's decision should not therefore be interfered with.

Hare v Marcar [2006] EWHC 82 (Admin)

Facts

Councillor Hare acted, in what he described as 'his private capacity', as a representative for a resident at land registry arbitration proceedings to determine whether the resident had by adverse possession acquired title to land owned by the Council.

In the land registry proceedings, the councillor had made references to a Council report which was confidential and, when asked by the Council's solicitor not to use information obtained in confidence, thereafter made a number of serious accusations against the solicitor and other officers.

He was found to have breached the Code by using the confidential information and by failing to treat others with respect

Issue

Cllr Hare argued that he should not have been suspended, or should have been suspended for a shorter period

Decision

There were serious aggravating features in the case namely, 'allegations of an essentially criminal nature against professional staff in senior positions of trust in a major body', the failure of the appellant to apologise, and the view of the Tribunal as the fact finders, who had seen and heard the appellant that 'the lack of understanding and insight shown by the [appellant] caused the Case Tribunal serious concern that this conduct was likely to be repeated'.

The sanction was upheld.

CRIMINAL PROCEEDINGS AGAINST COUNCILLORS

Jones v Swansea City Council [1990] I WLR 1453

Facts

The Claimant alleged that councillors had been guilty of misfeasance in public office, when they decided to reverse a prior decision taken under different political control, to grant the Claimant permission, under a lease, to change the use of a site owned by the Council from an office and showroom to a club.

The Claimant was in business with her husband, who, at the time of the prior decision permitting the change of use, was a councillor representing the majority group on the council. At local authority elections which then took place, the Claimant's husband did not stand for re-election and several of his party colleagues lost their seats.

The Claimant alleged that the members of the new administration which made the decision bore a grudge against her husband and were motivated by malice.

The proof of that allegation depended on proving that the Leader of the Council had been activated by malice and also on showing that, either directly or indirectly, expressly or by implication from the circumstances, he as an individual and as leader of the group had caused the other councillors in his group to vote as they did.

The trial judge held that, though the leader of the Council had animosity towards the Claimant, he had not been motivated by malice. Further, the judge accepted the evidence of three other councillors that they did not know of the leader's attitude to the Claimant, did not vote in accordance with his instructions and did not vote according to a party whip, whether imposed at his instigation or otherwise so that the Claimant's allegation that all of the councillors were tainted by the Leader's motivation could not in any event be made out.

The Court of Appeal ordered a new trial because they thought it open to the court at the new trial to find that the Leader was activated by malice and that the majority of the councillors voting against the Claimant's interests were infected by that malice, by the exercise of the whip or by party solidarity.

Issue

Whether the trial judge had been right to find that there was not sufficient evidence on which it could be said that the decision was motivated by malice.

Decision

The House of Lords, reversing the Court of Appeal's decision, held that there was no error of law in the trial judge's finding that, although the possibility of malice could not be dismissed, it was not proved on the balance of probability that the Leader of the Council or any other member of the group was motivated by malice towards the Claimant or her husband in the strict legal sense of wishing and intending to cause them harm.

There were sound planning reasons for refusing the grant of permission to alter the use of the premises and his motivation for reversing the decision was his belief that permission should never have been granted in the first place (and was only granted because of the Claimant's husband's role in the Council), his desire to have his own way on this issue and to fulfil the pledge which he had made to have the matter reversed and to be seen, as he saw it, to be 'doing justice'. It was held that he had an honest and sincere belief that a developer of property who had acquired a lease from the defendant Council should be obliged to keep to the use for which that property had been originally advertised.

Secondly, even if the Leader of the Council was motivated by malice, the Claimant had pleaded her case on the basis that all of the councillors who voted for the resolution were (at the least) infected by their leader's malice. That case failed and it would be wrong now to give her a further opportunity, which was open to her at the trial, of making a new case based on the submission that a majority (as opposed to all) of the council were infected by malice.

Thirdly, even if the case had been pleaded on that alternative 'majority' basis, the evidence of the three councillors who did not know anything of the Leader's feelings towards the matter would have disposed of the claim.

Barnard v Restormel BC [1998] 3 PLR 27

Facts

The Claimant and another had submitted 'rival' applications for planning permission. At a meeting of the Council's planning committee, the application of the Claimant's rival was approved. The Claimant brought a claim for damages in respect of misfeasance in public office on various bases including that the chairman of the committee had failed to declare an interest in the application, and that the committee had been misled by the negligent and fraudulent actions of the Mayor.

The Claimant's claim as regards negligence and breach of statutory duty were struck out at a preliminary hearing. However, the judge at that hearing refused to strike out the claim in the tort of misfeasance in public office and deceit/fraud because in his view, the pleadings disclosed an arguable case

Issue

Whether misfeasance in public office and deceit/fraud can be established against a local authority, when the factual allegation is that some but not a majority of those who took the decision complained of were actuated by malice.

Decision

The Court held that the case should have been struck out at the preliminary hearing.

While there was no doubt that if a majority of those who took the decision were malicious, that would make the decision itself malicious, that was not the Claimant's case (which was that three members (a minority) of the committee were malicious).

The judge had erred in placing weight on the 'seriousness' of the allegation against a particular member and the fact that one member of the planning committee (the Chairman) was allegedly the agent for the rival applicant.

The Court held that this was the wrong approach:

> 'If it is necessary to show that both A and B were malicious, the seriousness or intensity of A's malice does not establish anything against B unless it can be shown that in some way B partook of that malice.'

The Claimant's case in deceit failed because one of the ingredients of the tort was that a false representation was made to the Claimant who relied on it. Here, it was not alleged that a representation had been made to the Claimant.

DPP v Burton, The Times, June 8, 1995

Facts

Four councillors were charged with failing to disclose poll tax arrears and voting at a meeting held to determine the level of poll tax contrary to the Local Government Finance Act 1992, s 106(2).

The Magistrate found that there was no case to answer because each of the Councillors had, under regulation 17(3) of the Community Charges (Administration and Enforcement) Regulations 1989, reached an agreement as to the repayment of arrears, and that it was only if a payment under that agreement remained unpaid for at least two months that the obligations in s 106 of the Local Government Finance Act 1992 arose.

Issues

(1) Whether the Magistrate misdirected himself when ruling that s 106(3) of the Local Government Finance Act 1992 created one offence which could be committed in two ways, either: (a) failing to disclose arrears, or (b) voting having failed to disclose those arrears or whether both elements needed to be made out.

(2) Whether he misdirected himself when ruling that in relation to agreements under Regulation 17(3) the sums referred to in s 106 of the Local Government Finance Act 1992 must remain unpaid for at least two months from the date on which payment is due under the agreement, before s 106 of the Local Government Finance Act 1992 applied.

Decision

The High Court allowed the appeal of the prosecutor.

The Court upheld the magistrate's decision that s 106(3) of the Local Government Finance Act 1992 created one offence which could be committed in two ways, either: (a) failing to disclose, or (b) having failed to disclose, voting. It was not necessary for both elements to be made out.

However, the court found that an agreement under regulation 17(3) referred to payment in the future and not to amounts which should already have been paid. Section 106 of the Local Government Finance Act 1992 therefore applied where a person was in arrears even if they had entered into an arrangement for their repayment.

R v Speechley [2004] EWCA 3067

Facts

Councillor Speechley was the leader of a county council who owned a plot of land which could be affected by the re-alignment of a road. He had made a number of planning applications which were refused because the land was separated from the adjoining village by a road which was the cause of accidents. The appellant took part in discussions about proposals to realign the road with officers and attended meetings of various council committees without declaring his interest. In the course of discussions he proposed an alteration of the route which would favour his plot of land.

Subsequently the appellant admitted that he had failed to declare his interest. He was sentenced to 18 months' imprisonment and ordered to pay £25,000 costs of the prosecution.

Issues

The issues included:

(1) Whether the judge should have given a direction to the jury to the effect that it was not sufficient for the defendant merely to know that he was going to gain some personal benefit 'by a side wind', if he was honestly seeking a legitimate goal.

(2) Whether the sentence was manifestly excessive.

Decision

The trial judge had not erred in his direction to the jury. The judge had made clear that it was necessary for the jury to be satisfied that the defendant's actions were 'dishonest'. If dishonesty was the driving force in the appellant's mind, and his motivation was dishonest, he cannot have been someone honestly seeking a legitimate goal but knowing that if he succeeded he was going to get some personal benefit by a side wind.

The appeal against sentence was also dismissed:

'If the new by-pass followed the off-line route many people, including the appellant, believed that it would substantially increase the value of the appellant's land. That is clear from the finding of the jury, having regard to the way in which they were directed by the judge. With that knowledge the appellant, as Leader of the County Council, chose to conceal his interest and to press for the off-line route using the full weight of his office and his personality to further the case. This was not a case of oversight. His conduct, as the jury found, involved dishonesty. Indeed, it was dishonesty that was the driving force. Advice was ignored. Any official who attempted to withstand the appellant had also to consider his own position. As the judge said, the public must have confidence in our public institutions. When someone in a high position is convicted of this sort of misconduct a severe sentence is entirely appropriate. But for the mitigating factors [which included the defendant's age (67), his lack of previous convictions, his distinguished record in local government, the humiliation of the trial, the fact that there were sound reasons for advocating the proposed route and that the defendant had not, by selling the land, actually achieve a financial benefit] the sentence could well have been longer.'

PROCEDURE AT HEARINGS

Janik v Standards Board For England [2007] EWHC 835 (Admin)

Facts

Mr Janik was informed that a hearing had been listed before the Case Tribunal on a particular date. Five days before the hearing, Mr Janik wrote to the Tribunal to ask that the hearing be adjourned due to ill health and because he was due to have a medical appointment on the day of the hearing. Mr Janik was requested by the Tribunal to provide a copy of the medical note and appointment card. He provided a copy of the note but not the appointment card. The Tribunal adjourned the hearing for one month. Ten days before the hearing, Mr Janik wrote to 'formally request' legal assistance in the form of funding or the services of a barrister or solicitor. The Tribunal informed Mr Janik that they were used to situations where one party is unrepresented and to seeking to ensure that an unrepresented party is not disadvantaged.

One day before the hearing, Mr Janik wrote again to say that he was likely to be declared medically unfit to attend the hearing scheduled for the following day, that he had a doctor's appointment that morning and listed his medical complaints. The Tribunal asked Mr Janik to provide a medical report which explained why he was unable to attend the hearing. Mr Janik provided a copy of a medical note, but no report and said that the hearing should be adjourned.

The request for an adjournment was refused but the Tribunal offered to pay for a taxi to enable Mr Janik to attend the hearing. He did so and his request for an adjournment was refused. He withdrew and the hearing proceeded.

Mr Janik challenged the decision to proceed (but did not appear at the hearing to consider the challenge).

Issue

When should an adjournment on medical grounds be granted?

Decision

Where a councillor seeks an adjournment of a disciplinary hearing on medical grounds, supported by medical evidence, the normal approach would be to adjourn the hearing.

However, there may be exceptional circumstances where it would be appropriate to hear the matter and impose a disqualification in the councillor's absence. Here, the Tribunal had considered the appropriate matters.

On the one hand, it recognised that Councillor Janik had produced some medical evidence that he was not fit to attend the hearing.

> 'On the other however, the Case Tribunal took into account that despite the previous directions, the medical evidence did not adequately address the nature or severity of his condition and in particular the prognosis for how

long this might continue. The significance of this was that, given the cause of the stress was the hearing itself, this raised the possibility that Councillor Janik would not for some significant period of time, or indeed ever, be fit to attend the hearing. The Case Tribunal had to take into account the public interest in this matter being resolved within a reasonable period of time. [...] There had already been extensive delays partly on account of the length of time the investigation had taken but also on account of the earlier adjournment. Further, the Case Tribunal had received representations both from the ESO and the Council that Councillor Janik was continuing in the course of conduct which had given rise to the current allegations, that is, that he was continuing to cause difficulty and upset amongst Council officers and thereby impede Council business. The Case Tribunal also took into account that Councillor Janik was continuing with his weekly surgery for residents such that he was able to carry out some of his Councillor related functions.

The Case Tribunal balanced the difficulties faced by Councillor Janik on account of the stress with the need for this matter to be resolved. It noted that resolution of the matter would be operative in ending the stress faced by Councillor Janik. The Case Tribunal took account of the fact that Councillor Janik had at no stage availed himself of the opportunity of responding to the allegations, either by way of written representations or interview with the Standards Board or by making a response to the reference. [...] The Case Tribunal considered that, if he had been unable or unwilling to prepare for the hearing in the last six months, there was little likelihood that he would do so in any further adjournment. The Case Tribunal felt that, given the unusual circumstances leading up to this request for an adjournment, the public interest would not be served by any further delay.'

The Court held that the Tribunal also had a right to take into account that the material before the Tribunal (that is to say the evidence which was relied upon in support of the allegations made against Mr Janik) was almost entirely in writing, if not entirely in writing. It was not a case in which the outcome depended on questions of credibility, conflicts of evidence which could only fairly be resolved by hearing oral evidence. Secondly, the Tribunal was informed that the kind of conduct which formed the substance of the allegations against Mr Janik was continuing. That added to the need to resolve the issues as soon as reasonably possible.

The decision to proceed was the correct one.

Wales

Contents

LOCAL GOVERNMENT ACT 2000, PART 3, CHAPTERS, 1, 3, 4 AND 5, SS 49–54, 56, 68–83

49. Principles governing conduct of members of relevant authorities

(2) The National Assembly for Wales may by order specify the principles which are to govern the conduct of members and co-opted members of relevant authorities

(2D) An order under subsection (2)–

(a) may specify principles which are to apply to a person at all times;

(b) may specify principles which are to apply to a person otherwise than at all times.

(5) Before making an order under this section, the National Assembly for Wales must consult–

(a) such representatives of relevant authorities [...] as it considers appropriate,

(b) the Auditor General for Wales ,

(c) the Public Services Ombudsman for Wales , and

(d) such other persons (if any) as it considers appropriate.

(6) In this Part 'relevant authority' means–

(a) a county council in Wales,

(b) a county borough council,

(f) a community council,

(l) a fire and rescue authority in Wales constituted by a scheme under section 2 of the Fire and Rescue Services Act 2004 or a scheme to which section 4 of that Act applies, or

(p) a National Park authority [in Wales] established under section 63 of the Environment Act 1995.

(7) In this Part 'co-opted member', in relation to a relevant authority, means a person who is not a member of the authority but who–

(a) is a member of any committee or sub-committee of the authority, or

(b) is a member of, and represents the authority on, any joint committee or joint sub-committee of the authority,

and who is entitled to vote on any question which falls to be decided at any meeting of that committee or sub-committee.

50. Model code of conduct

[...]

(2) The National Assembly for Wales may by order issue a model code as regards the conduct which is expected of members and co-opted members of relevant authorities in Wales other than police authorities (also referred to in this Part as a model code of conduct).

(3) The power under subsection (1) or (2) to issue a model code of conduct includes power to revise any such model code which has been issued.

(4) A model code of conduct–

(a) must be consistent with the principles for the time being specified in an order under section 49(1) or 49(2) as the case may be),

(b) may include provisions which are mandatory, and

(c) may include provisions which are optional.

(4E) A model code of conduct issued under subsection (2) may include–

(a) provisions which are to apply to a person at all times;

(b) provisions which are to apply to a person otherwise than at all times.

(5) Before making an order under this section, [...] the National Assembly for Wales must carry out such consultation as is required, by virtue of section 49, before an order is made under that section.

[...]

51. Duty of relevant authorities to adopt codes of conduct.

(1) It is the duty of a relevant authority, before the end of the period of six months beginning with the day on which the first order under section 50 which applies to them is made, to pass a resolution adopting a code as regards the conduct which is expected of members and co-opted members of the authority (referred to in this Part as a code of conduct).

(2) It is the duty of a relevant authority, before the end of the period of six months beginning with the day on which any subsequent order under section 50 which applies to them is made, to pass a resolution–

(a) adopting a code of conduct in place of their existing code of conduct under this section, or

(b) revising their existing code of conduct under this section.

(3) A relevant authority may by resolution–

(a) adopt a code of conduct in place of their existing code of conduct under this section, or

(b) revise their existing code of conduct under this section.

(4) A code of conduct or revised code of conduct–

(a) must incorporate any mandatory provisions of the model code of conduct which for the time being applies to that authority,

(b) may incorporate any optional provisions of that model code, and

(c) may include other provisions which are consistent with that model code.

[(4C) The provisions which may be included under subsection (4)(c) [...] 2 include–

(a) provisions which are to apply to a person at all times;

(b) provisions which are to apply to a person otherwise than at all times.

(5) Where a relevant authority fail to comply with the duty under subsection (1) or (2) before the end of the period mentioned in that subsection–

(a) they must comply with that duty as soon as reasonably practicable after the end of that period, and

(b) any mandatory provisions of the model code of conduct which for the time being applies to the authority are to apply in relation to the members and co-opted members of the authority for so long as the authority fail to comply with that duty.

(6) As soon as reasonably practicable after adopting or revising a code of conduct under this section, a relevant authority must–

(a) ensure that copies of the code or revised code are available at an office of the authority for inspection by members of the public at all reasonable hours,

(b) publish in one or more newspapers circulating in their area a notice which–

(i)   states that they have adopted or revised a code of conduct,

(ii)   states that copies of the code or revised code are available at an office of the authority for inspection by members of the public at such times as may be specified in the notice, and

(iii)   specifies the address of that office, and

(c) send a copy of the code or revised code–

[...]

(ii)   [...] to the [Public Services Ombudsman for Wales].

(7) Where a relevant authority themselves publish a newspaper, the duty to publish a notice under subsection (6)(b) is to be construed as a duty to publish that notice in their newspaper and at least one other newspaper circulating in their area.

(8) A relevant authority may publicise their adoption or revision of a code of conduct under this section in any other manner that they consider appropriate.

(9) A relevant authority's function with respect to the passing of a resolution under this section may be discharged only by the authority (and accordingly, in the case of a relevant authority to which section 101 of the Local Government Act 1972 applies, is not to be a function to which that section applies).

52. Duty to comply with code of conduct

(1) A person who is a member or co-opted member of a relevant authority at a time when the authority adopt a code of conduct under section 51 for the first time–

(a) must, before the end of the period of two months beginning with the date on which the code of conduct is adopted, give to the authority a written undertaking that he will observe the authority's code of conduct for the time being under section 51, and

(b) if he fails to do so, is to cease to be a member or co-opted member at the end of that period.

(2) The form of declaration of acceptance of office which may be prescribed by an order under section 83 of the Local Government Act 1972 [in relation to a relevant authority] may include an undertaking by the declarant that he will observe the authority's code of conduct for the time being under section 51.

(3) A person who becomes a member of a relevant authority to which section 83 of that Act does not apply at any time after the authority have adopted a code of conduct under section 51 for the first time may not act in that office unless he has given the authority a written undertaking that he will observe the authority's code of conduct for the time being under section 51.

(4) A person who becomes a co-opted member of a relevant authority at any time after the authority have adopted a code of conduct under section 51 for the first time may not act as such unless he has given the authority a written

undertaking that he will observe the authority's code of conduct for the time being under section 51.

(5) In relation to a relevant authority whose members and co-opted members are subject to mandatory provisions by virtue of section 51(5)(b)–

(a) the references in subsections (2) to (4) to the authority's code of conduct for the time being under section 51 include the mandatory provisions which for the time being apply to the members and co-opted members of the authority, and

(b) the references in subsections (3) and (4) to any time after the authority have adopted a code of conduct under section 51 for the first time are to be read as references to any time after the coming into force of section 184 of the Local Government and Public Involvement in Health Act 2007.

53. Standards committees

(1) Subject to subsection (2), every relevant authority must establish a committee (referred to in this Part as a standards committee) which is to have the functions conferred on it by or under this Part.

(2) Subsection (1) does not apply to a [...] community council.

[...]

(11) The National Assembly for Wales may by regulations make provision–

(a) as to the size and composition of standards committees of relevant authorities [...] (including provision with respect to the appointment to any such committee of persons who are not members of the relevant authority concerned),

(b) as to the term of office of members of any such committees,

(c) as to the persons who may, may not or must chair any such committees,

(d) as to the entitlement to vote of members of any such committee who are not members of the relevant authority concerned,

(e) for or in connection with treating any such committees as bodies to which section 15 of the Local Government and Housing Act 1989 does not apply,

(f) with respect to the access of the public to meetings of such committees,

(g) with respect to the publicity to be given to meetings of such committees,

(h) with respect to the production of agendas for, or records of, meetings of such committees,

(i) with respect to the availability to the public or members of relevant authorities of agendas for, records of or information connected with meetings of any such committees,

(j) as to the proceedings and validity of proceedings of any such committees,

(k) for or in connection with requiring relevant authorities [...] to send to [the Public Services Ombudsman for Wales] statements which set out the terms of reference of their standards committees.

(12) The provision which may be made by virtue of subsection [...] (11)(f) to (i) includes provision which applies or reproduces (with or without modifications) any provisions of Part VA of the Local Government Act 1972.

54. Functions of standards committees

(1) The general functions of a standards committee of a relevant authority are–

(a) promoting and maintaining high standards of conduct by the members and co-opted members of the authority, and

(b) assisting members and co-opted members of the authority to observe the authority's code of conduct.

(2) Without prejudice to its general functions, a standards committee of a relevant authority has the following specific functions–

(a) advising the authority on the adoption or revision of a code of conduct,

(b) monitoring the operation of the authority's code of conduct, and

(c) advising, training or arranging to train members and co-opted members of the authority on matters relating to the authority's code of conduct.

(3) A relevant authority may arrange for their standards committee to exercise such other functions as the authority consider appropriate.

[(3A) In relation to a relevant authority whose members and co-opted members are subject to mandatory provisions by virtue of section 51(5)(b), references in subsection (1)(b) and (2)(b) and (c) to the authority's code of conduct are to those mandatory provisions.]

[...]

(5) The National Assembly for Wales may by regulations make provision with respect to the exercise of functions by standards committees of relevant authorities [...].

[...]

(7) The National Assembly for Wales may issue guidance with respect to the exercise of functions by standards committees of relevant authorities [...].

[54A Sub-committees of standards committees

(1) A standards committee of a relevant authority may appoint one or more sub-committees for the purpose of discharging any of the committee's functions, whether or not to the exclusion of the committee.

(2) Subsection (1) does not apply to functions under [section 56].

(3) A sub-committee under subsection (1) shall be appointed from among the members of the standards committee by which it is appointed [...].

[...]

(5) As regards sub-committees appointed under subsection (1) by a standards committee of a relevant authority [...]—

(a) regulations under section 53(11) may make provision in relation to such sub-committees, and

(b) section 54(5) and (7) apply in relation to such sub-committees as they apply in relation to standards committees.

(6) Subject to [...]

any provision made by regulations under [section 53(11)(a)] (as applied by this section)—

(a) the number of members of a sub-committee under subsection (1), and

(b) the term of office of those members,

are to be fixed by the standards committee by which the sub-committee is appointed.]

56. Standards committees or sub-committees for community councils

(1) A standards committee of a county council in Wales is to have the same functions in relation to–

(a) the community councils which are situated in the area of the county council, and

(b) the members of those community councils,

as the standards committee has under section 54(1) and (2) in relation to the county council and the members of the county council.

(2) A standards committee of a county borough council is to have the same functions in relation to–

(a) the community councils which are situated in the area of the county borough council, and

(b) the members of those community councils,

as the standards committee has under section 54(1) and (2) in relation to the county borough council and the members of the county borough council.

(3) A standards committee of a county council or county borough council may appoint a sub-committee for the purpose of discharging all of the functions conferred on the standards committee by this section.

(4) In deciding whether it will be their standards committee, or a sub-committee of their standards committee, which is to discharge the functions conferred by this section, a county council or county borough council must consult the community councils which are situated in their area.

(5) Regulations under section 53(11) may make provision in relation to sub-committees appointed under this section.

(6) Subsections (5) and (7) of section 54 apply in relation to sub-committees of standards committees appointed under this section as they apply in relation to standards committees.

(7) Any function which by virtue of the following provisions of this Part is exercisable by or in relation to the standards committee of a relevant authority which is a community council is to be exercisable by or in relation to–

(a) the standards committee of the county council or county borough council in whose area the community council is situated, or

(b) where that standards committee has appointed a sub-committee under this section, that sub-committee;

and any reference in the following provision of this Part to the standards committee of a relevant authority which is a community council is to be construed accordingly.

68. [Public Services Ombudsman for Wales]

(1) [The Public Services Ombudsman for Wales] is to have the functions conferred on him by this Part and such other functions as may be conferred on him by order made by the National Assembly for Wales under this subsection.

(2) [The Public Services Ombudsman for Wales] –

(a) may issue guidance to relevant authorities [...] on matters relating to the conduct of members and co-opted members of [those] authorities,

(b) may issue guidance to relevant authorities [...] in relation to the qualifications or experience which monitoring officers should possess, and

(c) may arrange for any such guidance to be made public.

[(3) The National Assembly for Wales may by regulations make provision which, for the purpose of any provisions of the Public Services Ombudsman (Wales) Act 2005 specified in the regulations, treats–

(a) functions of the Public Services Ombudsman for Wales under that Act as including his functions under this Part, or

(b) expenses of the Public Services Ombudsman for Wales under that Act as including his expenses under this Part.]

(4) The provision which may be made by virtue of subsection (3) includes provision which modifies, or applies or reproduces (with or without modifications), any provisions of [...] that Act.

[...]

69. [Investigations by the Public Services Ombudsman for Wales]

(1) [The Public Services Ombudsman for Wales] may investigate–

(a) cases in which a written allegation is made to him by any person that a member or co-opted member (or former member or co-opted member) of

269

a relevant authority [...] has failed, or may have failed, to comply with the authority's code of conduct, and

(b) other cases in which he considers that a member or co-opted member (or former member or co-opted member) of a relevant authority [...] has failed, or may have failed, to comply with the authority's code of conduct and which have come to his attention as a result of an investigation under paragraph (a).

(2) If [the Public Services Ombudsman for Wales] considers that a written allegation under subsection (1)(a) should not be investigated, he must take reasonable steps to give written notification to the person who made the allegation of the decision and the reasons for the decision.

(3) The purpose of an investigation under this section is to determine which of the findings mentioned in subsection (4) is appropriate.

(4) Those findings are–

(a) that there is no evidence of any failure to comply with the code of conduct of the relevant authority concerned,

(b) that no action needs to be taken in respect of the matters which are the subject of the investigation,

(c) that the matters which are the subject of the investigation should be referred to the monitoring officer of the relevant authority concerned, or

(d) that the matters which are the subject of the investigation should be referred to the president of the Adjudication Panel for Wales for adjudication by a tribunal falling within section 76(1).

(5) Where a person is no longer a member or co-opted member of the relevant authority concerned but is a member or co-opted member of another relevant authority [...] , the reference in subsection (4)(c) to the monitoring officer of the relevant authority concerned is to be treated as a reference either to the monitoring officer of the relevant authority concerned or to the monitoring officer of that other relevant authority (and accordingly [if the Public Services Ombudsman for Wales reaches a finding under subsection (4)(c)] must decide to which of those monitoring officers to refer the matters concerned).

70. Investigations: further provisions

(1) The National Assembly for Wales may by order make provision with respect to investigations under section 69 (including provision with respect to the obtaining or disclosure of documents or information).

(2) The provision which may be made by virtue of subsection (1) includes provision which applies or reproduces (with or without modifications)–

(a) any provisions of sections 60 to 63 [as those sections had effect immediately before their repeal by the Localism Act 2011], or

[(b) any provisions of sections 13 to 15, 25 to 27 and 32 of the Public Services Ombudsman (Wales) Act 2005.]

(3) [The Public Services Ombudsman for Wales] may cease an investigation under section 69 at any stage before its completion.

(4) Where [the Public Services Ombudsman for Wales] 4 ceases an investigation under section 69 before its completion, he may refer the matters which are the subject of the investigation to the monitoring officer of the relevant authority concerned.

(5) Where a person is no longer a member or co-opted member of the relevant authority concerned but is a member or co-opted member of another relevant authority [...], [the Public Services Ombudsman for Wales] may, if he thinks it more appropriate than making such a reference as is mentioned in subsection (4), refer the matters which are the subject of the investigation to the monitoring officer of that other relevant authority.

71. Reports etc

(1) Where [the Public Services Ombudsman for Wales] determines in relation to any case that a finding under section 69(4)(a) or (b) is appropriate–

(a) he may produce a report on the outcome of his investigation,

(b) he may provide a summary of any such report to any newspapers circulating in the area of the relevant authority concerned,

(c) he must send to the monitoring officer of the relevant authority concerned a copy of any such report, and

(d) where he does not produce any such report, he must inform the monitoring officer of the relevant authority concerned of the outcome of the investigation.

(2) Where [the Public Services Ombudsman for Wales] determines in relation to any case that a finding under section 69(4)(c) is appropriate he must–

(a) produce a report on the outcome of his investigation,

(b) subject to subsection (4)(b), refer the matters which are the subject of the investigation to the monitoring officer of the relevant authority concerned, and

(c) send a copy of the report to the monitoring officer, and the standards committee, of the relevant authority concerned.

(3) Where [the Public Services Ombudsman for Wales] determines in relation to any case that a finding under section 69(4)(d) is appropriate he must–

(a) produce a report on the outcome of his investigation,

(b) refer the matters which are the subject of the investigation to the president of the Adjudication Panel for Wales for adjudication by a tribunal falling within section 76(1), and

(c) send a copy of the report to the monitoring officer of the relevant authority concerned and to the president of the Adjudication Panel for Wales.

(4) Where a person is no longer a member or co-opted member of the relevant authority concerned but is a member or co-opted member of another relevant authority [...] –

(a) the references in subsections (1)(b), (c) and (d), (2)(c) and (3)(c) to the relevant authority concerned are to be treated as including references to that other relevant authority, and

(b) [if the Public Services Ombudsman for Wales reaches a finding under section 69(4)(c) he] must refer the matters concerned either to the monitoring officer of the relevant authority concerned or to the monitoring officer of that other relevant authority.

(5) A report under this section may cover more than one investigation under section 69 in relation to any members or co-opted members (or former members or co-opted members) of the same relevant authority.

(6) [The Public Services Ombudsman for Wales] must–

(a) inform any person who is the subject of an investigation under section 69, and

(b) take reasonable steps to inform any person who made any allegation which gave rise to the investigation,

of the outcome of the investigation.

72. Interim reports

(1) Where he considers it necessary in the public interest, [the Public Services Ombudsman for Wales] may, before the completion of an investigation under section 69, produce an interim report on that investigation.

(2) An interim report under this section may cover more than one investigation under section 69 in relation to any members or co-opted members (or former members or co-opted members) of the same relevant authority.

(3) Where the prima facie evidence is such that it appears to [the Public Services Ombudsman for Wales]–

(a) that the person who is the subject of the interim report has failed to comply with the code of conduct of the relevant authority concerned,

(b) that the nature of that failure is such as to be likely to lead to disqualification under section 79(4)(b), and

(c) that it is in the public interest to suspend or partially suspend that person immediately,

the interim report may include a recommendation that that person should be suspended or partially suspended from being a member or co-opted member of the relevant authority concerned for a period which does not exceed six months or (if shorter) the remainder of the person's term of office.

(4) Where [the Public Services Ombudsman for Wales] produces an interim report under this section which contains such a recommendation as is mentioned

in subsection (3), he must refer the matters which are the subject of the report to the president of the Adjudication Panel for Wales for adjudication by a tribunal falling within section 76(2).

(5) A copy of any report under this section must be given–

(a) to any person who is the subject of the report,

(b) to the monitoring officer of the relevant authority concerned, and

(c) to the president of the Adjudication Panel for Wales.

(6) Where a person is no longer a member or co-opted member of the relevant authority concerned but is a member or co-opted member of another relevant authority [...]–

(a) the second reference in subsection (3) to the relevant authority concerned is to be treated as a reference to that other relevant authority, and

(b) the reference in subsection (5)(b) to the relevant authority concerned is to be treated as including a reference to that other relevant authority.

73. Matters referred to monitoring officers

(1) The National Assembly for Wales may by regulations make provision in relation to the way in which any matters referred to the monitoring officer of a relevant authority under [section 70(4) or (5) or 71(2) or (4)] are to be dealt with.

(2) The provision which may be made by regulations under subsection (1) includes provision for or in connection with–

(a) enabling a monitoring officer of a relevant authority to conduct an investigation in respect of any matters referred to him,

(b) enabling a monitoring officer of a relevant authority to make a report, or recommendations, to the standards committee of the authority in respect of any matters referred to him,

(c) enabling a standards committee of a relevant authority to consider any report or recommendations made to it by a monitoring officer of the authority (including provision with respect to the procedure to be followed by the standards committee),

(d) enabling a standards committee of a relevant authority, following its consideration of any such report or recommendations, to take any action prescribed by the regulations (including action against any member or co-opted member (or former member or co-opted member) of the authority who is the subject of any such report or recommendation),

(e) the publicity to be given to any such reports, recommendations or action.

(3) The provision which may be made by virtue of subsection (2)(a) includes provision for or in connection with–

(a) conferring powers on a monitoring officer of a relevant authority to enable him to conduct an investigation in respect of any matters referred to him,

(b) conferring rights (including the right to make representations) on any member or co-opted member (or former member or co-opted member) of a relevant authority who is the subject of any such investigation.

(4) The provision which may be made by virtue of subsection (2)(d) includes provision for or in connection with–

(a) enabling a standards committee of a relevant authority to ensure a member or co-opted member (or former member or co-opted member) of the authority,

(b) enabling a standards committee of a relevant authority to suspend or partially suspend a person from being a member or co-opted member of the authority for a limited period,

(c) conferring a right of appeal on a member or co-opted member (or former member or co-opted member) of a relevant authority in respect of any action taken against him.

(5) Nothing in subsection (2), (3) or (4) affects the generality of the power under subsection (1).

[...]

(7) Where [the Public Services Ombudsman for Wales] refers any matters to the monitoring officer of a relevant authority under [section 70(4) or (5) or 71(2) or (4)] 1 he may give directions to the monitoring officer as to the way in which those matters are to be dealt with.

74. Law of defamation

For the purposes of the law of defamation, any statement (whether written or oral) made by [the Public Services Ombudsman for Wales] in connection with the exercise of his functions under this Part shall be absolutely privileged.

75. [Adjudication Panel for Wales]

[...]

(2) There is to be a panel of persons, known as the Adjudication Panel for Wales or Panel Dyfarnu Cymru, eligible for membership of tribunals drawn from the Panel.

[...]

(5) The members of the Adjudication Panel for Wales are to be appointed by the National Assembly for Wales on such terms and conditions as it may determine.

(6) The National Assembly for Wales–

(a) must appoint one of the members of the Adjudication Panel for Wales as president of the Panel, and

(b) may appoint one of those members as deputy president of the Panel.

[...]

(8) Such members of the Adjudication Panel for Wales as the National Assembly for Wales thinks fit must possess such qualifications as may be determined by the National Assembly for Wales.

[...]

(10) The president and deputy president (if any) of the Adjudication Panel for Wales are to be responsible–

(a) for training the members of the Panel,

(b) for issuing guidance on how tribunals drawn from the Panel are to reach decisions.

[...]

76. Case tribunals and interim case tribunals

(1) Adjudications in respect of matters referred to the president of the [Adjudication Panel for Wales] under [section 71(3)] are to be conducted by tribunals (referred to in this Part as case tribunals) consisting of not less than three members of the Panel.

(2) Adjudications in respect of matters referred to the president of the [Adjudication Panel for Wales] under [section 72(4)] are to be conducted by tribunals (referred to in this Part as interim case tribunals) consisting of not less than three members of the Panel.

(3) The president of the [Adjudication Panel for Wales] (or in his absence the deputy president) is to appoint the members of any case tribunal or interim case tribunal.

(4) A case tribunal drawn from the [Adjudication Panel for Wales] may conduct a single adjudication in relation to two or more matters which are referred to the president of the Panel under [section 71(3)].

(5) An interim case tribunal drawn from the [Adjudication Panel for Wales] may conduct a single adjudication in relation to two or more matters which are referred to the president of the Panel under [section 72(4)].

(6) The president or the deputy president of the [Adjudication Panel for Wales] may be a member of a case tribunal or interim case tribunal drawn from the Panel.

(7) A member of the [Adjudication Panel for Wales] may not at any time be a member of a case tribunal or interim case tribunal drawn from the Panel which is to adjudicate on a matter relating to a member or co-opted member (or former member or co-opted member) of a relevant authority if, within the period of five years ending with that time, the member of the Panel has been a member or an officer of the authority or a member of any committee, sub-committee, joint committee or joint sub-committee of the authority.

(8) A member of the [Adjudication Panel for Wales] who is directly or indirectly interested in any matter which is, or is likely to be, the subject of an adjudication conducted by a case tribunal or interim case tribunal–

(a) must disclose the nature of his interest to the president or deputy president of that Panel, and

(b) may not be a member of a case tribunal or interim case tribunal which conducts an adjudication in relation to that matter.

(9) Where there is no deputy president of the [Adjudication Panel for Wales], the reference in subsection (3) and (8) to the deputy president is to be treated as a reference to such member of the Panel as [...] the National Assembly for Wales may specify.

[...]

(10) A person who is a member of an interim case tribunal which, as a result of an investigation under [section 69], conducts an adjudication in relation to any person may not be a member of a case tribunal which, on the conclusion of that investigation, subsequently conducts an adjudication in relation to that person.

[...]

(13) The National Assembly for Wales may issue guidance with respect to the composition of case tribunals or interim case tribunals drawn from the Adjudication Panel for Wales.

(14) The National Assembly for Wales may incur expenditure for the purpose of providing administrative support to the Adjudication Panel for Wales.

[...]

77. Adjudications

(1) A person who is the subject of an adjudication conducted by a case tribunal or interim case tribunal may appear before the tribunal in person or be represented by–

(a) counsel or a solicitor, or

(b) any other person whom he desires to represent him.

[...]

(4) The National Assembly for Wales may by regulations make such provision as appears to it to be necessary or expedient with respect to adjudications by case tribunals or interim case tribunals drawn from the Adjudication Panel for Wales.

(5) The president of the Adjudication Panel for Wales may, after consultation with the National Assembly for Wales, give directions as to the practice and procedure to be followed by tribunals drawn from the Panel.

(6) Regulations under this section may, in particular, include provision–

(a) for requiring persons to attend adjudications to give evidence and produce documents and for authorising the administration of oaths to witnesses,

(b) for requiring persons to furnish further particulars,

(c) for prescribing the procedure to be followed in adjudications, including provision as to the persons entitled to appear and to be heard on behalf of persons giving evidence,

(d) for the award of costs or expenses (including provision with respect to interest and provision with respect to the enforcement of any such award),

(e) for taxing or otherwise settling any such costs or expenses (and for enabling such costs to be taxed in [the county court]),

(f) for the registration and proof of decisions and awards of tribunals.

(7) A person who without reasonable excuse fails to comply with any requirement imposed by virtue of subsection (6)(a) or (b) [...] is guilty of an offence and liable on summary conviction to a fine not exceeding level 3 on the standard scale.

(8) In this section any reference to documents includes a reference to information held by means of a computer or in any other electronic form.

78. Decisions of [...] interim case tribunals

(1) [In adjudicating on any of the matters which are the subject of an interim report, [...] an interim case tribunal] must reach one of the following decisions–

(a) that the person to whom the recommendation mentioned in [section 72(3)] relates should not be suspended or partially suspended from being a member or co-opted member of the relevant authority concerned,

(b) that that person should be suspended or partially suspended from being a member or co-opted member of the [relevant authority concerned] 3 for a period which does not exceed six months or (if shorter) the remainder of the person's term of office.

[(2) If the decision of [the interim case tribunal] is as mentioned in subsection (1) (a), the tribunal must give notice of its decision to the standards committee of the relevant authority concerned.

(3) If the decision of [the interim case tribunal] is as mentioned in subsection (1)(b), the tribunal must give notice to the standards committee of the relevant authority concerned stating that the person concerned is suspended or partially suspended for the period, and in the way, that the tribunal has decided.

(3A) The effect of a notice given under subsection (3) is to suspend or partially suspend the person concerned as mentioned in subsection (3).]

[...]

(5) A decision of an interim case tribunal under this section shall not prevent [the Public Services Ombudsman for Wales] from continuing with the investigation under section 69 which gave rise to the interim report concerned and producing a report under section 71, or a further interim report under section 72, in respect of any matters which are the subject of the investigation.

(6) The suspension or partial suspension of any person under this section shall not extend beyond the day on which a notice [is given by virtue of [section 79]]

to the standards committee of the relevant authority concerned with respect to that person.

(7) A copy of any notice under this section must be given–

(a) to any person who is the subject of the notice, and

(b) to the monitoring officer of the relevant authority concerned.

[(8) Where the person concerned is no longer a member or co-opted member of the relevant authority concerned, but is a member or coopted member of another relevant authority–

(a) the references in subsection (1) to the relevant authority concerned are to be treated as references to that other authority,

(b) the references in subsections (2) and (7)(b) to the relevant authority concerned are to be treated as including a reference to that other relevant authority,

(c) the duty under subsection (3) to give notice to the standards committee of the relevant authority concerned is to be treated as a duty–

   (i) to give that notice to the standards committee of that other relevant authority, and

   (ii) to give a copy of that notice to the standards committee of the relevant authority concerned.

(8A) Subsection (8) does not apply unless–

[...]

(b) [...] the other relevant authority is also in Wales.]

(9) [An] interim case tribunal must take reasonable steps to inform any person who made any allegation which gave rise to the investigation under [section 69] of its decision under this section.

[...]

(10) [Where a person is suspended or partially suspended under this section by a decision of an interim case tribunal, the person] may appeal to the High Court–

(a) against the suspension or partial suspension, or

(b) against the length of the suspension or partial suspension.

[(11) An appeal may not be brought under subsection (10) except with the leave of the High Court.]

79. [Decisions of case tribunals: Wales]

[(A1)In this section 'Welsh case tribunal' means a case tribunal drawn from the Adjudication Panel for Wales.]

(1) A [Welsh case tribunal] which adjudicates on any matter must decide whether or not any person to which that matter relates has failed to comply with the code of conduct of the relevant authority concerned.

(2) Where a [Welsh case tribunal] decides that a person has not failed to comply with the code of conduct of the relevant authority concerned, it must give notice to that effect to the standards committee of the relevant authority concerned.

(3) Where a [Welsh case tribunal] decides that a person has failed to comply with the code of conduct of the relevant authority concerned, it must decide whether the nature of the failure is such that the person should be suspended or disqualified in accordance with subsection (4).

(4) A person may be–

(a) suspended or partially suspended from being a member or co-opted member of the relevant authority concerned, or

(b) disqualified for being, or becoming (whether by election or otherwise), a member of that or any other relevant authority.

(5) Where a [Welsh case tribunal] makes such a decision as is mentioned in subsection (4)(a), it must decide the period for which the person should be suspended or partially suspended (which must not exceed one year or, if shorter, the remainder of the person's term of office).

(6) Where a [Welsh case tribunal] makes such a decision as is mentioned in subsection (4)(b), it must decide the period for which the person should be disqualified (which must not exceed five years).

(7) Where a [Welsh case tribunal] decides that a person has failed to comply with the code of conduct of the relevant authority concerned but should not be suspended or disqualified as mentioned in subsection (4), it must give notice to the standards committee of the relevant authority concerned–

(a) stating that the person has failed to comply with that code of conduct, and

(b) specifying the details of that failure.

(8) Where a [Welsh case tribunal] decides that a person has failed to comply with the code of conduct of the relevant authority concerned and should be suspended or partially suspended as mentioned in subsection (4)(a), it must give notice to the standards committee of the relevant authority concerned–

(a) stating that the person has failed to comply with that code of conduct,

(b) specifying the details of that failure, and

(c) stating that the person [is suspended or partially suspended] for the period, and in the way, which the tribunal has decided.

[(9) The effect of a notice given to the standards committee of a relevant authority under subsection (8) is to suspend or partially suspend the person concerned as mentioned in subsection (8)(c).]

(10) Where a [Welsh case tribunal] decides that a person has failed to comply with the code of conduct of the relevant authority concerned and should be disqualified as mentioned in subsection (4)(b), it must give notice to the standards committee of the relevant authority concerned–

279

(a) stating that the person has failed to comply with that code of conduct,

(b) specifying the details of that failure, and

(c) stating that the person is disqualified for being, or becoming (whether by election or otherwise), a member of that or any other relevant authority for the period which the tribunal has decided.

(11) The effect of a notice given to the standards committee of a relevant authority under subsection (10) is to disqualify the person concerned as mentioned in subsection (10)(c).

(12) A copy of any notice under this section–

[(a) must be given to the Public Services Ombudsman for Wales,]

(b) must be given to any person who is the subject of the decision to which the notice relates, and

(c) must be published in one or more newspapers circulating in the area of the relevant authority concerned.

(13) Where the person concerned is no longer a member or co-opted member of the relevant authority concerned but is a member or co-opted member of another relevant authority [...]–

(a) a copy of any notice under subsection (2), (7) or (10) must also be given to the standards committee of that other relevant authority,

[(b) the reference in subsection (4)(a) to the relevant authority concerned is to be treated as a reference to that other relevant authority,]

(c) the duty to give notice to the standards committee of the relevant authority concerned under subsection (8) is to be treated as a duty–

    (i)   to give that notice to the standards committee of that other relevant authority, and

    (ii)   to give a copy of that notice to the standards committee of the relevant authority concerned,

(d) the reference in subsection (12)(c) to the relevant authority concerned is to be treated as including a reference to that other relevant authority.

(14) A Welsh case tribunal must take reasonable steps to inform any person who made any allegation which gave rise to the adjudication of the decision of the Welsh case tribunal under this section.

(15) Where a Welsh case tribunal decides under this section that a person has failed to comply with the code of conduct of the relevant authority concerned, that person may appeal to the High Court against that decision, or any other decision under this section which relates to him.

(16) An appeal may not be brought under subsection (15) except with the leave of the High Court.

80. Recommendations by case tribunals

(1) Where a case tribunal has adjudicated on any matter under this Act, it may make recommendations to a relevant authority about any matters relating to–

(a) the exercise of the authority's functions,

(b) the authority's code of conduct, or

(c) the authority's standards committee.

(2) A case tribunal must send a copy of any recommendations it makes under subsection (1) to the relevant person.

(3) A relevant authority to whom recommendations are made under subsection (1) must consider the recommendations and, within a period of three months beginning with the day on which the recommendations are received, prepare a report for the Public Services Ombudsman for Wales giving details of what action the authority have taken or are proposing to take as a result of the recommendations.

(4) A relevant authority's function of considering a report under subsection (3) may be discharged only by the authority or by the standards committee of that authority (and accordingly, in the case of a relevant authority to which section 101 of the Local Government Act 1972 applies, is not to be a function to which that section applies).

(5) If the Public Services Ombudsman for Wales is not satisfied with the action the relevant authority have taken or propose to take in relation to the recommendations, the Public Services Ombudsman for Wales may require the authority to publish a statement giving details of the recommendations made by the tribunal and of the authority's reasons for not fully implementing the recommendations.

81. Disclosure and registration of members' interests etc

(1) The monitoring officer of each relevant authority must establish and maintain a register of interests of the members and co-opted members of the authority.

(2) The mandatory provisions of the model code applicable to each relevant authority ('the mandatory provisions') must require the members and co-opted members of each authority to register in that authority's register maintained under subsection (1) such financial and other interests as are specified in the mandatory provisions.

(3) The mandatory provisions must also–

(a) require any member or co-opted member of a relevant authority who has an interest specified in the mandatory provisions under subsection (2) to disclose that interest before taking part in any business of the authority relating to that interest,

(b) make provision for preventing or restricting the participation of a member or co-opted member of a relevant authority in any business of the authority to which an interest disclosed under paragraph (a) relates.

(4) Any participation by a member or co-opted member of a relevant authority in any business which is prohibited by the mandatory provisions is not a failure to comply with the authority's code of conduct if the member or co-opted member has acted in accordance with a dispensation from the prohibition granted by the authority's standards committee in accordance with regulations made under subsection (5).

(5) The Welsh Ministers may prescribe in regulations the circumstances in which standards committees may grant dispensations under subsection (4).

(6) A relevant authority must ensure that copies of the register for the time being maintained by their monitoring officer under this section are available at an office of the authority for inspection by members of the public at all reasonable hours.

(7) As soon as practicable after the establishment by their monitoring officer of a register under this section, a relevant authority must–

(a) publish in one or more newspapers circulating in their area a notice which–

  (i) states that copies of the register are available at an office of the authority for inspection by members of the public at all reasonable hours, and

  (ii) specifies the address of that office, and

[...]

(c) inform the Public Services Ombudsman for Wales that copies of the register are so available.

82. Code of conduct for local government employees

[...]

(2) The National Assembly for Wales may by order issue a code as regards the conduct which is expected of qualifying employees of relevant authorities.

(3) The power under subsection (2) to issue a code includes power–

(a) to issue a separate code for council managers (within the meaning of Part II of this Act), and

(b) to revise any code which has been issued.

(6) Before making an order under this section, the National Assembly for Wales must consult–

(a) such representatives of relevant authorities, and of employees of those authorities, as it considers appropriate,

(b) the Auditor General for Wales, and

(c) the Public Services Ombudsman for Wales.

(7) The terms of appointment or conditions of employment of every qualifying employee of a relevant authority (whether appointed or employed before or after the commencement of this section) are to be deemed to incorporate any code for the time being under this section which is applicable.

(8) In this section 'qualifying employee', in relation to a relevant authority, means an employee of the authority other than an employee falling within any description of employee specified in regulations under this subsection.

(9) The power to make regulations under subsection (8) is to be exercised–

[...]

(b) by the National Assembly for Wales.

82A. Monitoring officers: delegation of functions under Part 3

(1) This section applies to functions of a monitoring officer of a relevant authority in relation to matters referred to him under section 70(4) or (5) or 71(2) or (4).

(2) Where the monitoring officer considers that in a particular case he himself ought not to perform particular functions to which this section applies, those particular functions shall in that case be performed personally by a person nominated for the purpose by the monitoring officer.

(3) Where a deputy nominated by the monitoring officer under section 5(7) of the Local Government and Housing Act 1989 (nomination of member of monitoring officer's staff to act as deputy when monitoring officer absent or ill) considers that in a particular case he himself ought not to perform particular functions—

(a) to which this section applies, and

(b) which, by reason of the absence or illness of the monitoring officer, would but for this subsection fall to be performed by the deputy,

those particular functions shall, while the monitoring officer continues to be unable to act by reason of absence or illness, be performed in that case personally by a person nominated for the purpose by the deputy.

(4) Where functions to which this section applies are to be performed by a person nominated under subsection (2) or (3) who is an officer of the relevant authority, the authority shall provide the officer with such staff, accommodation and other resources as are, in the officer's opinion, sufficient to allow those functions to be performed.

(5) Where functions to which this section applies are to be performed by a person nominated under subsection (2) or (3) who is not an officer of the relevant authority, the authority shall—

(a) pay the person a reasonable fee for performing the functions,

(b) reimburse expenses properly incurred by the person in performing the functions, but only to the extent that the amount of the expenses is reasonable, and

(c) provide the person with such staff, accommodation and other resources as are reasonably necessary for the person's performance of the functions.

83. Interpretation of Part III

(1) In this Part–

'case tribunal' has the meaning given by section 76(1),

'code of conduct' means a code of conduct under section 51,

'co-opted member' has the meaning given by section 49 (7),

'elected mayor' and 'elected executive member' have the meaning given by section 39(1) and (4),

'executive' is to be construed in accordance with section 11,

'executive arrangements' has the meaning given by section 10,

'executive leader' has the meaning given by section 11(2A)(a) or (3)(a),

'interim case tribunal' has the meaning given by section 76(2),

'model code of conduct' is to be construed in accordance with section 50(2),

'relevant authority' has the meaning given by section 49(6).

(2) Any reference in this Part to a committee of a relevant authority, in the case of a relevant authority to which Part II of this Act applies, includes a reference to a committee of an executive of the authority.

(3) Any reference in this Part to a member of a relevant authority, in the case of a relevant authority to which Part II of this Act applies, includes a reference to an elected mayor or elected executive member of the authority.

[...]

(5) Any reference in this Part to a joint committee or joint sub-committee of a relevant authority is a reference to a joint committee on which the authority is represented or a sub-committee of such a committee.

(6) Any reference in this Part to a failure to comply with a relevant authority's code of conduct includes a reference to a failure to comply with the mandatory provisions which apply to the members or co-opted members of the authority by virtue of section 51(5)(b).

(7) Any reference in this Part to a person being partially suspended from being a member or co-opted member of a relevant authority includes a reference to a person being prevented from exercising particular functions or having particular responsibilities as such a member or co-opted member.

(8) The reference in subsection (7) to particular functions or particular responsibilities as a member of a relevant authority, in the case of a relevant authority to which Part II of this Act applies, includes a reference to particular functions or particular responsibilities as a member of an executive of the authority.

(9) A person who is suspended under this Part from being a member of a relevant authority shall also be suspended from being a member of any committee, sub-committee, joint committee or joint sub-committee of the authority, but this subsection does not apply to a person who is partially suspended under this Part.

(10) A person who is suspended under this Part from being a member of a relevant authority to which Part II of this Act applies shall also be suspended, if he is a member of an executive of the authority, from being such a member; but this subsection does not apply to a person who is partially suspended under this Part.

(11) A person who is disqualified under this Part for being or becoming a member of a relevant authority shall also be disqualified–

(a) for being or becoming a member of any committee, sub-committee, joint committee or joint sub-committee of the authority, and

(b) if the authority is one to which Part II of this Act applies, for being or becoming a member of an executive of the authority.

[...]

(13) Any function which by virtue of this Part is exercisable by or in relation to the monitoring officer of a relevant authority which is a community council is to be exercisable by or in relation to the monitoring officer of the county council or county borough council in whose area the community council is situated; and any reference in this Part to the monitoring officer of a relevant authority which is a community council is to be construed accordingly.

(14) Any functions which are conferred by virtue of this Part on a relevant authority to which Part II of this Act applies are not to be the responsibility of an executive of the authority under executive arrangements.

CONDUCT OF MEMBERS (PRINCIPLES) (WALES) ORDER 2001, SI 2001/2276

1. Citation, commencement and application

(1) This Order may be cited as the Conduct of Members (Principles) (Wales) Order 2001 and shall come into force on 28 July 2001.

(2) This Order applies to each relevant authority in Wales.

2. Interpretation

In this Order–

'co-opted member' ('aelod cyfetholedig'), in relation to a relevant authority, means a person who is not a member of the authority but who–

(a) is a member of any committee or sub-committee of the authority, or

(b) is a member of, and represents the authority on, any joint committee or joint sub-committee of the authority,

and who is entitled to vote on any question which falls to be decided at any meeting of that committee or sub-committee;

'member' ('aelod') includes a co-opted member; and

'relevant authority' ('awdurdod perthnasol') means–

(a) a county council,

(b) a county borough council,

(c) a community council,

[(d) a fire and rescue authority constituted by a scheme under section 2 of the Fire and Rescue Services Act 2004 or a scheme to which section 4 of that Act applies, and]

(e) a National Park authority established under section 63 of the Environment Act 1995.

3. Principles governing conduct of members of relevant authorities

The principles which are to govern the conduct of members of a relevant authority in Wales are set out in the Schedule to this Order.

1. Selflessness

Members must act solely in the public interest. They must never use their position as members to improperly confer advantage on themselves or to improperly confer advantage or disadvantage on others.

2. Honesty

Members must declare any private interests relevant to their public duties and take steps to resolve any conflict in a way that protects the public interest.

3. Integrity and Propriety

Members must not put themselves in a position where their integrity is called into question by any financial or other obligation to individuals or organisations that might seek to influence them in the performance of their duties. Members must on all occasions avoid the appearance of such behaviour.

4. Duty to Uphold the Law

Members must act to uphold the law and act on all occasions in accordance with the trust that the public has placed in them.

5. Stewardship

In discharging their duties and responsibilities members must ensure that their authority's resources are used both lawfully and prudently.

6. Objectivity in Decision-making

In carrying out their responsibilities including making appointments, awarding contracts, or recommending individuals for rewards and benefits, members must make decisions on merit. Whilst members must have regard to the professional advice of officers and may properly take account of the views of others, including their political groups, it is their responsibility to decide what view to take and, if appropriate, how to vote on any issue.

7. Equality and Respect

Members must carry out their duties and responsibilities with due regard to the need to promote equality of opportunity for all people, regardless of their gender, race, disability, sexual orientation, age or religion, and show respect and consideration for others.

8. Openness

Members must be as open as possible about all their actions and those of their authority. They must seek to ensure that disclosure of information is restricted only in accordance with the law.

9. Accountability

Members are accountable to the electorate and the public generally for their actions and for the way they carry out their responsibilities as a member. They must be prepared to submit themselves to such scrutiny as is appropriate to their responsibilities.

10. Leadership

Members must promote and support these principles by leadership and example so as to promote public confidence in their role and in the authority. They must respect the impartiality and integrity of the authority's statutory officers and its other employees.

LOCAL GOVERNMENT INVESTIGATIONS (FUNCTIONS OF MONITORING OFFICERS AND STANDARDS COMMITTEES) (WALES) REGULATIONS 2001, SI 2001/2281

1. Name, commencement and application

(1) These Regulations are called the Local Government Investigations (Functions of Monitoring Officers and Standards Committees)(Wales) Regulations 2001 and they come into force on the 28th July 2001.

(2) The regulations apply to relevant authorities in Wales only.

2. Interpretation

In these Regulations:

'relevant authority' ('awdurdod perthnasol') means:

- a county council,
- a county borough council,
- a community council,
- [a fire and rescue authority constituted by a scheme under section 2 of the Fire and Rescue Services Act 2004 or a scheme to which section 4 of that Act applies], and

- a National Park authority established under section 63 of the Environment Act 1995; and

'the 2000 Act' ('Deddf 2000') means the Local Government Act 2000.

3. Functions of monitoring officers

(1) Where any matter is referred to the monitoring officer of a relevant authority under section 70(4) of the 2000 Act, the monitoring officer must in respect of that matter:

(a) conduct an investigation; and

(b) report, and if appropriate make recommendations, to the Standards Committee of the relevant authority.

(2) Where any matter is referred to the monitoring officer of a relevant authority under section 71(2) of the 2000 Act, the monitoring officer must consider any report sent to him or her by [the Public Services Ombudsman for Wales] and, if appropriate, make recommendations to the Standards Committee of the relevant authority.

4. Investigations

(1) When conducting an investigation under Regulation 3(1)(a) above the monitoring officer may follow such procedures as he or she considers appropriate in the circumstances of the case and in particular may:

(a) make such enquiries of any person as he or she thinks necessary for the purposes of carrying out the investigation,

(b) require any person to provide him or her with such information, explanation or documents as he or she considers necessary,

(c) require any member or co-opted member or officer of a relevant authority to appear before him or her for the purposes of paragraph (a) and (b) above.

(2) In conducting the investigation, the monitoring officer may be assisted by any person.

(3) The monitoring officer may also where necessary obtain expert or other advice from any person who is in his or her opinion particularly qualified to assist in conducting the investigation.

(4) Where a person has attended before the monitoring officer or provided information or assistance for the purposes of the investigation in accordance with paragraphs (1) or (2) above, the monitoring officer may, subject to the Standards Committee's authorisation, pay to that person

(a) such sums in respect of expenses properly incurred by him or her, and

(b) such allowances by way of compensation for the loss of his or her time, as may be determined by the [Welsh Ministers].

(5) Where a person has given advice in accordance with paragraph (3) above, the monitoring officer may pay to that person such fees or allowances incurred subject to the maxima set out in the relevant authority's allowances scheme.

5. Restrictions on disclosure of information

(1) Information obtained by a monitoring officer when conducting an investigation must not be disclosed unless:

(a) the disclosure is made for the purposes of enabling a monitoring officer or standards committee to perform their functions under these Regulations;

(b) the disclosure is made for the purpose of enabling [the Public Services Ombudsman for Wales] to carry out his or her functions;

(c) the person to whom the information relates has consented to its disclosure;

(d) the information has previously been disclosed to the public with lawful authority;

(e) the disclosure is for the purposes of criminal proceedings in any part of the United Kingdom and the information in question was not obtained as a result of personal enquiries of the person subject to the criminal proceedings under Regulation 4 above; [...]

(f) the disclosure is made to the Audit Commission for the purposes of any function of the Audit Commission or an auditor under the Audit Commission Act 1998 [; or]

[(g) the disclosure is made to the Auditor General for Wales for the purposes of any function of his or hers or of an auditor under Part 2 of the Public Audit (Wales) Act 2004.]

(2) In this Regulation and in Regulation 4 above, any reference to documents includes a reference to information held by means of a computer or in any other electronic form.

6. Reports

After concluding an investigation, the monitoring officer must:

(a) produce a report on the findings of his or her investigation and, if appropriate, may make recommendations to the Standards Committee of the relevant authority concerned,

(b) send a copy of the report to any person who is the subject of the investigation, and

(c) take reasonable steps to send a copy of the report to any person who made any allegation which gave rise to the investigation.

7. Functions of the Standards Committee

After receiving a report and any recommendations from the monitoring officer, or a report from [the Public Services Ombudsman for Wales] together with any recommendations of the monitoring officer, the Standards Committee must determine either:

(a) that there is no evidence of any failure to comply with the code of conduct of the relevant authority concerned and must notify any person who is the subject of the investigation, any person who made any allegation which gave rise to the investigation and the [Public Services Ombudsman for Wales] 2 accordingly; or

(b) that any person who is the subject of the investigation should be given the opportunity to make representations, either orally or in writing in respect of the findings of the investigation and any allegation that he or she has failed, or may have failed, to comply with the relevant authority's code of conduct.

8. Procedure and Powers of Standards Committees

(1) Subject to any express provision in these Regulations or in the Standards Committees (Wales) Regulations 2001, the practice and procedure to be followed in exercising its functions under these Regulations shall be for the Standards Committee of the relevant authority to decide.

[(2) Paragraphs (3) to (3D) apply—

(a) in respect of the Public Services Ombudsman for Wales in the case of an investigation undertaken by the Public Services Ombudsman for Wales and referred to the monitoring officer of the relevant authority under section 71(2) of the 2000 Act; and

(b) in respect of the monitoring officer of the relevant authority in the case of an investigation referred to the monitoring officer under section 70(4) of the 2000 Act.

(3) The Public Services Ombudsman for Wales and the monitoring officer are entitled to attend before the Standards Committee for the purposes of—

(a) presenting the report and/or explaining any of the matters in it; and

(b) otherwise playing such part or assisting the Standards Committee as the Standards Committee considers appropriate.

(3A) The Standards Committee may request the Public Services Ombudsman for Wales or the monitoring officer to attend before it for the purposes of—

(a) presenting the report and/or explaining any of the matters in it; and

(b) otherwise playing such part or assisting the Standards Committee as the Standards Committee considers appropriate.

(3B) A request under paragraph (3A) must not be unreasonably refused and if such request is refused the Public Services Ombudsman for Wales or monitoring officer must give reasons in writing to the Standards Committee for not complying with the request to attend.

(3C) The attendance shall be when the Standards Committee of the relevant authority is considering any representations made by the person who is the subject of the investigation or, if no such representations are made, at any reasonable time.

(3D) The Public Services Ombudsman for Wales and monitoring officer may be represented by counsel or a solicitor.]

(4) If any person who is the subject of the investigation fails to make representations in accordance with Regulation 7(b) above, the Standards Committee may:

(a) unless it is satisfied that there is sufficient reason for such failure, consider the monitoring officer's report and make a determination in that person's absence; or

(b) give that person a further opportunity to make representations.

(5) Where appropriate, and in accordance with the provisions of these Regulations, the Standards Committee has power to censure any member or co-opted member (or former member or co-opted member) of the relevant authority, or suspend or partially suspend a member or co-opted member for a period not exceeding 6 months.

(6) Any period of suspension or partial suspension shall commence on the day after:

(a) the expiry of the time allowed to lodge a notice of appeal under Regulation 10(2) below,

(b) receipt of notification of the conclusion of any appeal in accordance with Regulation 12(a)(i) or (b) below, or

(c) a further determination by the Standards Committee made after receiving a recommendation from an appeals tribunal under Regulation 12(a)(ii) below, whichever occurs last.

9. Determinations of the Standards Committee

(1) After considering any representations, a Standards Committee must determine:

(a) that there is no evidence of any failure to comply with the code of conduct of the relevant authority and that therefore no action needs to be taken in respect of the matters which are the subject of the investigation;

(b) that a member or co-opted member (or former member or co-opted member) of a relevant authority has failed to comply with the relevant authority's code of conduct but that no action needs to be taken in respect of that failure;

(c) that a member or co-opted member (or former member or co-opted member) of the relevant authority has failed to comply with the authority's code of conduct and should be censured, or

(d) that a member or co-opted member of a relevant authority has failed to comply with the authority's code of conduct and should be suspended or partially suspended from being a member or co-opted member of that authority for a period not exceeding six months.

(2) Where an appeals tribunal drawn from the Adjudication Panel for Wales makes a recommendation in accordance with Regulation 12(a)(ii) below that a different penalty should be imposed, the Standards Committee must also determine whether or not it should uphold its original determination or accept the recommendation.

(3) After making a determination in accordance with paragraph (1) or (2) above the Standards Committee must notify any person who is the subject of the investigation, any person who made any allegation which gave rise to the investigation and the [Public Services Ombudsman for Wales] accordingly, giving reasons for the decision.

(4) After making a determination in accordance with paragraph (2) above the Standards Committee must also notify the president of the Adjudication Panel for Wales.

10. Right of appeal

(1) Where a Standards Committee determines under Regulation 9(1) above that a person has failed to comply with the code of conduct of the relevant authority concerned, that person may appeal against the determination to an appeals tribunal drawn from the Adjudication Panel for Wales.

(2) The appeal must be instigated by giving notice in writing within 21 days of receiving notification of the Standard Committee's determination to this address:

[The President
Adjudication Panel for Wales
Welsh Assembly Government
Cathays Park
Cardiff
CF10 3NQ]

(3) The notice of appeal must specify:

(a) the grounds for appeal; and

(b) whether or not the person giving notice of appeal consents to the appeal being conducted by way of written representations.

11. Appeals

(1) Appeals from a determination of a Standards Committee will be conducted:

(a) by an appeals tribunal consisting of not less than three members of the Adjudication Panel for Wales,

(b) by way of an oral hearing unless every person who has given notice of appeal consents to the appeal being conducted by way of written representations in accordance with Regulation 10(3)(b) above.

(2) The president of the Adjudication Panel for Wales (or in his absence the deputy president) is to appoint the members of any appeals tribunal, and the president or deputy president may be a member of a tribunal.

(3) A member of the Adjudication Panel for Wales may not at any time be a member of an appeals tribunal drawn from the Panel which is to adjudicate on a matter relating to a member or co-opted member (or former member or co-opted member) of a relevant authority if, within the period of five years ending with that time, the member of the Panel has been a member or an officer of the authority or a member of any committee, sub-committee, joint committee or joint sub-committee of the authority.

(4) A member of the Adjudication Panel for Wales who is directly or indirectly interested in any matter which is, or is likely to be, the subject of an appeal conducted by an appeals tribunal:

(a) must disclose the nature of his interest to the president of the Panel, and

(b) may not be a member of the appeals tribunal which considers an appeal in relation to that matter.

(5) Subject to any express provision in these Regulations, the practice and procedure to be followed by appeals tribunals drawn from the Adjudication Panel for Wales will be such as the president of the Panel, after consultation with the [Welsh Ministers], will decide.

12. Conclusions of an appeals tribunal

An appeals tribunal must:

(a) uphold the determination of the relevant authority's Standards Committee that any person who was subject to the investigation breached the code of conduct and either:

    (i) endorse any penalty imposed, or

    (ii) refer the matter back to the Standards Committee with a recommendation that a different penalty be imposed; or,

(b) overturn the determination of the relevant authority's Standards Committee that any person has breached the code of conduct, and must inform any person subject to the investigation, the [Public Services Ombudsman for Wales] and the Standards Committee of the relevant authority accordingly, giving reasons for the decision.

13. Publication

(1) A Standards Committee must cause to be produced within 14 days after:

(a) the expiry of the time allowed to lodge a notice of appeal under Regulation 10(2) above,

(b) receipt of notification of the conclusion of any appeal in accordance with Regulation 12(a)(i) or (b) above, or

(c) a further determination by the Standards Committee made after receiving a recommendation from an appeals tribunal under Regulation 12(a)(ii) above, whichever occurs last, a report on the outcome of the investigation and send a copy to the [Public Services Ombudsman for Wales], the monitoring officer of the relevant authority concerned, any person subject to the investigation and take reasonable steps to send a copy to any person who made any allegation which gave rise to the investigation.

(2) Upon receipt of the report of the Standards Committee, the monitoring officer of the relevant authority shall:

(a) for a period of 21 days publish the report on the relevant authority's website and make copies available for inspection by the public without charge at all reasonable hours at one or more of the authority's offices, where any person shall be entitled to take copies of, or extracts from, the report when made so available,

(b) supply a copy of the report to any person on request if he or she pays such charge as the relevant authority may reasonably require, and

(c) not later than 7 days after the report is received from by the Standards Committee, give public notice, by advertisement in newspapers circulating in the area and such other ways as appear to him or her to be appropriate, that copies of the report will be available as provided by sub-paragraphs (a) and (b) above, and shall specify the date (being a date not more than seven days after public notice is first given) from which the period of 21 days will begin.

14. Representation

A person who makes oral representations to a Standards Committee or who appeals against a decision of a Standards Committee to an appeals tribunal drawn from the Adjudication Panel for Wales may appear before the Committee or tribunal in person or be represented by–

(a) counsel or a solicitor, or

(b) any other person he or she desires.

15. Costs

(1) The Standards Committee of a relevant authority shall have no power to make an award of any Costs or expenses arising from any of its proceedings.

(2) An appeals tribunal shall not normally make an order awarding costs or expenses, but may, subject to paragraph (3), make such an order:

(a) against a person if it is of the opinion that that person has acted frivolously or vexatiously, or that his or her conduct in pursuing an appeal was wholly unreasonable;

(b) as a result of the postponement or adjournment of a hearing.

(3) No order shall be made under paragraph (2)(a) above against a person without that person having been given an opportunity to make representations against the making of such an order.

THE ADJUDICATIONS BY CASE TRIBUNALS AND INTERIM CASE TRIBUNALS (WALES) REGULATIONS 2001, SI 2001/2288

1. Name, commencement and application

(1) The name of these Regulations is the Adjudications by Case Tribunals and Interim Case Tribunals (Wales) Regulations 2001 and they shall come into force on 28th July 2001.

(2) These Regulations apply to adjudications by case tribunals and interim case tribunals in Wales only.

2. Adjudications

The provisions set out in the Schedule to these Regulations shall apply to adjudications carried out by case tribunals or interim case tribunals.

SCHEDULE

1. Interpretation

In this Schedule–

'accused person' ('person a gyhuddwyd') means a person who is the subject of the investigation which gave rise to the reference to the Adjudication Panel for Wales under section 71(3) or 72(4) of the Act;

[...]

'register' ('cofrestr') means the register of adjudications and decisions kept in accordance with these provisions;

'registrar' ('cofrestrydd') means the person for the time being acting as a registrar of tribunals and includes any person authorised for the purpose by the president of the Adjudication Panel for Wales;

'report' ('adroddiad') means the report produced by [the Public Services Ombudsman for Wales] in accordance with section 71(3)(a) or 72(1) of the Act, a copy of which has been sent or given to the president of the Adjudication Panel for Wales in accordance with section 71(3)(c) or 72(5)(c) of the Act;

'the Act' ('y Ddeddf') means the Local Government Act 2000; and

'tribunal' ('tribiwnlys') means a case tribunal established under section 76(1) of the Act or an interim case tribunal established under section 76(2) of the Act (as the case may be).

2. Acknowledgement, registration and notification

Following a reference by [the Public Services Ombudsman for Wales] under section 71(3) or 72(4) of the Act the registrar shall–

(a) send to the [Public Services Ombudsman for Wales] an acknowledgement of its receipt;

(b) enter particulars of it in the register;

(c) give written notice to any accused person of the reference, the case number entered in the register (which shall constitute the title of the adjudication) and the address to which notices and other communications to the tribunal shall be sent; and

(d) send with the notice a copy of the report and such other information as is appropriate to the case including information about the delivery of a reply.

3. Reply

(1) An accused person must deliver to the registrar a written reply acknowledging receipt of the notice and stating–

(a) whether or not that person intends

    (i)   to attend or be represented at the hearing, or

    (ii)   to dispute the contents of the report and, if so, on what grounds;

(b) the name and address and the profession of any person who is to represent him or her and whether such address is to be his or her address for service for the purposes of the adjudication; and

(c) whether that person wishes the hearing to be conducted in English or Welsh.

(2) Such reply shall be signed either by the accused person or by his or her nominated representative and shall be delivered to the address for the tribunal specified in the notice given under paragraph 2(c) above not later than 21 days after the date on which the notice was received or by such later date as the tribunal may allow.

(3) If no reply is received by the registrar within the specified time or any extension of time allowed by the tribunal, or if the accused person states in his or her reply that he or she does not intend either to attend or be represented at the hearing or to dispute the contents of the report, the tribunal may determine the adjudication without a hearing.

4. Written representations

An accused person who has delivered to the registrar a written reply stating that he or she does not intend to attend or be represented at the hearing or to dispute the contents of the report may send to the registrar written representations which shall be considered by the tribunal before a decision on the case is reached.

5. Directions in preparation for a hearing

(1) The tribunal may at any time, on the application of an accused person or of its own motion, give directions to enable that person to prepare for the hearing or to assist the tribunal to determine the issues.

(2) An application for directions shall be made in writing to the registrar.

6. Particulars

The tribunal may give directions requiring any person to provide such particulars as may be reasonably required for the determination of the adjudication.

7. Disclosure of documents and other material

The tribunal may give directions requiring any person to deliver to the tribunal any document or other material which the tribunal may require and which it is in the power of that person to deliver.

8. Summoning of witnesses

The tribunal may by summons require any person in the United Kingdom (with the exception of [the Public Services Ombudsman for Wales] and any member of the staff of [the Public Services Ombudsman for Wales]) to attend as a witness at the hearing of an adjudication at such time and place as may be specified in the summons and at the hearing to answer any questions or produce any documents or other material in his or her custody or control which relate to any matter in question in the adjudication, provided that–

(a) no person shall be required to attend in obedience to such a summons unless he or she has been given at least fourteen days' notice of the hearing or, if less than fourteen days, has informed the tribunal that he or she accepts such notice as has been given; and

(b) no person, other than an accused person, shall be required in obedience to such a summons to attend and give evidence or to produce any document unless the necessary expenses of his or her attendance are paid or tendered to him or her.

[9. Attendance of the Public Services Ombudsman for Wales

(1) The Public Services Ombudsman for Wales is entitled to attend, and the tribunal may request the Public Services Ombudsman for Wales to attend, the hearing of an adjudication for the purposes of—

(a) presenting the report and/or explaining any of the matters in it; and

(b) otherwise playing such part or assisting the tribunal at the hearing as the tribunal considers appropriate.

(2) A request under sub-paragraph (1) must not be unreasonably refused and if such request is refused the Public Services Ombudsman for Wales must give reasons in writing to the tribunal for not complying with a request to attend a hearing.

(3) The Public Services Ombudsman for Wales may be represented by counsel or a solicitor.

10. Experts

(1) Where the tribunal considers that any question arises on which it would be desirable to have the assistance of an expert, it may make arrangements for a

person with appropriate qualifications to enquire into and report on the matter and, if the tribunal so requires, to attend the hearing and to give evidence.

(2) A copy of a report received from an expert shall be supplied to each accused person before the hearing or any resumed hearing.

(3) The fees of an expert shall be borne by the tribunal.

11. Varying or setting aside directions

Where a person to whom a direction (including any summons) is addressed had no opportunity of objecting to the making of the direction, he or she may apply to the tribunal to vary it or set it aside but the tribunal shall not so do without first notifying the person who applied for the direction and considering any representations made by him or her.

12. Pre-hearing review

(1) Where it appears to the tribunal that an adjudication would be facilitated by the holding of a pre-hearing review, it may, of its own motion or on the application of an accused person, give directions for such a review to be held. The registrar shall give each accused person at least fourteen days notice of the time and place of the review.

(2) The review shall be held in private unless the tribunal directs otherwise and any accused person may appear and be represented by any other person.

(3) On a review:

(a) the tribunal or, subject to sub-paragraph (4), the registrar shall give all such directions as appear to be necessary or desirable to secure the just, expeditious and economical conduct of the adjudication;

(b) the tribunal or, subject to sub-paragraph (4), the registrar shall endeavour to secure that any accused person makes all such admissions and agreements as ought reasonably to be made in relation to the adjudication; and

(c) the tribunal may, if every accused person agrees, determine the adjudication on the documents and statements then before it without any further hearing.

(4) The registrar shall exercise the powers given to him or her by sub-paragraph (3)(a) and (b) in accordance with the directions of the tribunal and any direction given by the registrar may be set aside or varied by the tribunal of its own motion or on the application of an accused person.

13. Notice of place and time of hearing

(1) The registrar shall fix the date, time and place of the hearing and, not less than twenty one days before that date, shall send to any accused person notice of the hearing.

(2) The registrar shall include in or with the notice of hearing–

(a) information and guidance, in a form approved by the president of the Adjudication Panel for Wales, as to attendance at the hearing of witnesses, the bringing of documents, and the right of representation by another person; and

(b) a statement explaining the possible consequences of non-attendance and of the right of any accused person who has delivered a reply but who does not attend and is not represented to make representations in writing.

(3) The tribunal may postpone a hearing and the registrar shall give to any accused person not less than seven days notice of any such postponement.

(4) The tribunal may from time to time adjourn a hearing and, if the time and place of the adjourned hearing are announced before the adjournment, no further notice shall be required.

14. Public notice of hearings

The registrar shall make available for public inspection a list of all adjudications for which an oral hearing is to be held and of the date, time and place of the hearing.

15. Power to determine an adjudication without a hearing

(1) The tribunal may–

(a) if every accused person so agrees in writing, or

(b) in the circumstances described in paragraph 3(3) above, determine an adjudication, or any particular issue, without a hearing.

(2) The provisions of paragraphs 17(2) and 18(6) shall apply in respect of the determination of an adjudication, or any particular issue, in accordance with this paragraph.

16. Hearings to be public: exceptions

(1) All hearings by a tribunal shall be held in public except where the tribunal considers that publicity would prejudice the interests of justice.

(2) The following persons shall be entitled to attend a hearing whether or not it is in private–

(a) the president and members of the Adjudication Panel for Wales notwithstanding that they do not constitute the tribunal for the purpose of the hearing;

(b) [...]

(c) [the Public Services Ombudsman for Wales] or the representative of [the Public Services Ombudsman for Wales]; and

(d) the monitoring officer of an authority of which the accused person is a member or co-opted member [or the representative of the monitoring officer].

299

(3) The tribunal may permit any other person to attend a hearing which is held in private.

(4) Without prejudice to any other powers which it may have, a tribunal may exclude from a hearing, or part of it, any person whose conduct has disrupted or is likely, in the opinion of the tribunal, to disrupt the hearing.

17. Failure of parties to attend hearing

(1) If an accused person fails to attend or be represented at a hearing of which he or she has been duly notified, the tribunal may–

(a) unless it is satisfied that there is sufficient reason for such absence, hear and determine the adjudication in that person's absence; or

(b) adjourn the hearing; and may make such order as to costs and expenses as it thinks fit.

(2) Before deciding to determine an adjudication in the absence of an accused person, the tribunal shall consider any representations in writing submitted by that person in response to the notice of hearing and, for the purpose of this paragraph, any reply shall be treated as a representation in writing.

18. Procedure at hearing

(1) At the beginning of the hearing the chairperson shall explain the order of proceeding which the tribunal proposes to adopt.

(2) Subject to this paragraph, the tribunal shall conduct the hearing in such manner as it considers most suitable to the clarification of the issues before it and generally to the just handling of the adjudication; it shall so far as appears to it appropriate seek to avoid formality in its proceedings.

(3) The hearing may be conducted in either English or Welsh as the tribunal directs and in making such a direction the tribunal shall take account of and, so far as is reasonably practicable, give effect to any preference stated by an accused person in a reply delivered under paragraph 3. In either case an instantaneous translation service shall be provided for any person attending the hearing who requests it.

(4) Any accused person shall be entitled to give evidence, to call witnesses, to question any witnesses and to address the tribunal both on the evidence and generally on the subject matter of the adjudication.

(5) Evidence before the tribunal may be given orally or, if the tribunal so orders, by affidavit or written statement, but the tribunal may at any stage of the proceedings require the personal attendance of any deponent or maker of a written statement.

(6) The tribunal may receive evidence of any fact which appears to the tribunal to be relevant notwithstanding that such evidence would be inadmissible in proceedings before a court of law but shall not refuse to admit any evidence which is admissible at law and is relevant.

(7) A tribunal may require any witness to give evidence on oath or affirmation and for that purpose there may be administered an oath or affirmation in due form.

19. Decision of Tribunal

(1) A decision of a tribunal may be taken by a majority and the decision shall record whether it was unanimous or taken by a majority.

(2) The decision of a tribunal may be given orally at the end of the hearing or reserved and, in any event, whether there has been a hearing or not, shall be recorded forthwith in a document which shall also contain a statement of the reasons for its decision and which shall be signed and dated by the chairperson.

(3) Subject to sub-paragraph (4), every document referred to in this paragraph shall, as soon as may be, be entered in the register.

(4) Where any such document refers to any evidence that has been heard in private, only a summary of the document shall be entered in the register, omitting such material as the tribunal may direct.

(5) Except where a decision is announced at the end of the hearing, the document recording it shall be treated as having been made on the date on which it is entered in the register.

20. Orders for costs and expenses

(1) Save as provided by paragraph 17(1) the tribunal shall not normally make an order awarding costs and expenses, but may, subject to sub-paragraph (2), make such an order against a person if it is of the opinion that that person has acted frivolously or vexatiously or that his or her conduct has been wholly unreasonable.

(2) No order shall be made under sub-paragraph (1) against a person without that person having been given an opportunity to make representations against the making of the order.

(3) An order under sub paragraph (1) may require the person against whom it is made to pay another person either a specified sum in respect of the costs and expenses incurred by that other person in connection with the adjudication or the whole or part of such costs as assessed (if not otherwise agreed).

(4) Any costs required by an order under this paragraph to be assessed shall be assessed in the county court on the standard basis.

(5) The specified or assessed amount of any costs and expenses awarded by a tribunal shall, unless set aside and subject to any variation on appeal or review, carry interest from the fourteenth day after the date of the award at the rate for the time being prescribed under section 69 of the County Courts Act 1984.

(6) The specified or assessed amount of any costs and expenses and any interest thereon shall be recoverable by execution issued from a county court.

21. Irregularities

(1) Any irregularity resulting from failure to comply with any of these provisions or of any direction of the tribunal before the tribunal has reached its decision shall not of itself render the adjudication void.

(2) Where any such irregularity comes to the attention of the tribunal, the tribunal may, and if it considers that any person may have been prejudiced by the irregularity shall, give such directions as it thinks just before reaching its decision to cure or waive the irregularity.

(3) Clerical mistakes in any document recording a direction or decision of the tribunal, or errors arising in such a document from an accidental slip or omission, may be corrected by the chairperson by certificate under his hand.

22. The register and publication of decisions

(1) The register shall be kept at the address of the Adjudication Panel for Wales and shall be open to the inspection of any person without charge at all reasonable hours.

(2) The tribunal may make arrangements for the publication of its decisions as it considers appropriate but, in doing so, shall have regard to the need to preserve the confidentiality of any evidence heard in private and for that purpose may make any necessary amendments to the text of a decision.

23. Proof of documents and certificate of decisions

(1) Any document purporting to be a document duly executed or issued by the registrar on behalf of the tribunal shall, unless the contrary is proved, be deemed to be a document so executed or issued as the case may be.

(2) A document purporting to be certified by the registrar to be a true copy of any entry of a decision in the register shall, unless the contrary is proved, be sufficient evidence of the entry and of matters contained therein.

24. Method of sending, delivering or serving documents, etc

(1) Any document required or authorised by these provisions to be sent or delivered to, or served on, any person shall be duly sent, delivered or served on that person–

(a) if it is sent to that person at his or her proper address by post in a registered letter or by recorded delivery;

(b) if it is sent to him or her at that address by facsimile transmission or any other means which produces a document containing a text of the communication, in which event the document shall be regarded as sent when it is received in a legible form; or

(c) if it is delivered to him or her or left at his or her address.

(2) Any document required or authorised to be sent or delivered to, or served on, an incorporated company or body shall be duly sent, delivered or served if sent or delivered to or served on the secretary of the company or body.

(3) The proper address of any person to or on whom any such document is to be sent, delivered or served shall, in the case of a secretary of any incorporated company or body, be that of the registered or principal office of the company or body and, in any other case, be the last known address of the person in question.

THE LOCAL AUTHORITIES (MODEL CODE OF CONDUCT) (WALES) ORDER 2008, SI 2008/788

1. Title, commencement and application

(1) The title of this Order is the Local Authorities (Model Code of Conduct) (Wales) Order 2008 and it comes into force on 18 April 2008.

(2) This Order applies to each relevant authority in Wales.

2. Interpretation

In this Order—

'the Act' ('y Ddeddf') means the Local Government Act 2000;

'co-opted member' ('aelod cyfetholedig') has the meaning set out in Part 1 of the model code in the Schedule to this Order;

'member' ('aelod') has the meaning set out in Part 1 of the model code in the Schedule to this Order; and

'relevant authority' ('awdurdod perthnasol') has the meaning set out in Part 1 of the model code in the Schedule to this Order.

3. Model Code of Conduct

(1) A model code as regards the conduct which is expected of members of a relevant authority is set out in the Schedule to this Order.

(2) For the purposes of section 50(4) of the Act, the provisions of the model code are to be regarded as mandatory.

4. Provisions to be disapplied

(1) Where a relevant authority which is a county, county borough or community council or fire and rescue authority has adopted a code of conduct or such a code applies to it, the following will, where applicable to the relevant authority, be disapplied as respects that authority—

(a) sections 94 to 98 and 105 of the Local Government Act 1972; and

(b) any regulations made or code issued under sections 19 and 31 of the Local Government and Housing Act 1989.

(2) Where a relevant authority which is a National Park authority has adopted a code of conduct or such a code applies to it, the following will, where applicable to the relevant authority, be disapplied as respects that authority—

(a) paragraphs 9 and 10 of Schedule 7 to the Environment Act 1995; and

(b) any regulations made or code issued under sections 19 and 31 of the Local Government and Housing Act 1989.

(3) Section 16(1) of the Interpretation Act 1978 will apply to a disapplication under paragraph (1) or (2) above as if it were a repeal, by an Act, of an enactment.

5. Revocation

The following orders are revoked:

(a) the Conduct of Members (Model Code of Conduct) (Wales) Order 20011 ;

(b) the Conduct of Members (Model Code of Conduct) (Amendment) (Wales) Order 2004; and

(c) the Conduct of Members (Model Code of Conduct) (Wales) (Amendment) (No. 2) Order 2004.

6. Transitional Provisions and Savings

The orders referred to in article 5 continue to have effect for the purposes of and for purposes connected with—

(a) the investigation of any written allegation under Part 3 of the Act, where that allegation relates to conduct that occurred before the date when, pursuant to section 51 of the Act—

    (i) the relevant authority adopts a code of conduct incorporating the mandatory provisions of the model code of conduct in the Schedule to this Order in place of its existing code of conduct;

    (ii) the relevant authority revises its existing code of conduct to incorporate the mandatory provisions of the model code of conduct in the Schedule to this Order; or

    (iii) the mandatory provisions of the model code of conduct in the Schedule to this Order apply to members or co-opted members of the relevant authority under section 51(5)(b) of that Act;

(b) the adjudication (or determination) of a matter raised in such an allegation; and

(c) an appeal against the decision of a standards committee, an interim case tribunal or case tribunal in relation to such an allegation.

PART 1

INTERPRETATION

1.

(1) In this code—

'co-opted member' ('aelod cyfetholedig'), in relation to a relevant authority, means a person who is not a member of the authority but who—

(a) is a member of any committee or sub-committee of the authority, or

(b) is a member of, and represents the authority on, any joint committee or joint sub-committee of the authority,

and who is entitled to vote on any question which falls to be decided at any meeting of that committee or sub-committee;

'meeting' ('cyfarfod') means any meeting—

(a) of the relevant authority,

(b) of any executive or board of the relevant authority,

(c) of any committee, sub-committee, joint committee or joint sub-committee of the relevant authority or of any such committee, sub-committee, joint committee or joint sub-committee of any executive or board of the authority, or

(d) where members or officers of the relevant authority are present other than a meeting of a political group constituted in accordance with regulation 8 of the Local Government (Committees and Political Groups) Regulations 1990,

and includes circumstances in which a member of an executive or board or an officer acting alone exercises a function of an authority;

'member' ('aelod') includes, unless the context requires otherwise, a co-opted member;

['registered society' means a society, other than a society registered as a credit union, which is—

(a) a registered society within the meaning given by section 1(1) of the Co-operative and Community Benefit Societies Act 2014; or

(b) a society registered or deemed to be registered under the Industrial and Provident Societies Act (Northern Ireland) 1969;]

'relevant authority' ('awdurdod perthnasol') means—

(a) a county council,

(b) a county borough council,

(c) a community council,

(d) a fire and rescue authority constituted by a scheme under section 2 of the Fire and Rescue Services Act 2004 or a scheme to which section 4 of that Act applies,

(e) a National Park authority established under section 63 of the Environment Act 1995;

'you' ('chi') means you as a member or co-opted member of a relevant authority; and

'your authority' ('eich awdurdod') means the relevant authority of which you are a member or co-opted member.

(2) In relation to a community council, references to an authority's monitoring officer and an authority's standards committee are to be read, respectively, as references to the monitoring officer and the standards committee of the county or county borough council which has functions in relation to the community council for which it is responsible under section 56(2) of the Local Government Act 2000.

PART 2

GENERAL PROVISIONS

2.

(1) Save where paragraph 3(a) applies, you must observe this code of conduct—

(a) whenever you conduct the business, or are present at a meeting, of your authority;

(b) whenever you act, claim to act or give the impression you are acting in the role of member to which you were elected or appointed;

(c) whenever you act, claim to act or give the impression you are acting as a representative of your authority; or

(d) at all times and in any capacity, in respect of conduct identified in paragraphs 6(1)(a) and 7.

(2) You should read this code together with the general principles prescribed under section 49(2) of the Local Government Act 2000 in relation to Wales.

3.

Where you are elected, appointed or nominated by your authority to serve—

(a) on another relevant authority, or any other body, which includes a police authority or Local Health Board you must, when acting for that other authority or body, comply with the code of conduct of that other authority or body; or

(b) on any other body which does not have a code relating to the conduct of its members, you must, when acting for that other body, comply with this code of conduct, except and insofar as it conflicts with any other lawful obligations to which that other body may be subject.

4.

You must—

(a) carry out your duties and responsibilities with due regard to the principle that there should be equality of opportunity for all people, regardless of their gender, race, disability, sexual orientation, age or religion;

(b) show respect and consideration for others;

(c) not use bullying behaviour or harass any person; and

(d) not do anything which compromises, or which is likely to compromise, the impartiality of those who work for, or on behalf of, your authority.

5.

You must not—

(a) disclose confidential information or information which should reasonably be regarded as being of a confidential nature, without the express consent of a person authorised to give such consent, or unless required by law to do so;

(b) prevent any person from gaining access to information to which that person is entitled by law.

6.

(1) You must—

(a) not conduct yourself in a manner which could reasonably be regarded as bringing your office or authority into disrepute;

(b) report, whether through your authority's confidential reporting procedure or direct to the proper authority, any conduct by another member or anyone who works for, or on behalf of, your authority which you reasonably believe involves or is likely to involve criminal behaviour (which for the purposes of this paragraph does not include offences or behaviour capable of punishment by way of a fixed penalty);

(c) report to the Public Services Ombudsman for Wales and to your authority's monitoring officer any conduct by another member which you reasonably believe breaches this code of conduct;

(d) not make vexatious, malicious or frivolous complaints against other members or anyone who works for, or on behalf of, your authority.

(2) You must comply with any request of your authority's monitoring officer, or the Public Services Ombudsman for Wales, in connection with an investigation conducted in accordance with their respective statutory powers.

7.

You must not—

(a) in your official capacity or otherwise, use or attempt to use your position improperly to confer on or secure for yourself, or any other person, an advantage or create or avoid for yourself, or any other person, a disadvantage;

(b) use, or authorise others to use, the resources of your authority—

    (i)   imprudently;

    (ii)   in breach of your authority's requirements;

    (iii) unlawfully;

      (iv)   other than in a manner which is calculated to facilitate, or to be conducive to, the discharge of the functions of the authority or of the office to which you have been elected or appointed;

      (v)   improperly for political purposes; or

      (vi)   improperly for private purposes.

8.

You must—

(a) when participating in meetings or reaching decisions regarding the business of your authority, do so on the basis of the merits of the circumstances involved and in the public interest having regard to any relevant advice provided by your authority's officers, in particular by—

      (i)   the authority's head of paid service;

      (ii)   the authority's chief finance officer;

      (iii) the authority's monitoring officer;

      (iv)   the authority's chief legal officer (who should be consulted when there is any doubt as to the authority's power to act, as to whether the action proposed lies within the policy framework agreed by the authority or where the legal consequences of action or failure to act by the authority might have important repercussions);

(b) give reasons for all decisions in accordance with any statutory requirements and any reasonable additional requirements imposed by your authority.

9.

You must—

(a) observe the law and your authority's rules governing the claiming of expenses and allowances in connection with your duties as a member;

(b) avoid accepting from anyone gifts, hospitality (other than official hospitality, such as a civic reception or a working lunch duly authorised by your authority), material benefits or services for yourself or any person which might place you, or reasonably appear to place you, under an improper obligation.

PART 3

INTERESTS

Personal Interests

10.

(1) You must in all matters consider whether you have a personal interest, and whether this code of conduct requires you to disclose that interest.

(2) You must regard yourself as having a personal interest in any business of your authority if—

(a) it relates to, or is likely to affect—

   (i)   any employment or business carried on by you;

   (ii)   any person who employs or has appointed you, any firm in which you are a partner or any company for which you are a remunerated director;

   (iii) any person, other than your authority, who has made a payment to you in respect of your election or any expenses incurred by you in carrying out your duties as a member;

   (iv) any corporate body which has a place of business or land in your authority's area, and in which you have a beneficial interest in a class of securities of that body that exceeds the nominal value of £25,000 or one hundredth of the total issued share capital of that body;

   (v)   any contract for goods, services or works made between your authority and you or a firm in which you are a partner, a company of which you are a remunerated director, or a body of the description specified in sub-paragraph (iv) above;

   (vi) any land in which you have a beneficial interest and which is in the area of your authority;

   (vii) any land where the landlord is your authority and the tenant is a firm in which you are a partner, a company of which you are a remunerated director, or a body of the description specified in sub-paragraph (iv) above;

  (viii) any body to which you have been elected, appointed or nominated by your authority;

   (ix) any—

      (aa) public authority or body exercising functions of a public nature;

      (bb) company, [registered society], charity, or body directed to charitable purposes;

      (cc) body whose principal purposes include the influence of public opinion or policy;

      (dd) trade union or professional association; or

      (ee) private club, society or association operating within your authority's area,

    in which you have membership or hold a position of general control or management;

   (x)   any land in your authority's area in which you have a licence (alone or jointly with others) to occupy for 28 days or longer;

(b) a member of the public might reasonably perceive a conflict between your role in taking a decision, upon that business, on behalf of your authority as a whole and your role in representing the interests of constituents in your ward or electoral division; or

(c) a decision upon it might reasonably be regarded as affecting—

    (i) your well-being or financial position, or that of a person with whom you live, or any person with whom you have a close personal association;

    (ii) any employment or business carried on by persons as described in 10(2)(c)(i);

    (iii) any person who employs or has appointed such persons described in 10(2)(c)(i), any firm in which they are a partner, or any company of which they are directors;

    (iv) any corporate body in which persons as described in 10(2)(c)(i) have a beneficial interest in a class of securities exceeding the nominal value of £5,000; or

    (v) any body listed in paragraphs 10(2)(a)(ix)(aa) to (ee) in which persons described in 10(2)(c)(i) hold a position of general control or management, to a greater extent than the majority of—

        (aa) in the case of an authority with electoral divisions or wards, other council tax payers, rate payers or inhabitants of the electoral division or ward, as the case may be, affected by the decision; or

        (bb) in all other cases, other council tax payers, ratepayers or inhabitants of the authority's area.

Disclosure of Personal Interests

11.

(1) Where you have a personal interest in any business of your authority and you attend a meeting at which that business is considered, you must disclose orally to that meeting the existence and nature of that interest before or at the commencement of that consideration, or when the interest becomes apparent.

(2) Where you have a personal interest in any business of your authority and you make—

(a) written representations (whether by letter, facsimile or some other form of electronic communication) to a member or officer of your authority regarding that business, you should include details of that interest in the written communication; or

(b) oral representations (whether in person or some form of electronic communication) to a member or officer of your authority you should disclose the interest at the commencement of such representations, or when it becomes apparent to you that you have such an interest, and confirm the representation and interest in writing within 14 days of the representation.

(3) Subject to paragraph 14(1)(b) below, where you have a personal interest in any business of your authority and you have made a decision in exercising a function of an executive or board, you must in relation to that business ensure that any written statement of that decision records the existence and nature of your interest.

(4) You must, in respect of a personal interest not previously disclosed, before or immediately after the close of a meeting where the disclosure is made pursuant to sub-paragraph 11(1), give written notification to your authority in accordance with any requirements identified by your authority's monitoring officer from time to time but, as a minimum containing—

(a) details of the personal interest;

(b) details of the business to which the personal interest relates; and

(c) your signature.

(5) Where you have agreement from your monitoring officer that the information relating to your personal interest is sensitive information, pursuant to paragraph 16(1), your obligations under this paragraph 11 to disclose such information, whether orally or in writing, are to be replaced with an obligation to disclose the existence of a personal interest and to confirm that your monitoring officer has agreed that the nature of such personal interest is sensitive information.

(6) For the purposes of sub-paragraph (4), a personal interest will only be deemed to have been previously disclosed if written notification has been provided in accordance with this code since the last date on which you were elected, appointed or nominated as a member of your authority.

(7) For the purposes of sub-paragraph (3), where no written notice is provided in accordance with that paragraph you will be deemed as not to have declared a personal interest in accordance with this code.

Prejudicial Interests

12.

(1) Subject to sub-paragraph (2) below, where you have a personal interest in any business of your authority you also have a prejudicial interest in that business if the interest is one which a member of the public with knowledge of the relevant facts would reasonably regard as so significant that it is likely to prejudice your judgement of the public interest.

(2) Subject to sub-paragraph (3), you will not be regarded as having a prejudicial interest in any business where that business—

(a) relates to—

    (i)   another relevant authority of which you are also a member;

    (ii)   another public authority or body exercising functions of a public nature in which you hold a position of general control or management;

(iii)   a body to which you have been elected, appointed or nominated by your authority;

(iv)   your role as a school governor (where not appointed or nominated by your authority) unless it relates particularly to the school of which you are a governor;

(v)   your role as a member of a Local Health Board where you have not been appointed or nominated by your authority;

(b)   relates to—

(i)   the housing functions of your authority where you hold a tenancy or lease with your authority, provided that you do not have arrears of rent with your authority of more than two months, and provided that those functions do not relate particularly to your tenancy or lease;

(ii)   the functions of your authority in respect of school meals, transport and travelling expenses, where you are a guardian, parent, grandparent or have parental responsibility (as defined in section 3 of the Children Act 1989) of a child in full time education, unless it relates particularly to the school which that child attends;

(iii)   the functions of your authority in respect of statutory sick pay under Part XI of the Social Security Contributions and Benefits Act 1992, where you are in receipt of, or are entitled to the receipt of such pay from your authority;

(iv)   the functions of your authority in respect of an allowance or payment made under sections 22(5), 24(4) and 173 to 176 of the Local Government Act 1972, an allowance or pension under section 18 of the Local Government and Housing Act 1989 or an allowance or payment under section 100 of the Local Government Act 2000;

(c)   your role as a community councillor in relation to a grant, loan or other form of financial assistance made by your community council to community or voluntary organisations up to a maximum of £500.

(3) The exemptions in subparagraph (2)(a) do not apply where the business relates to the determination of any approval, consent, licence, permission or registration.

Overview and Scrutiny Committees

13.

You also have a prejudicial interest in any business before an overview and scrutiny committee of your authority (or of a sub-committee of such a committee) where—

(a)   that business relates to a decision made (whether implemented or not) or action taken by your authority's executive, board or another of your authority's committees, sub-committees, joint committees or joint sub-committees; and

(b) at the time the decision was made or action was taken, you were a member of the executive, board, committee, sub-committee, joint-committee or joint sub-committee mentioned in sub-paragraph (a) and you were present when that decision was made or action was taken.

Participation in Relation to Disclosed Interests

14.

(1) Subject to sub-paragraphs (2), (3) and (4), where you have a prejudicial interest in any business of your authority you must, unless you have obtained a dispensation from your authority's standards committee—

(a) withdraw from the room, chamber or place where a meeting considering the business is being held—

   (i) where sub-paragraph (2) applies, immediately after the period for making representations, answering questions or giving evidence relating to the business has ended and in any event before further consideration of the business begins, whether or not the public are allowed to remain in attendance for such consideration; or

   (ii) in any other case, whenever it becomes apparent that that business is being considered at that meeting;

(b) not exercise executive or board functions in relation to that business;

(c) not seek to influence a decision about that business;

(d) not make any written representations (whether by letter, facsimile or some other form of electronic communication) in relation to that business; and

(e) not make any oral representations (whether in person or some form of electronic communication) in respect of that business or immediately cease to make such oral representations when the prejudicial interest becomes apparent.

(2) Where you have a prejudicial interest in any business of your authority you may attend a meeting but only for the purpose of making representations, answering questions or giving evidence relating to the business, provided that the public are also allowed to attend the meeting for the same purpose, whether under a statutory right or otherwise.

(3) Sub-paragraph (1) does not prevent you attending and participating in a meeting if—

(a) you are required to attend a meeting of an overview or scrutiny committee, by such committee exercising its statutory powers; or

(b) you have the benefit of a dispensation provided that you—

   (i) state at the meeting that you are relying on the dispensation; and

   (ii) before or immediately after the close of the meeting give written notification to your authority containing—

(aa)   details of the prejudicial interest;

(bb)   details of the business to which the prejudicial interest relates;

(cc)   details of, and the date on which, the dispensation was granted; and

(dd)   your signature.

(4) Where you have a prejudicial interest and are making written or oral representations to your authority in reliance upon a dispensation, you must provide details of the dispensation within any such written or oral representation and, in the latter case, provide written notification to your authority within 14 days of making the representation.

PART 4

THE REGISTER OF MEMBERS' INTERESTS

Registration of Financial and Other Interests and Memberships and Management Positions

15.

(1) Subject to sub-paragraph (3), you must, within 28 days of—

(a)   your authority's code of conduct being adopted or the mandatory provisions of this model code being applied to your authority; or

(b)   your election or appointment to office (if that is later),

register your financial interests and other interests, where they fall within a category mentioned in paragraph 10(2)(a) in your authority's register maintained under section 81(1) of the Local Government Act 2000 by providing written notification to your authority's monitoring officer.

(2) You must, within 28 days of becoming aware of any new personal interest or change to any personal interest registered under sub-paragraph (1), register that new personal interest or change by providing written notification to your authority's monitoring officer.

(3) Sub-paragraphs (1) and (2) do not apply to sensitive information determined in accordance with paragraph 16(1).

(4) Sub-paragraph (1) will not apply if you are a member of a relevant authority which is a community council when you act in your capacity as a member of such an authority.

Sensitive information

16.

(1) Where you consider that the information relating to any of your personal interests is sensitive information, and your authority's monitoring officer agrees,

you need not include that information when registering that interest, or, as the case may be, a change to the interest under paragraph 15.

(2) You must, within 28 days of becoming aware of any change of circumstances which means that information excluded under sub-paragraph (1) is no longer sensitive information, notify your authority's monitoring officer asking that the information be included in your authority's register of members' interests.

(3) In this code, 'sensitive information' ('gwybodaeth sensitif') means information whose availability for inspection by the public creates, or is likely to create, a serious risk that you or a person who lives with you may be subjected to violence or intimidation.

Registration of Gifts and Hospitality

17.

You must, within 28 days of receiving any gift, hospitality, material benefit or advantage above a value specified in a resolution of your authority, provide written notification to your authority's monitoring officer of the existence and nature of that gift, hospitality, material benefit or advantage.

THE CODE OF CONDUCT FOR MEMBERS OF LOCAL AUTHORITIES IN WALES: GUIDANCE FROM THE PUBLIC SERVICES OMBUDSMAN FOR WALES FOR MEMBERS OF COUNTY AND COUNTY BOROUGH COUNCILS, FIRE AND RESCUE AUTHORITIES, AND NATIONAL PARK AUTHORITIES

Preface

This revised guide from me as Public Services Ombudsman for Wales provides an overview of the Model Code of Conduct (the Code) introduced in 2008. It is intended to help you as a member to understand your obligations under the Code. The Code applies to all members and co-opted members of local authorities, community councils, fire and rescue authorities and national park authorities in Wales. As a member, you are required to sign up to it as part of your declaration of acceptance of office. The Code does not apply to the actions of authorities as a whole, or to the conduct of their officers and employees. There is a separate code of conduct applying to officers of local authorities in Wales.

This is the second version of this guidance, and it will be adapted from time to time to reflect case law and any changes to the Code. This section includes, for the first time, guidance on local arrangements for dealing with member on member complaints, and any arrangements for referring local services complaints for local consideration. It also excludes guidance which only relates to town and community councillors, for whom I have now issued separate guidance. It contains examples drawn from recent cases considered by the Adjudication Panel for Wales and standards committees across Wales.

315

The following pages aim to provide you with a general understanding of the Code and its requirements. Section 1 provides an introduction, while Section 2 outlines your obligations under the Code, referencing specific paragraphs for further information. Sections 3 and 4 deal with general issues surrounding interests, and aim to clarify a number of provisions which you will find in Parts 3 & 4 of the Code. You can obtain a copy of the Code by downloading it from your authority's website or contacting your Monitoring Officer.

The guide is intended to help you to understand the Code and how it applies, but it cannot hope to cover every conceivable circumstance. Ultimately, it is your responsibility to take specific advice from your Monitoring Officer and to make a decision as to the most suitable course of action.

I have used examples throughout to help to bring the guidance to life. These examples are drawn from actual cases considered by my office and also include decisions reached by local standards committees and the Adjudication Panel for Wales.

As a member you will be offered training on the Code whether by a Monitoring Officer or from a representative body. I expect all members to take advantage of such training, including refresher courses, to ensure that they are fully aware of the provisions of the Code and its interpretation.

In issuing this advice I am very conscious of the importance of standards in ensuring the future health and effectiveness of our democratic institutions. It is important that we should all work collaboratively to drive up standards and to create a culture where members are respected for their selflessness, objectivity and respectful behaviour. If we do so we can build public confidence in our democratic institutions and promote good governance for the benefit of the people of all of our communities.

Peter Tyndall
Public Services Ombudsman for Wales
September 2012

This statutory guidance is issued by the Public Services Ombudsman for Wales under Section 68 of the

Local Government Act 2000 for elected, co-opted and appointed members of:

- county and county borough councils;

- fire and rescue authorities, and

- national park authorities in Wales.

Acknowledgement

This guidance draws on guidance prepared and issued by Standards for England on the former English Code of Conduct. It has been extended and amended to refer to the Welsh Code and to the Welsh context. It also reflects responses to the consultation I have undertaken.

Separate guidance is available for members of community councils.

First published April 2010.

This edition published September 2012.

1. Introduction

The Local Government Act 2000 created a new ethical framework for local government in Wales. It created a power for the National Assembly for Wales to issue a model code of conduct to apply to members and co-opted members of all relevant authorities in Wales. This power was transferred to the Welsh Ministers by the Government of Wales Act 2006. In 2008, Welsh Ministers issued the current Model Code of Conduct which all relevant authorities are required to adopt.

Authorities were required to adopt the Code in its model form in its entirety, but could make additions to the Code, provided these were consistent with the Model. This was intended to give certainty to members and the public as to what standards are expected. It helps to ensure consistency throughout relevant authorities, avoiding confusion for members on more than one authority and for the public.

Standards committees of principal councils are required to assist members and co-opted members of their authorities, together with members of town and community councils in their area, to observe the Code and to arrange for advice and training to be provided. I strongly recommend that all members should attend training and take advice where it is offered. I support individual authorities which require members to attend training on the Code before they can join certain decision-making bodies such as planning committees.

Ultimately, as a member, you are responsible for the decisions you take and can be held to account for them. However, this doesn't imply that you can take decisions which breach the Code or contrary to advice simply because the decision is yours to take. This guidance explains the constraints you are expected to act within to ensure members of the public can be confident in the way in which authorities in Wales reach their decisions.

It is my role as Public Services Ombudsman to investigate complaints that members of local authorities in Wales have breached the Code. In determining whether to investigate a complaint or whether to continue an investigation of a breach of the Code I will use a two-stage test. In the first instance, I will aim to establish whether there is evidence that a breach actually took place.

The second test I will apply is whether the breach alleged would be likely to lead to a sanction. I have discretion as to whether to investigate or not. I have adopted this test in order to explain how I will usually exercise my discretion and to secure a degree of consistency. In using my discretion, I will take account of the outcomes of previous cases considered by standards committees across Wales and decide accordingly.

If whilst assessing a complaint or at any point where I have commenced an investigation I consider that the second limb of the two stage test has not been met I will invite the Monitoring Officer (in conjunction with the Standards

Committee) to consider whether a local investigation is appropriate. If so I will formally refer the matter to the Monitoring Officer for investigation under section 70(4) of the Local Government Act 2000.

However, if I am aware of previous complaints about the same member and believe these may be indicative of a pattern of breaches, I will then often choose to investigate. Where there is prima facie evidence of a breach of the Code, and I do not decide to investigate, I will almost always write to the member concerned making it clear that my decision should not in any way be regarded as approval for any breach of the Code and making clear that I will take it into account if there are further reported breaches.

The process I use for investigating complaints is on my website at www. ombudsman-wales.org.uk. If I find that a complaint is justified, I may refer it either to your Standards Committee or to a tribunal convened by the Adjudication Panel for Wales. If it then finds the complaint proven, it can impose a range of sanctions.

Local Resolution Process

During the course of the life of this guidance I expect local authorities across Wales to have implemented local resolution procedures to deal with low level complaints which are made by a member against a fellow member. Typically these complaints will be about alleged failures to show respect and consideration for others as required by paragraph 4(b) of the Code or the duty not to make vexatious, malicious or frivolous complaints against other members under paragraph 6(1)(d) of the Code. Whilst a member may still complain directly to me about a fellow member if the matter being complained about concerns paragraphs 4b and 6(1)(d) I am likely to refer the matter back to the Council's Monitoring Officer for consideration under this process.

In my view such complaints are more appropriately resolved informally and locally in order to speed up the complaints process and to ensure that my resources are devoted to the investigation of serious complaints. The aim of local resolution is to resolve matters at an early stage so as to avoid the unnecessary escalation of the situation which may damage personal relationships within the authority and the authority's reputation. The process may result in an apology being made by the member concerned. However, where a member has repeatedly breached their authority's local protocol then I would expect the Monitoring Officer to refer the matter back to me.

When I have investigated a complaint I may refer the matter to a Standards Committee or the Adjudication Panel for Wales which have the following roles:

Standards Committee

Where a Standards Committee concludes that a member or co-opted member has failed to comply with the relevant authority's code of conduct, it may determine that:

1. no action needs to be taken in respect of that failure;

2. the member or co-opted member should be censured; or

3. the member or co-opted member should be suspended or partially suspended from being a member of that authority for a period not exceeding six months.

A censure takes the form of a public rebuke of the member concerned.

Standards committees are made up of independent lay members and of elected members of the authority. Matters which have arisen in the Council chamber which may be drawn to the attention of a Standards Committee via its local resolution process, may have been witnessed by many of the elected members of an authority. In these circumstances a Monitoring Officer may decide that it would be permissible for any elected members who have witnessed the events complained about and who are members of the Standards Committee to consider the matter via any local resolution process. However, if I were to investigate the matter, it is likely that those witnesses will have been interviewed as part of the investigation. If I were then decided to formally refer the matter to the Standards Committee I consider that the rules of natural justice dictate that it would not be appropriate for those members who witnessed the events to play any part in any subsequent hearing of the matter.

A member may appeal against the determination of a standards committee to the Adjudication Panel for Wales.

Adjudication Panel for Wales

The powers available to the tribunal when it determines that a member or co-opted member has failed to comply with the Code are:

1. to disqualify the respondent from being, or becoming, a member of the relevant authority concerned or any other relevant authority for a period of up to five years;

2. to suspend or partially suspend the respondent from being a member or co-opted member of the relevant authority concerned for up to 12 months, or

3. to take no action in respect of the breach.

Where either a standards committee or a tribunal suspends or partly suspends a member or co-opted member that member or co-opted member is still subject to the code of conduct, in particular the provisions set out in paragraphs 6(1) (a) (bringing the office of member or authority into disrepute) and paragraph 7 (improperly using the position of member).

The Principles

The Local Government Act empowered the National Assembly to issue principles to which you must have regard in undertaking your role as a member. The Code is based on these principles which are designed to promote the highest possible standards. These principles draw on the 7 Principles of Public Life which were set out in the Nolan Report 'Standards of Conduct in Local Government in England, Scotland and Wales'. Three more were added to these: a duty to uphold the law, proper stewardship of the Council's resources and equality and respect for others.

Members elected to local authorities give generously of their time and commitment for the benefit of their communities. The principles provide a framework for channelling your commitment in a way which will reflect well on you and your authority, and which will give your communities confidence in the way that your authority is governed.

The individual sections of the Code are designed to support the implementation of the Principles. For example, the Selflessness principle is covered by Section 7 of the Code – Selflessness and Stewardship.

The current principles were set out in a statutory instrument[1] and are detailed below.

1. **Selflessness**

   Members must act solely in the public interest. They must never use their position as members to improperly confer advantage on themselves or to improperly confer advantage or disadvantage on others.

2. **Honesty**

   Members must declare any private interests relevant to their public duties and take steps to resolve any conflict in a way that protects the public interest.

3. **Integrity and Propriety**

   Members must not put themselves in a position where their integrity is called into question by any financial or other obligation to individuals or organisations that might seek to influence them in the performance of their duties. Members must on all occasions avoid the appearance of such behaviour.

4. **Duty to Uphold the Law**

   Members must act to uphold the law and act on all occasions in accordance with the trust that the public has placed in them.

5. **Stewardship**

   In discharging their duties and responsibilities members must ensure that their authority's resources are used both lawfully and prudently.

6. **Objectivity in Decision-making**

   In carrying out their responsibilities including making appointments, awarding contracts, or recommending individuals for rewards and benefits, members must make decisions on merit. Whilst members must have regard to the professional advice of officers and may properly take account of the views of others, including their political groups, it is their responsibility to decide what view to take and, if appropriate, how to vote on any issue.

7. **Equality and Respect**

   Members must carry out their duties and responsibilities with due regard to the need to promote equality of opportunity for all people, regardless of their gender, race, disability, sexual orientation, age or religion, and show respect and consideration for others.

---

1   The Conduct of Members (Principles) (Wales) Order 2001, SI 2001/2276 (W.166).

8. **Openness**

Members must be as open as possible about all their actions and those of their authority. They must seek to ensure that disclosure of information is restricted only in accordance with the law.

9. **Accountability**

Members are accountable to the electorate and the public generally for their actions and for the way they carry out their responsibilities as a member. They must be prepared to submit themselves to such scrutiny as is appropriate to their responsibilities.

10. **Leadership**

Members must promote and support these principles by leadership and example so as to promote public confidence in their role and in the authority. They must respect the impartiality and integrity of the authority's statutory officers and its other employees.

The principles are not part of the Model Code, and failure to comply with the Principles is not of itself, therefore, indicative of a breach of the Code. However, it is likely that a failure, for example, to adhere to the principle concerning equality and respect would constitute a breach of the requirements of paragraphs 4 (a) and (b) in the Code in respect of equality of opportunity and respect.

In any event, the Principles offer a sound basis for your conduct in office and I encourage members to have regard to them at all times.

Deciding when the Code applies to you

See paragraphs 2 and 3

The Code applies to you:

1. Whenever you act in your official capacity, including whenever you are conducting the business of your authority or acting, claiming to act, or give the impression you are acting, in your official capacity as a member or as a representative of your authority.

2. At any time, if you conduct yourself in a manner which could reasonably be regarded as bringing your office or your authority into disrepute or if you use or attempt to use your position to gain an advantage or avoid a disadvantage for yourself or any other person or if you misuse your authority's resources.

Where you act as a representative of your authority on another relevant authority, or any other body, you must, when acting for that other authority, comply with their Code of Conduct. When you are nominated by your authority as a trustee of a charity you are obliged when acting as such to do so in the best interests of that charity, in accordance with charity law and with the guidance which has been produced by the Charity Commission (see its website: www.charity-commission.gov.uk).

If you are acting as a representative of your authority on another body, for example on the board of a housing association, which doesn't have a code of conduct relating to its members, you must comply with your authority's own code unless it conflicts with any legal requirements that the other body has to comply with.

If you refer to yourself as Councillor, the Code will apply to you. This applies in conversation, in writing, or in your use of electronic media. There has been a significant rise in complaints to me concerning the use of Facebook, blogs and Twitter. If you refer to your role as councillor in any way or comments you make are clearly related to your role then the Code will apply to any comments you make there. Even if you do not refer to your role as councillor, your comments may have the effect of bringing your office or authority into disrepute and could therefore breach paragraph 6(1)(a) of the Code of Conduct.

If you are nominated by your authority as the director of a company (a stock transfer housing association for example) you are obliged to act in the best interests of the company. If it has a code of conduct for its directors you must abide by it. If it doesn't, you must comply with your authority's code, except on the rare occasions where it conflicts with any legal obligations the company may have.

If you are suspended from office for any reason, you must still observe those elements of the Code which apply, particularly as set out in paragraph 2(1)(d), while you are suspended.

Example

Councillor B was nominated by a County Borough Council to serve as a board member of a stock transfer housing association. The Chief Executive of the housing association copied all board members into a confidential e-mail to the Chief Executive of the Council. Councillor B admitted sending the e-mail to the local press and said that he had done so because he felt that his duty as a councillor over-rode his duty as a board member of the housing association. Councillor B was found to have breached paragraph 3(a) of the Council's Code by disclosing the e-mail in breach of the board's own code of conduct. He was also found to have brought his office and authority into disrepute by making a misleading statement that 'he recently had to withdraw' from the board of the housing association when he had been removed with immediate effect for the serious breach of confidentiality.

An on-line poll about a person accused of murder which contained inappropriate language was set up using Councillor B's Council-provided laptop, internet access and his council e-mail address. Councillor B said he personally had not set up the poll. However, as the Council had provided him with the laptop he was responsible for it. He also made disparaging comments about housing benefit claimants on his Facebook page when responding to a request for advice in his councillor role. The Adjudication Panel found that Councillor B had acted in his official capacity because he had used his Council-provided equipment and e-mail address. Therefore, he could reasonably be regarded as representing himself as a councillor.

2. General obligations under the Code of Conduct

Equality

See paragraph 4(a)

You must carry out your duties with due regard to the principle that there should be equality of opportunity for all people regardless of their gender, race, disability, sexual orientation, age or religion. Although the Code is not explicit about trans-gender status, I will normally consider it to be included under the gender category, and expect the principle of equal opportunity to be applied.
You should at all times seek to avoid discrimination. There are four main forms of discrimination:

- Direct discrimination: treating people differently because of their gender, race, disability, sexual orientation, age or religion.

- Indirect discrimination: treatment which does not appear to differentiate between people because of their gender, race, disability, sexual orientation, age or religion, but which disproportionately disadvantages them.

- Harassment: engaging in unwanted conduct on the grounds of gender, race, disability, sexual orientation, age or religion, which violates another person's dignity or creates a hostile, degrading, humiliating or offensive environment.

- Victimisation: treating a person less favourably because they have complained of discrimination, brought proceedings for discrimination, or been involved in complaining about or bringing proceedings for discrimination.

The introduction of the Equality Act 2010 reinforces the importance of this part of the Code. It imposes positive duties to eliminate unlawful discrimination and harassment and to promote equality. Under equality laws, your authority may be liable for any discriminatory acts which you commit. This will apply if you do something in your official capacity in a discriminatory manner.

You must be careful not to act in a way which may amount to any of the prohibited forms of discrimination, or to do anything which hinders your authority's fulfilment of its positive duties under equality laws. Such conduct may cause your authority to break the law, and you may find yourself subject to a complaint that you have breached this paragraph of the Code.

You must also be mindful that at all times including when acting in your private capacity you must not act in a way that would bring your Council into disrepute. It is likely that engaging in behaviour which could be considered to be in breach of the Equality Act in your private capacity is likely to fall into this category.

Example

A member of a County Council was a member of the Council's Recruitment Panel to appoint a new Chief Executive. Five applicants were shortlisted. After one candidate had finished his presentation and left the room Councillor A said 'good candidate, shame he's black'. The Adjudication Panel for Wales found that paragraph 4(a) of the Code had been breached and that Councillor A had brought the office of member and his authority into disrepute (in breach of paragraph 6(1) (a) of the Code).

Treating others with respect and consideration

See paragraph 4(b)

Political groupings in authorities are expected to campaign for their ideas, and they may also seek to discredit the policies and action of their opponents. Criticism of ideas and opinion is part of democratic debate, and it is unlikely that such comments would ever be considered to be a breach of the Code of Conduct for failing to treat someone with respect and consideration.

Furthermore, a member's freedom of expression attracts enhanced protection when his comments are political in nature. 'Political' comments are not confined to those made within the Council chamber and, for example, include comments members may generally make on their authority's policies or about their political opponents. Therefore, unless the comments are highly offensive or outrageous, it is unlikely that I will investigate complaints made in this context and councillors need a 'thicker skin' in dealing with, and responding to, politically motivated comments.

Likewise, when members raise 'political' issues with officers, particularly those holding senior positions, for example Chief Executives or Heads of Services, depending on the circumstances of the case I may also decline to investigate if I take the view that the member was entitled to question the officer concerned and the conduct was not sufficiently serious to amount to a failure to show respect and consideration.

However, I do expect members to afford colleagues, opponents and officers the same courtesy and consideration as they show to others in their everyday lives. Whilst I recognise that political debate can, at times, become heated, the right to freedom of expression should not be used as an excuse for poor conduct generally. Such poor conduct can only discredit the role of councillor in the eyes of the public.

Whilst it is acknowledged that some members of the public can make unreasonable demands on members, members should always treat members of the public courteously and with consideration. Rude and offensive behaviour lowers the public's expectation and confidence in its elected representatives. This is the case in face to face settings such as meetings as well as when communicating by phone, letter, e-mail or other electronic means.

Example

The Adjudication Panel upheld a finding of a Standards Committee for failing to show respect and consideration for others by posting comments about other councillors and the way in which the Council was run.

The member sought judicial review of this decision. The Court found that whilst the comments which were posted were sarcastic and mocking and the tone ridiculed his fellow members, because the majority of the comments related to the way in which the Council was run, how its decisions were recorded and the competence of the councillors, the comments were 'Political Expression'. The ruling said no account had been taken of the need for politicians to have 'thicker skins'. In view of the member's freedom of expression and the fact that the majority of comments were directed at fellow councillors the finding of a breach in this case was a disproportionate interference with the member's rights under Article 10 of the European Convention on Human Rights. The Standards Committee's decision to censure the member was therefore set aside.

Example

A member of a town council wrote to a Deputy Minister of the Welsh Assembly Government about an employee ('Mr Smith') of a county council, which was also copied to the Council. In the letter the member questioned Mr Smith's competence and motivation and he made a number of comments of a disparaging and personal nature about Mr Smith and his associates. He raised the issue of homosexuality and referred to it as a 'notorious disability' and that 'homosexuality is only a demon which can be driven out'. The member was referred to the Adjudication Panel for Wales.

The Panel found that the member had breached paragraph 4(b) in that he had failed to show respect and consideration for others. It also found that by his use of words he had brought the office of member into disrepute in breach of paragraph 6(1)(a) of the Code.

The member was disqualified for 12 months from being or becoming a member of a local authority.

Bullying and harassment

See paragraph 4(c)

You must not use any bullying behaviour or harass any person including other councillors, council officers or members of the public.

Harassment is repeated behaviour which upsets or annoys people. Bullying can be characterised as offensive, intimidating, malicious, insulting or humiliating behaviour. Such behaviour may happen once or be part of a pattern of behaviour directed at a weaker person or person over whom you have some actual or perceived influence. Bullying behaviour attempts to undermine an individual or a group of individuals, is detrimental to their confidence and capability, and may adversely affect their health.

This can be contrasted with the legitimate challenges which a member can make in questioning policy or scrutinising performance. An example of this would be debates in the chamber about policy, or asking officers to explain the rationale for the professional opinions they have put forward. You are entitled to challenge fellow councillors and officers as to why they hold their views.

I will always consider allegations of bullying and harassment from the perspective of the alleged victim. The question to be answered is whether the individual was reasonably entitled to believe they were being bullied rather than whether the person accused of bullying thought that he or she was doing so. Bullying is often carried out face to face, but increasingly, it can be carried out in print or using electronic media. The standards of behaviour expected are the same, whether you are expressing yourself verbally or in writing.

You need to ensure that your behaviour does not cross the line between being forceful and bullying. There can be no hard and fast rules governing every set of circumstances but the relative seniority of the officer will be a factor in some cases. As outlined under paragraph 4(b) very senior officers can be involved in robust discussion with members and be well placed to put their own point of view forcefully. The same is not true of more junior officers and members need to be aware of this. This is not to say that I condone the bullying of senior officers, only that the greater the power difference between the officer and the member the greater the likelihood that the officer will consider behaviour to constitute bullying.

It's also evident that there are appropriate channels for expressing concern about the performance of an officer, and doing so in the context of a meeting with others present, especially if they are from outside bodies or are members of the public, is not acceptable. Neither is it acceptable to do so in the media, in your own publications or using blogs, tweets, Facebook or other electronic means. It is important that you raise issues about poor performance in the correct way and proper forum. However, if your criticism is a personal attack or of an offensive nature, you are likely to cross the line of what is acceptable behaviour.

Compromising the impartiality of officers of the authority

See paragraph 4(d)

You must not compromise, or attempt to compromise, the impartiality of anyone who works for, or on behalf of, your authority.

You should not approach anyone who works for, or on behalf of, the authority with a view to pressurising them to carry out their duties in a biased or partisan way. They must be neutral and should not be coerced or persuaded to act in a way that would undermine their neutrality. For example, you should not get officers to help you prepare party political material, or to help you with matters relating to your private business. You should not provide or offer any incentive or reward in return for acting in a particular way or reaching a particular decision or threaten someone if they are not minded to act in a particular way. As well as avoiding pressurising officers in person, you need to avoid doing so in writing, using electronic media or in the press.

Although you can robustly question officers in order to understand, for example, their reasons for proposing to act in a particular way, or the content of a report that they have written, you must not try and force them to act differently, change their advice, or alter the content of that report, if doing so would prejudice their professional integrity.

If a member develops a close personal relationship with an officer, this becomes a personal and possibly a prejudicial interest under the Code. I would encourage you to adhere to any protocol developed by your authority that deals with relationships between members and officers.

Example

The son and daughter-in-law of a member of a county borough council were neighbours of a family who were tenants of the Council. Complaints had been made about the family's conduct. The member contacted officers of the Council regarding the family's occupancy of the council property and its impact on his son's family on a number of occasions, sometimes outside office hours. The calls were made in his role as elected member and he had direct access to officials because he was a member.

He received a warning from the Deputy Monitoring Officer as to his conduct, which emphasised the powerful position elected members occupy when dealing with members of staff.

Despite this he continued to contact officers about the matter including requesting an officer to visit his family 'there and then' and accusing an officer of 'tipping off' the family being complained about that noise monitoring equipment was being installed.

The Adjudication Panel found that the conduct of the member was a persistent course of conduct over a period of 6 months intended to bring undue pressure upon council officials. It found that by his actions he had sought to compromise the impartiality of officers of the Council. It also found that the member had failed to show respect and consideration for others and that his actions amounted to harassment and he had used his position improperly to promote the interests of his own family. Given the accumulative nature of his dealing with officers and his making a false allegation that an officer had 'tipped off' the family he had also brought the office of member into disrepute.

The member was suspended from office for 12 months.

Disclosing confidential information

See paragraph 5(a)

You must not disclose confidential information, or information which should be reasonably regarded to be of a confidential nature, except in any of the following circumstances:

- You have the consent of the person authorised to give it.

- You are required by law to do so.

The Information Commissioner has issued helpful guidance on the Freedom of Information Act and Data Protection Act which is available on his website at www.ico.gov.uk or by calling 0303 123 1113.

As a member, you may be party to confidential information about individuals or organisations including personal or commercially sensitive matters. This might include information about people's employment, or personal matters arising from social services work, for instance. Sometimes, these will be marked confidential. On other occasions, this will not be the case, but you must not disclose them even if they are not marked. If you are in any doubt, always ask your Monitoring Officer.

As a general rule, you should treat items discussed in the confidential sections of meetings (exempt items) as confidential. These reports have usually been assessed by the author as containing sensitive information, following expert legal advice. The sensitivity of the information may decline over time, but you are strongly urged to take proper legal advice before disclosing it. Similarly, legal advice, whether provided by external lawyers or your authority's in-house legal staff, is almost always covered by legal privilege and should not be disclosed.

Example

A member of a county borough council who sat on the Council's adoption panel disclosed publicly details of a person who had applied to the panel to adopt a child. He could only have become aware of the information he disclosed by virtue of his membership of the panel. The Adjudication Panel found that the member had disclosed confidential information in breach of the Code. It suspended the member from the Council for 6 months.

Preventing access to information

See paragraph 5(b)

You must not prevent any person from accessing information which they are entitled to by law. This includes information under the Freedom of Information Act 2000 or those copies of minutes, agendas, reports and other documents of your authority which they have a right to access. To find out more about what types of information the public can access, contact the Information Commissioner's Office by visiting www.ico.gov.uk or by calling 0303 123 1113 or for specific queries, you should ask your Monitoring Officer or Clerk.

Any information that you produce in your official capacity is liable to be subject to the disclosure requirements of the Freedom of Information Act, and your authority may be required to release it in response to a request. If you do not provide the information to the relevant officer of your authority on request, you will be in breach of the Code.

Your authority needs to decide whether to disclose information or whether it may be covered by an exemption. Even if you believe that information you hold is exempt, you must provide it to your authority's relevant officer to allow the authority to reach a decision. As well as being a breach of the Code, it is a criminal offence if information is destroyed after a Freedom of Information Act request has been received.

Example

A leader of a county council refused to give the Council's Information Officer a letter he had written to the Wales Audit Office on behalf of the Council's

Executive. As a result the Council could not respond appropriately to a Freedom of Information Act request which resulted in a complaint being made to the Information Commissioner's Office. The member continued to refuse to disclose the letter despite having received clear and unequivocal advice from the Information Officer. His refusal led to an adverse finding from the Information Commissioner's Officer. The Adjudication Panel found that the member had breached paragraphs 5(b) and 6(1)(a) (disrepute) in respect of this matter and other related matters. By the time the case was considered by the Panel the member had resigned from office. He was disqualified from holding office for 12 months.

Disrepute

See paragraph 6(1)(a)

You must not behave in a way which could reasonably be regarded as bringing your office or authority into disrepute at any time.

As a member, your actions and behaviour are subject to greater scrutiny than those of ordinary members of the public. You should be aware that your actions in both your public and private life might have an adverse impact on your office or your authority.

Dishonest and deceitful behaviour will bring your authority into disrepute, as may conduct which results in a criminal conviction, especially if it involves dishonest, threatening or violent behaviour, even if the behaviour happens in your private life. Making unfair or inaccurate criticism of your authority in a public arena might well be regarded as bringing your authority into disrepute. Inappropriate e-mails to constituents might well bring the office of member into disrepute.

As outlined in the case example on page 12 above, you must also conduct yourself in an appropriate manner with others within the confines of a council's building, regardless of whether or not your conduct is likely to be in the public domain.

Example

A Community Councillor had been abusive to a shop proprietor and two members of her staff and had attempted to obtain a discount on a private purchase by saying it was being bought on behalf of the Community Council, and when his request for a discount was refused he had made threats against the business. The Adjudication Panel found that the member had brought the office of member into disrepute and suspended him for 9 months.

Reporting breaches of the Code

See paragraph 6(1)(c)

If you reasonably believe that a breach of the Code has occurred, you must report it to me and to your Monitoring Officer. In order to have a reasonable belief that a breach has occurred, you will need to have evidence which supports this. If you are in doubt as to whether a breach has occurred, you should consult your Monitoring Officer as soon as possible. Where the breach is a very minor or technical one, or where there is no clear evidence that a breach occurred, your Monitoring Officer may advise you of the likely threshold I will set. Nonetheless, the decision as to whether to investigate a breach rests with me. The balance of any doubt should always favour reporting. It is helpful if you specify which aspect of the Code you believe has been breached, but this is not essential.

Where a member has reported a fellow member to their Monitoring Officer under the authority's local resolution process, there is no need to report the matter to me as well.

To report a breach, you can contact my office by phone at 0845 6010987, by e-mail to ask@ombudsman-wales.org.uk or via the website at www.ombudsman-wales.org.uk. A special leaflet on making complaints about alleged breaches of the Code is available on request or on the website.

In determining whether to investigate a complaint of a breach I will use the two stage test which I have outlined on pages 5 and 6 above. You should ensure that you provide any evidence you have available when you make a complaint including minutes of meetings, correspondence, contemporaneous notes or e-mails. If there are other individuals who have witnessed the alleged breach, you should let us know who they are. This latter point is especially important as if I only have one person's word against another's, it's usually not possible for me to make a finding that a breach has occurred, and in the absence of independent confirmation, I won't usually begin an investigation.

Vexatious complaints

See paragraph 6(1)(d)

You must not make complaints against other members or staff members or people working on behalf of your authority which are not founded in fact and which are motivated by malice (a desire to do them harm) or by political rivalry. Unfortunately, there have been instances where members have sought to bring complaints about rivals which are designed to disadvantage them, sometimes in the run-up to elections, and where the evidence of any breach is thin or non-existent. I consider that in the first instance such conduct should be considered under the relevant authority's local resolution process.

Where specific details of such complaints are passed to local press and media, this may prejudice an investigation and so also may be a breach of the Code. You must report well-founded alleged breaches to me and to your Monitoring Officer, not to your local newspaper or radio station. The press will properly cover the business of any hearings and their outcomes, and members making allegations should not generate publicity in advance of these.

You should also avoid making complaints which have little or no substance (frivolous complaints) or which are designed mainly to annoy the person complained about.

Example

A member of a county borough council claimed that the leader of the Council had offered to provide another councillor and his group of members with office facilities if that councillor supported the leader's preferred candidate for the post of Chief Executive. The evidence supported the leader's position that the two matters were unconnected and that therefore the complaint was malicious. The Adjudication Panel suspended the member making the complaint for 12 months.

Co-operating with investigations

See paragraph 6(2)

You must co-operate with an investigation when it is being conducted by me or by your Monitoring Officer using our statutory powers. Not to do so is itself a breach of the code. This means that you should reply promptly to all correspondence and telephone calls, make yourself available for interview if required and make available copies of any requested documents. My office and your Monitoring Officer will make reasonable allowances for urgent pressures you face and arrangements previously made, e.g. for holidays. However, they will expect you to give priority to their investigations, to avoid matters being needlessly drawn out. The requirement to co-operate with an investigation applies whether you are a witness or the subject of the investigation.

(In the course of my work I have unfortunately become aware of instances where members accused of breaches of the Code have sought to put pressure on the individuals making the complaint or on other witnesses. I regard such behaviour as entirely unacceptable. You must not intimidate or attempt to intimidate any person who is or is likely to be a complainant, a witness, or involved in the administration of any investigation or proceedings relating to a failure to comply with the Code.

However much you may be concerned about allegations that you or a fellow councillor failed to comply with the Code, it is always wrong to bully, intimidate or attempt to intimidate any person involved in the investigation or hearing. Even though you may not have breached the Code, you will have your say during any independent investigation or hearing, and you should let these processes follow their natural course.

If you intimidate a witness in an investigation about your conduct, for example, you may find yourself subject to another complaint that you have breached paragraph 4 (c) of the Code with regard to bullying or harassment, for example, or paragraph 6(1)(a) in respect of bringing the office of member into disrepute.)

Using your position improperly

See paragraph 7(a)

You must not use, or attempt to use, your position improperly to the advantage or disadvantage of yourself or anyone else. This paragraph applies at all times and not just when you are carrying out your duties as a member. You should not use, or attempt to use, your public office either for your or anybody else's personal gain or loss. For example, your behaviour would be improper if you sought to further your own private interests through your position as a member. This also applies if you use your office to improve your wellbeing at the expense of others.

Members who own land, or whose close personal associates own land, need to be particularly cautious where planning matters are concerned. If you are in any doubt, you should take advice.

This applies equally to members of community councils when your Council is consulted on planning matters. Similarly, while it is reasonable to expect members to help constituents apply to the Council e.g. for housing, it is quite inappropriate to seek to influence the decision to be taken by the officers.

The provisions of the Bribery Act 2010 apply to members carrying out their public functions. Should a member be convicted of a criminal offence under this Act then it is likely that they will also have used their position improperly (in breach of paragraph 7(a)) and be likely to have brought the office of member or their authority into disrepute in breach of paragraphs 6(1)(a) and (b). If any complaint which is made to me concerns conduct which may amount to a criminal offence then I am likely to refer the matter to the police.

Example

A member of a county council had requested that land in his ownership in Village A be included as suitable for development in the Council's Local Development Plan (LDP). When the Council was considering suitable settlement areas for inclusion in the LDP, officers recommended that land in the neighbouring village (Village B) be included in the draft plan instead. Despite having received very clear advice from the Council's Monitoring Officer on his prejudicial interest the member e-mailed the Council's planning policy officer and outlined a number of arguments which he claimed favoured the inclusion of his land in Village A as opposed to the land in Village B. At the relevant time the draft plan had been disclosed to members of the Council on a confidential basis and had not been disclosed publicly.

The Adjudication Panel found that by sending the e-mail the member had breached paragraph 7(a) of the Code by attempting to use his position improperly for his own advantage. At the hearing he sought to apportion blame on the Council's Monitoring Officer for failing to advise and train him properly on the Code when this clearly was not the case. His actions also brought his office and the Council into disrepute. The member was disqualified from holding office for 18 months for this and other breaches of the Code.

The authority's resources

See paragraph 7(b)

You must only use or authorise the use of the resources of the authority in accordance with its requirements.

Where your authority provides you with resources (for example telephone, computer and other IT facilities, transport or support from council employees), you must only use these resources or employees for carrying out your local authority business and any other activity which your authority has authorised you to use them for.

You must be familiar with the rules applying to the use of these resources made by your authority. Failure to comply with your authority's rules is likely to amount to a breach of the Code.

If you authorise someone (for example a member of your family) to use your authority's resources, you must take care to ensure that this is allowed by your authority's rules.

Using resources for proper purposes only

See paragraphs 7(b)(v) and 7(b)(vi)

You must make sure you use the authority's resources for proper purposes only. It is not appropriate to use, or authorise others to use, the resources for political purposes, including party political purposes. When using the authority's resources, you must have regard, if applicable, to any guidance issued by your authority.

You should never use authority resources for purely political purposes, including designing and distributing party political material produced for publicity purposes.

However, your authority may authorise you to use its resources and facilities for political purposes in connection with your authority's business, for example, holding meetings of your political group.

In this case, you must be aware of the limitations placed upon such use for these purposes. Members should also have regard to the fact that periods leading up to local government elections are particularly sensitive in this regard. Using your authority's resources outside of these limitations is likely to amount to a breach of the Code of Conduct. Some authorities will permit members to use authority-supplied IT equipment such as laptops for ancillary use. Provided that such usage is in line with the authority's requirements, there would not be a breach, but sending mass e-mails as part of an election campaign, for example, would not be appropriate.

Where, however, there is no policy or the policy is silent you may not use these resources for any political or private purposes.

Example

A member of a county council was found in breach of the code for making improper use of his Council-issued computer equipment for private purposes by downloading inappropriate adult pornographic images and sending a number of letters to a local newspaper, which he falsely represented as being from members of the public. The Adjudication Panel found that the member had misused the council equipment in breach of the Code and had brought the office of member into disrepute. He was disqualified from being or becoming a member of a local authority for 2 years and 6 months.

Example

A member of a county borough council was found in breach of the Code for using his council-issued mobile phone excessively for private purposes. Whilst limited personal use was permitted under the Council's IT policy a bill in excess of £1000 was incurred in respect of private calls which the member had made. The Adjudication Panel suspended the member for 9 months for this and other breaches.

Reaching decisions objectively

See paragraph 8

When taking part in meetings of your authority, or when arriving at decisions relating to the authority's business, you must do so with an open mind and objectively. During the decision-making process you must act fairly and take proper account of the public interest.

In some decisions, such as those taken by planning committees, you are required always to make your decisions on the basis of the facts in front of you, and not to have made your mind up in advance to such an extent that you're entirely unprepared to consider all of the evidence and advice you receive. Having a completely closed mind is known as pre-determination. You are entitled to hold a preliminary view about a particular matter in advance of a meeting (pre-disposition) as long as you keep an open mind and are prepared to consider the merits of all the arguments and points made about the matter under consideration before reaching your decision.

Pre-determination on the other hand would be where you have clearly decided on a course of action in advance of a meeting and are totally unwilling to consider the evidence and arguments presented on that matter during the meeting. Pre-determination could not only invalidate the decision, it would also amount to a breach of the Code.

Section 78 of the Local Government (Wales) Measure 2011 prohibits a member of an overview or scrutiny committee meeting from voting on a question at a meeting, if before the meeting, the member has been given a party whip relating to the question.

In order for me to investigate complaints of 'whipping' of votes by political groups there must be written evidence or other corroborative evidence available of the whip. Suppositions based upon the voting patterns of particular groups will not be sufficient evidence of a whip.

(The now defunct body Standards for England prepared a very useful guidance note on this subject entitled 'Understanding pre-determination and bias' which is available for reference on my website at www.ombudsman-wales.org.uk)

Considering advice provided to you and giving reasons

See paragraph 8

You must have regard to all of the advice you receive from your authority's officers, especially advice from the Chief Executive, Chief Finance Officer, Monitoring Officer and Chief Legal Officer where they give it under their statutory duties. Such advice may also be contained in policy and guidance documents produced by your authority. This is a complex area and there are provisions within other legislation which underpin it, but in general, it goes well beyond a requirement to simply consider and reject advice if it's not welcome. I expect members to follow the advice unless there are strong reasons not to do so, and where a decision is made not to follow advice, it is highly advisable to record the reasons for not doing so.

It is worth reflecting also that this places a considerable onus on statutory officers to consider their formal advice carefully, and again, where they believe it is likely to be contentious, to keep a record of it. There may be isolated cases where advice is given to a member which, when followed, leads to a breach of the Code. In investigating such cases, if the evidence suggests that there has been a breach, I would generally regard the flawed advice as a factor in mitigation, rather than as evidence that no breach occurred.

It is always helpful, if you can, to get advice as early as possible. If you can, ask for advice in good time before a meeting, rather than at the meeting or immediately before it starts. Make sure you give the officer concerned all of the information they need to take into account when giving you advice.

If you seek advice, or advice is offered to you, for example, on whether or not you should register a personal interest, you should have regard to this advice before you make your mind up. Failure to do so may be a breach of the Code.

You must give reasons for all decisions in accordance with any statutory requirements and any reasonable requirements imposed by your authority. Giving reasons for decisions is particularly important in relation to regulatory decisions and decisions where people's rights are affected but it is not confined to these.

As a matter of good practice, where you disagree with officer recommendations in making a decision, you should give clear reasons for your decision. This applies to decisions to vote against the advice of the statutory officers, even if you lose the vote. If you decide to vote against their advice, you should ensure that your reasons for doing so are recorded in the relevant minutes. You should be aware that voting against the advice of the statutory officers without good reason may be a breach of the Code.

In reaching decisions where the advice is not provided by the statutory officers, you should still have regard to the advice provided by officers and take it into account in reaching your decision. You may also wish to have regard to other advice you have received and, of course, to the position adopted by a political group of which you are a member. In some circumstances, such as planning decisions, you must not vote on the basis of a 'whip' imposed by your group. In others, it is reasonable to do so but you should avoid having an entirely closed mind prior to a debate. Again, whatever the reasons for voting against officer advice, it's highly advisable to record them.

Example

A member of a county council who chaired a Council meeting refused to allow the Council's Monitoring Officer to advise members during a debate about the Council's 'Annual Letter' from the Wales Audit Office. Also, when the Monitoring Officer did manage to intervene to express grave concerns about the way in which the proceedings were being conducted, he failed to have regard to the limited advice she was allowed to offer and simply said that he 'noted her comments'.

The member was found to have breached paragraph 8(a)(iii) of the Code. The Adjudication Panel took into account the member's full apology and expressions of remorse for his behaviour and indicated that had the member not already accepted his wrongdoing it would have imposed a greater sanction than the 4 months' suspension it imposed.

Expenses

See paragraph 9(a)

You need to follow the law and your authority's requirements in claiming expenses and allowances. If you are in any doubt about your entitlements, or the proper way to claim, you should ask for advice. You need to keep proper records of expenditure supported by receipts where appropriate, so that you can properly evidence your claims. Even if a particular scheme does not require you to submit receipts, you are strongly advised to keep these so that you can prove how much you have actually spent on the items you are claiming for e.g. childcare.

Example

A member of a county borough council was alleged to have used the Child/ Dependent Care Allowance to pay his wife to look after their daughter. During the investigation it transpired that he had paid his adult son (from a previous marriage) a regular weekly income to care for the child as and when required. The member was able to provide proof of the payments through receipts and cheque counterfoils. In view of this there was no evidence of any failure on the part of the member to comply with the Code.

Gifts and hospitality

See paragraph 9(b)

It's important that you don't accept any gifts or hospitality for yourself, or on behalf of others, which would place you under obligation or appear to do so. Accepting such gifts or hospitality could be regarded as compromising your objectivity when you make decisions or carry out the work of your Council. This is also true of any services or gifts in kind.

This does not prevent you from attending official events such as a civic reception or working lunch where these are authorised by your authority.

(See also the section on registering gifts and hospitality at page 37)

3. Personal and prejudicial interests

The elements of the Code which cover personal and prejudicial interests give rise to many questions from members. They are designed to safeguard the principles of selflessness and objectivity. They are intended to give members of the public confidence that decisions are being taken in their best interests, and not in the best interests of members of authorities or their close personal associates.

Personal interests relate to issues where you or a close personal associate may have some link to a matter under discussion. These interests become prejudicial where an informed independent observer could conclude that the interest would influence your vote, or your decision. Guidance on registering interests is at Section 4.

The paragraphs below are designed to offer guidance on a very complex subject. I would strongly recommend that if you are in any doubt about whether you have a personal or prejudicial interest, and what you need to do if so, you should ask your Monitoring Officer for advice.

Personal Interests

See paragraph 10

While you are carrying out your duties, you need to decide if you have a personal interest, and if so, whether you need to disclose it. Most members know that you need to disclose personal interests at meetings, but as you will read below, there are other occasions, such as when speaking to your authority's officers about the matter concerned, when you may also need to do so.

You have a **personal interest** in any business of your authority, including when making a decision, where it relates to or is likely to affect:

1. your job or your business;

2. your employer, or any firm in which you are a partner or paid director;

3. any person who has paid towards the cost of your election or your expenses as a member;

4. any company in which you hold shares with a nominal value of more than £25,000 or where your holding is more than 1% of the total issued share capital, which has premises or land in your authority's area;

5. any contract that your authority makes with a firm in which you are a partner, paid director or hold shares in as described in 4;

6. any land in which you have an interest and which is in your authority's area (this is especially important in all planning matters including strategic plans);

7. any land let by your authority to a firm in which you're a partner, paid director or a body as set out in 4;

8. any body to which you've been elected, appointed or nominated by your authority;

9. any

    - public authority or body exercising functions of a public nature,

    - company, industrial and provident society, charity or body directed to charitable purposes,

    - body whose main role is influencing public opinion or policy,

    - trade union or professional association,

    - private club, society or association operating in your authority's area in which you have membership or are in a position of general control or management, or

10. any land in your authority's area which you have a license to occupy for at least 28 days. It is always safer to declare an interest, however, if in doubt consult your Monitoring Officer.

Ward and electoral division issues – including paragraph 10 (2)(b)

If a member of the public could reasonably conclude that when you're taking a decision on behalf of the authority as a whole you are more influenced by issues in your ward or electoral division than by the interests of the authority as a whole eg if the authority needs to make a provision but you don't think it should be in your ward or electoral division, then you would have a personal interest.

This paragraph has given rise to great interpretative difficulties. The crux of the problem is that a strict interpretation of the paragraph, as worded, could well preclude members from participating in any decision affecting their ward – whereas the underlying policy intention had been to limit the scope of this provision to decisions made by individual councillors in the exercise of executive functions.

I do not believe that it would be in the public interest, or in the interests of local democracy, to adopt a literal interpretation as a matter of course. Therefore as a general rule, in exercising my discretion, the decision as to whether or not to investigate will be based on the assumption that the paragraph is actually directed at individual members making decisions in the exercise of executive functions and decisions such as those made at planning or licensing committees.

Whilst s 25 of the Localism Act 2011 outlines circumstances when members should not be regarded as having a closed mind when taking decisions I do not consider that this impacts upon the provisions of the Code. However I will review this in light of any future decisions and case law on the effect of this provision.

Example

The Adjudication Panel considered a case concerning this provision of the Code. The member had declared his opposition to a controversial planning application in his election manifesto pledging to 'work tirelessly on issues of concern' and to 'oppose the current development proposal'. Having been elected the member voted against the first planning application which the Council considered when the application was refused. He was subsequently quoted in the local and national press defending his decision to oppose the development. The Adjudication Panel found that the member had acted in such a way that a member of the public might reasonably perceive a conflict between his role as a local councillor and his role in taking a decision on behalf of his authority. It suspended the member from the planning committee for a period of 3 months.

Matters affecting your well being or financial position

If a decision might be seen as affecting your well being or financial position or the well being or financial position of any person who lives with you or with whom you have a close personal association to a greater extent than other people in your ward or, for members of authorities which do not have wards (e.g. national parks) in your authority's area, you also have a personal interest.

Examples of decisions of this kind include obvious issues like contracts being awarded to your partner's company but also issues about the location of developments, where it might make a big difference to where you or your close personal associates live. Examples have included the location of playgrounds, where elected members have opposed them near their houses because of issues about noise.

What is 'a body exercising functions of a public nature'?

The phrase 'a body exercising functions of a public nature' has been subject to broad interpretation by the courts for a variety of different purposes. Although it is not possible to produce a definitive list of such bodies, here are some of the criteria to consider when deciding whether or not a body meets that definition:

- Does that body carry out a public service?

- Is the body taking the place of local or central government in carrying out the function e.g. a care home with residents supported by social services?

- Is the body (including one outsourced in the private sector) exercising a function delegated to it by a public authority e.g. a private company collecting refuse for the authority?

- Is the function exercised under legislation or according to some statutory power?

- Can the body be judicially reviewed?

Unless you answer 'yes' to one of the above questions, it is unlikely that the body in your case is exercising functions of a public nature. Examples of bodies included in this definition: health bodies, council-owned companies exercising public functions and school governing bodies. If you need further information or specific advice on this matter, please contact your Monitoring Officer.

What does 'affecting well-being or financial position' mean?

The term 'well-being' can be described as a condition of contentedness and happiness. Anything that could affect your quality of life, either positively or negatively, is likely to affect your well-being.

A personal interest can affect you or your close personal associates positively and negatively. So if you or they have the potential to gain or lose from a matter under consideration, you need to declare a personal interest in both situations.

Who is a close personal associate?

Close personal associates include people such as close friends, colleagues with whom you have particularly strong connections, business associates and close relatives. It does not include casual acquaintances, distant relatives or people you simply come in contact with through your role as member or your work in the local community.

Close personal associates can also include someone with whom you have been in dispute, or whom you may be regarded as having an interest in disadvantaging. For example, being a member of the same golf club as another person would not of itself constitute a close personal association but having that person as a weekly golf partner might well do. If you are in doubt, you should ask your Monitoring Officer.

What if I belong to an authority without wards or electoral divisions?

If you are a member of an authority that does not have wards or electoral divisions, you will need to declare a personal interest whenever you consider a matter in a meeting of your authority if it affects the well-being or financial position of you or one or more of your close personal associates, more than it would affect other people in your authority's area. If you are a local authority member of a fire authority, for example, you would need to declare an interest under this heading on matters concerning your nominating authority's area.

'Twin hatted' members

If you are a member of both a community council and a county council you are not prevented from discussing the same matters at both. You may, for example, take part in a discussion about a planning application about which your community council has been consulted and still go on to participate in a decision about the application if you sit on the planning committee of your county council.

If you do so, you would be well advised to state at the community council meeting that you would be looking at the matter afresh when you consider it at the county council, and that you would take into account all of the information and advice provided to you. At the planning committee, you should make it clear that you are not bound by the views of the community council. The advice about objective decision making in respect of paragraphs 8 and 10(2)(b) of the Code is also relevant here.

Obviously, if the application was one submitted by the community council, then you would have both a personal and a prejudicial interest, and you would be required to declare it and withdraw in line with the guidance on 'what to do if you have a prejudicial interest' below.

Example

Councillor F participated in a meeting which was considering whether to approve the complainant's nomination for the post of school governor; Councillor F's husband had also applied for the post. Not only did the Adjudication Panel find that she should have declared a personal interest in the item of business by virtue of her close personal association with her husband, but it also took the view that as there had been a history of animosity directed towards the member by the complainant which had been reported publicly, she also had a personal interest by virtue of her close personal association with the complainant.

A further element to this complaint was that after the complainant had made a complaint to me about the member, the member sat on the Council's Standards Committee when it considered a separate complaint from the complainant against another member. The Adjudication Panel took the view that, in light of the acrimonious relationship between the member and the complainant, the member's participation in the Standards Committee hearing could reasonably have been regarded as affecting the complainant's wellbeing because she was entitled to a fair and unbiased hearing of her complaint.

What if I am not aware of my personal interest?

Your obligation to disclose a personal interest to a meeting only applies when you are aware of or reasonably ought to be aware of the existence of the personal interest.

Clearly you cannot be expected to declare something of which you are unaware. It would be impractical to expect you to research into the employment, business interests and other activities of all your close associates and relatives. However, you should not ignore the existence of interests which, from the point of view of a reasonable and objective observer, you should have been aware.

If you declare a personal interest you can remain in the meeting, speak and vote on the matter, unless your personal interest is also a **prejudicial interest**.

What constitutes a prejudicial interest is outlined in a following section.

Disclosing personal interests

See paragraph 11

At meetings, you must declare that you have a personal interest, and the nature of that interest, before the matter is discussed or as soon as it becomes apparent to you except in limited circumstances. Even if your interest is on the register of interests, you must declare it orally in the meetings where matters relating to that interest are discussed.

If you're making representations in writing (including e-mails, faxes etc.) to another member or an officer, you must include details of any personal interests you have.

Similarly, if you're speaking with an officer or member in person, by phone or video conference you should tell them about any personal interest you have before making representations or when the interest becomes apparent. You are obliged to confirm your interest by e-mail or in writing to the officer concerned and to the Monitoring Officer within 14 days. The Ombudsman would generally expect officers to make a record of any conversation in which a member has declared an interest and attach it to the appropriate file.

If you're making a decision as part of an executive or board, you must make sure that the written record of that decision (eg minutes of a cabinet meeting) includes details of your interest.

If you have disclosed an interest at a meeting which has not previously been recorded, you must give it in writing to your authority in line with the arrangements set out by your Monitoring Officer. Normally, this will mean before, or immediately after the meeting concerned or as soon as possible thereafter. As a minimum, you need to say in writing what the interest is, what business considered by the meeting it relates to and you need to sign it.

If you have agreed with your Monitoring Officer that the information about your personal interest is sensitive information then you should disclose the existence of a personal interest, and confirm that the Monitoring Officer has agreed that the information about it is sensitive. More information about this is included in the separate section below.

Prejudicial Interests

See paragraph 12

What is a prejudicial interest?

Your personal interest will also be a prejudicial interest in a matter if either of the following conditions applies:

- the matter does not fall within one of the exempt categories of business, or

- the matter relates to a licensing or regulatory matter (see paragraph 12(3)),

and a member of the public, who knows the relevant facts, would reasonably think your personal interest is so significant that it is likely to prejudice your judgement of the public interest.

What is so significant that it is likely to prejudice your judgement?

If a reasonable member of the public with knowledge of all the relevant facts would think that your judgement of the public interest might be prejudiced, then you have a prejudicial interest. This is an objective test. You must decide not whether you would take the decision without prejudice, but whether you would be seen as doing so.

You must ask yourself whether a member of the public – if he or she knew all the relevant facts – would think that your personal interest was so significant that it would be likely to prejudice your judgement. In other words, the interest must be perceived as likely to harm or impair your ability to judge the public interest.

The mere existence of local knowledge, or connections within the local community, will not normally be sufficient to meet the test. There must be some factor that might positively harm your ability to judge the public interest objectively. The nature of the matter is also important, including whether a large number of people are equally affected by it or whether you or a smaller group are particularly affected.

Some general principles must be remembered when applying this test. You should clearly act in the public interest and not in the interests of any close personal associates. You are a custodian of the public purse and the public interest and your behaviour and decisions should reflect this responsibility.

You would have a prejudicial interest in a planning application proposal if a close personal associate of yours (e.g. your son or a good friend) lives next to the proposed site. This is because your close personal associate would be likely to be affected by the application to a greater extent than the majority of the inhabitants of the ward or electoral division affected by the decision (or authority, if your authority does not have wards) and this gives you a personal interest in the issue. The close personal association means a reasonable member of the public might think that it would prejudice your view of the public interest when considering the planning application. It does not matter whether it actually would or not.

In other cases, where there has been a dispute between you and an individual who could be disadvantaged by a decision, an informed reasonable member of the public might conclude that you would be inclined to vote accordingly, whether this is the case or not.

Exempt categories of business

Paragraph 12(2) of the Code states that a member will not have a prejudicial interest in any business that relates to:

- another relevant authority of which you are also a member;

- another public authority or a body exercising functions of a public nature in which you hold a position of general control or management;

- a body to which you've been elected, appointed or nominated by your authority;

- your role as school governor where you haven't been appointed or nominated by your authority (eg a parent governor) unless the business specifically relates to your school;

- your role as a member of a health board where you haven't been appointed by your authority.

- Housing, if you hold a tenancy or lease with the authority, as long as the matter does not relate to your particular tenancy or lease and you don't have arrears of rent of more than 2 months.

- School meals or school transport and travelling expenses, if you are a parent, guardian, grandparent of, or have parental responsibility for, a child in full-time education unless it relates particularly to the school your child attends.

- Decisions about statutory sick pay if you receive or are entitled to receive it from your authority.

- An allowance or payment for members. (I do not consider a member being put forward for election to a council office which attracts a Special Responsibility Allowance to have a prejudicial interest as I consider them to be covered by this dispensation.)

These exemptions will not apply where the business you are considering is about determining an approval, consent, license, permission or regulation. I consider these descriptions to refer to a narrow category of decisions, such as granting planning consent and licensing decisions. A wider interpretation of approval, for example, would cover almost every aspect of your authority's business and was clearly not intended.

Example

Two members of a county borough council, who were sisters, were found by the Council's Standards Committee to have failed to declare both personal and prejudicial interests when they decided to allocate funds from their Members' Small Payments Scheme to a company, in respect of which one of the members was a non-paid director. During my investigation one of the members disputed the fact that she had received advice from the Monitoring Officer about the disclosure of such interests, and the other member had, despite receiving advice on the declaration of interests, falsely declared that she had no interest in the company on the nomination form. The Standards Committee considered the breaches of the code to be serious ones. It decided to censure both members.

Overview and Scrutiny Committees

See paragraph 13

Please note: this section does not apply to fire and rescue authorities, and national park authorities. You have a prejudicial interest in any business before an overview and scrutiny committee or sub-committee meeting where both of the following requirements are met:

- That business relates to a decision made (whether implemented or not) or action taken by your authority's executive, board or another of your authority's committees, sub-committees, joint committees or joint sub-committees.

- You were a member of that decision-making body at that time and you were present at the time the decision was made or action taken.

If the overview and scrutiny committee is checking a decision which you were involved in making you may be called to attend the meeting to give evidence or answer questions on the matter, and you may do so providing it is acting under its statutory powers.

What to do when you have a prejudicial interest

See paragraph 14

Even where you have a prejudicial interest, the Code supports your role as a community advocate and enables you in certain circumstances to represent your community and to speak on issues important to them and to you.

Key points:

If you have a **prejudicial interest** in a matter being discussed at a meeting, you must, having declared your personal interest in the matter, leave the room (or any other venue in which the meeting is being held including, for example, the location of a site meeting), **unless members of the public are allowed to make representations, give evidence or answer questions about the matter**, by statutory right or otherwise. If that is the case, you can also attend the meeting for that purpose.

However, you must immediately leave the room or chamber once the period for considering representations has finished, and before any discussion on the item begins, even if members of the public are allowed to remain. You cannot remain in the public gallery to observe the vote on the matter.

In addition, you must not seek to influence a decision in which you have a prejudicial interest. This rule is similar to your general obligation not to use your position as a member improperly to your or someone else's advantage or disadvantage. This means that as well as leaving meetings where the item is discussed, you should also not write or make any oral representations about the matter.

Do I have a statutory right to speak to the meeting?

The Code does not provide you with a general right to speak to a meeting where you have a prejudicial interest. However, in limited circumstances, legislation may provide you with a right to speak (for example, licensing hearings and standards hearings) which the Code recognises. If so, you will be allowed to exercise that right to speak. Your Monitoring Officer should be able to confirm whether this is relevant to your case.

If I don't have a statutory right, will I be allowed to speak to the meeting?

The Code aims to provide members with the same rights as ordinary members of the public to speak on certain matters in meetings, despite having a prejudicial interest. These rights are usually governed by your authority's constitution, procedure rules or standing orders, and may be subject to conditions including time limits or the fact that representations can only be made in writing.

If an ordinary member of the public would be allowed to speak to a meeting about an item, you should be provided with the same opportunity. You will be able to make representations, answer questions or give evidence, even if you have a prejudicial interest in the item. You may not take part in the discussion or observe the vote.

When must I leave the place where the meeting is held?

You must leave immediately when the time for making representations, giving evidence or answering questions is finished, and before any debate starts.

What does influencing a decision mean?

You must not make any representations or have any involvement with decisions in which you have a prejudicial interest, except where you are entitled to speak as described above.

What if the public are not allowed to speak to the meeting on the matter?

If an ordinary member of the public is not allowed to speak on the matter, you cannot do so if you have a prejudicial interest. You must leave the place where the debate is being held and not seek to influence the debate in any way.

This may be the case, for example, where your authority is discussing a confidential matter in closed session or does not have procedure rules or standing orders in place that allow members of the public to speak at a meeting of your authority. Like the public, you are not allowed to participate if you have a prejudicial interest. However, where the public may be allowed to sit in the public gallery to observe the meeting, you will be required to leave the room during the debate and vote.

What if I am summoned to attend a scrutiny committee to discuss business in which I have a prejudicial interest?

If you're asked to attend by the committee exercising its statutory powers, then you may attend and participate in the meeting.

Executive or cabinet roles

Please note: this section will not apply to fire and rescue authorities or national park authorities, unless in the latter case there are executive arrangements in place.

If you are a leader or cabinet member of an authority operating executive arrangements, you must follow the normal rules for executive members who have personal and prejudicial interests.

If your interest is personal but not prejudicial, you can advise the executive on the issue and take part in executive discussions and decisions as long as you declare your interest. You can also exercise delegated powers in the matter as long as you record the existence and nature of your personal interest.

If you are an executive member who can take individual decisions, and you have a prejudicial interest in a decision, your authority may make other arrangements as set out in ss 14–16 of the Local Government Act 2000. This means that the decision can be taken by an officer, another cabinet member, the full executive, or a committee of the executive.

Although you have a prejudicial interest in a matter, you may be able to make representations, answer questions and give evidence as long as a member of the public would have the same rights, but you are barred from decision-making about that matter individually or in cabinet. You also should not participate in any early consideration of it, or exercise any delegated powers in relation to it. If you have delegated powers in that area, you should refer the consideration and any decisions on the matter to the cabinet to avoid the perception of improper influence.

Dispensations

If I have a prejudicial interest, can I obtain a dispensation to allow me to take part in the meeting?

You can apply in writing to your authority's Standards Committee for a dispensation on one or more of the following grounds:

- at least 50 per cent of the authority or committee members would be prevented from taking a full part in a meeting because of prejudicial interests;

- at least half of the cabinet would be so prevented (the leader should be included in the cabinet in calculating the proportion);

- in the case of a county/county borough council, the political balance at the meeting would be upset to such an extent that the outcome would be likely to be affected;

- the nature of your interest is such that your participation wouldn't harm public confidence;

- your interest is common to a significant proportion of the general public;

- you have a particular role or expertise which would justify your participation;

- the business is being considered by an overview or scrutiny committee and you don't have a pecuniary interest;

- the business relates to the finances or property of a voluntary organisation and you sit on its board or committee in your own right and you don't have any other interest, although in this instance, any dispensation won't let you vote on the matter; or

- the committee believes that your participation would be in the interests of the people in your authority's area and that the committee notifies Welsh Ministers within seven days.

You can apply for a dispensation individually and in certain circumstances, you can make joint applications where a number of members want to obtain a dispensation to speak or vote on the same matter. If the Standards Committee approves your application, it must grant the dispensation in writing and before the meeting is held. If you need a dispensation, you should apply for one as soon as is reasonably possible.

Only the Standards Committee can grant the dispensation and will do so at its discretion. The Standards Committee will need to balance the public interest in preventing members with prejudicial interests from taking part in decisions, against the public interest in decisions being taken by a reasonably representative group of members of the authority. If failure to grant a dispensation will result in an authority or committee not achieving a quorum, this may well constitute grounds for granting a dispensation.

Where you hold a dispensation, you can also make written representations but you must provide details of the dispensation in any correspondence. If you make oral representations, whether in person or by phone, you must refer to the dispensation and confirm this in writing within 14 days.

4. Registration of Interests

Key points:

All members of authorities have to provide a record of their interests in a public register of interests. If you are a member of a county or county borough council, fire authority or national park authority, you must tell your Monitoring Officer in writing within 28 days of taking office, or within 28 days of any change to your register of interests, of any interests which fall within the categories set out in the Code, outlined below.

You need to register your interests so that the public, authority staff and fellow members know which of your interests might give rise to a conflict of interest. The register is a document that can be consulted when (or before) an issue arises, and so allows others to know what interests you have, and whether they might give rise to a possible conflict of interest.

The register also protects you. You are responsible for deciding whether or not you should declare an interest in a meeting, but it can be helpful for you to know early on if others think that a potential conflict might arise. It is also important that the public know about any interest that might have to be declared by you or other members, so that decision making is seen by the public as open and honest. This helps to ensure that public confidence in the integrity of local governance is maintained.

As previously mentioned, unless you are a community councillor, you must tell your Monitoring Officer in writing within 28 days of taking office, or within 28 days of any change to your register of interests, of any interests which fall within the categories set out in the Code. These categories include:

- Your job(s) or business(es).
- The name of your employer or people who have appointed you to work for them.

- The name of any person who has made a payment to you in respect of your election or expenses you have incurred in carrying out your duties.

- The name of any person, company or other body which has a place of business or land in the authority's area, and in which you have a shareholding of more than £25,000 (nominal value) or have a stake of more than 1/100th of the share capital of the company.

- Any contracts between the authority and yourself, your firm (if you are a partner) or a company (if you are a paid director or if you have a shareholding as described above) including any lease, licence from the authority and any contracts for goods, services or works. Where the contract relates to use of land or a property, the land must be identified on the register.

- Any land and property in the authority's area in which you have a beneficial interest (or a licence to occupy for more than 28 days) including, but not limited to, the land and house you live in and any allotments you own or use.

- Your membership or position of control or management in:
  - any other bodies to which you were elected, appointed or nominated by the authority;
  - any bodies **exercising functions of a public nature** (described above), or directed to charitable purposes, or whose principal purposes include the influence of public opinion or policy, including any political party or trade union;
  - Any private club, society or association operating within your authority's area.

Sensitive information

Key points:

You may be exempt from having to include sensitive information on your register of interests. If your personal interest in a matter under discussion at a meeting is sensitive information, you will need to declare that you have a personal interest but you will not have to give any details about the nature of that interest.

Sensitive information may include your sensitive employment (such as certain scientific research or the Special Forces) or other interests that are likely to create a serious risk of violence or intimidation against you or someone who lives with you should they become public knowledge.

You should provide this information to your Monitoring Officer and explain your concerns regarding the disclosure of the sensitive information; including why it is likely to create a serious risk that you or a person who lives with you will be subjected to violence or intimidation. You do not need to include this information in your register of interests, if your Monitoring Officer agrees. Ultimately, you must decide what information to include on your publicly available register of interests. If information on your register ceases to be sensitive, you must notify your Monitoring Officer within 28 days asking them to amend the information accordingly.

349

Gifts and hospitality

Key points:

You must register any gifts or hospitality worth more than the amount specified by your authority that you receive in connection with your official duties as a member, and the source of the gift or hospitality.

You must register the gift or hospitality and its source within 28 days of receiving it.

Like other interests in your register of interests, you may have a **personal interest** in a matter under consideration if it is likely to affect a person who gave you a gift or hospitality that is registered. If that is the case, you must declare the existence and nature of the gift or hospitality, the person who gave it to you, how the business under consideration relates to that person, and then decide whether that interest is also a **prejudicial interest**.

It is also good practice to provide a note of any offers of gifts which you have declined.

Is the gift or hospitality connected to my official duties as a member?

You should ask yourself, would I have been given this if I was not on the council? If you are in doubt as to the motive behind a gift or hospitality, we recommend that you register it or speak to your Monitoring Officer.

You do not need to register gifts and hospitality which are not related to your role as a member, such as Christmas gifts from your friends and family, or gifts which you do not accept. However, you should always register a gift or hospitality if it could be perceived as something given to you because of your position or if your authority requires you to.

What if I do not know the value of a gift or hospitality?

The general rule is, if in doubt as to the value of a gift or hospitality, you should register it, as a matter of good practice and in accordance with the principles of openness and accountability in public life.

You may have to estimate how much a gift or hospitality is worth. Also, an accumulation of small gifts you receive from the same source over a short period that add up to the value specified by your authority or over should be registered.

The Code also refers to material benefit or advantage. The measure of this would be if an informed independent observer could conclude that you might be perceived to be better off as a consequence.

Public Services Ombudsman for Wales
1 Ffordd yr Hen Gae
Pencoed
CF35 5LJ

Tel: 01656 641150

Fax: 01656 641199

E-mail: ask@ombudsman-wales.org.uk

Web: www.ombudsman-wales.org.uk

THE CODE OF CONDUCT FOR MEMBERS OF LOCAL AUTHORITIES IN WALES: GUIDANCE FROM THE PUBLIC SERVICES OMBUDSMAN FOR WALES FOR MEMBERS OF COMMUNITY COUNCILS

Preface

This revised guide from me as Public Services Ombudsman for Wales provides an overview of the Model Code of Conduct (the Code) introduced in 2008. It is intended to help you as a member to understand your obligations under the Code. The Code applies to all members and co-opted members of local authorities, community councils, fire and rescue authorities and national park authorities in Wales. As a member, you are required to sign up to it as part of your declaration of acceptance of office. The Code does not apply to the actions of authorities as a whole, or to the conduct of their officers and employees. There is a separate code of conduct applying to officers of local authorities in Wales.

This is a separate version of this guidance aimed at Community and Town Councillors (referred to throughout this guidance as Community Councillors). The guidance differs in many parts from the original document (and the guidance to County Councillors) as it recognises the different role that Community Councillors undertake. The Guidance will be adapted from time to time to reflect case law and any changes to the Code. It contains examples drawn from recent cases considered by the Adjudication Panel for Wales and standards committees across Wales.

The following pages aim to provide you with a general understanding of the Code and its requirements. Section 1 provides an introduction, while Section 2 outlines your obligations under the Code, referencing specific paragraphs for further information. Sections 3 and 4 deal with general issues surrounding interests, and aim to clarify a number of provisions which you will find in Parts 3 & 4 of the Code. You can obtain a copy of the Code by contacting your Clerk.

The guide is intended to help you to understand the Code and how it applies, but it cannot hope to cover every conceivable circumstance. Ultimately, it is your responsibility to take specific advice from your Clerk or Monitoring Officer and to make a decision as to the most suitable course of action.

I have used examples throughout the report to help to bring the guidance to life. These examples are drawn from actual cases considered by my office and also include decisions reached by local standards committees and the Adjudication Panel for Wales.

As a member you will be offered training on the Code whether by your Clerk, a Monitoring Officer or from a representative body. I expect all members to take advantage of such training, including refresher courses, to ensure that they are fully aware of the provisions of the Code and its interpretation.

In issuing this advice I am very conscious of the importance of standards in ensuring the future health and effectiveness of our democratic institutions. It is important that we should all work collaboratively to drive up standards and to create a culture where members are respected for their selflessness, objectivity and respectful behaviour. If we do so we can build public confidence in our democratic institutions and promote good governance for the benefit of the people of all of our communities.

Peter Tyndall
Public Services Ombudsman for Wales
September 2012

This statutory guidance is issued by the Public Services Ombudsman for Wales under Section 68 of the Local Government Act 2000 for elected, co-opted and appointed members of Community and Town Councils in Wales.

Separate guidance is available for elected, co-opted and appointed members of County Councils, Fire and Rescue authorities and National Park authorities in Wales.

Acknowledgement

This guidance draws on the guidance prepared and issued by Standards for England on the former English Code of Conduct. It has been extended and amended to refer to the Welsh Code and to the Welsh context. It also reflects responses to the consultation I have undertaken.

First published April 2010.

This edition published September 2012.

1. Introduction

The Local Government Act 2000 created a new ethical framework for local government in Wales.

It created a power for the National Assembly for Wales to issue a model code of conduct to apply to members and co-opted members of all relevant authorities in Wales. This power was transferred to the Welsh Ministers by the Government of Wales Act 2006. In 2008, Welsh Ministers issued the current Model Code of Conduct which all relevant authorities are required to adopt.

Authorities were required to adopt the Code in its model form in its entirety, but could make additions to the Code, provided these were consistent with the Model. This was intended to give certainty to members and the public as to what standards are expected. It helps to ensure consistency throughout relevant authorities, avoiding confusion for members on more than one authority and for the public.

Standards committees of principal councils are required to assist members and co-opted members of town and community councils in their area to observe the Code, and to arrange for advice and training to be provided. I strongly recommend that all members should attend training and take advice where it is offered.

Whilst Community Councillors do not act on decision-making bodies such as planning committees you will be called upon to take decisions on the allocation of funding from your precept and to offer guidance, drawing on your valuable local knowledge, to the County Council about the impact of planning applications.

It is imperative therefore, that you are fully aware of the Code of Conduct and its implications for your decision-making and indeed, whether you should be involved in making a decision. In light of this I recommend training on the Code of Conduct for all Councillors as early in their term of office as possible.

Ultimately, as a member, you are responsible for the decisions you take and can be held to account for them. However, this doesn't imply that you can take decisions which breach the Code or contrary to advice simply because the decision is yours to take. This guidance explains the constraints you are expected to act within to ensure members of the public can be confident in the way in which authorities in Wales reach their decisions.

It is my role as Public Services Ombudsman to investigate complaints that members of local authorities in Wales have breached the Code. In determining whether to investigate a complaint or whether to continue an investigation of a breach of the Code I will use a two-stage test. In the first instance, I will aim to establish whether there is evidence that a breach actually took place.

The second test I will apply is whether the breach alleged would be likely to lead to a sanction. I have discretion as to whether to investigate or not. I have adopted this test in order to explain how I will usually exercise my discretion and to secure a degree of consistency. In using my discretion, I will take account of the outcomes of previous cases considered by standards committees across Wales and decide accordingly.

If whilst assessing a complaint or at any point where I have commenced an investigation I consider that the second limb of the two stage test has not been met I will invite the Monitoring Officer (in conjunction with the Standards Committee) to consider whether a local investigation is appropriate. If so I will formally refer the matter to the Monitoring Officer for investigation under s 70(4) of the Local Government Act 2000.

However, if I am aware of previous complaints about the same member and believe these may be indicative of a pattern of breaches, I will then often choose to investigate. Where there is prima facie evidence of a breach of the Code, and I do not decide to investigate, I will almost always write to the member concerned making it clear that my decision should not in any way be regarded as approval for any breach of the Code and making clear that I will take it into account if there are further reported breaches.

The process I use for investigating complaints is on my website at www. ombudsman-wales.org.uk. If I find that a complaint is justified, I may refer it either to your Standards Committee or to a tribunal convened by the Adjudication Panel for Wales. If it then finds the complaint proven, it can impose a range of sanctions.

In this guidance I have tried, where possible, to use examples of cases which have been referred to me and which are relevant to Community Councils. Where this has not been possible I have given examples of theoretical scenarios that indicate how the Code of Conduct may be breached whilst you are undertaking your role.

Local Resolution Process

During the course of the life of this guidance I expect principal local authorities across Wales to have implemented local resolution procedures to deal with low level complaints which are made by a member against a fellow member. These mechanisms are initially being adopted by principal councils, but I am supportive of this extending to cover community councils in due course. Typically these complaints will be about alleged failures to show respect and consideration for others as required by paragraph 4(b) of the Code or the duty not to make vexatious, malicious or frivolous complaints against other members under paragraph 6(1)(d) of the Code. Whilst a member may still complain directly to me about a fellow member if the matter being complained about concerns paragraphs 4b and 6(1)(d) I am likely to refer the matter back to the Council's Monitoring Officer for consideration under this process.

In my view such complaints are more appropriately resolved informally and locally in order to speed up the complaints process and to ensure that my resources are devoted to the investigation of serious complaints. The aim of local resolution is to resolve matters at an early stage so as to avoid the unnecessary escalation of the situation which may damage personal relationships within the authority and the authority's reputation. The process may result in an apology being made by the member concerned. However, where a member has repeatedly breached their authority's local protocol then I would expect the Monitoring Officer to refer the matter back to me.

When I have investigated a complaint I may refer the matter to a Standards Committee or the Adjudication Panel for Wales which have the following roles:

Standards Committee

Where a standards committee concludes that a member or co-opted member has failed to comply with the relevant council's code of conduct, it may determine that:

1. no action needs to be taken in respect of that failure;

2. the member or co-opted member should be censured; or

3. the member or co-opted member should be suspended or partially suspended from being a member of that council for a period not exceeding six months.

A censure takes the form of a public rebuke of the member concerned.

A member may appeal against the determination of a standards committee to the Adjudication Panel for Wales.

Adjudication Panel for Wales

The powers available to the tribunal when it determines that a member or co-opted member has failed to comply with the Code are:

1. to disqualify the respondent from being, or becoming, a member of the relevant council concerned or any other relevant council for a period of up to five years;

2. to suspend or partially suspend the respondent from being a member or co-opted member of the relevant council concerned for up to 12 months;

3. to take no action in respect of the breach.

Where either a standards committee or a tribunal suspends or partly suspends a member or co-opted member that member or co-opted member is still subject to the code of conduct, in particular the provisions set out in paragraphs 6(1)(a) (bringing the office of member or authority into disrepute) and paragraph 7 (improperly using the position of member).

The Role of the Clerk

The Clerk is employed by your Council and undertakes a number of tasks including providing administrative support to the Council, advising on the development of policies and procedures and advising the Council on implementing and using its procedures. The Clerk acts in a supporting role and is the person you should turn to in the first instance if you need any advice.

The Clerk has a complex role and will be able to advise Councillors on relevant legislation, including matters relating to the Code of Conduct, and on the Council's standing orders. The Clerk will work closely with the Chair to ensure that appropriate procedures are followed at meetings and that all necessary information is available to Councillors so that they may make informed decisions. Clerks may approach their relevant County Council's Monitoring Officer for advice (see below).

The Clerk is an employee of the Council and is not required to abide by the Code of Conduct. Any issues regarding the performance of the Clerk are personnel matters and should be addressed using appropriate employment procedures. The Ombudsman cannot consider complaints regarding the performance of the Clerk; this is a matter for the Council as the Clerk's employer.

The Role of the Monitoring Officer

The Monitoring Officer is an officer employed by the County Council. Among many other things they advise and assist County Councillors. Monitoring Officers may offer some training to Community Councils.

The Monitoring Officer has a significant role in the local resolution process outlined above and they will also work closely in advising the Standards Committee.

You should always ask your Clerk in the first instance for any guidance or information. The Monitoring Officer may be able to provide information if your Clerk is unavailable.

The Principles

The Local Government Act empowered the National Assembly to issue principles to which you must have regard in undertaking your role as a member. The Code is based on these principles which are designed to promote the highest possible standards. These principles draw on the 7 Principles of Public Life which were set out in the Nolan Report 'Standards of Conduct in Local Government in England, Scotland and Wales'. Three more were added to these: a duty to uphold the law, proper stewardship of the Council's resources and equality and respect for others.

Members elected to local authorities give generously of their time and commitment for the benefit of their communities. The principles provide a framework for channelling your commitment in a way which will reflect well on you and your council, and which will give your communities confidence in the way that your council is governed.

The individual sections of the Code are designed to support the implementation of the Principles. For example, the Selflessness principle is covered by Section 7 of the Code – Selflessness and Stewardship.

The current principles were set out in a statutory instrument[2] and are detailed below.

1. **Selflessness**
   Members must act solely in the public interest. They must never use their position as members to improperly confer advantage on themselves or to improperly confer advantage or disadvantage on others.

2. **Honesty**
   Members must declare any private interests relevant to their public duties and take steps to resolve any conflict in a way that protects the public interest.

3. **Integrity and Propriety**
   Members must not put themselves in a position where their integrity is called into question by any financial or other obligation to individuals or organisations that might seek to influence them in the performance of their duties. Members must on all occasions avoid the appearance of such behaviour.

4. **Duty to Uphold the Law**
   Members must act to uphold the law and act on all occasions in accordance with the trust that the public has placed in them.

5. **Stewardship**
   In discharging their duties and responsibilities members must ensure that their authority's resources are used both lawfully and prudently.

6. **Objectivity in Decision-making**
   In carrying out their responsibilities including making appointments, awarding contracts, or recommending individuals for rewards and benefits, members must make decisions on merit. Whilst members must have regard to the professional advice of officers and may properly take account of the views of others, including their political groups, it is their responsibility to decide what view to take and, if appropriate, how to vote on any issue.

7. **Equality and Respect**
   Members must carry out their duties and responsibilities with due regard to the need to promote equality of opportunity for all people, regardless of their

2   The Conduct of Members (Principles) (Wales) Order 2001, SI 2001/2276 (W.166).

gender, race, disability, sexual orientation, age or religion, and show respect and consideration for others.

8. Openness

Members must be as open as possible about all their actions and those of their authority. They must seek to ensure that disclosure of information is restricted only in accordance with the law.

9. Accountability

Members are accountable to the electorate and the public generally for their actions and for the way they carry out their responsibilities as a member. They must be prepared to submit themselves to such scrutiny as is appropriate to their responsibilities.

10. Leadership

Members must promote and support these principles by leadership and example so as to promote public confidence in their role and in the authority. They must respect the impartiality and integrity of the authority's statutory officers and its other employees.

The principles are not part of the Model Code, and failure to comply with the Principles is not of itself, therefore, indicative of a breach of the Code. However, it is likely that a failure, for example, to adhere to the principle concerning equality and respect would constitute a breach of the requirements at paragraphs 4 (a) and (b) in the Code in respect of equality of opportunity and respect.

In any event, the Principles offer a sound basis for your conduct in office and I encourage members to have regard to them at all times.

Deciding when the Code applies to you

See paragraphs 2 and 3

The Code applies to you:

1. Whenever you act in your official capacity, including whenever you are conducting the business of your council or acting, claiming to act, or give the impression you are acting, in your official capacity as a member or as a representative of your council.

2. At any time, if you conduct yourself in a manner which could reasonably be regarded as bringing your office or your council into disrepute or if you use or attempt to use your position to gain an advantage or avoid a disadvantage for yourself or any other person or if you misuse your council's resources.

Where you act as a representative of your council on another relevant authority, or any other body, you must, when acting for that other authority, comply with their Code of Conduct. When you are nominated by your council as a trustee of a charity you are obliged when acting as such to do so in the best interests of that charity, in accordance with charity law and with the guidance which has been produced by the Charity Commission (see its website: www.charity-commission.gov.uk).

If you are acting as a representative of your council on another body, for example on an event committee, which doesn't have a code of conduct relating to its members, you must comply with your council's own code unless it conflicts with any legal requirements that the other body has to comply with.

If you refer to yourself as councillor, the Code will apply to you. This applies in conversation, in writing, or in your use of electronic media. There has been a significant rise in complaints to me concerning the use of Facebook, blogs and Twitter. If you refer to your role as councillor in any way or comments you make are clearly related to your role then the Code will apply to any comments you make there. Even if you do not refer to your role as councillor, your comments may have the effect of bringing your office or authority into disrepute and could therefore breach paragraph 6(1)(a) of the Code of Conduct.

If you are suspended from office for any reason, you must still observe those elements of the Code which apply, particularly as set out in paragraph 2(1)(d), while you are suspended.

Example

Councillor A made remarks about Councillor B at a committee meeting organising a waterfront parade. The parade was being arranged by a group of volunteers which had asked the Community Council to provide representatives to help it remain aware of Community issues when making the arrangements.

I was satisfied that Councillor A was acting in his capacity as a Councillor at the committee meeting, as his role on the committee was as the Council's representative and were it not for this fact he would not have been present at the meeting. However, in this case I was satisfied that the comments made by Councillor A were not sufficiently serious that, if proven, it would lead to a sanction being imposed on the accused member by a Standards Committee, therefore I did not investigate this complaint.

Conversely a complaint was received that Councillor J was intoxicated and behaving inappropriately at a street party. It was established that Councillor J did not have to undertake any action on behalf of the Council at the party. Therefore, in my view, she attended the party as a member of the public and as she did not seek to rely on her status as a Councillor in any way the Code of Conduct did not apply (except for paragraph 6(1)(a). Whilst her behaviour may have been considered inappropriate by some it was not relevant to her role as a Councillor and in my view did not bring the Council into disrepute so paragraph 6(1)(a) also did not apply. I did not investigate this complaint.

2. General obligations under the Code of Conduct

Equality

See paragraph 4(a)

You must carry out your duties with due regard to the principle that there should be equality of opportunity for all people regardless of their gender, race, disability, sexual orientation, age or religion. Although the Code is not explicit about trans-gender status, I will normally consider it to be included under the gender category, and expect the principle of equal opportunity to be applied.

You should at all times seek to avoid discrimination. There are four main forms of discrimination:

- Direct discrimination: treating people differently because of their gender, race, disability, sexual orientation, age or religion.

- Indirect discrimination: treatment which does not appear to differentiate between people because of their gender, race, disability, sexual orientation, age or religion, but which disproportionately disadvantages them.

- Harassment: engaging in unwanted conduct on the grounds of gender, race, disability, sexual orientation, age or religion, which violates another person's dignity or creates a hostile, degrading, humiliating or offensive environment.

- Victimisation: treating a person less favourably because they have complained of discrimination, brought proceedings for discrimination, or been involved in complaining about or bringing proceedings for d iscrimination.

The introduction of the Equality Act 2010 reinforces the importance of this part of the Code. It imposes positive duties to eliminate unlawful discrimination and harassment and to promote equality. Under equality laws, your council may be liable for any discriminatory acts which you commit. This will apply if you do something in your official capacity in a discriminatory manner.

You must be careful not to act in a way which may amount to any of the prohibited forms of discrimination, or to do anything which hinders your council's fulfilment of its positive duties under equality laws. Such conduct may cause your council to break the law, and you may find yourself subject to a complaint that you have breached this paragraph of the Code.

You must also be mindful that at all times including when acting in your private capacity you must not act in a way that would bring your Council into disrepute. It is likely that engaging in behaviour which could be considered to be in breach of the Equality Act in your private capacity is likely to fall into this category.

Example

A member of a County Council was a member of the Council's Recruitment Panel to appoint a new Chief Executive. Five applicants were shortlisted. After one candidate had finished his presentation and left the room Councillor A said 'good candidate, shame he's black'. The Adjudication Panel for Wales found that paragraph 4(a) of the Code had been breached and that Councillor A had brought the office of member and his authority into disrepute (in breach of paragraph 6(1)(a) of the Code). Having taken into consideration mitigating factors on behalf of the member the Panel decided that no further action was necessary.

Treating others with respect and consideration

See paragraph 4(b)

You must show respect and consideration for others.

Political groupings in authorities are expected to campaign for their ideas, and they may also seek to discredit the policies and action of their opponents. Criticism of ideas and opinion is part of democratic debate, and it is unlikely that such comments would ever be considered to be a breach of the Code of Conduct for failing to treat someone with respect and consideration.

Furthermore, members' freedom of expression attracts enhanced protection when their comments are political in nature. 'Political' comments are not confined to those made within council meetings and, for example, include comments members may generally make on their council's policies or about their political opponents. Therefore, unless the comments are highly offensive or outrageous, it is unlikely that I will investigate complaints made in this context and councillors need a 'thicker skin' in dealing with, and responding to, politically motivated comments.

Likewise, when members raise 'political' issues with officers, eg the Clerk to a Council, depending on the circumstances of the case I may also decline to investigate if I take the view that the member was entitled to question the officer concerned and the conduct was not sufficiently serious to amount to a failure to show respect and consideration.

Whilst it is acknowledged that some members of the public can make unreasonable demands on members, members should always treat members of the public courteously and with consideration. Rude and offensive behaviour lowers the public's expectation and confidence in its elected representatives. This is the case in face to face settings such as meetings as well as when communicating by phone, letter, e-mail or other electronic means.

Example

The Adjudication Panel upheld a finding of a Standards Committee about a Councillor who was accused of failing to show respect and consideration for others by posting comments about other Councillors and the way in which the Council was run.

The member sought judicial review of this decision. The Court found that whilst the comments which were posted were sarcastic and mocking and the tone ridiculed his fellow members, because the majority of the comments related to the way in which the Council was run, how its decisions were recorded and the competence of the Councillors, the comments were 'Political Expression'. The ruling said no account had been taken for the need for politicians to have 'thicker skins'. In view of the member's freedom of expression and the fact that the majority of comments were directed at fellow Councillors the finding of a breach in this case was a disproportionate interference with the member's rights under Article 10 of the European Convention on Human Rights. The Standards Committee's decision to censure the member was therefore set aside.

Example

A member of a town council wrote to a Deputy Minister of the Welsh Assembly Government about an employee ('Mr Smith') of a county council, which was also copied to the Council. In the letter the member questioned Mr Smith's competence and motivation and he made a number of comments of a disparaging and personal nature about Mr Smith and his associates. He raised the issue of homosexuality and referred to it as a 'notorious disability' and that 'homosexuality is only a demon which can be driven out'. The member was referred to the Adjudication Panel for Wales.

The Panel found that the member had breached paragraph 4(b) in that he had failed to show respect and consideration for others. It also found that by his use of words he had brought the office of member into disrepute in breach of paragraph 6(1)(a) of the Code.

The member was disqualified for 12 months from being or becoming a member of a local authority.

Bullying and harassment

See paragraph 4(c)

You must not use any bullying behaviour or harass any person including other councillors, council officers (the Clerk or Proper Officer) or members of the public.

Harassment is repeated behaviour which upsets or annoys people. Bullying can be characterised as offensive, intimidating, malicious, insulting or humiliating behaviour. Such behaviour may happen once or be part of a pattern of behaviour directed at a weaker person or person over whom you have some actual or perceived influence. Bullying behaviour attempts to undermine an individual or a group of individuals, is detrimental to their confidence and capability, and may adversely affect their health.

I will always consider allegations of bullying and harassment from the perspective of the alleged victim. The question to be answered is whether the individual was reasonably entitled to believe they were being bullied rather than whether the person accused of bullying thought that he or she was doing so. Bullying is often carried out face to face, but increasingly, it can be carried out in print or using electronic media. The standards of behaviour expected are the same, whether you are expressing yourself verbally or in writing.

Example

Community Councillor P disagreed with the County Council's arrangements for the enforcement of parking breaches within the town. Councillor P used disrespectful and abusive language and behaved in a bullying and intimidating manner towards Council Civil Enforcement Officers on four occasions. He also sought to use his position as a Councillor improperly in relation to a parking offence. The Standards Committee found that Councillor P had breached paragraph 4c of the Code of Conduct as he had pursued a course of conduct of threatening behaviour towards the County Council employees. The Standards Committee also established that Councillor P breached paragraphs 4(b), 7(a) and 6(1)(a) of the Code of Conduct. He was suspended from acting as a Councillor for 12 months.

Compromising the impartiality of officers of the authority

See paragraph 4(d)

You must not compromise, or attempt to compromise, the impartiality of anyone who works for, or on behalf of, your Council.

You should not approach anyone who works for, or on behalf of, the Council with a view to pressurising them to carry out their duties in a biased or partisan way. They must be neutral and should not be coerced or persuaded to act in a way that would undermine their neutrality. For example, you should not get officers to help you prepare party political material, or to help you with matters relating to your private business. You should not provide or offer any incentive or reward in return for acting in a particular way or reaching a particular decision or threaten someone if they are not minded to act in a particular way.

If a member develops a close personal relationship with an officer, this becomes a personal and possibly a prejudicial interest under the Code.

Hypothetical Scenario

The Clerk is responsible for allocating allotments from a waiting list, the allotments are very popular and vacancies very rarely arise. The Clerk advised the Council that an allotment had become vacant and that they would consult the list and allocate the allotment to the person who had been waiting the longest in accordance with the Council's allotment allocation procedure. Councillor D's father had been waiting for an allotment for almost seven years. Councillor D approached the Clerk after the meeting and asked to see the list. He noted that one person was ahead of his father by only one month. Councillor D asked the Clerk to give the vacant allotment to his father, he said that as so much time had elapsed since his father and the other person had applied, the other person was unlikely to question who was first and in any event it would not be difficult to retype the list. Councillor D suggested that in return for this favour he would encourage the Council to look favourably on the charity suggested by the Clerk when it came time to decide where to allocate funds raised at a fun day the following month.

Disclosing confidential information

See paragraph 5(a)

You must not disclose confidential information, or information which should be reasonably regarded to be of a confidential nature, except in any of the following circumstances:

- You have the consent of the person authorised to give it.
- You are required by law to do so.

The Information Commissioner has issued helpful guidance on the Freedom of Information Act and Data Protection Act which is available on his website at www.ico.gov.uk or by calling 0303 123 1113.

As a Community Councillor you may have sight of sensitive information, for example of a commercial nature. You must also be mindful that, as a Councillor, you hold a position of trust and you may find that members of the public will provide you with information that could reasonably be regarded as confidential and you should always confirm (where possible obtain an agreement in writing) that you have the permission to disclose such information before doing so.

As a general rule, you should treat items discussed in the confidential sections of meetings (exempt items) as confidential. Similarly, legal advice is almost always covered by legal privilege and should not be disclosed.

Example

A Community Councillor (S) received an e-mail from another Councillor (T) regarding the employment of the caretaker. The e-mail was marked as confidential. Councillor s disclosed the e-mail to the caretaker's wife, information in the e-mails was subsequently used against the Council in a tribunal hearing relating to the caretaker's employment. I concluded that Councillor s might have breached paragraph 5(a) of the Code of Conduct.

Preventing access to information

See paragraph 5(b)

You must not prevent any person from accessing information which they are entitled to by law. This includes information under the Freedom of Information Act 2000 or those copies of minutes, agendas, reports and other documents of your Council which they have a right to access. To find out more about what types of information the public can access, contact the Information Commissioner's Office by visiting www.ico.gov.uk or by calling 0303 123 1113 or for specific queries, you should ask your Monitoring Officer or Clerk.

Any information that you produce in your official capacity is liable to be subject to the disclosure requirements of the Freedom of Information Act, and your Council may be required to release it in response to a request. If you do not provide the information to the Clerk on request, you will be in breach of the Code.

Your Council needs to decide whether to disclose information or whether it may be covered by an exemption. Even if you believe that information you hold is exempt, you must provide it to your Clerk if requested to allow the council to reach a decision. As well as being a breach of the Code, it is a criminal offence if information is destroyed after a Freedom of Information Act request has been received.

Example

A leader of a county council refused to give the Council's Information Officer a letter he had written to the Wales Audit Office on behalf of the Council's

Executive. As a result the Council could not respond appropriately to a Freedom of Information Act request which resulted in a complaint being made to the Information Commissioner's Office. The member continued to refuse to disclose the letter despite having received clear and unequivocal advice from the Information Officer. His refusal led to an adverse finding from the Information Commissioner's Office. The Adjudication Panel found that the member had breached paragraphs 5(b) and 6(1)(a) (disrepute) in respect of this matter and other related matters. By the time the case was considered by the Panel the member had resigned from office. He was disqualified from holding office for 12 months.

Disrepute

See paragraph 6(1)(a)

You must not behave in a way which could reasonably be regarded as bringing your office or authority into disrepute at any time.

As a member, your actions and behaviour are subject to greater scrutiny than those of ordinary members of the public. You should be aware that your actions in both your public and private life might have an adverse impact on your Council.

Dishonest and deceitful behaviour will bring your Council into disrepute, as may conduct which results in a criminal conviction, especially if it involves dishonest, threatening or violent behaviour, even if the behaviour happens in your private life. Making unfair or inaccurate criticism of your Council in a public arena might well be regarded as bringing your Council into disrepute. Inappropriate e-mails to constituents might well bring the office of member into disrepute.

Example

A Community Councillor had been abusive to a shop proprietor and two members of her staff and had attempted to obtain a discount on a private purchase by saying it was being bought on behalf of the Community Council, and when his request for a discount was refused he had made threats against the business. The Adjudication Panel found that the member had brought the office of member into disrepute and suspended him for 9 months.

Example

A member of a County Borough Council who regularly wrote an article for a local monthly publication referred in his article to a recent road traffic accident in which a 10 year old boy was injured. The complainant was the mother of the boy who was with the injured child. After the article was published she telephoned the Councillor who she said was abusive towards her during the call. In a subsequent e-mail exchange the Councillor told her that she had 'failed to take any responsibility for her child allowing him out alone', that her 'ill educated in the highway code son' was to blame and said 'don't you dare try and shift your inadequacies as a parent upon me'.

The member was found in breach of paragraphs 4(b) (respect & consideration) and 6(1)(a) (disrepute). The matter was referred to the Adjudication Panel for

Wales. Although the member had claimed to have apologised for his behaviour what he had actually said was 'I have nothing to apologise for... I do apologise if, for some reason it upset you'.

The Panel found that the member had breached paragraphs 4(b) (treating others with respect) and 6(1) (a) (disrepute). He had previously been suspended by the Panel for 2 months for sending inappropriate e-mails in 2006. He was suspended for 12 months in respect of these breaches.

Reporting breaches of the Code

See paragraph 6(1)(c)

If you reasonably believe that a breach of the Code has occurred, you must report it to me and to your Monitoring Officer. In order to have a reasonable belief that a breach has occurred, you will need to have evidence which supports this. If you are in doubt as to whether a breach has occurred, you should consult your Monitoring Officer as soon as possible. Where the breach is a very minor or technical one, or where there is no clear evidence that a breach occurred, your Monitoring Officer may advise you of the likely threshold I will set. Nonetheless, the decision as to whether to investigate a breach rests with me. The balance of any doubt should always favour reporting. It is helpful if you specify which aspect of the Code you believe has been breached, but this is not essential.

To report a breach, you can contact my office by phone at 0845 6010987, by email to ask@ombudsman-wales.org.uk or via the website at www.ombudsman-wales.org.uk. A special leaflet on making complaints about alleged breaches of the Code is available on request or on the website.

In determining whether to investigate a complaint of a breach I will use the two stage test which I have outlined on pages 5 and 6 above. You should ensure that you provide any evidence you have available when you make a complaint including minutes of meetings, correspondence, contemporaneous notes or e-mails. If there are other individuals who have witnessed the alleged breach, you should let us know who they are. This latter point is especially important as if I only have one person's word against another's, it's usually not possible for me to make a finding that a breach has occurred, and in the absence of independent confirmation, I won't usually begin an investigation.

Vexatious complaints

See paragraph 6(1)(d)

You must not make complaints against other members or staff members or people working on behalf of your Council which are not founded in fact and which are motivated by malice (a desire to do them harm) or by political rivalry. Unfortunately, there have been instances where members have sought to bring complaints about rivals which are designed to disadvantage them, sometimes in the run-up to elections, and where the evidence of any breach is thin or non-existent. I consider that in the first instance such conduct should be considered under the relevant authority's local resolution process if there is one in place.

Where specific details of such complaints are passed to local press and media, this may prejudice an investigation and so also may be a breach of the Code. You must report well-founded alleged breaches to me and to your Monitoring Officer, not to your local newspaper or radio station. The press will properly cover the business of any hearings and their outcomes, and members making allegations should not generate publicity in advance of these.

You should also avoid making complaints which have little or no substance (frivolous complaints) or which are designed mainly to annoy the person complained about.

It became necessary during the year to correspond with the Clerk of a Council in relation to our mutual concern about the number of complaints I had received in respect of its members. During 2011/12, I received 65 complaints about members of this Council out of a total of 206, representing 32% of the complaints about Community Councils. This level of complaints is entirely disproportionate. Such a level of complaints, in my view, reflected a very hostile set of interactions between councillors and must inevitably lower the esteem in which the Council was held by its electors. I urged the Council to reflect on the culture which gave rise to these complaints and how behaviour might be changed to reverse this trend. I made clear that if there was no reduction in the number of complaints by members against other members I would not hesitate to investigate the matter under paragraph 6(1)(d) of the Code.

You should note that the Code of Conduct only applies to those who have been elected, co-opted or otherwise appointed to a body which is covered by the Code of Conduct. It does not apply to members of the public. Whilst I appreciate that it can be frustrating if a member of the public makes repeated complaints against you which you consider to be vexatious or frivolous in nature, I am required to consider each complaint on its own merit. However, it is likely that such complaints would not pass the two stage test and result in an investigation.

Co-operating with investigations

See paragraph 6(2)

You must co-operate with an investigation when it is being conducted by me or by your Monitoring Officer using our statutory powers. Not to do so is itself a breach of the code. This means that you should reply promptly to all correspondence and telephone calls, make yourself available for interview if required and make available copies of any requested documents. My office and your Monitoring Officer will make reasonable allowances for urgent pressures you face and arrangements previously made, eg for holidays. However, they will expect you to give priority to their investigations, to avoid matters being needlessly drawn out. The requirement to co-operate with an investigation applies whether you are a witness or the subject of the investigation.

In the course of my work I have unfortunately become aware of instances where members accused of breaches of the Code have sought to put pressure on the individuals making the complaint or on other witnesses. I regard such behaviour as entirely unacceptable. You must not intimidate or attempt to intimidate any person who is or is likely to be a complainant, a witness, or involved in the administration of any investigation or proceedings relating to a failure to comply with the Code.

However much you may be concerned about allegations that you or a fellow councillor failed to comply with the Code, it is always wrong to bully, intimidate or attempt to intimidate any person involved in the investigation or hearing. Even though you may not have breached the Code, you will have your say during any independent investigation or hearing, and you should let these processes follow their natural course.

If you intimidate a witness in an investigation about your conduct, for example, you may find yourself subject to another complaint that you have breached paragraph 4(c) of the Code with regard to bullying or harassment, for example, or paragraph 6(1)(a) in respect of bringing the office of member into disrepute.

Using your position improperly

See paragraph 7(a)

You must not use, or attempt to use, your position improperly to the advantage or disadvantage of yourself or anyone else. This paragraph applies at all times and not just when you are carrying out your duties as a member. You should not use, or attempt to use, your public office either for your or anybody else's personal gain or loss. For example, your behaviour would be improper if you sought to further your own private interests through your position as a member. This also applies if you use your office to improve your wellbeing at the expense of others.

Members who own land, or whose close personal associates own land, need to be particularly cautious where planning matters are concerned. If you are in any doubt, you should take advice.

This applies equally to members of community councils when your Council is consulted on planning matters. Similarly, while it is reasonable to expect members to help constituents apply to the Council e.g. for housing, it is quite inappropriate to seek to influence the decision to be taken by the officers.

The provisions of the Bribery Act 2010 apply to members carrying out their public functions. Should a member be convicted of a criminal offence under this Act then it is likely that they will also have used their position improperly (in breach of paragraph 7(a)) and be likely to have brought the office of member or their authority into disrepute in breach of paragraphs 6(1)(a) and (b). If any complaint which is made to me concerns conduct which may amount to a criminal offence then I am likely to refer the matter to the police.

Example

Councillor D was a 'joint co-ordinator' of a community group. Councillor D did not notify the Council of her position in this group. She took part in the considerations and voted on the decision to negotiate a new lease in respect of a workshop used by this community group. A Standards Committee found that she had used her position on the Council improperly as the decision on which she voted benefitted a group in which she clearly had an interest which she had not made the Council aware of. She was found in breach of paragraph 7(a) of the Code of Conduct and suspended from acting as a Councillor for four weeks.

The authority's resources

See paragraph 7(b)

You must only use or authorise the use of the resources of the Council in accordance with its requirements.

If your Council provides you with access to resources (for example telephone, computer and other IT facilities), you must only use these resources for carrying out your council business and any other activity which your Council has authorised you to use them for.

You must be familiar with the rules applying to the use of these resources made by your Council. Failure to comply with your Council's rules is likely to amount to a breach of the Code.

If you authorise someone (for example a member of your family) to use your Council's resources, you must take care to ensure that this is allowed by your Council's rules.

Using resources for proper purposes only

See paragraphs 7(b)(v) and 7(b)(vi)

You must make sure you use the Council's resources for proper purposes only. It is not appropriate to use, or authorise others to use, the resources for political purposes, including party political purposes. When using the Council's resources, you must have regard, if applicable, to any guidance issued by your Council.

Example

A member of a county council was found in breach of the Code for making improper use of his council-owned computer equipment for private purposes by downloading inappropriate adult pornographic images and sending a number of letters to a local newspaper, which he falsely represented as being from members of the public. The Adjudication Panel found that the member had misused the Council equipment in breach of the Code and had brought the office of member into disrepute. He was disqualified from being or becoming a member of a local authority for 2 years and 6 months.

Reaching decisions objectively

See paragraph 8

When taking part in meetings of your Council, or when arriving at decisions relating to the Council's business, you must do so with an open mind and objectively. During the decision-making process you must act fairly and take proper account of the public interest.

Most decisions taken by a Community Council relate to local matters and funding of local projects. Although the amounts of money being spent are smaller than at County level all decisions must be taken on the basis of the facts in front of you, and you must not have made your mind up in advance to such an extent that you're entirely unprepared to consider all of the evidence and advice you receive. Having a completely closed mind is known as pre-determination. You are entitled to hold a preliminary view about a particular matter in advance of a meeting (pre-disposition) as long as you keep an open mind and are prepared to consider the merits of all the arguments and points made about the matter under consideration before reaching your decision.

Pre-determination on the other hand would be where you have clearly decided on a course of action in advance of a meeting and are totally unwilling to consider the evidence and arguments presented on that matter during the meeting. Pre-determination could not only invalidate the decision, it would also amount to a breach of the Code.

Considering advice provided to you and giving reasons

See paragraph 8

You must have regard to all of the advice you receive from your Clerk. The Clerk is usually also the Proper Officer and it is part of their role to research the policy, guidelines and legislation relevant to advice given when taking decisions.

It is always helpful, if you can, to get advice as early as possible. If you can, ask for advice in good time before a meeting, rather than at the meeting or immediately before it starts. Make sure you give the Clerk all of the information they need to take into account when giving you advice.

If you seek advice, or advice is offered to you, for example, on whether or not you should register a personal interest, you should have regard to this advice before you make your mind up. Failure to do so may be a breach of the Code.

As a matter of good practice, where you disagree with the Clerk's recommendations in making a decision, you should give clear reasons for your decision. If you decide to vote against their advice, you should ensure that your reasons for doing so are recorded in the relevant minutes.

Expenses

See paragraph 9(a)

You need to follow the law and your Council's requirements in claiming expenses and allowances. If you are in any doubt about your entitlements, or the proper way to claim, you should ask your Clerk for advice. You need to keep proper records of expenditure supported by receipts where appropriate, so that you can properly evidence your claims. Even if a particular scheme does not require you to submit receipts, you are strongly advised to keep these so that you can prove how much you have actually spent on the items you are claiming for.

Gifts and hospitality

See paragraph 9(b)

It's important that you don't accept any gifts or hospitality for yourself, or on behalf of others, which would place you under obligation or appear to do so. Accepting such gifts or hospitality could be regarded as compromising your objectivity when you make decisions or carry out the work of your Council. This is also true of any services or gifts in kind.

This does not prevent you from attending official events such as a civic reception or working lunch where these are authorised by your Council.

3. Personal and prejudicial interests

The elements of the Code which cover personal and prejudicial interests give rise to many questions from members. They are designed to safeguard the principles of selflessness and objectivity. They are intended to give members of the public confidence that decisions are being taken in their best interests, and not in the best interests of members of authorities or their close personal associates.

Personal interests relate to issues where you or a close personal associate may have some link to a matter under discussion. These interests become prejudicial where an informed independent observer could conclude that the interest would influence your vote, or your decision. Guidance on registering interests is at Section 4.

The paragraphs below are designed to offer guidance on a very complex subject. I would strongly recommend that if you are in any doubt about whether you have a personal or prejudicial interest, and what you need to do if so, you should ask your Clerk for advice.

Personal Interests

See paragraph 10

While you are carrying out your duties, you need to decide if you have a personal interest, and if so, whether you need to disclose it. Most members know that you need to disclose personal interests at meetings, but as you will read below, there are other occasions, such as when speaking to the Clerk about the matter concerned, when you may also need to do so.

You have a **personal interest** in any business of your Council, including when making a decision, where it relates to or is likely to affect:

1.   your job or your business;

2.   your employer, or any firm in which you are a partner or paid director;

3.   any person who has paid towards the cost of your election or your expenses as a member;

4.   any company in which you hold shares with a nominal value of more than £25,000 or where your holding is more than 1% of the total issued share capital, which has premises or land in your Council's area;

5. any contract that your Council makes with a firm in which you are a partner, paid director or hold shares in as described in 4;

6. any land in which you have an interest and which is in your Council's area (this is especially important in all planning matters including strategic plans);

7. any land let by your Council to a firm in which you're a partner, paid director or a body as set out in 4;

8. any body to which you've been elected, appointed or nominated by your Council;

9. any:

   - public authority or body exercising functions of a public nature,

   - company, industrial and provident society, charity or body directed to charitable purposes,

   - body whose main role is influencing public opinion or policy,

   - trade union or professional association,

   - private club, society or association operating in your Council's area in which you have membership or are in a position of general control or management, or

10. any land in your Council's area which you have a license to occupy for at least 28 days. It is always safer to declare an interest, however, if in doubt consult your Monitoring Officer.

Matters affecting your well being or financial position

If a decision might be seen as affecting your well being or financial position or the well being or financial position of any person who lives with you or with whom you have a close personal association to a greater extent than other people in your Council's area, you also have a personal interest.

Examples of decisions of this kind include obvious issues like contracts being awarded to your partner's company but also issues about the location of developments, where it might make a big difference to where you or your close personal associates live. Examples have included the location of playgrounds, where elected members have opposed them near their houses because of issues about noise.

What is 'a body exercising functions of a public nature'?

The phrase 'a body exercising functions of a public nature' has been subject to broad interpretation by the courts for a variety of different purposes. Although it is not possible to produce a definitive list of such bodies, here are some of the criteria to consider when deciding whether or not a body meets that definition:

- Does that body carry out a public service?

- Is the function exercised under legislation or according to some statutory power?

- Can the body be judicially reviewed?

When conducting Community Council business it is likely that you will be acting on a body which is exercising functions of a public nature. You may also be doing this if you have been appointed to act on behalf of the Council on a community project or interest group.

What does 'affecting well-being or financial position' mean?

The term 'well-being' can be described as a condition of contentedness and happiness. Anything that could affect your quality of life, either positively or negatively, is likely to affect your well-being.

A personal interest can affect you or your close personal associates positively and negatively. So if you or they have the potential to gain or lose from a matter under consideration, you need to declare a personal interest in both situations.

Who is a close personal associate?

Close personal associates include people such as close friends, colleagues with whom you have particularly strong connections, business associates and close relatives. It does not include casual acquaintances, distant relatives or people you simply come in contact with through your role as member or your work in the local community.

Close personal associates can also include someone with whom you have been in dispute, or whom you may be regarded as having an interest in disadvantaging. For example, being a member of the same golf club as another person would not of itself constitute a close personal association but having that person as a weekly golf partner might well do. If you are in doubt, you should ask your Monitoring Officer.

'Twin hatted' members

If you are a member of both a community council and a county council you are not prevented from discussing the same matters at both. You may, for example, take part in a discussion about a planning application about which your community council has been consulted and still go on to participate in a decision about the application if you sit on the planning committee of your county council.

If you do so, you would be well advised to state at the community council meeting that you would be looking at the matter afresh when you consider it at the county council, and that you would take into account all of the information and advice provided to you. At the planning committee, you should make it clear that you are not bound by the views of the community council. The advice about objective decision making in respect of paragraph 8 of the Code is also relevant here.

Obviously, if the application was one submitted by the community council, then you would have both a personal and a prejudicial interest, and you would be required to declare it and withdraw in line with the guidance on 'what to do if you have a prejudicial interest' below.

Example

Councillor F participated in a meeting which was considering whether to approve the complainant's nomination for the post of school governor; Councillor F's husband had also applied for the post. Not only did the Adjudication Panel find that she should have declared a personal interest in the item of business by virtue of her close personal association with her husband, but it also took the view that as there had been a history of animosity directed towards the member by the complainant which had been reported publicly, she also had a personal interest by virtue of her close personal association with the complainant.

A further element to this complaint was that after the complainant had made a complaint to me about the member, the member sat on the Council's Standards Committee when it considered a separate complaint from the complainant against another member. The Adjudication Panel took the view that, in light of the acrimonious relationship between the member and the complainant, the member's participation in the Standards Committee hearing could reasonably have been regarded as affecting the complainant's wellbeing because she was entitled to a fair and unbiased hearing of her complaint.

What if I am not aware of my personal interest?

Your obligation to disclose a personal interest to a meeting only applies when you are aware of or reasonably ought to be aware of the existence of the personal interest.

Clearly you cannot be expected to declare something of which you are unaware. It would be impractical to expect you to research into the employment, business interests and other activities of all your close associates and relatives. However, you should not ignore the existence of interests which, from the point of view of a reasonable and objective observer, you should have been aware.

Disclosing personal interests

See paragraph 11

At meetings, you must declare that you have a personal interest, and the nature of that interest, before the matter is discussed or as soon as it becomes apparent to you except in limited circumstances. You must declare any interest orally if discussing a matter with the Clerk or another Member as soon as you become aware of the interest and subsequently confirm it in writing within 14 days.

If you have agreed with your Monitoring Officer that the information about your personal interest is sensitive information then you should disclose the existence of a personal interest, and confirm that the Monitoring Officer has agreed that the information about it is sensitive. More information about this is included in the separate section below.

Prejudicial Interests

See paragraph 12

If you declare a personal interest you can remain in the meeting, speak and vote on the matter, unless your personal interest is also a prejudicial interest.

What is a prejudicial interest?

Your personal interest will also be a prejudicial interest in a matter if a member of the public, who knows the relevant facts, would reasonably think your personal interest is so significant that it is likely to prejudice your judgement of the public interest. There are exemptions to this which are contained in paragraph 12(2) of the Code of Conduct although many of the examples are unlikely to apply to business undertaken by a community council.

What is so significant that it is likely to prejudice your judgement?

If a reasonable member of the public with knowledge of all the relevant facts would think that your judgement of the public interest might be prejudiced, then you have a prejudicial interest. This is an objective test. You must decide not whether you would take the decision without prejudice, but whether you would be seen as doing so.

You must ask yourself whether a member of the public – if he or she knew all the relevant facts – would think that your personal interest was so significant that it would be likely to prejudice your judgement. In other words, the interest must be perceived as likely to harm or impair your ability to judge the public interest.

The mere existence of local knowledge, or connections within the local community, will not normally be sufficient to meet the test. There must be some factor that might positively harm your ability to judge the public interest objectively. The nature of the matter is also important, including whether a large number of people are equally affected by it or whether you or a smaller group are particularly affected.

Some general principles must be remembered when applying this test. You should clearly act in the public interest and not in the interests of any close personal associates. You are a custodian of the public purse and the public interest and your behaviour and decisions should reflect this responsibility.

You would have a prejudicial interest in the consideration and decision on whether to support a planning application proposal if a close personal associate of yours (e.g. your son or a good friend) lives next to the proposed site. This is because your close personal associate would be likely to be affected by the application to a greater extent than the majority of the inhabitants of your council area and this gives you a personal interest in the issue. The close personal association means a reasonable member of the public might think that it would prejudice your view of the public interest when considering the planning application. It does not matter whether it actually would or not.

In other cases, where there has been a dispute between you and an individual who could be disadvantaged by a decision, an informed reasonable member of the public might conclude that you would be inclined to vote accordingly, whether this is the case or not.

Community Councillors don't have a prejudicial interest in decisions made by their council in respect of grants, loans or other financial assistance to community groups or voluntary organisations where the value doesn't exceed £500. Furthermore community councillors who have been appointed to the community group or voluntary organisation concerned by their community council e.g. to the board of a community hall, will not have a prejudicial interest in decisions made by their council in respect of any grants, loans or other financial assistance. If, on the other hand, you are on such a board in your own capacity and haven't been appointed by your Council, then you will have a prejudicial interest.

What to do when you have a prejudicial interest

See paragraph 14

Even where you have a prejudicial interest, the Code supports your role as a community advocate and enables you in certain circumstances to represent your community and to speak on issues important to them and to you.

Key points:

If you have a **prejudicial interest** in a matter being discussed at a meeting, you must, having declared your personal interest in the matter, leave the room (or any other venue in which the meeting is being held including, for example, the location of a site meeting), **unless members of the public are allowed to make representations, give evidence or answer questions about the matter**, by statutory right or otherwise. If that is the case, you can also attend the meeting for that purpose.

However, you must immediately leave the room or chamber once the period for considering representations has finished, and before any discussion on the item begins, even if members of the public are allowed to remain. You cannot remain in the public gallery to observe the vote on the matter.

In addition, you must not seek to influence a decision in which you have a prejudicial interest. This rule is similar to your general obligation not to use your position as a member improperly to your or someone else's advantage or disadvantage. This means that as well as leaving meetings where the item is discussed, you should also not write or make any oral representations about the matter.

The Code does not provide you with a general right to speak to a meeting where you have a prejudicial interest.

The Code aims to provide members with the same rights as ordinary members of the public to speak on certain matters in meetings, despite having a prejudicial interest. These rights are usually governed by your Council's constitution, procedure rules or standing orders, and may be subject to conditions including time limits or the fact that representations can only be made in writing.

If an ordinary member of the public would be allowed to speak to a meeting about an item, you should be provided with the same opportunity. You will be able to make representations, answer questions or give evidence, even if you have a prejudicial interest in the item. You may not take part in the discussion or observe the vote.

When must I leave the place where the meeting is held?

You must leave immediately after the time for making representations, giving evidence or answering questions is finished, and before any debate starts.

What does influencing a decision mean?

You must not make any representations or have any involvement with decisions in which you have a prejudicial interest, except where you are entitled to speak as described above.

What if the public are not allowed to speak to the meeting on the matter?

If an ordinary member of the public is not allowed to speak on the matter, you cannot do so if you have a prejudicial interest. You must leave the place where the debate is being held and not seek to influence the debate in any way.

This may be the case, for example, where your Council is discussing a confidential matter in closed session or does not have procedure rules or standing orders in place that allow members of the public to speak at a meeting of your Council. Like the public, you are not allowed to participate if you have a prejudicial interest. However, where the public may be allowed to sit in the public gallery to observe the meeting, you will be required to leave the room during the debate and vote.

Example

Councillor R attended a workshop with the Local Park Authority relating to the consideration of land for inclusion in the Local Development Plan (LDP). Councillor R had previously submitted an application for land he owned to be included in the LDP. I considered that Councillor R had a prejudicial interest in the item which was being discussed as the outcome could have a significant impact on his property and could affect his financial well being. The Standards Committee found that he was in breach of paragraph 14(1)(a) of the Code of Conduct by not declaring an interest and leaving the room when discussions concerning the area in which his own land was situated took place.

Dispensations

If I have a prejudicial interest, can I obtain a dispensation to allow me to take part in the meeting?

You can apply in writing to your County Council's Standards Committee for a dispensation on one or more of the following grounds:

- at least 50 per cent of the council or committee members would be prevented from taking a full part in a meeting because of prejudicial interests;

- the nature of your interest is such that your participation wouldn't harm public confidence;

- your interest is common to a significant proportion of the general public;

- you have a particular role or expertise which would justify your participation;

- the business relates to the finances or property of a voluntary organisation and you sit on its board or committee in your own right and you don't have any other interest, although in this instance, any dispensation won't let you vote on the matter, or

- the committee believes that your participation would be in the interests of the people in your Council's area and that the committee notifies Welsh Ministers within seven days.

You can apply for a dispensation individually and in certain circumstances, you can make joint applications where a number of members want to obtain a dispensation to speak or vote on the same matter. If the Standards Committee approves your application, it must grant the dispensation in writing and before the meeting is held. If you need a dispensation, you should apply for one as soon as is reasonably possible.

Only the Standards Committee can grant the dispensation and will do so at its discretion. The Standards Committee will need to balance the public interest in preventing members with prejudicial interests from taking part in decisions, against the public interest in decisions being taken by a reasonably representative group of members of the Council. If failure to grant a dispensation will result in a council or committee not achieving a quorum, this may well constitute grounds for granting a dispensation.

Where you hold a dispensation, you can also make written representations but you must provide details of the dispensation in any correspondence. If you make oral representations, whether in person or by phone, you must refer to the dispensation and confirm this in writing within 14 days.

4. Registration of Interests

Gifts and hospitality

Key points:

You must notify your Clerk of any gifts or hospitality worth more than the amount specified by your Council that you receive in connection with your official duties as a member, and the source of the gift or hospitality.

Like other interests in your register of interests, you may have a **personal interest** in a matter under consideration if it is likely to affect a person who gave you a gift or hospitality that is registered. If that is the case, you must declare the existence and nature of the gift or hospitality, the person who gave it to you, how the business under consideration relates to that person, and then decide whether that interest is also a **prejudicial interest**.

It is also good practice to provide a note of any offers of gifts which you have declined.

Is the gift or hospitality connected to my official duties as a member?

You should ask yourself, would I have been given this if I was not on the Council? If you are in doubt as to the motive behind a gift or hospitality, we recommend that you register it or speak to your Clerk.

You do not need to your Clerk gifts and hospitality which are not related to your role as a member, such as Christmas gifts from your friends and family, or gifts which you do not accept. However, you should always notify your Clerk of any a gift or hospitality if it could be perceived as something given to you because of your position or if your Council requires you to.

What if I do not know the value of a gift or hospitality?

The general rule is, if in doubt as to the value of a gift or hospitality, you should notify your Clerk of it, as a matter of good practice and in accordance with the principles of openness and accountability in public life.

You may have to estimate how much a gift or hospitality is worth. Also, an accumulation of small gifts you receive from the same source over a short period that add up to the value specified by your Council or over should be registered.

The Code also refers to material benefit or advantage. The measure of this would be if an informed independent observer could conclude that you might be perceived to be better off as a consequence.

Public Services Ombudsman for Wales
1 Ffordd yr Hen Gae
Pencoed
CF35 5LJ

Tel: 01656 641150

Fax: 01656 641199

E-mail: ask@ombudsman-wales.org.uk

Web: www.ombudsman-wales.org.uk

Index

[References are to paragraph numbers]